GW00360942

Iran on the Brink

Iran on the Brink

Rising Workers and Threats of War

ANDREAS MALM
and
SHORA ESMAILIAN

Pluto Press

LONDON • ANN ARBOR, MI

First published 2007 by Pluto Press
345 Archway Road, London N6 5AA
and 839 Greene Street, Ann Arbor, MI 48106

www.plutobooks.com

Copyright © Andreas Malm and Shora Esmailian 2007

The right of Andreas Malm and Shora Esmailian to be identified as the authors
of this work has been asserted by them in accordance with the Copyright,
Designs and Patents Act 1988.

British Library Cataloguing in Publication Data
A catalogue record for this book is available from the British Library

Hardback
ISBN-13   978 0 7453 2604 7
ISBN-10   0 7453 2604 8

Paperback
ISBN-13   978 0 7453 2603 0
ISBN-10   0 7453 2603 X

Library of Congress Cataloging in Publication Data applied for

10 9 8 7 6 5 4 3 2 1

Designed and produced for Pluto Press by
Chase Publishing Services Ltd, Fortescue, Sidmouth, EX10 9QG, England
Typeset from disk by Stanford DTP Services, Northampton, England
Printed and bound in the European Union by
Antony Rowe Ltd, Chippenham and Eastbourne, England

Contents

LIST OF FIGURES

Chronology

1906 The Shah is forced to accept the formation of a parliament, Majles, entitled to write a new constitution for Iran. The Constitutional Revolution unleashes a wave of democratic movements in the country. In cities, towns, and villages, so called "anjumans", or councils, assume power.

1907 Britain and Russia carve up Iran in one British zone of influence in the south, one Russian in the north. Their agreement is known as the Anglo-Russian Convention, and fiercely resisted by the revolutionary forces in the country.

1908 The Shah stages a coup and counter-revolution against the Majles and the anjumans. There ensues a civil war. In the same year, a British entrepreneur discovers oil in Khuzestan.

1911 The Constitutional Revolution is brought to an end when Russian forces march on Tehran and massacre revolutionaries in the northern parts of the country.

1920 The jangalists proclaim a Soviet Socialist Republic in the province of Gilan.

1921 Cossack commander Reza Khan rises to power, supported by the British, soon calling himself Shah Reza Pahlavi. During his decades on the throne, no opposition activities are allowed in Iran.

1941 Reza Shah is deposed by incoming allied forces. Iran is occupied, but basic democratic liberties allow trade unions and newspapers to flourish. The communist party Tudeh is formed.

1946 A general strike among the oil workers in Khuzestan manifests the power of Tudeh and the labour movement.

1951 Democratically elected liberal prime minister Muhammad Mossadeq nationalises oil in Iran, previously owned and controlled by the British. A tense confrontation with Britain ensues.

1953 CIA stages a coup d'état against Mossadeq. He is replaced by the son of Reza Shah, Mohammed Reza Shah. Absolute dictatorship is reinstated, relying on American military and financial support. Tudeh is exiled, and all opposition activities are severely repressed.

1963   The ulama, among them Ayatollah Khomeini, lead an uprising against the Shah's policies. Khomeini is expelled from the country.

1971   Fedaiyan, a Marxist guerrilla, launches a campaign of armed struggle against the Shah's regime.

1978   The Shah's regime starts crumbling. Bazaari and ulama take to the streets, are massacred by royal troops in great numbers, and are soon joined by workers. In the autumn, a wave of strikes overflows Iran, while millions of people demonstrate against the monarchy. At the end of the year, the economy is paralysed by an all-encompassing general strike.

1979   On 16 January, the Shah leaves Iran, never to return. On 11 February, his Immortal Guards are defeated by the Fedaiyan. The monarchy collapses. Ayatollah Khomeini rises to power and creates an Islamic Republic, while in the workplaces, councils or "shoras" take control over the means of production. In practice, they run the economy for most of the year. On 4 November, the US embassy is seized by Islamist students; the American diplomats are taken hostages. The revolution enters a new, purely Islamic phase.

1980   Iraq unilaterally sends its army into Iran. It is the start of the longest conventional war in the twentieth century. Fedaiyan splits in two, the Majority and the Minority. Strikes are banned and Pasdaran mobilised to rout the shoras.

1982   The shora movement is essentially quashed. The US starts giving financial aid to Saddam Hussein's Iraq, in a first major escalation of the American engagement on Iraq's side in the war. Iran re-conquers all lost territory and is offered a truce by Iraq, but Khomeini chooses to continue the war.

1983   Khomeini crushes Tudeh and Fedaiyan Majority. With the exception of the Kurdish guerrillas, no substantial opposition to the Islamic Republic is alive.

1988   The Iran-Iraq war ends without any changes in the border. Thousands of political prisoners of the Left are executed in the Evin prison.

1989   Ayatollah Khomeini dies. He is succeeded in the post as faqih, or Supreme Leader, by Ayatollah Khamene'i, while Hashemi Rafsanjani is elected president. Rafsanjani soon announces a programme of economic liberalisation, but it is essentially stalled.

1997 Mohammad Khatami is elected president on a programme of political reform. It is the beginning of a short-lived thaw in the Islamic Republic. The reformist movement, led by Khatami, opens up spaces for some political debate. However, at the point of production, nothing changes, as Khatami has no idea about trade union rights, nor any economic agenda.

1999 A major student uprising in Tehran is brutally repressed by Pasdaran. Khatami condemns the students.

2002 With the continued rise of the oil price, the great millionaire mullah bonanza sets in. The existence of a secret nuclear plant at Natanz is revealed. American president George W. Bush includes Iran in the "axis of evil".

2003 Iraq is occupied by US-led "coalition forces". Iran voluntarily suspends its programme for enrichment of uranium and enters into co-operation and negotiations with IAEA and EU. Reports of Israel planning military strikes against nuclear installations in Iran surface in the media. *Reading Lolita in Tehran* is published.

2004 Massacre at the copper plant in Khatonabad, teachers' strike, May Day demonstrations, workers' control in Gilan. Birth of a new labour movement. In the Majles elections in February, the reformists are banned from running. It is the end of the reform project. Iran revises its oil reserves upwards. American drones are seen in the sky in northern Iran.

2005 Major civil uprisings in Kurdistan and Khuzestan, followed by armed campaigns in both provinces. Rising strike wave, new initiatives for organising workers independently of the state, radicalisation of the women's movement. In June, Mahmoud Ahmadinejad is elected new president of Iran. Iran resumes enrichment of uranium, entering into a period of escalating confrontation with the West.

Glossary

Anjuman – Persian for "association", "council". The term used for the local councils during the Constitutional Revolution, 1906–1911.

Ayatollah – "Sign of Allah". A high-ranking Shiite cleric.

Basiji – Paramilitary, plainclothes street-gangs of Pasdaran, connected to local mosques.

Bazaari – A social segment comprised of the various professions active in the bazaar, primarily merchants, retailers, artisans, and money-lenders.

Bonyad – "Foundation". The bonyads are religious, quasi-governmental holding companies with some philanthropic functions besides their businesses.

Chador – "Tent". A black cloth covering all of the woman's body, except for the face. The preferred dress for all women, in the eyes of the Islamic Republic.

Evin – Infamous prison in Tehran, with a huge section for political prisoners.

Faqih – "Jurisprudent". An Islamic cleric versed in jurisprudence and interpretation of the Koran and the Sunna. Al-Faqih signifies the Supreme Leader of the Islamic Republic, that is, the ayatollah leading the state apparatus.

Fatwa – An Islamic decree; a legal pronouncement based on interpretation of sharia.

Hadith – The collected traditions of the sayings and deeds of the prophet Muhammad.

Halal – Permissible, approved, according to Islam.

Haram – Prohibited, sinful, according to Islam.

Hijab – "Barrier, screen". Veil, scarf carried by women in Islamic countries; mandatory for all women in public in the Islamic Republic of Iran.

Hezbollahi – A person committed to the politics of Ayatollah Khomeini and the leadership of the Islamic Republic, ready to be mobilised by basiji or Pasdaran.

Hojatoleslam – "Proof of Islam". A middle-ranking Shiite cleric.

Imam – In Sunni Islam: a prayer leader in the mosque. In Shia, and in Iran: a man who is a perfect example in everything and therefore able to lead the umma in all matters on a mandate from Allah. According to Twelver Shia, the state religion of Iran since the accession of the Safavid dynasty in 1501, there were twelve imams succeeding the prophet Muhammad, starting with Imam Ali and ending with Mehdi.

Itjihad – Independent interpretation of the Koran and the Sunna, usually in the form of applying known principles and rules on new problems facing Muslims, thereby reaching a conclusion on what is the right thing to do.

Khane-ye Karegar – "House of Labour". Originally a headquarters for the councils of workers and unemployed in Tehran during the revolution, since then the governmental "trade union". It is a federation of shora-ye eslami.

Khod kafai – "Self-sufficiency". The economic goal set up for Iran by Ayatollah Khomeini.

Komiteh – Originally civil defence groups during the revolution, thereafter transformed into neighbourhood organs of the Pasdaran, whereby Islamic volunteers supervise their neighbours' behaviour and promote the ideals of the Islamic Republic.

Kouffiyeh – Traditional cloth headdress donned by Arab (and Kurdish) men; associated with the Palestinian and other Arab liberation struggles since the Great Revolt in Palestine 1936, when anti-zionist activists first used it to hide their faces and show their national pride.

Madrasa – Literally "school", though often signifying centres for study of the Koran.

Majles – "Parliament", used to connote the Iranian parliament ever since the Constitutional Revolution in 1906, when the first Majles was formed.

Marg bar... – Literally "Death to", figuratively "Down with". A common first part of political chants in Iran: *Marg bar Amrika*, *Marg bar Jomhurie Eslamie* (the Islamic Republic), and so on.

Mehdi – According to Shia, the twelfth and last Imam, born in 868 AD. At the age of eight, the Mehdi left the umma and went into "occultation". He is still living somewhere on earth, but hidden to the human eye. He will return to a state of visible presence near the day of judgement, take up leadership of the umma again, and redeem mankind.

Mojahedin – Literally "struggler", someone who engages in jihad; figuratively and historically, a term applied to many freedom fighters of various brands in the Islamic world.

Mostazafin – The "oppressed" or "deprived".

Mullah – A Shiite cleric.

Pasdaran – The Revolutionary Guards. A voluntary force instituted by Ayatollah Khomeini in 1979 as the armed wing of the Islamic revolution. Its specific mission is generally said to be the protection of the revolution, whereas that of the regular Iranian army is the protection of the territory, meaning that Pasdaran is a partisan, political military force. It has been deployed against all sorts of opponents to the rule of the Islamic Republic, including in combat during the Iran-Iraq war.

Peshmerga – "Those who face death". Kurdish militias.

Savak – The security service of Muhammad Reza Shah Pahlavi, created in 1957 with the assistance of CIA and Mossad. Infamous for extreme ruthlessness and torture methods.

Shah – "King".

Sharia – Islamic law.

Shora – "Council". Refers to the grass roots councils that proliferated in Iran during the 1979 revolution. A shora is constituted through a general assembly of all employees in a workplace, squatters in a squat, neighbours in a neighbourhood, soldiers in a military unit, peasants on a piece of land, etcetera. Most often, the term refers to workers' councils.

Shora-ye eslami – "Islamic council". A form of workplace association, comprising both employees and employers, set up by the Islamic Republic to replace the independent shoras. Today, it is the only allowed workers' organisation in Iran, though its task is not to represent the workers against the employer or the state, but rather to supervise and police them.

Shora-ye mahallat – "Council of the people". Refers specifically to the neighbourhood shoras in the 1979 revolution.

Shukr Allah – "Thanks to Allah."

Siqe – Temporary marriage: an institution peculiar to Shia Islam. A man and a woman may enter a siqe-contract, and thereby gain the right to have proper sexual relations for a certain period of time, ranging from one hour to 99 years.

Sofreh – Traditional dining cloth, unrolled over the floor, in Iran.

Sunna – The collections of the hadiths, see "hadith".

Suq – "Bazaar" or "market", in Arabic.

Ulama – Islamic clerics and scholars.

Umma – The community of Islamic believers.

Velayat al-faqih – "The rule of the jurisprudent". The particular doctrine laid down by Ayatollah Khomeini, stating that the umma should be ruled by an infallible ayatollah.

Preface

Every year, the Swedish weekly publication *Arbetaren* ("The Worker") asks two of its reporters to travel to a Third World country and write an extensive dispatch. In 2004, it was our turn, and we wanted to go to Iraq. This must be, we were certain, the place where momentous stories lay waiting to be unearthed. However, the Iraqi resistance had adopted the tactic of kidnapping Westerners, including journalists, and as the date of our travel approached, the stream of gruesome pictures of beheadings and silently terrified hostages was in full spate and our editor forbade us from going.

Looking around for alternative destinations, we recalled words of something afoot in Iran, a place more familiar to us. Shora was born in Tehran and lived there until the age of nine, and we had travelled the country before, most recently during the student riots of 2003. Through the uncertain channels of communication with people in Iran, vague reports of unrest on May Day had reached us earlier in the year; now, we made some inquiries in Iranian diaspora networks, found a few email contacts inside the country, and set off.

We stumbled straight into a teeming new underground of militant labour activism. Iran's workplaces were seething with rage. The monolithic dictatorship of the Islamic Republic, which had emerged from the 1990s eminently victorious in shaking off every attempt to reform the system from within, was being challenged by a desperate working class. As in the early days of every other labour movement, this one had its victories and setbacks, won a strike here and lost another one there, made inroads into the working population and broke new political ground. Only one thing was peculiar: this movement faced an extremely repressive regime that was at the same time the product of one of the most popular and democratic revolutions in history. In this paradox, the workers' movement was beginning to coalesce.

Some 18 months after we had arrived in Iran, the new labour movement surfaced in mainstream world media. As thousands of striking bus drivers battled the regime's forces on the streets of Tehran in some of the worst disturbances seen since the Islamic Republic had taken power, and as pickets and protests were held outside Iranian embassies across the world, even the *Wall Street Journal* and the US State Department began to pay close attention.

In the meantime, Iran had moved to the centre stage of world politics. Its alleged ambition to acquire a nuclear bomb had brought it to the brink of a war with the West. During a few hours of alarm on 16 February 2005, after a huge blast near a nuclear power plant in the southern part of Iran, many thought the bombings had actually begun; it later proved to be an accident.[1] But the country was on tenterhooks and remained so, as threats of an air assault were either openly communicated, or implicitly alluded to, by the US and Israel. From the autumn of 2004 to the spring of 2006, the diplomatic row over the nuclear issue intensified, as Iran was appointed "the next big issue", in the words of George W. Bush.

At the time of writing, combat has not yet begun, and none is sure to come. But one thing is for certain: Iran is already profoundly affected by the threat of war, and it has been locked into a vicious circle of antagonistic conflicts of interests with the West.

One could think of Iran, with its vast territory and 70 million inhabitants, as a huge prison. Inside its high walls, the inmates are trying various methods of liberation. Some dig tunnels, some gear up for a riot, others have gone on hunger strike; yet another group is studying maps of the premises to find the prison's weak spots. Outside the walls, an army of bulldozers approaches, threatening to *flatten* the prison and all within it. This book is a study of Iran at that particular moment. Corresponding to the timing of developments in recent years, this book moves in a sequence from the inside to the outside; first investigating the conditions inside the prison, then stepping outside to examine the forces that are on their way to crash into the prison walls.

The first chapters of this book, however, deal with the genesis of the situation: the popular revolution in 1979. While the world has since become used to the phenomenon of Islamism, this was the first time in modern history that Islamism appeared on the scene as a movement with immense energies. Its claims to be the proponent of a just society, where the wretched and oppressed of the earth – the *mostazafin* – would be released and redeemed, were no less assertive and grandiose than those once made by the socialist movement. Almost three decades after the 1979 Islamic Revolution, the allure and power of its vision makes Islamism the most energetic revolutionary project in the world today, and Iran remains its birthplace. Partly, this book is therefore a study of the substance of its claims; a view of the society that Islamism has created in Iran, not primarily from the point of intellectuals, students, or pleasure-seeking youth – already the objects of numerous studies – but from the point of the mostazafin themselves, that is, the poor and the workers.

By starting in the revolutionary moments of Iranian history, we wish to highlight a certain tradition in the politics of the country that has not achieved the attention it deserves. Inside Iran, it is by no means forgotten, nor is it dead. It contains as many fascinating moments, appalling mistakes, political lessons and strategic subjects of contention as any of the canonised equivalents in the history of the western world. Today, this tradition is on the threshold of a comeback. But it not only faces a repressive domestic regime; before it there is also a foreign force with a capacity for extreme destruction. The second part of this book attempts to come to grips with this force and the factors impelling it towards Iran. It attempts to analyse from where both the West and Iran entered into the current state of escalating confrontation.

When we returned from Iran in late 2004, and had written our much publicised report and spoken out against the regime, we faced a problem. The regime is known to have many eyes and ears, and a second trip to further study the labour movement would be extremely risky, certainly for Shora who holds Iranian citizenship.[2] Therefore, our account of the labour movement is based on the field research conducted in the autumn of 2004, and on regular interviews by phone or email since then with movement figures inside and outside Iran, as well as, of course, printed and electronic sources. These are cited in the endnotes. For security reasons, most names of activists have been either withheld or replaced by the pseudonyms they have requested.

Stockholm,
June 2006

Acknowledgements

This book could not have been written without the commitment of many people. First of all, we would like to thank those workers and labour activists who opened the way for us into Iran, sharing their secrets and their homes with exceptional generosity: *movafaq bashid!* Maziar Razi of the Iranian Workers Solidarity Network in London most kindly has been helping us with contacts, comments and encouragement throughout this project. Javad has always, with an inexhaustible generosity and patience, been available for all sorts of assistance. Thanks to Massood, Foad, Nazem and others that cannot be mentioned, in particular those of you who have helped us with contacts in Iran; you all know how deeply we appreciate your contributions. Thanks to Mahmoud for making it possible to reach out to the Iranian communities, to David Jonstad (who drew the diagrams) and all the other comrades at *Arbetaren* for assistance and solidarity, to Frida and Fred for help at the last minute. Shora wishes to express gratitude to Kassandra for encouragement and for always coming up with new ideas in the highest of spirits. Andreas pays a special tribute to Rikard, who made the first discovery, at Sveavägen 98, and who never flinches from the cause. Last but not least, thanks to Mahnaz for inspiration, help – and the name!

Acknowledgements

Part I
Workers in Iran

1
May Day in the Children's Park

On May Day 2004, while thousands of workers unfolded their banners along the busy, noisy highway that passes through western Tehran's seemingly endless zone of warehouses, round-the-clock assembly lines and factory construction sites, the streets of Saqqez, in western Iran, lay eerily silent. The town had been cordoned off; the leafy alleys near the Children's Park were empty. Somewhere in Saqqez, contingents of police and soldiers were hiding. Uneasy at their invisible presence, people stayed inside longer than planned, although they were not exactly surprised that a massive force had been deployed into this remote corner of the Kurdish province.

Months earlier, groups of workers in Saqqez – seamstresses, bakers, brick-makers – set up a *shora*, or council. They linked up with labour activists in Tehran and five other cities, primarily in northern Iran, and began exchanging ideas and penning demands. After secret meetings and coordination, a resolution had been agreed upon and the decision taken: on May Day, workers would demonstrate simultaneously in all seven cities. Ignoring police instructions, the workers would break through decades-old barriers of fear, and manifest their discontent with the hardships imposed upon them by the Islamic Republic. Nothing of the sort had happened before during the Republic's regime.

To the Western mind, Iran appears to be clad in black. A morose mullah in a dark robe has evil plans in mind, a rancorous president maniacally spits conspiracy theories, woeful women covered in monotonous *chadors* amble through gloomy streets: these are some of the images conjured up by the word "Iran". Lately, to these impressions have been added the images of a smiling young couple holding hands, an excited blogger expressing his admiration for Western pop stars, a female student pulling back her *hijab* to uncover a seductive curl of hair, only to throw it all off as she enters the villa where the next party will take place, hidden from the views of Islamic virtue.

These images do not necessarily make the whole picture more accurate. Iran is first and foremost, by all quantitative standards, inhabited by ordinary people trying to make a living. They worry about how to cover their rising rent, how to get some time with their children, how to persuade the manager to change a temporary contract into a permanent one. They expect accidents at work, suspect that the company is in the process of being downsized and sold, and resent the glaring riches amassed by the ruling elite; in recent years, more of them have started to do what so many others in their situation have done before. They organise. On 1 May 2004, some of them went public.

The shora of Saqqez had applied to the local authorities for a May Day celebration. Their application had been rejected. The activists had proceeded anyway, putting up posters and distributing red-coloured leaflets. As the appointed hour approached, people gathered in small groups on the fringes of the Children's Park, speaking quietly, waiting. When Saqqez's well-known labour leader finally arrived, everyone started to move into the park, while more people from the streets joined in.

Then the silence was shattered. From a half-finished building near the mosque, police charged the crowd. They waved batons, hurled insults, chased men and women through the park, pulling them down to the ground. When the crowd had vanished from the park, forty demonstrators lay pressed to the ground, hands tied on their backs. Within an hour they would all be behind bars.

No May Day was celebrated in Saqqez.[1] But the event, related through underground networks for many months, gradually assumed the character of a symbolic inauguration of the most sustained period of labour unrest since Iran's clerical regime secured power in the early 1980s. This unrest came to afflict the regime as its major internal menace.

But the menace didn't emerge from a vacuum. Iran's history is steeped in the actions of working people taking society's matters in their own hands.

2
After Spring Comes Winter

A SPIRIT OF RESISTANCE TO ALL AUTHORITY

Modern Iranian history appears to follow the form of a strange weather cycle: spring arrives, popular aspirations to self-rule stir, intensely democratic structures emerge from the ground; workers' organisations begin to flourish, things warm up along social frontiers – at which point winter sets in. A new regime establishes a chilling stranglehold over all of Iranian society and everything freezes. The freeze permeates the grass roots, for what seems like an everlasting ice age. Then the cycle starts anew.

An early spring asserted itself in 1906. At that time, Iran was auto-cratically ruled by the long-standing Qajjar dynasty, which had agreed to auction off the country piece by piece to imperialist powers, mainly Britain and Russia. Strikes and animated protests from the merchant community of Tehran in early 1906 forced the king, or *Shah*, to take a step back. He acceded to the formation of a parliament, or *Majles*, that was to write a constitution for the country and specify the powers of the throne within strict parameters. To supervise the elections to the Majles – an affair for merchant guilds and other proprietary classes – local councils, or *anjumans*, were set up in the cities. But they would accept no straitjacket. Beginning in the northern Azeri city of Tabriz, the anjumans remained in session after the elections, opened up their proceedings to the populace, and widened their activities to such areas as tax collection, establishment of pension funds, and the construction of schools, roads and health clinics.[1]

The Tabriz anjuman was like the sun thawing a frozen Iran. The people of Tabriz participated in daily meetings, tending to their interests through a radicalisation of the council, which enforced reductions in the prices of basic commodities, such as meat and bread. Landowners and merchants who didn't comply found their stock expropriated; gradually, the anjuman took control over the distribution of grain and other necessities in the province. As other anjumans throughout the country emulated these practices, what is known as the "Constitutional Revolution" of Iran entered its social phase. In her monumental study of the period, *The Iranian*

5

Constitutional Revolution, 1906–1911, Janet Afary shows how the classes initially in support of the reshuffle of power – merchants, clergy, wealthy landowners – now realised that the ideas of a parliament and a constitution had released the genie of a very different concept of democracy, one implemented through daily participation by the lay masses of peasants, artisans, workers and petty traders, including women.[2]

Iran's embittered leaders turned against the revolution. Commanding the front was Tehran's highest-ranking cleric, Sheikh Fazlullah Nuri, who in 1907 proposed an amendment to the constitution. It was an ominous portent of what was to come many decades later: an appointed assembly of learned clerics would receive the bills presented to the Majles and check their concordance with (its own interpretations of) *sharia* law, equipped with the authority to veto any law deemed un-Islamic. This would pave the way for what Nuri envisioned as a "theocratic government". Since it constituted the antithesis of the anjumans' existing power, the passing of the amendment triggered a renewal of the revolution. In Tabriz, the anjuman announced a general strike against the con- stitutional revisions and expelled leading clerics, delineating an absolute separation between religious and political affairs. From the city, news of the anjuman's general empowerment beamed out across the country. Local rulers were pilloried, suspicious clerics censured, and arms deposits seized.

Britain's consul in Tehran, Sir Cecil A. Spring-Rice, wrote in consternation:

In every town there is an independent Assembly [anjuman], which acts without consulting the Governor or the Central Assembly [Majles] at Tehran. One after another, unpopular Governors have been expelled, and the Central Government and the Tehran Assembly have found themselves powerless to resist. The danger of universal disorganisation seems a real one. A spirit of resistance to oppression and even to all authority is spreading throughout the country. The leaders are unknown.[3]

Naturally, the Shah abhorred this steady dissolution of power and wanted all anjumans disbanded. This was wishful thinking on the royal court's part, whose authority remained severely curtailed; more remarkably, the Majles did what it could to rein in the councils. It promulgated laws limiting the number of officially approved anjumans, brusquely refused the requests of many towns and villages to form councils of their own, and prohibited all anjumans from dealing with political matters. The latter decree was equally futile and ludicrous, in a country where not only political but economic matters were increasingly in the hands of the anjumans. And the councils continued to proliferate, in towns as well as in villages. The Tabriz anjuman was, correctly, singled out by the central government as the instigator of village councils – used by peasants to undermine feudal relations – but the principle was firmly defended by the anjuman's preacher, Sayyid Javad Natiq:

In every civilised nation, according to our Muslim traditions, people are allowed to form organisations. In every city, region, community, and village, people exchange ideas about their affairs, whether they relate to their interests, better cultivation of their land, raising their children, opening schools, or even harassment by government and overseers, in order to stop such action. Why is it then that the people of Dikhvaragan [a village in the area] are to be deprived of such a public right and that whatever the cruel landowners and governors wish to do to the poor peasants, it is to be endured and not stopped?[4]

Such was the spirit among the grass roots when the Constitutional Revolution restrained the monarchy. They grew even more impassioned as the Shah attempted to regain what he had lost through a *coup d'état* in July 1908. The Shah's forces bombarded the Majles, which was defended by thousands of *mojahedin* revolutionaries and anjuman activists. However, Russian Cossack brigades engaged by the Shah eventually cleared the streets of Tehran. There ensued a civil war between reactionaries entrenched in the capital, and progressives – all the more socially defined – centred in Tabriz, ending with the liberation of Tehran one year after the coup.

During what is known as the "second constitutional period", a new grouping appeared in the expanding variety of popular associations. In June 1910, the printers of all the major newspapers in Tehran went on a general strike, and announced the formation of the first trade union in Iran. They confronted their employers with a list of 14 demands, among them a working day of nine hours, one free day a week, and increased compensation for night work. Other demands read as premonitions of the working conditions that would plague the Iranian working class into the twenty-first century: "in the case of illness a workman must receive his full wage", "above all, the wages must be paid regularly", and, most tellingly, "managers must treat their employers with politeness".[5]

All of this organising came to an abrupt end in 1911, when Russian forces occupied northern Iran. The monarchy was restored, free of restrictions. However, at the end of the First World War – which brought more occupations, battlefield destruction and extreme famine to Iran – the heat from intense social struggles rose again. From the mountain forests of the northern province of Gilan, a peasant-based partisan army called the *jangalists* or "forest-dwellers" descended on the country. In June 1920, backed up by Red Army troops and led by the legendary bearded horseman Khuzek Khan, the jangalists proclaimed a Soviet Socialist Republic in the province.[6] Parts of this movement formed a communist party along Bolshevik lines – the first of its kind in Asia – and an ambitious programme of land reform and democratic institutions was embarked upon, with the aim of spreading the party's message to all of Iran. At about the same time, socialists and communists united various workers' collectives into the Central Council of Federated Trade Unions; popular associations and political debates once again flourished.

It required the iron fist of a resolute new Shah to quell the movement. In 1921, self-made Cossack commander Reza Khan imposed himself upon the throne. His top priorities were to crush the jangalist movement, which threatened to march on Tehran, wipe out the tribal forces that roamed freely in the peripheries of the country, and put an end to the contagion of trade unions. By constructing a strong, centralised army – his main achievement – Reza Shah managed to undo all the post-war upheavals within a few years. In 1925, he felt confident enough to invoke the ancient Persian dynasty of "Pahlavi", adding the title to his name. Reza Shah Pahlavi now monopolised power in his own hands, with the Majles' role reduced to a façade, dissidents jailed, and the ever expanding army tightening its grip on the country; strikes, unions and political debate were banned. All opposition activities were frozen, and all might was reinstated at the top.[7] A first cycle of thaw and freeze had been completed.

THE STRIKE THAT SPREAD LIKE WILDFIRE

Spring arrived again with the next war. In 1941, the avidly pro-Nazi Reza Shah, who conspired with the Germans to open his territory for their troops en route to the Soviet Union, was deposed by incoming Allied forces.[8] When the jails were opened, labour organisers, immured for up to two decades, walked straight out to the coalfields, textile workshops and metal factories and picked up the threads of unionisation. Other ex-prisoners, mainly intellectuals, formed a new communist party called *Tudeh*, "the masses". In reality, however, the party was fostered by the Soviet military authorities occupying the northern parts of the country, to be used as Moscow's pawn in the country. None the less, the Tudeh established a genuine base among the masses, by fusing its party apparatus with the trade unions.[9]

During the later war years, union activists successfully penetrated Iran's new economic centre: the oil fields of Khuzestan. Tens of thousands of highly combative oil workers, operating what were at the time the world's biggest oil refineries, were recruited as the muscle of the labour movement; in a show of their strength in 1946 they held what has been labelled "the largest industrial strike in Middle Eastern history".[10] The Central Council of Iranian Trade Unions likewise became the largest union federation in Middle Eastern history, and Tudeh the strongest communist party.

This critical period of Iranian history reached its zenith in 1951. Buoyed on a wave of popular support, as expressed in democratic elections, mass demonstrations, strikes and *fatwas*, Prime Minister Muhammad Mossadeq ejected Britain from the oil fields and nationalised them. Instead of fettering the Iranians in foreign domination and poverty, this source of immeasurable wealth would henceforth belong to the people. In the eyes of the imperialist powers, Mossadeq's action was regarded as a mortal sin. The British, having lost their black gold mine, hatched plans to retake what they considered rightfully theirs, but they could succeed only after the CIA had invested its logistic resources in the enterprise. In 1953, US agents, armed with briefcases stuffed with millions of dollars, entered Iran and connected with the network of stooges left idle by the departing British. They bought news presses to spread lies about Mossadeq, bribed ayatollahs to turn against him, suborned generals and key people in government positions. On 19 April 1953, Mossadeq's opponents mobilised military units on the CIA's payroll and a mob hired for a good day's wage. Led by the national team of weightlifters, they encircled the prime minister's home (after the street battle, some were found with fresh 500-rial notes in their pockets).[11] For the CIA, the day of the coup was "a day that should never have ended, for it carried with it such a sense of excitement, of satisfaction, and of jubilation that it is doubtful any other can come up to it".[12]

The Tudeh didn't lift a finger. Although its reach had extended deep into the military, the party made no attempt to resist the coup; none of its hundreds of thousands of members and sympathisers were mobilised. During the nationalisation process, the Tudeh had been wavering in its support for Mossadeq; the party preferred a solution where not Britain but rather *the USSR* would be accorded access to Iran's oil. Consequently, when the coup was set off, the leadership of the Tudeh simply departed for Moscow, leaving the rank and file in the lurch. Some leaders, though, preferred to stay and cooperate with the new military authorities by handing over information about the party and the unions, which were subsequently annihilated.[13]

In Mossadeq's place, the son of pro-Nazi Reza, who had been designated the inheritor of the crown since the age of 12, was now anointed almighty king of Iran by the US. He was to be known as Mohammed Reza Shah Pahlavi. For modern Iran, this coronation would form the primordial national trauma: the oil was returned to the British and, above all, to the Americans, who now succeeded Britain as the dominant power in Iran. The Shah was Washington's man, hailed throughout the Western world as the progressive "moderniser" of a backward country. Indeed, following in the footsteps of his father, the Shah's goal was "modernisation from above", by means of a tightly centralised state, where the Majles was once again a façade, and the Shah's power enforced by the new murderous security service, Savak. From the early 1960s onwards, the Shah used this state apparatus to initiate a rapid industrialisation of the Iranian economy. This industrialisation was based on a permanent war against labour. After the coup in 1953, the workplaces were turned into army barracks. Soldiers were permanently stationed at big factories, and colonels-cum-managers routinely used batons and other physical means to repress the workers, while blue-collar Savak agents listened closely to all suspicious conversations on the shop-floor.

All trade union activity was a criminal offence. The only "unions" allowed were the "syndicates", whose representatives were selected by the state and whose only task was to inculcate reverence for the Shah into the labour force. All Persians were one flock, the Shah its benevolent shepherd. Class was a non-Persian concept. Employers were granted legal powers to dismiss workers at will, a normal working day was 10–12 hours long, and wages stagnated on subsistence levels.[14] For decades, workers' strikes were virtually unheard of. Sometimes the Shah would complain that labour failed in its duty to do its utmost for the fatherland: "This is intolerable in contemporary Iran. We shall take those who do not work by the tails and throw them out like mice." But in general, he had every reason to be satisfied with the arrangements. In March 1977, he boasted,

"The difficulties of the West are due to lack of discipline and the way work is managed; whereas in Iran, there is not one minute of worker's strikes."[15] The US was deeply impressed; in December 1977, President Jimmy Carter gave a toast to the Shah at one of many state visits: "Iran, because of the great leadership of the Shah, is an island of stability in one of the more troubled areas of the world. This is a great tribute to you, Your Majesty, and to your leadership and to the respect and admiration and love which your people give to you."[16]

Twelve months later, the Shah's kingdom was in crisis. A general strike had shut down the national economy. In the spring of 1978, after sudden protest activities among certain sectors of Iranian society, the freeze showed unexpected signs of thawing. Workers cautiously tried the ground outside the den in which they had been shut up for so long; strikes tentatively appeared in the spring. But it was September before they started in earnest. Tens of thousands of machine-tool workers in Tabriz walked out of their plant, followed by workers at the giant steel mills in Esfahan and Ahwaz and the Tehran oil refinery. Within six weeks, in a country where strikes were illegal, these workers were joined by others, from water and electricity installations, from General Motors, from Caterpillar; from fisheries, ministries, metal factories; courts, ports, copper mines; banks, schools, universities; post offices, customs offices, even studios where actors dubbed foreign films and television programmes. On one October day, 65 new strikes were reported; on the next, another 110.[17]

Initially, their demands were of an economic nature, as workers and white-collar employees alike took the first chance in 25 years to call for wage hikes. But it wasn't long before other demands were raised. In October, the Esfahan steel workers called for the expulsion of all Savak agents and military personnel from the complex, the dissolution of the syndicate, and the dismissal of "feudal" managers. At another steel plant, striking workers distributed a leaflet asking for support from the community: "Come and see that we are working under the shadow of tanks, cannons, rifles and bayonets ... Entering the factory premises is like stepping into a concentration camp."[18]

In November 1978, the Shah made a desperate attempt to subdue his subjects by establishing untrammelled military rule. This served only to spread the general strike even further, and to direct its force against one single target: the Shah himself. He, and his regime, had to go. In early 1979, every striking group rallied behind this ultimate demand. At the forefront were the tens of thousands of oil workers concentrated in the Khuzestan fields; in December, they had refined their grievances – "dissolution of Savak", "end to discrimination against women staff ", "unconditional release of all political prisoners" – into a single demand for complete regime change. Army troops tried to force oil workers back into the installations at bayonet point, to no effect; when the new year arrived, not a drop of oil was extracted. With no fuel for transport, and crucial oil export revenues cut off, the country was at a standstill. The doomed monarchy fell on 11 February 1979.[19]

WE WANTED TO BECOME OUR OWN MASTERS

The general strike – one of the most all-encompassing in world history – had sprung up from nothing: Iran had had no labour movement, no trade unions or any other organisations. In the absence of unions, calls for strikes were spread through the casual networks: "One would inform another; he would inform the next, and so on. In this way the strike would get started", one worker related afterwards.[20] As the regime crumbled, and censorship and other repressive measures disappeared, striking workers gradually began to communicate openly. Learning from others – but first and foremost as a response to their own practical needs – workers in a given enterprise would assemble in a mass meeting, formulate demands, and elect their representatives. In practice, it was these thousands of spontaneously formed strike committees that handed the death sentence to the autocratic regime.[21]

Two days after the fall of the Shah's regime, the strike committees were instructed to disband. The man ordering all work to resume instantly was not based in any factory, nor in any other kind of workplace, but was universally recognised as the leader of the Iranian people's revolution: the revered Ayatollah Khomeini. On 13 February 1979, he issued his first diktat – get back to work – and the workers heeded him. Within three days, all factories were up and running again.[22]

However, nothing could remain the same in the workplaces. The returning workers were jubilant, energised after decades of apathy, amazed and euphoric over their own power to destroy despotism. They were not ready to go back to work as usual, or, as one metal worker put it: "After the revolution, the workers noticed that the country belonged to them."[23] Upon their return, they found many factories empty. Their horrified owners had fled the country in panic, taking with them as much money as they could.

In other factories, workers ran into the old managers nervously clinging to the helm. This untenable situation soon ignited into confrontation. At one factory, Eirfo, the returning workers presented the managers with a list of demands for higher wages and job security. When the managers refused to accept, they were taken hostage. Such was the course taken in scores of factories. In others, when obstinate workers demanded retroactive payment for the strike period, managers would decline, pointing out that no wage should be paid for no work; the workers would then declare that they had been preoccupied with saving the country – and without further ado, they would open the financial books of the company, and wages were paid.[24]

Whether managers were absent or present, compliant or uncooperative, the logical outcome and only practicable arrangement was the same: the workers gained control over production. The strike committees were not dissolved, but institutionalised, and now adopted the title *shora*.

A shora comprised the whole workforce of a given enterprise, manual workers and professionals, men and women, and constituted itself through general assemblies. In the assembly, an executive committee was elected, a constitution drafted, and major decisions taken. The executive committee reported back to the assembly, and mandates could be revoked at any time. The scheduling of general assemblies ranged from once a week to once a month; similarly, the actual structure of the shoras varied, from ones where the representatives took on full-time administrative responsibilities, to those where they continued working on the shopfloor. In some factories, the old management actually remained in place, but it was invariably reduced to a shadow of its former self, as the shoras pressed their demands for wages, holidays and job security, constantly interfering in the administration of the enterprise. But in the majority of factories, the shoras wielded power on their own and were in full control.[25]

During the months after the revolution, Iran thus entered the most comprehensive experiment in workers' control in the Third World seen to this day. Whereas their past equivalents in more advanced economies (that is, in the West) belong to the canon of radical political history, only one volume is exclusively devoted to the study of the shora movement. Assef Bayat's *Workers and Revolution in Iran* is a breathless tour through the factories while they were still under workers' control: "I had to adopt a guerrilla-type tactic of research – ask and run."[26] But the phenomenon did attract the attention of other observers, became the subject of a number of essays, and figures in every well-informed account of the revolution.[27] From these accounts a clear picture emerges. For most of 1979, the shoras ran the national economy of Iran. "There seem to have been as many different instances of 'workers' control' as there are factories", said one astounded reporter.[28]

The key to shora power was the right to hire and dismiss personnel. After the conquest of the workplace, a shora usually set up a committee to investigate those who were associated with the old authoritarian relations – foremen, Savak agents, directors with connections to the Shah's army. They were stood before a "proletarian tribunal" at the general assembly. The verdict on those found guilty was simple: dismissal. Workers who had been sacked by the old management, often for political reasons, were concurrently rehired.[29]

In a common procedure, the Fanoos factory in Tehran divided its executive branch into seven subcommittees, with responsibilities for the overseeing of supplies, production and distribution, for security, cultural activities and other aspects of factory life. According to its constitution, the Fanoos shora should "raise the level of output in the interests of the public", "organise the factory to cut the dependency ties [to advanced economies]", and secure "a just distribution of the products throughout the country".[30] At General Motors, the shora began switching production from private cars to public buses; at Caterpillar, it sent a team to Geneva to purchase raw materials; at uncounted shoras, all workers were provided with perks such as free lunches and transportation, literacy classes and parking lots, and increased house allowances. Though female workers had to struggle for proper representation in the shoras, these provided an arena for furthering their particular demands, such as workplace nurseries, which enabled women to continue working after childbearing, and were now regularly established in or adjacent to their workplaces.[31]

The pay gap between blue-collar and white-collar employees was radically narrowed. Productivity increases of up to 50 per cent were recorded.[32] For such miracles, a worker at the Melli shoe plant gave Assef Bayat an explanation: "Nowadays you don't need to tell a worker to go and work. He works himself. Why? The reason why he didn't work [under the Shah] was because he was under the boss's thumb. He couldn't speak out. Now, he'll say: 'the work is my own. I'll work.'"[33]

From his interviews and readings of shora constitutions, Bayat collects statements made in the same spirit. In the Leyland factory shora's constitution, the shora was inscribed as the expression of "the sovereignty of people over their own destiny". At another plant, a worker told Bayat: "Look, the reason why the Revolution was made at all was because we wanted to become our own masters; to determine our own destiny ... We did not want a situation where one or a few make decisions for two thousand."[34]

Bayat concludes that the shora was the product of a mood among workers during the months of the revolution, the "feeling that now was the time to rebuild *their* society, *their* country, *their* factory according to their own ideas", or, an "ambiguous ideology of possession and anti-authoritarianism".[35] Another scholar of the phenomenon, Valentine M. Moghadam, concurs: "Here was a situation that was fundamentally different from that before the Revolution, when there was no criticism, no open airing of grievances, enormous wage differentials between workers and managers, no participation in finances or production goals, and a rigid and authoritarian division of labour within the factory."[36]

While the factories were the nuclei of the shora concept, the revolution ensured its spread to other spheres of society. In his sequel *Street Politics*, Assef Bayat details how *shora-ye mahallat*, or "neighbourhood councils", flowered in the poor districts of the cities from January 1979 onwards, as the prolonged general strike brought about a state of emergency. No fuel, a dearth of basic commodities, social services in disarray: people had to gather together and come up with makeshift solutions. Idle youngsters were sent to requisition what fuel they could find and deliver it, as well as fresh bread and foodstuffs, to families' doorsteps, free of charge for the sick, elderly and otherwise penniless.

After the crisis had settled down, the neighbourhood shoras, whose leaders were either freely elected or appointed by trusted community figures, did not disband. They began digging wells, installing electricity, clearing areas for picnic places, and in many other ways upgrading the shantytowns of the urban poor. In spring 1980, Esfahan was divided into administrative areas, 70 per cent of them run directly by the shoras.[37]

The initial chaos of the revolution was the wellspring of more kinds of associations. In the months of the death struggle of the regime, bloody street battles, attacks on revolutionary neighbourhoods by diehard thugs loyal to the Shah, and the disintegration of the police forces made security an urgent priority. With the approval of the neighbourhood councils, so-called *komitehs* of lightly armed young men enthusiastically shouldered the task. Later on, in an altered guise, these komitehs would play a decisive role in the new Iran.

Homeless families and poor tenants occupied deserted luxury villas and hotels and set up shoras for their squats and blocks, unemployed workers assembled in councils, as did students and revolutionary soldiers; though only in two provinces – Kurdistan and the Turkmen areas of Golestan – peasants reclaimed land.[38] Wherever a shora was formed, it was the scene of heated discussions about the revolution, in its macro- as much as its micro-dimensions. The shoras were so many laboratories for democracy, at the most basic units of society, or, as Valentine M. Moghadam, called them: the "seeds of a new social order".[39]

BARREN SEEDS

These "seeds of a new order" possessed a number of fatal weaknesses. Lacking experience in trade unions or other forms of labour politics, the workers' councils were an improvised creation. They followed no single blueprint or received wisdom, since none had been allowed to accumulate; rather, the councils were developed as ad hoc responses to exigencies by a working class caught up in revolutionary fervour. Administering one's own factory proved to be within the capabilities of the shoras. Administering the country did not. No one knew how to implement ongoing coordination between workplaces.

During the spring of 1979, the idea of the shora as the cornerstone of a new national administration travelled on the revolutionary wind. "*Shoraism*" was in the air. Already in the weeks before the regime collapsed, a committee representing the oil workers in Khuzestan pushed for "workers' participation in the political affairs of the country" as the only forum for "genuine construction" of an Iranian republic.[40] Attempts to articulate such demands were made by gathering delegates from shoras all over the country. These gatherings took place in a Tehran building that would come to play a very different role a few years later: the *Khane-ye Karegar*, or "Workers' House". In the late spring and early summer of 1979, it functioned as the headquarters for the shoras of workers and the unemployed. While their representatives issued political statements calling for the full recognition of the councils, thousands of people made it a habit to pop in to the House for lunch, fiery discussions, or even shelter for the night. With slogans such as "Workers Democracy is Limitless",

Khane-ye Karegar unleashed a massive demonstration on the streets of Tehran on May Day 1979.[41]

The ideas of the shora movement were picked up by the one leading left-leaning cleric, Ayatollah Taleqani, who was immensely popular at the time. In April 1979, in what would be his last speech, he proposed a new constitution based on the shoras as the vehicles of popular self-government.[42] But none of these ideas came to fruition. In reality, every singular shora was acting on its own. There was no economic cooperation on a national scale, no pooling of resources, no institutionalised higher councils projecting the concept into the future. There weren't even organisational links with all those shoras outside the factory gates, only metres away.[43]

Perhaps even more noxious than the atomised character of the shoras was the influence of the parties of the left. After the exodus of the Tudeh and the militarisation of the factories in the early 1950s, Iranian Marxists had been fenced off from any contact with the working class. The repressive apparatus of the Shah remained successful in keeping that fence impenetrable. When a new generation of Iranian Marxists appeared on university campuses, they opted for a strategy in vogue throughout the Third World at that time.

In 1971, a small group of rebels, the *Fedaiyan*, descended from the very same mountains where the earlier jangalists had been based, and attacked a royal gendarmerie post in the village of Siyahkal. The Fedaiyan's intellectuals, influenced by Che Guevara's strategy of "focoism", excluded the possibility of any self-activity among Iranian workers. The power of the autocracy, they claimed, was "absolute", the powerlessness of the proletariat equally "absolute", and the only way forward was armed guerrilla struggle.[44] The Fedaiyan suffered a military defeat in the mid-1970s, but regrouped in 1978 and emerged onto the streets of central Tehran on 10 February 1979, when the Immortal Guard of the Shah made a final sortie. The Fedaiyan defeated the Guard, putting the last nail in the regime's coffin; they soon attracted up to half a million people to their rallies on the streets of Tehran.[45]

The Fedaiyan was the most substantial organisation on the Left after the revolution. The returning Tudeh, initially much less reputable than the valiant Fedaiyan, was the second most popular group. But these two were not alone in vying for the souls of Iran's rising workers. As can be gathered from Figure 2, the divisions on the Left soon reached absurd proportions. Maziar Behrooz, chronicler of the Iranian Left, puts the number of Marxist groups active in

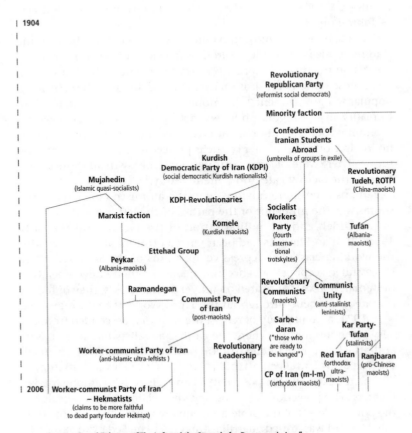

Sources: Saeed Rahnema: "The Left and the Struggle for Democary in Iran",
p. 250-279 in Cronin; Behrooz; Left Parties of the World: Iran, www.broadleft.org.ir

Figure 2   The genealogy of the Iranian Left: a selection

Iran after the revolution at 80, all of them Marxist-Leninist.[46] With
the exception of perhaps three, all of them were also avowedly
Stalinist. The Fedaiyan had never questioned Tudeh's trust in Stalin as
paragon – only Tudeh's unwavering loyalty to the Soviet Union *after*
Stalin – and copied the practices of crackdown on internal dissent,
violent purges, and paeans to Stalin as "the great teacher" and "iron
will of the world proletariat". Fedaiyan sympathisers received their
Marxism distilled through the words of Lenin and, even more so, of
Stalin, Tudeh adding the works of Khruschev and Brezhnev; neither

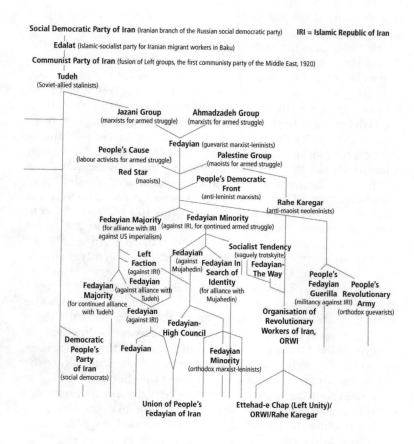

Social Democratic Party of Iran (Iranian branch of the Russian social democratic party) IRI = Islamic Republic of Iran

Edalat (Islamic-socialist party for Iranian migrant workers in Baku)

Communist Party of Iran (fusion of Left groups, the first communisty party of the Middle East, 1920)

Tudeh
(Soviet-allied stalinists)

Jazani Group
(marxists for armed struggle)

Ahmadzadeh Group
(marxists for armed struggle)

Fedayian (guevarist marxist-leninists)

People's Cause
(labour activists for armed struggle)

Palestine Group
(maoists for armed struggle)

Red Star
(maoists)

People's Democratic
Front
(anti-leninist marxists)

Rahe Karegar
(anti-maoist neoleninists)

Fedayian Majority
(for alliance with IRI
against US imperialism)

Fedayian Minority
(against IRI, for continued armed struggle)

Left
Faction
(against IRI)

Fedayian
(against
Mujahedin)

Socialist Tendency
(vaguely trotskyite)

Fedayian In
Search of
Identity
(for alliance with
Mujahedin)

Fedayian-
The Way

People's
Fedayian
Guerilla
(militancy against IRI)

People's
Revolutionary
Army
(orthodox guevarists)

Fedayian
Majority
(for continued alliance
with Tudeh)

Fedayian
(against alliance with
Tudeh)

Organisation of
Revolutionary
Workers of Iran,
ORWI

Fedayian
(against IRI)

Fedayian-
High Council

Democratic
People's
Party
of Iran
(social democrats)

Fedayian

Fedayian
Minority
(orthodox marxist-leninists)

Union of People's
Fedayian of Iran

Ettehad-e Chap (Left Unity)/
ORWI/Rahe Karegar

group produced creative analyses of their own country. The Iranian twentieth-century political Left actually stands out for its lack of any significant influences from anti-Stalinist currents of socialism: a legacy from the close ties between the northern parts of the country and Russia, including the occupation of 1941.[47]

Now the Marxists overwhelmed the fences around the factories. How did they respond to the shoras? On the one hand, here was the proletariat in person, bold and confident, acting in a way reminiscent of that great revolution in 1917. On the other hand, the shoras were spontaneous – that is, naïve – by nature, and seemed totally ignorant of the most basic need of their class: a Communist Party. Consequently, most leftist groups shared a common indecisiveness regarding the shora phenomenon, vacillating between fascination and condescension.

The Tudeh was the only party which decidedly disparaged the shoras, pursuing the policy of replacing them with traditional trade unions as quickly as possible, under the auspices of the party itself, as in its golden era of the 1940s. The party most receptive to the shora concept was, in the very early months after the revolution, the Fedaiyan. But in the spring of 1980, the organisation split in two. The Majority entered into a compact with Tudeh, joining the agitation for immediate dissolution of the shoras. The radical Minority viewed the shoras as useful, insofar as they facilitated the building of a Communist Party – and that was, indeed, the strategy of the vast majority of the leftist groups. The shoras had to be recruited as appendages to the Communist Party. Since this party was closer to being eighty parties than one, this strategy translated into the export of splits, confusion and mutual animosities to the factories. [48]

No single party was able to decisively and consistently maintain that the shora institution was valuable *as such*, regardless of its political content. They insisted on assessing the councils not in terms of the power they wielded, but rather the affiliations of their leading activists: in the eyes of the Fedaiyan Minority, one particular shora was beneficial as the Minority happened to have a footing there; in the eyes of the Maoist Peykar, it was malicious for the same reason, and so on. The fight was not for the defence and expansion of the shoras' authority; it was for authority over the shoras. [49]

Far from contributing to unification, leftist agitation in the factories – naturally effective in a revolutionary situation like this – served to further fracture the councils. The Peykar accused the Fedaiyan of reformism, while the Fedaiyan denounced the Peykar as anarchists using violence against rival agitators inside the factories. Members of the Fedaiyan Majority and Minority stopped talking to each other after the split, and ideological and tactical quibbles fragmented them and other groups into ever smaller particles. Maziar Behrooz sums up the relationship between organised Marxism and Iranian workers: "Imagine a situation in which workers are preparing for a strike: one group is arguing against the whole idea, another is proposing ideas so unrealistic that it has to be ejected from the meeting, a third is more concerned with isolating the first than organising the strike, all of this at a time when workers and management loyal to factory owners are doing their best to stop the whole venture." [50]

Such were the defence lines of the shoras when the onslaught began.

THE DAY AFTER TOMORROW

At first, the nascent Islamic state tolerated the shoras, since they were at the hub of society. In April 1979, even Ayatollah Beheshti, one of Khomeini's closest colleagues, commented that "if factories could be better organised with councils, they should be accepted … It is not possible to run a factory with bayonets."[51] At its innermost core, however, the Islamic state sensed the existential danger of the shoras from day one.

It wasn't long before Khomeini's first prime minister, the liberal Mehdi Bazargan, issued a first declaration of war. In May, he lashed out against those who claimed that "councils [should] run the affairs of the nation, and that people must be in a state of revolution all the time. If this goes on we will have no alternative but to resign."[52] His labour minister repeated that "the Ministry of Labor is either my place of work or the councils'."[53] To prevent the country from falling into anarchy, Bazargan promised that shora activists disturbing the proper management of factories would be "severely pursued by the authorities". Hence the government began appointing reliable managers and sending them off to the factories, accompanied by special police forces, to wrest power from the councils and make sure they were quietly suppressed.[54] On this issue, all factions, liberals as well as Islamists in and around the government concurred: it was either the new state or the shoras.

The first battleground was the Khuzestan oil fields. As early as February and March 1979, in the weeks after the end of the general strike, the provisional government had to deal with mutinous oil workers demanding control over production, or at least participation in all decision making. Without the oil flow, the new state would be as unfortunate as the old, and Khomeini had to use threat against the wilful workers: "Any disobedience from, and sabotage of the implementation of the plans of the Provisional Government will be regarded as opposition against the genuine Islamic Revolution. The provocateurs and agents will be introduced to the people as counter-revolutionary elements, so that the nation itself will decide about them, as they did about the counter-revolutionary regime of the Shah."[55]

The oil fields were one of the few strongholds of the Tudeh, which advised the workers to drop their loyalty to the shora and reconcile with the state. By the early summer of 1979, the oil shoras caved in to the pressure; stubborn activists were arrested as business returned to "normal", and the state regained full control.[56]

At this point, however, the overwhelming majority of shoras were still powerful enough to repel intruders. Most of Bazargan's managers were banished from the factories. It wasn't until November 1979 that the balance of forces started to shift throughout the country. This followed the occupation of the US embassy in Tehran – fearing a repetition of the coup in 1953, revolutionary students had decided to pre-empt any US plots – whereby the Iranian revolution entered its pure Islamic phase. Khomeini exploited the 444 days of the embassy occupation, parading the American hostages before the world's media; to strengthen his rule over the country, he replaced Bazargan's liberals with the truly faithful. The government now opted for another approach: it co-opted the popular idea of the shora and gave it a suitable twist. Alluding to Koranic verses on the value of *shura* – meaning "counsel" rather than "council" – Khomeini and his fellow mullahs introduced the concept of *shora-ye eslami*, or "Islamic council".

From the outset of the revolution, there had certainly been genuine workers' councils leaning towards Khomeini, but shora-ye eslami was something different. By this phrase, the government referred to organs consisting of workers *and* managers. They were supposed not to govern the workplaces, but to cancel out disagreements and foster the values of the Islamic *umma*. Brotherhood between all Muslims, sacrifice as the only way to prosperity, and, above all else, devout submission to the leadership of the clergy: these were the mandatory virtues of a shora-ye eslami.[57] It would not be difficult to distinguish from a shora proper – or as a member of the government's labour committee noted: "As long as workers' councils act to defend class interests, they cannot be allowed to operate in an Islamic society. Order in an Islamic society is based on guardianship."[58]

In August 1980, the state enacted a shora-ye eslami law, stating that a workplace had the right to form such an organ – and nothing else. All other rights, including the right to draft the constitution of the shora-ye eslami, set up its constituent body, and screen all its candidates and members, would reside with the Ministry of Labour. Armed with this law, the government moved to dismantle the workers' councils.

In 1980 and 1981, Islamic councils were established in the factories, alongside the shoras. A tense coexistence ensued. Gradually, the independent councils' powers were rolled back and the Islamic ones promoted. Since the revolution, the government had acquired a method for extortion: most industry had been nationalised, and any workforce that tried to stay in charge through its own shora could easily be cut off from credit, international transactions, or supplies of components. In this way, dozens of shoras were brought to their knees, while others caved in at the mere threat. If they survived as organising bodies at all (if not for the whole workforce, then for the most committed activists), the shoras receded into the shadow, as barely tolerated quasi-unions, while the power rested in the Islamic management.[59]

During this tug-of-war between the state and the shoras, lasting from the autumn of 1979 into 1982, workers responded bitterly with waves of strikes and other actions. They were roundly condemned. In August 1979, Ayatollah Khomeini found it necessary to chastise his people: "In these days after the revolution when all social strata should cooperate to reconstruct the country ... strike after strike, sit-in after sit-in, march after march, and lie after lie are prevailing attempts to weaken the government with deceit and rumours. Those who incite others to strike and sit in to weaken the government are opponents of our movement and supporters of foreigners."[60]

The next step, a legal ban on all strikes, was implemented in March 1980. "Representatives" of Islamic councils were summoned to echo the commandment that strikes are *haram*, sinful to Islam. Then the new state mobilised its sharpest weapon: the *Pasdaran*, or "Revolutionary Guards", a volunteer force of Islamist militants loyal to Khomeini, created precisely to "guard the revolution" against its internal enemies. It was deployed to break strikes and cleanse the national economy of intransigent shoras. In late 1980, the Pasdaran toured the factories of the northern provinces, where the shoras were most steadfast, sealing offices and making sure activists were sacked, arrested, or even worse. Assef Bayat happened to be present at the Fanoos factory in Tehran in late 1981 when Pasdaran forces burst in and took away shora members; that was the end of that particular council.[61] Twenty-three years later, a worker in a car factory in Tehran recalled how in those days "you would turn on the radio and hear nothing but names of executed shora activists being read out with contempt."[62]

The dismantling of the workers' councils was mirrored in the neighbourhoods, squats and centres for the unemployed. The shoras, likewise debilitated by divisions between political factions, were co-opted into the swelling Islamic apparatus, purged of opposition elements or starved by the withholding of economic resources. Just six months after they had assumed power, the governorate of Esfahan decided to cut all budget allowances to the neighbourhood shoras.[63]

But the crucial battleground was the sphere of production, where the state now directed its forces from a new headquarters: the Khane-ye Karegar. In summer 1981, the building was impounded by the Pasdaran. A coordinating body of the Islamic councils took up residence in it and adopted its name; the basement was henceforth used for the state's correctional method of choice: flogging. It became ever more difficult to differentiate between the shora-ye eslami and the Pasdaran. Armed guardians of the Islamic Revolution were permanently installed in the factories, as plainclothes agents and security staff, or, attached to the biggest factories, as soldiers in military encampments.

Farkhonde Ashena, now living in exile, was one of seven elected representatives of the shora at a textile plant in Tehran. This is her story, fairly typical, of how it all ended:

One day in 1982 they took me to the prayer-room in the factory's basement. People from the shora-ye eslami accused me of having spit on a picture of Ayatollah Khomeini. I felt ill at ease after the interrogation, and my co-workers agreed that from now on we should all prevent the guards from taking people away; if they wanted to ask us questions, they had to do it on the shop-floor. When I came home, I got rid of all the leaflets and workers' bulletins in my belongings. But two nights later, the Pasdaran showed up at our house. They broke in and took me away.[64]

After one year of torture, two years in isolation, and five more years in the notorious Evin prison, Farkhonde Ashena was finally released in 1990. Again from 1982, a worker at a metal factory in Tehran recalls a far from extraordinary incident, illustrating the state of permanent fear that had settled upon the working class, which was to last for decades:

They flogged one of my colleagues to death. They accused him of having cursed Imam Ali. First they brought him to prison, but then they dragged him to the factory and bound him to a machine. All production was stopped and we were ordered to appear in front of the scene. I could only stand to have my eyes on him for two lashes. Then blood was gushing from his wounds. He died after 50, 60 lashes. He was about 50 years old.[65]

Winter was back with a vengeance.

3
The Sword that Chopped Off America's Hand

EVERYONE AGAINST THE COMPRADORS

In 1979, a whole nation rose to free itself from tyranny. The working class, creating the shora institution on its own home ground, was but one of the protagonists. In his seminal study *Social Origins of the Iranian Revolution*, Misagh Parsa describes the revolution's character as something of a scramble. Or, perhaps one could say it was a *siqe*, that is, a temporary marriage of convenience between the constituents of the Iranian nation: different classes and groups rushed to struggle for their own interests, at a certain stage found each other fighting a common enemy and, for a short euphoric period, fell in passionate love, only to violently divorce as soon as the enemy was overthrown.[1]

As it happened, the working class actually arrived rather late to the revolution. When it muscled in, it dealt the mortal blow to the stability of the Shah's regime, and gave the event a distinctly proletarian flavour. Indeed, here was a revolution unlike any other in the world after 1945: it was urban-based, comparatively advanced in socio-economic context, initiated, sustained and brought to the final triumph by mass actions such as general strikes and street demonstrations. Unlike in China, Cuba, Nicaragua, and other well-known Third World revolutions, peasant mobilisation was never decisive in Iran, and armed struggle only ensued at the very last moment. In fact, the revolution was one of the most popular in world history, with a participation rate some five times higher than in the French and ten times higher than in the Russian revolutions.[2]

But the leadership was not based in the working class. Coming late, it had little choice but to take its place in the ranks arranged by others. Lacking organisational infrastructure, a union, a party, a charismatic figure or any other spearhead entity, workers rallied behind the revolutionary leadership already in place, namely Ayatollah Khomeini.[3] As the general strike drew to a close and demands became political, the workers staked their own class interests in Khomeini, pledging allegiance to him and calling for his return from exile. Parsa reports a typical case from mid-December 1978, when "workers in the Bandar-e Abbas steel complex walked out. They acknowledged Ayatollah Khomeini's leadership and vowed to fight for a democratic government based on the votes of the working classes."[4] In the rallies, people would shout "Hail to Khomeini!" one moment, "Workers' government!" the next, with no sense of incompatibility. An oil worker explained to a US correspondent: "We want Khomeini. He will take power from the rich and give it to us." In January 1979, revolutionary oil workers stated that "led by Ayatollah Khomeini, they [the workers of Iran] will take control of their factories in the days after the revolution and forever leave behind the exploiters and the imperialists."[5]

In terms of an individual, the common enemy was Muhammad Reza Shah Pahlavi. In terms of class, the enemy was the "comprador bourgeoisie", that is, a bourgeoisie reliant on capital and power emanating from the centres of world capitalism, and serving as their extension in the peripheral country. Such was the structure of the ruling class in Pahlavi's Iran. The Shah derived his regency from the intervention of the US state, which made good use of him as the policeman of the Persian Gulf, fighting off leftist guerrillas in Oman and hosting the US regional espionage centre in Tehran. To fulfil its role, Iran was equipped with the latest high-tech hardware from the armouries of the West; from the British, the Shah received more Chieftain tanks than the UK kept for its own armed forces. But it was the US who predominated, as Grumman, Lockheed and the other corporate giants of militarism took up forward positions in the Iranian economy. These corporations were faithfully followed by a flow of capital from the US into the Pahlavi kingdom in the guise of huge loans and "aid" packages, as well as banks buying Iranian banks and businesses, agribusiness corporations taking over Iranian markets for grain and agricultural equipment, and engineers and technicians ensconcing themselves in the prosperous Western enclaves in Tehran.

Thus the state-centred accumulation of the Pahlavi period was realised through American capital. Iranian industry became heavily dependent on intermediate and capital goods primarily from the US, from where financial capital was raised and returned. Foreign – that is, primarily US – investors were granted such benefits as subsidised bank credits, the right to full repatriation of profits, five years' tax exemption, and complete exemption from duty on all necessary imports. In addition, US military personnel stationed in

Iran enjoyed juridical immunity. These people were, in the Shah's time, the untouchable proprietors of the country.[6]

And they basked in the Iranian sun. Harvard economists advised the Shah that extreme profit levels were the key to wealth accumulation. Brochures enticing foreigners to invest in Iran brandished profit rates never below 30 per cent, and often as high as 200 per cent, and it worked, in so far as Iran experienced exceptional growth in the 1970s. But this wealth never accrued to ordinary Iranians. Their living standards were kept in check with a complete ban on strikes and trade unions. However, the wealth was shared with *some* Iranians, namely, the perversely rich royal court and its retinue of families. These were the domestic representatives of the class in charge of capital accumulation, sharing ownership of private industries, estates and lands, and enjoying international contacts: the Iranian face of General Motors was the Akhavan family, Caterpillar's was Vahabzadeh, Toshiba's was Barkhodar, and so on.[7]

During the Islamic Revolution, this comprador bourgeoisie was to be obliterated. All other groups in Iranian society, including the workers, had everything to gain from banishing the US masters and their Iranian compradors. As the workers joined the uprising, they naturally directed their grievances against the comprador bourgeoisie, their counterpart and material adversaries in the relations of production. Consequently, the striking oil workers of Khuzestan demanded that "all foreign employees must leave the country", "all communications must be in Persian", along with "punishment of corrupt high government officials and ministers".[8] Strike committees all over the country standardised the definition of their struggle as "anti-despotic *and anti-imperialist*".[9]

Anti-imperialism was indeed the link between the workers and Ayatollah Khomeini, who made every effort to concentrate the energies of the masses on purifying the country of all foreign influence. However, by simultaneously forcing the revolution through the palaces of the comprador bourgeoisie *and advancing the national leadership of Khomeini*, the striking working class unwittingly contributed to the building of a new cage for the workers.[10] For in the emptied palace, another ruling class would enthrone itself.

THE BAZAARI ROLLS OUT THE BANDWAGON

One of the first groups to roll out the revolutionary bandwagon, by instigating street demonstrations in early 1978, was one peculiar to the Iranian social formation: the *bazaari*. Its abode is the city's central bazaar. The bazaar is a maze of narrow, shadowy alleys under vaulted roofs, where hundreds (in Tehran, tens of thousands) of small shops offer their goods. They are owned by merchants, each one proud of their expertise in the one commodity they deal in – be it carpets, textiles, veils, pistachio, spices, pewter – or manufacture right on the spot, often in the same workshop where their fathers' fathers once perfected the skills of a coppersmith, goldsmith, tinsmith, shoemaker, bookbinder, or saddler. The bazaari move easily between their roles as wholesalers, retailers and artisans, as well as money lenders and stock exchange speculators. In the latter functions, they determine prices – in Tehran, national prices – through constant market transactions.

Every commodity has its own section in the bazaar, as the home of that particular guild. The bazaar is thus a labyrinthine shopping mall with multifarious scents, colours, noises and the omnipresent sound of endless haggling. If the assembly line, or the coal mine, is the historically ideal space for the fostering of proletarian class consciousness – workers being densely packed together, in perpetual communication with each other and forced by material necessity to develop a sense of fellowship – then the bazaar is the equivalent for the petty bourgeoisie.

But the bazaar stretches beyond the confines of this class category. In the bazaar, there are guesthouses, public baths, teahouses, courtyards, and, most importantly, mosques and *madrasas* interspersed among the shops, making it a place for much more than trade and commerce: the bazaar is a community centre, the sediment of centuries of social life in Persia. Therefore, it is not only a greenhouse for the growth of petty bourgeoisie self-awareness, but for its articulation or trans-figuration into a wider community interest.[11]

Hence a major theme running through the history of modern Iran is the activism of the bazaari. Time after time, the bazaari has been inflamed by the encroachment of foreign capital, or by government regulations, or a combination of the two. The Constitu-tional Revolution was triggered by the Tehran bazaari, after the Shah's police forces had publicly beaten sugar merchants for not reducing prices as stipulated; with this incident, the bazaari felt it had had enough of the Shah and his desire to satisfy European merchants with the one hand while manhandling Persians with the other. They demanded and received a Majles, of which they initially made up about 40 per cent.[12]

The prelude to the next great revolution was very similar. In late 1977, the bazaari had been drawn into a fight with the highest stakes. The Shah's plans for capital accumulation included the construction of a new commercial sector outside the bazaar, with large banks, shopping malls and supermarkets selling cheap machine-made carpets and other commodities, imported through wide-open channels from the US or Europe. In industry, the Shah favoured equally large and technologically advanced enterprises. The royally protected class of foreigners and their compradors thus threatened to crowd out the bazaari from their ancient economic turf. One observer wrote: "With the import of the Pepsi Cola factory, all lemonade workshops disappeared; with the growth of factories engaged in the production of household goods, the furniture and other workshops closed down; with the setting up of shoemaking factories, shoemakers went out of business."[13]

The Shah made it seem a virtue to bulldoze the bazaari – "[they] are a fanatic lot, highly resistant to change because their locations afford a lucrative monopoly" – as well as the bazaar itself, when in 1976 a proposal was tabled to flatten the bazaar of Tehran and build a new market modelled on London's New Covent Garden. Even before this, the Shah had made the bazaari a scapegoat for galloping inflation (in reality caused by the inflow of petrodollars) by imposing special price restrictions on them and systematically punishing those who were caught price-fixing or overcharging by fining them, closing down their shops and deporting them to remote villages. Still, the bazaari were in control of most of the retail trade within the country. But if the Shah was to carry on with his programme, clearly there would be no space left for them.[14]

The bazaari were forced to mobilise for survival – and knew where to turn for support. For centuries, the bazaari were tethered to the *ulama*, the Shia clergy. Any city's central mosque was always adjacent to or built into the bazaar structure. Local ulama and bazaari belonged to the same families, and through honourable donations the bazaari – always proud of their piety – financed the vast infra-structure of mosques, shrines and madrasas, as well as the communal ceremonies in the holy month of Muharram and other feasts. One hand paid the money, the other the blessings. As they were in daily contact with lay believers, the bazaari functioned as intermediaries between the populace and the ayatollahs; to have an audience with a revered ayatollah, the best path was through recommendations from a respected bazaari figure. One knew the way to the heart of the other.

Already in 1963, the bazaari and the ulama had joined forces in protest against the policies of the Shah. He had reacted by expelling a fiery cleric named Khomeini. In late 1977, as they were threatened in their very existence as a class, the bazaari knocked on their brothers' doors and asked that something be done against this wicked regime which ruled at the beck and call of the infidels.[15]

OBEY THOSE IN AUTHORITY AMONG YOU

In January 1978, the Shah created the opportunity for the formation of a bazaari-ulama alliance. An official newspaper published the most malicious vilification of Ayatollah Khomeini, portraying him as a man "without faith", agent of the Arabs and the British. Theology students loyal to the ayatollah took to the streets in the holy city of Qom, and were massacred. First to react were the bazaari, who shut down bazaars all over the country in protest, as a first show of their power to disrupt the national economy. On the fortieth day after the Qom massacre, marking the end of the Muslim mourning period, they shut them down again, marched with Khomeini's followers through the streets, and were again repelled with murderous force. For the rest of the year, bazaari strikes and huge rallies were synchronised in rising tidal waves – usually in forty-day intervals – flooding the country as other groups rallied behind, ready to receive the Shah's bullets. This all took place before the workers dared to begin to go on strike.[16]

During this concentration of forces, by no means all ulama were in favour of revolutionary action. The highest-ranking ayatollahs within the country actually attempted to dissuade the movement from escalation. But whatever they might do to put on the brakes, the forces remained in motion, and accelerated, driven primarily by the bazaari, but also facilitated by religious amenities. The mosques were the only infrastructure available: apolitical as they originally were, they had been left all but untouched by Savak. While the Tudeh, the Fedaiyan, and all other expressions of autonomous political life had been viciously repressed, the publication of religious journals and books continued and legions of mullahs were drilled in Qom, the clergy preaching to the masses every Friday. In 1978, more than ten thousand mosques provided the only space that was fairly safe from attack where people could discuss the latest events, mourn their losses, and prepare for the next demonstration. Under the cover of Ramadan prayers, they would gather for riot. The parties of the Left, emaciated by the years of clandestine existence, didn't stand a chance against this formidable organisational power.[17]

It was through analogous conditions that Ayatollah Khomeini established himself as the focal point of revolution. Because he resided outside Iran, he was relatively immune to the Shah's repression; first from Najaf in Iraq, and then from Paris, he could preach freely and shower the Shah with plentiful amounts of vitriol. His message reached Iran in audio cassettes. Thanks to this privilege of exile, all through the 1960s and 1970s Khomeini built a reputation not as an ayatollah more deft in esoteric exegesis than the rest, but as the one uncompromising, undaunted enemy of the Shah. Attacking the US domination of the Iranian economy, the losses of bazaari markets, the imperialist pillage of natural resources, the indiscriminate killing of demonstrators, and never flinching from the belief that the entire regime must go, his power was magnified by actual events. At the end of 1978, there was a national outcry for his sword, to cut Iran's Gordian knot, and bring forth an Islamic republic.[18] The transition to this idea was seamless:

How can we stay silent and idle today when we see that a band of traitors and usurpers, the agents of foreign powers, have appropriated the wealth and the fruits of labour of hundreds of millions of Muslims – thanks to the support of their masters and through the power of the bayonet – granting the Muslims not the least right to prosperity? It is the duty of Islamic scholars and all Muslims to put an end to this system of oppression and, for the sake of the well-being of hundreds of millions of human beings, to overthrow these oppressive governments and form an Islamic government.[19]

Theologically, Khomeini's idea of an Islamic republic was cloaked in the term *velayat al-faqih*, or "rule of the jurisprudent". According to Shia Islam, the twelfth imam, Mehdi, left the umma to take up residence at some place invisible to the human eye – that is, "in occultation" – from which he will return in the last of days to instate a reign of divine justice. Until that day, the umma wanders without an earthly leader. Or does it really? During his studies, Khomeini came to the conclusion that a deputy should be appointed. Mehdi could in fact have a representative on earth – just as Mehdi himself is the representative of Allah – and this human being of flesh and blood could be none other than the most erudite and inspired ayatollah, who had full insight into the inner meaning of the Koran and the teachings of the imams. Khomeini pointed to Koranic injunctions such as "Obey God and the Messenger and those in authority among you", and Imam Ali's commandment to "obey my successors", whom Ali defined as "those who transmit my statements and my traditions and teach them to the people". To the successor was due unrestricted authority to guide the umma in every matter political, social and religious, an authority derived not from the US, but ultimately from Allah. And that person was, of course, Khomeini himself.[20]

As the revolution unfolded, the idea of velayat al-faqih took root in the ulama of Iran. Modest ayatollahs, preferring a compromise such as a pre-Pahlavi constitutional monarchy, were sidelined by the marching forces. The radical ulama, those who adhered to Khomeini, possessed unsurpassable leadership resources. Shia Islam elevates suffering at the hands of tyrants and the glorification of martyrdom, modelled on Mohammad's grandson Imam Hussein's courageous death in the battle against the evil caliph Yazid in Karbala in 680. This scenario serves as a thematic source for the faithful; radical clerics could easily use it to exhort the masses to intrepid action. As trustees of the de facto revolutionary infrastructure, the ulama were propelled into a position of national leadership, and through the hierarchical order of the mosques they could issue guidelines from the highest level – namely, Ayatollah Khomeini – straight to the populace.[21]

During the course of the revolution, this very infrastructure was redesigned step by step to become the new state apparatus, under the logo of Khomeini's Islamic Republican Party, the IRP. As soon as he had returned to Iran, rapturously greeted by 3 million people, Ayatollah Khomeini monopolised the power to appoint the Friday prayer leaders in all cities, placed his representatives in every government body, and staffed the judiciary with loyal mullahs. The komitehs, the civilian defence groups, were allied to the mosques and, in the summer of 1979, transformed into purely IRP groups. In Tehran, nearly 50,000 members of the komitehs were expelled for displaying lack of commitment to the "Imam's line" – "Imam" being the reverent name for Khomeini – as loyal followers were mobilised in the fight against his contenders. They were now reconstituted as the local neighbourhood branches of the Pasdaran, the iron fist of the Islamic republic, and were assigned as the watchdog over their neighbours, keeping an eye on them to ensure they refrained from any political or "immoral" acts.[22]

Such was the Islamic state in the making. But while the ulama certainly had accumulated a considerable amount of property during centuries of donations and inheritances, they should not be regarded as primarily a class, in the strict sense of the word. Rather, they were a phalanx uniquely equipped precisely for *state-building*, that is, for the construction of undisputed political and social authority.[23] Their first mission was to stamp out the alternative, parallel authority – the shoras – and negate its dissolution of power *by concentrating it all in the hands of the faqih*, the absolute jurisprudent, the Supreme Leader: Ayatollah Khomeini.

HONEYMOON IN THE PALACE

Throughout the Islamic Revolution, it was the bazaari who supplied its socio-economic backbone. They were the first to fill the mosques with their own class interests, pushing the ulama to action while maintaining the most intimate relations to Ayatollah Khomeini. Already in his first theological work, published in 1942, he had endorsed the sanctity of private property, naturally earning him the ear of the bazaari. During his exile in Najaf, he was financed by the bazaari community and outlined his ideas on velayat al-faqih in bazaari mosques. Back in Tehran, he invited an exclusive group to his headquarters once a week to give a speech on recent events, bazaari figures always in the front row.[24]

These were the partners in wedlock – no temporary marriage, this one – that seized the keys to the palace of the compradors, who either had been liquidated or were on the run. The takeover assumed the form of nationalisation. Beginning in July 1979, with the expropriation of Iran's 51 wealthiest families' assets, and at the end reaching out to more than 80 per cent of the country's major production units, the Islamic Republic concentrated the means of production in its own hands. But this should not be confused with anything related to socialism. Widespread nationalisation was a means of guaranteeing orderly succession, or, as one analyst put it: "[It] reflected not so much the new regime's ideological commitment to common ownership and public enterprise as a series of pragmatic and ad hoc responses emerging from the reality of one ruling-class coalition taking over power from another."[25]

But could the state really respect private property when it owned 80 per cent of production units? This respect was noted in the new Islamic constitution, but the reality was undeniably different. It was not until two decades later that the property formula invented by the new ruling class would be clearly developed.

To the bazaari, anyway, the destruction of the comprador bourgeoisie was a godsend. Space was cleared for expansion of its own businesses. As the Shah's henchmen disappeared, profits in the bazaar surged to the highest levels ever recorded. The sections of the Tehran bazaari that wholeheartedly backed Khomeini entered the highest levels of the body politic, such as, crucially, the Ministry of Commerce, now empowered to regulate all imports. The ministry became an office of guild organisations, the minister an influential bazaari. The system of bazaari donations to the ulama was augmented and remained a vital financial base even for the office of Al-Faqih. A special bazaari stronghold was established among the mullahs of the Council of Guardians, which was finally given the right proposed by Sheikh Fazlullah Nuri in 1907: to block every law interpreted as inconsistent with sharia. After the 1984 Majles elections, whose candidates had to be approved by the Council of Guardians, bazaari delegates were in the majority in that arm of government as well.

An Islamic leader of the Tehran bazaar, Sayyed Taghi Khamoushi, was promoted to be Khomeini's special head of guild affairs, while by chance his brother Mohandes Khamoushi was appointed as director of the body perhaps most indicative of the nature of the Islamic Republic: *Bonyad Mostazafin*, "The Foundation of the Oppressed". This holding company was established to appropriate all assets of the Pahlavi court – from cinemas to factories, even to real estate in New York – and to administer them in accordance with the commands of Al-Faqih.[26]

The booty was safely in the hands of the alliance. Bazaari and ulama had taken for themselves something they had never before possessed: direct state power. It had been achieved through the popular banishment of the comprador bourgeoisie, by *tearing Iran away from the orbit of dependency around the capitalist core, the US in particular*.[27] However, ghosts from that past would eventually return to haunt the republic.

POPULISM AND THE URBAN POOR

One of the very last groups to join the revolution was the shantytown dwellers, the landless men and women from the countryside who ended up in the festering slums of the cities, Tehran in particular – or, as they are usually called, "the urban poor". They certainly had their own bone to pick with the Shah – he had been determined to bulldoze their abodes as well – but it was not until the revolution had reached its very crescendo that its leaders broached their plight. Suddenly, Khomeini began employing the term *mostazafin*, "the oppressed" or "deprived", to appeal to them. At first, this focus on the urban poor was a way of safeguarding the revolution from the seductions of socialism, but after the victory of the Islamic Republic it was systematised, as Khomeini realised that the urban poor had a pivotal role to play in the new state apparatus. His rhetoric now became laden with dictums such as "In a truly Islamic society, there will be no shantytowns", "Islam represents the shantytown dwellers, not the palace dwellers", and "The duty of the ulama is to liberate the hungry from the clutches of the rich." Bonyad Mostazafin was instructed to use some of its holdings for social services, a programme of general improvement of communications between villages and cities was launched, and, of great importance for later developments, free electricity was granted to the poor and all fuel and petroleum products heavily subsidised.[28]

The role allotted to the urban poor and their rural cousins was, of course, to staff the Pasdaran. Recruited to this force of Revolutionary Guards – not as petty conscripts, but as the voluntarily zealous servants of Al-Faqih – they were offered a regular salary, a divinely appointed task, and overall power in their streets and neighbourhoods. This was an entirely new, and intoxicating, role. A considerable segment of the urban poor, either as members or as families dependent on their incomes, was absorbed by the Pasdaran and its different wings, such as the plainclothes "popular mobilisation" bands called the *basiji*.[29] As the Pasdaran was the pillar of the new state and held a monopoly on violence, this translated into a certain leverage for the urban poor *within* the state apparatus. It wasn't long before the potential for conflict with the bazaari became manifest. In the early 1980s, when the mostazafin or sansculotte phase of the revolution was at its height, the urban poor managed to revive the anti-profiteering policy of the Shah and flog some thousand bazaaris accused of ravenous over-pricing. The bazaari subsequently used *its* leverage within the same bloated apparatus to stop the floggings *and* kill consumer cooperatives in the poor neighbourhood mosques at the same time.[30]

At this juncture, the Islamic Republic was in the midst of a major discussion on the desirable extent of government interference in the economy. Al-Faqih himself saw fit to pass a judgement: "The things that the government is not able to do, the government should not do. But do not prevent the bazaar from doing the things it can do."[31] However, this was not really a final word, for a lasting tension had been built into the state, aggravated by the well-known logic that social conflicts repressed by a one-party system tend to reappear in sublimated forms within it. For decades to come, the intrigues between the ulama, the bazaari and the urban poor would engender frictions, plots and factional disputes inside the Islamic Republic that would remain obscure to the outside world.[32]

But over it all, there hovered the infinite wisdom of Al-Faqih. He knew how to satisfy his constituencies and maintain a relative harmony. The recipe for this tour de force has been eloquently defined by Ervand Abrahamian as *populism*, that is, "a middle-class movement that mobilises the masses with radical-sounding rhetoric against the external powers and entrenched classes. But in attacking the establishment, it is careful to respect private property and avoid concrete proposals that would undermine the petty bourgeoisie."[33]

More than 25 years after the revolution, the same delicately balanced mixture would, at another critical juncture, prop up the unity of the Islamic Republic.

A LETHAL LOVE

On one point, the Islamic Republic was perfectly unequivocal from its moment of birth. It was against the most basic rights of the working class. During the siqe that was the Iranian Revolution, this class performed matchlessly, but it fell prey to its own ex-partners. The bazaari and the ulama would never have come to power without the working class smashing the economic machine of the Shah, but they reciprocated by leaving the marriage at once and assailing the shoras, the right to strike, freedom of expression and all the other real or potential threats to their monopoly on power. When it came under attack, the working class was locked out of the same mosques – now megaphones of the state – that had recently welcomed them. The working class was forlorn, alone. Not even the urban poor would stand by its side; too many of them had found an outlet for their *ressentiment* in the Pasdaran.[34]

But more than anyone else, it was the Ayatollah-turned-Faqih who betrayed the illusions of the infatuated working class. These illusions had been stirred by the parties of the Left. During the revolution, all of them believed in the following deduction: our enemy is the comprador bourgeoisie; the "national bourgeoisie" – that is, the bazaari – is the enemy of the comprador bourgeoisie; hence the national bourgeoisie is our friend. Furthermore, we both wish to establish a national, Iranian economy; that is what all the "popular masses" are striving for. In a trenchant analysis, Valentine M. Moghadam writes, "Little did these groups know that a clerical regime, guided by a vague philosophy of Islamic populism, could accomplish all this and be profoundly anti-socialist and repressive as well ... The Left's focus on dependency and anti-imperialism blinded it to the exploitative nature of the Bazaar, and the politicisation of a clerical caste that was beginning to talk of Islamic government."[35]

The Iranians were a proud people, united in the attempt to free themselves from imperialism – and their leader was Khomeini. The Left, initially with one voice, extolled the Ayatollah's relentlessness and refusal to even consider a compromise with the enemy. To some degree, the Left's allegiance can be explained by the deceitful promises made while he was still in Paris. For example, in November 1978, he declared: "in Iran's Islamic government the media have the freedom to express all Iran's realities and events, and people have the freedom to form any form of political party and gathering that they like."[36] But the fundamental reason for the Left's loyalty was Khomeini's anti-imperialist stance; in that regard, he was seen as a hero.

Most confident in this position, and pursuing it to its absolute extreme, was the Tudeh party. It had learned from Moscow that "the clergy can play an objectively useful role to the extent that they are anti-comprador." Back in Iran, the Tudeh proclaimed that "Islam is the ideology of the anti-imperialist revolution", and, long after the departure of the compradors, sided with the clerical rule against anyone who might have any complaint against it.[37] "Uncovering the policies of the counter-revolution in the workplace, in the family [sic], and in any place where the masses are present is one of your most important duties", the leaders of Tudeh wrote to the party's supporters in August 1981.[38] Strikes were one of the ugly faces of this omnipresent counter-revolution. Tudeh subscribed to the banning of strikes on grounds identical to Khomeini's – that they were indeed objectively pro-imperialist acts of sabotage – and according to the same logic, intransigent shoras were of course equally counter-revolutionary.[39]

Tudeh actively promoted the split in the Fedaiyan. After affiliating with the Fedaiyan Majority, the two parties assisted the Islamic government by handing over inside information about the Fedaiyan Minority, as well as other leftist and Kurdish groups that had declared their opposition to Khomeini. "Never before", Maziar Behrooz concludes, "in the history of communism in Iran, and very rarely in other parts of the world has a Marxist organisation collaborated so closely with the state in the suppression of other Marxist groups."[40]

While the Tudeh and the Fedaiyan Majority disgraced themselves in their one-sided love affair (in 1983, a cunning Khomeini crushed them too), there were those on the Left who abandoned the illusion at a fairly early stage, most notably, the Fedaiyan Minority. Its reasons for opposing the Islamic Republic, however, were but an extension of the original deduction, now in the form of a *reductio ad absurdum*: the Islamic Republic purports to be freeing Iran from the imperialist enemy; the Islamic Republic is a lying enemy; hence it is a puppet of imperialism. The Fedaiyan Minority went into the mountains of Kurdistan and Gilan in order to resume armed struggle against the mullahs whom the Minority identified, contrary to all perceptible evidence, as *disguised compradors*. The Maoist party Peykar and a range of other radical leftist groups adopted the same analysis, thereby exposing themselves to a simple retort from the Islamic minions in the Tudeh and the Majority: how can you possibly explain all these obvious contradictions between the Islamic Republic and the US?[41]

The problem was, as Moghadam and many others have pointed out, the one-dimensional focus on anti-imperialism.[42] Completely ignorant of the concept of democracy, the Left was never able to formulate any coherent critique of the Islamic Republic with a bearing on the daily experiences of the working class. Instead, the anti-imperialist agitation resounded within the factories, where many a shora activist perceived the struggle against the compradors as their sole quest, their attention to the aspirations of the "national bourgeoisie" severely diluted.[43] Thus the stage was opened for the turbaned rulers.

Some commentators have judged this mistake so harshly as to put it on a par with that of the Komintern in the early 1930s, when the social democrats were regarded as the main enemy and the Nazis rose to power unchallenged.[44] There are undeniable parallels, not least of which are the implications of the question: what would have happened if the Left had behaved differently and managed to ward off the fascists? The Islamic Revolution of Iran was an epoch-making event, one that placed the Middle East on a political track it has never left. But it was built on the graveyard of another revolution.

There is, however, one lacuna in the analogy: enslavement under the US-backed compradors in Iran was a reality. Whereas the Komintern might have concocted most of the faults for which it blamed social democracy ("social fascism"), Iranian suffering under foreign dominance was painfully real. Behind all the errors and ignominies of the Iranian Left, there was a material dilemma; one experienced by progressive movements in most of the Third World, but perhaps nowhere as acutely as in Iran. How far must we go to close our ranks, how many brutes of our own breed – power-mad as they may be – is it rational to tolerate to keep a united front, when our nation is in the throes of fighting a foreign tyranny? If this dilemma was relatively easy to resolve at least after 11 February 1979, when the Shah and his compradors left the palace to the mullahs, it would, as we shall see, return in a much more complicated form many years later.

4

The Millionaire Mullah Bonanza

THE FUEL AND THE ENGINE

Early one morning in Iran, in 1908, the British geologist James B. Reynolds felt the earth shake beneath him; as he looked out from his tent, a 15-foot-high jet of black liquid shot up from the ground before him.[1] Since that morning, the history of Iran has been written in oil. What geologists had long suspected turned out to be true, and today, the Islamic Republic sits upon the second largest oil reserves in the world – only Saudi Arabia has more. Iran is similarly endowed with natural gas as well; the country's reserves are surpassed only by Russia's. The fortunes derived from these hydrocarbons are stored in the state's coffers. The Islamic Republic is keen to profess that, according to the Koran, what Allah has deposited beneath the surface of the earth can be the property of no individual human being; it shall be administered as a shared blessing of the umma. Hence, through the quartet of the National Iranian Oil, Gas, Petrochemical and Oil Refining and Distribution Companies, the Islamic state maintains a monopoly on every single drop in the ground.[2]

It hasn't always been a cornucopia. In 1979, the Iranian revolution – or, to be exact, the general strike of the Khuzestan oil workers – set off the most extreme price-hike ever seen in the global oil market. But, as the Islamic Republic made itself at home in the petroleum mansion, the price came crashing down and, with the exception of a few brief intervals, stayed low for two decades. During the 1980s and the 1990s, oil revenues were a far cry from what they had been during the Shah's last years; in 1988, the value of oil export revenues was down to a third of the 1977 level, which necessitated a great deal of economic austerity.[3]

But by 1999, cash came flowing from the sands. This was a first sign of the looming global oil peak – a topic to which we will return. Revenues slumped during the recession of 2000–01, only to rise with renewed force in 2002. Now, oil export revenues flowed as never before to Iran, the curve rising steeply: in 2005, they increased a staggering 45 per cent. Second in production only to Saudi Arabia, the Islamic Republic now receives slightly more than 10 per cent of all OPEC revenues. As of early 2006, that translated into between $40 billion and $60 billion dollars a year.[4] And there is no end in sight. The oil peak promises to extrapolate the curve into the foreseeable future: a true miracle for the Islamic Republic.

In the new millennium, oil makes up 60–70 per cent of the state income, compared to, for example, 35 per cent in 1998.[5] As taxes are closer to 20 per cent, many commentators have labelled Iran a "rentier state", signifying an idle parasite living on petroleum wealth.[6] However, the revenues are not all squandered. Ever since the reign of the Shah, investment levels have followed the swings of the oil price. In the republic today, the mechanism works like this: the state receives the revenues, places them in banks, and from there they are simply doled out to private or public companies as loans with truly virtuous interest rates. Through these channels, the oil money greases the wheels of actual capital accumulation.[7]

Most of Iran's petrodollars are deposited in the Oil Stabilisation Fund, a savings account opened by the state in 2000 to smooth out the ups and downs of oil prices. But in the age of seemingly perpetually high oil prices, there is no reason for hoarding. The Fund is cheerfully feasted upon. Like the boar of Valhalla that was butchered and eaten every night by the fallen Viking warriors, only to be found alive the next morning, Iran has now been blessed with its own national Särimner. The Fund is used for all kinds of purposes, such as expansion of the Pasdaran, new equipment for the police, grants to disabled war veterans – and private sector investment. The latter's share constitutes between 30 and 50 per cent of yearly withdrawals.[8] Added to the transfers to public companies, that means a preponderance for utilisation of oil revenues in productive areas such as mining and industry.

The upshot of these arrangements is a fundamental fact: the state is the engine of capital accumulation in Iran, and oil is its fuel.[9] This fact determines relations between the classes in Iran, as well as those between Iran and the world. It has been inherited from the Pahlavi era, but remoulded and given a new significance by the Islamic Republic.

UNEVEN DEVELOPMENT

In 1979, the hands of US capital in Iran were chopped off. Before the revolution, they were everywhere: in oil, armaments and banking, in the markets for high technology, agricultural equipment and consumer goods. The US was Iran's main and unrivalled trading partner. By 1986, the US share of Iran's markets stood at 0.5 per cent. After conquering Iran, the mullahs staged a major redirection of trade relations away from the US and the advanced capitalist countries, towards the developing world.[10] The severing of trade relations with the US was partly a function of American sanctions, but these were in a way a realisation of Iran's own intentions, for the very *raison d'être* of the new regime was the excision of American capital from the country. The other side of this program was a rapidly rising share of developing countries in Iranian imports: from 22 per cent at the time of the revolution to 46 per cent twenty years later. While 60 per cent of Iranian non-oil exports went to developed countries in 1979, the share was 36 per cent in late 1990s – even Germany's had been halved – with a correspondent doubling for developing countries, new major partners being the United Arab Emirates, China and Turkey.[11] America's hands were gone, while others were, deliberately, tied deep into the Iranian economy.

But the leitmotif of the Islamic Republic's economic policies became what Khomeini called *khod kafai*, "self-sufficiency": Iran should be able to construct the production hubs of an advanced economy entirely by itself. Reaching this goal, however, proved an uphill battle. Inscribed in the laws of path dependency, the patterns of importing high technology and other capital goods were difficult to break; plants built by US and other Western capital had to be operated with the same techniques and materials long after the Shah had departed. These factors slowed the shift to non-Western trading partners and the advancement of an Iranian industry.[12]

As a lever on the way to khod kafai, however, a general prohibition on imports of *all* goods that could be produced domestically was enforced in 1990. This was a considerable radicalisation of Iran's import-substitution policy, and it worked. During the years of depressed oil prices, the state was forced to look inwards and put its faith in domestic manufacturing; one stimulus was to create a closed market for its products, while another was to make loans more easily accessible. A new generation of small- and medium-sized manufacturing companies emerged and, uniting their efforts with the equally stimulated public sector, they managed to spur on Iran's lagging industrialisation.[13] The process was dramatically reinforced when oil revenues began to flow at the turn of the millennium. The combination of protective measures, readily available investment capital, and a positive demand-spiral already at work in the domestic market ushered in a period of industrial development unseen since the early 1970s. From a nadir of 32 per cent in 1986, the industry's share of GDP had been lifted to 41 per cent in 2004.[14]

The jewel in this particular turban is Iran Khodro, "Iran moving by itself", now the largest automobile manufacturer in the Middle East. This position has been reached by a shrewd expansion of joint ventures with Western automotive companies, a tactic earlier exercised by the compradors. In the 1990s, the state-owned Iran Khodro had engaged a host of multinationals such as Renault, Peugeot-Citroën and Hyundai (all presumably untainted by Satanic American ownership), in joint-venture agreements. To export cars to the Iranian market was strictly forbidden, but these companies were welcome to ship their components to Iran and let Iranian workers assemble them under the companies' supervision and training. The cars were thus relabelled as "Iranian" and given Persian names: *Pars*, *Peykan*, *Samand*.

From the Iranian side, the object was always the transfer of technology and know-how to Iran Khodro itself. Negotiations with multinationals itching for access to the Iranian market regularly ended up with pledges to undertake "full transfer of technology to the Iranian partner", as recently stated by Renault.[15] And, again, the tactic worked. A few years into the new millennium, Iran Khodro had learnt enough to begin the search for its own markets and joint-venture partners abroad. Exports increased rapidly during 2005, and are projected even higher for the years ahead, as the "national car" model Samand is sent out to conquer Russia, eastern Europe, central Asia and the Middle East. Samand is originally a Peugeot model, assembled in Tehran, with 68 per cent of its components now produced domestically. Before the revolution, all radiators, water pumps, pistons and electrical equipment were imported; now they are produced locally. This is a success story about wresting technology from Western to Iranian hands, the hoped-for goal being Iran identified as the regional hub for production of cars and buses. Half a million auto-workers are currently employed to achieve this goal, and between 1996 and 2003 the total sale of Iranian car products more than quadrupled. Iran now claims to rank eleventh among the world's auto-makers.[16]

With oil money bountifully distributed by the Stabilisation Fund and other foreign exchange reserves via the state-owned banks, Iranian industry has been driven to a qualitatively higher level of technological advancement. A range of advanced industries, from software to pharmaceuticals, have benefited from such benefits as eight-year loans with a 2 per cent interest rate, while large-scale projects in heavy industry such as steel and cement have been financed by the oil revenues.[17] When *Iran Daily*, one of the regime's English-language gazettes, boasted about Iranian progress in late 2004, the picture could be confirmed by independent sources: "Our industrial production is experiencing its highest levels in years. Today, we have access to technologies that we once wished for. We are the world's fourth largest dam builder and are capable of constructing large dams. We also have the capacity to build power plants, roads, railways, giant silos, petrochemical and oil facilities, etc."[18]

The auto industry is only one example of consolidated technological linkages *within* the national economy; another trend of the 1990s was increased satisfaction of the needs for intermediate goods at home. In 1977, 36 per cent of Iran's manufacturing products were intermediate goods and 60 per cent consumer goods; by 1997, the tables had turned, so that Iran was producing 28 per cent of its consumer goods, and 63 per cent intermediate.[19] A national economy that is supplying itself with means of production is the trajectory of a peripheral country moving away from dependency.

However, as in most nations following a radical import-substitution policy, Iranian industry – with a few exceptions, Iran Khodro foremost among them – would never stand a chance in a free market economic model.[20] In comparison with Western advanced economies, Iran's productivity levels remain low. In late 2005, *Iran Daily* candidly admitted that "productivity literally represents no share in Iran's overall economic growth".[21]

Outside the oases of large, well-nourished industrial enterprises, Iran's economy is still to a large extent a desert of backwardness. The textile industry – antique emblem of Persia – has failed to modernise; women still sew and weave in their homes.[22] Iranian textile production suffers heavy losses as Chinese goods flow into Iran, if not legally, then through the easily accessed routes used by endless caravans of smugglers.[23] The construction sector, on the other hand, is in a state of perpetual expansion. Iran is building everywhere, especially in its cities. But the technology is still primitive: hands, hammers and wheelbarrows are the standard tools. The same applies to brick production. The primary products for all construction are extracted and baked by approximately one million people working with their bare hands in temporary clay mills and plants.[24] Micro-production units – family homes, small workshops on street corners – still operate, following centuries-old traditions.

Light and heavy industries, traditional and modern methods, rural and metropolitan locations: uneven development makes Iran Janus-faced. In this regard, there is a certain continuity with the Shah's era. The face of the labour force has undergone only minor changes since then. Manufacturing makes up a fifth of employment, construction is up to a tenth, service has increased slightly to two-fifths, the diminished share being agriculture.[25] Capital does not accumulate evenly, and certainly not when oil is its fuel and the state its engine; rather, it tends to compartmentalise society, and this is truly the case with Iran.

THE MOST SECLUDED WONDER OF THE WORLD

Whatever happened to the compradors? The radical Left, banging its head against the Islamic Republic throughout the 1980s with no result other than its own further fragmentation, clung doggedly to the view that the compradors had never really left, the turbans being a mere cloak for the old American crown. The reality was otherwise. At the time of the Iranian Revolution, the entire periphery of world capitalism was in the process of being diverted from its experiments in building national economies, independent, or "de-linked", from the circuits of the core's capital; those economies would soon be fully reintegrated and accessible to Western investments, exports and financial speculation. At exactly the same time, Iran decided to move in the opposite direction.[26] In writing a new constitution for Iran, the Islamic Republic prohibited all "granting of concessions to foreign individuals and companies" and vowed to ensure the "prevention of foreign economic domination of the country's economy".[27] Under Khomeini's velayat al-faqih, the state kept a tight rein on exchange rates, trade permits, investment rights and all other economic dealings with the rest of the world.

After the death of its founder in June 1989, however, the profile of the Islamic Republic changed. As faqih, Khomeini was succeeded by Ayatollah Ali Khamene'i – a theological dabbler in comparison with the "Imam", unpopular and pale; as his second in command, Ali Akbar Hashemi Rafsanjani was elected president. They were a close-knit pair. As authorised by his captain, Rafsanjani began to dispense with Khomeini's revolutionary rhetoric regarding the mostazafin. Dismissing all reservations about "social justice", he praised private business as an "honourable profession", managerial skills the most noble of arts, and complained about the post-revolutionary atmosphere where entrepreneurs were "afraid to show their wealth".[28] Here was a president who cared nothing about the urban poor. He steered the Islamic state straight towards the wishes of the bazaari, and perhaps even further, as he hoisted the flag of economic liberalisation. Nationalised industries should now be privatised, trade regulations eased, the currency devalued, the Tehran Stock Exchange (closed since the revolution) reactivated, free trade zones established, money borrowed from the IMF, and, above all, foreign investors invited to return, in other words, the whole gamut of neoliberal economic policy.[29] Was Iran, ten years later, aiming to catch up with those Third World vassals of Washington? Some thought so. Anoushiravan Ehteshami, who wrote *After Khomeini*, a well-informed study of Iran, concluded that the republic was now moving "towards rapid reintegration into the Western-dominated capitalist world economy, and not away from it ... to the extent of inviting back to the Iranian market the exiled comprador classes which had been closely associated with the old, pro-Western, Pahlavi regime."[30]

However, full re-engagement with Western capital did not take place. The lofty proclamations of Rafsanjani ended in half-measures. Loans were procured from the IMF and the World Bank, but Iran repaid them dutifully and was never caught in the debt trap. The Tehran Stock Exchange renewed activities, but remained sluggish. Free trade zones were established in the Persian Gulf, most famously on the island of Kish, but these functioned more as havens for duty-free shopping than as magnets to attract investment. The most tangible result of "reintegration" was a property bubble in northern Tehran, where luxury villas and apartments were constructed in that prosperous enclave, high above the heavily polluted southern suburbs.[31]

Rather than retroactively confirming the suspicions of the ultra-Left, the Islamic Republic's rulers exhibited a prowess in opening its economy exactly where it suited its interest and keeping it shut exactly where it didn't, navigating gently between the risks and opportunities of integration. Trade is an illustrative case. Inside the state apparatus, there were vested interests in preserving strict regulations. Traders made huge profits on obtaining exclusive import licences, state-owned car, steel and textile corporations demanded continued protection, and there was every indication that high-level officials were actually cashing in on the illicit smuggling caravans, which had to pay up under the regulations.[32] Hence trade liberalisation made little progress during the 1990s. Instead, trade remains subject to the red tape of the Ministry of Commerce. The ministry continues to divide all goods into three categories: 1. permissible, that is, goods that can be imported freely (hardly any fall into this category); 2. prohibited, that is, luxury products such as beverages and fur coats, as well as carpets, dates, and others that compete with domestic producers, and 3. conditional goods, which *may* be imported. Those who import goods in the latter category, the largest, must pay fees for permits, tariffs and other duties – currently in the range of 170 to 300 per cent in the case of cars – and commercial profit taxes.[33] In late 1990s, taxes imposed the heaviest burden, but since 2000, tariffs are once again on the rise.[34]

Privatisation has been equally selective. It has gained momentum in recent years, and the state has now relinquished perhaps, at a high estimate, a fifth of its post-revolutionary assets. But it's not quite out of business. According to the IMF, 54 per cent of Iran's gross national income in 2003 was generated by enterprises entirely owned by the state, the Economist Intelligence Unit still complaining in 2006: "major sectors (such as oil and gas, transport, telecommunications, industry, and banking and finance) remain overwhelmingly under the purview of the state and its entities."[35]

Foreign direct investment (FDI) paints the same picture. The mullah's fingerprints are everywhere. Some of the paragraphs of the constitution most hostile to foreign investment were actually rescinded in 2002, after years of negotiating; while all foreign investments had been labelled *haram* after the revolution, some were now reinterpreted as *halal* – but only if properly authorised by the state. And the state offers irresistible brides. Levels of FDI are rising, in particular in the auto, oil and gas industries; in 2005, the sum equalled that of all FDI in the preceding ten years. The latest joint venture between Renault-Nissan and Iran Khodro at the time of writing constitutes the largest single French investment in Iran since the revolution, while Volkswagen has promised to build a car plant in the city of Bam, which was levelled by an earthquake in 2003; this factory will be integrated with Volkswagen's units in Brazil. Oil multinationals are present within the country (though none are American); among them are Shell, Total and Statoil. However, they and all other foreign investors have entered through the one and only gateway: deals with the state.[36] Inspections are meticulous, humility and lavish dowries mandatory. The state retains the right to rebuff suitors at any point.

The procedure of selecting a partner from the group of multinational giants eager to participate in the development of Iran's oil and gas fields is illustrative. The oil ministry makes a list of four to six bidders, examines their track record in developing a virgin field; it then assesses which corporation will allow Iranians to gain access to their technology. When the last bidders have been played off against each other, the remaining contestant is brought before a body run by the president and, finally, before Al-Faqih himself. If the bid is met with approval, the oil giant does not receive a concession but a "buyback contract": after rendering the state its services in developing a project, the corporation is reimbursed in the form of an entitlement to an amount of oil, to be cashed in on the market. The state misses no opportunity to extort the best conditions available, with a constant eye on appropriating the edges of visiting capital. And whatever the business, there is no way to bypass the state. The Majles reserves for itself the right to veto projects involving foreign investors, practically all capital transactions must collect bureaucratic permits, and the Tehran Stock Exchange, where privatised companies are put up for sale, is closed to foreigners.[37] The only way in is to ask the father and gatekeeper – the body politic of the Islamic Republic – and fastidious he is.

Read the international business press and whenever Iran is mentioned frustration is vented. Why don't they let us have a free taste, just like everyone else? Why do these mullahs persist in displaying such titillating objects of investments, without ever offering them for real? Every year, the Heritage Foundation and the *Wall Street Journal* present an *Index on Economic Freedom*, where the countries of the world are ranked by such criteria of accessibility for foreign capital as "property rights", "regulation" and "government intervention". Of 157 countries in 2006, Iran scored 156.[38] Only North Korea was lower. "Freer" than Iran are countries like Cuba, Burma, Zimbabwe, Laos, Syria, Uzbekistan, Venezuela, Haiti and Belarus. There is, however, one salient feature of the Iranian economy not shared by those of its superiors. It is booming. Of the 157 nations on the list, only *eight* have economies that are larger and growing more rapidly than Iran's.[39] In other words, if one somehow constructed an index where the economies were weighed on the combined criteria of size, growth and *inaccessibility for foreign capital*, Iran would probably be number one – the most secluded capitalist wonder of the world.

THE VAULTED MAZE OF THE BAZAAR

As long as the Islamic Republic remains in place, the comprador bourgeoisie is barred from returning to power. Instead, the last half-decade has witnessed the rise of an entirely original and domestic ruling class: the millionaire mullahs. The term was first coined in a report by Russian journalist Paul Klebnikov in *Forbes*, in July 2003; a year later, he was gunned down in Moscow, presumably by Russian mafia, but there were immediate suspicions involving Tehran.[40]

One particular millionaire mullah stands above the others: Hashemi Rafsanjani, generally believed to be the richest man in Iran. His family's list of connections would delight a bazaari-ulama family of the 1970s. Rafsanjani's cousin is managing director of the company that dominates the lucrative pistachio export market, a brother is governor of Qom, a nephew is a member of the Majles energy commission overseeing oil and gas policies. Rafsanjani's oldest son manages the company building Tehran's subway – one of the country's major ongoing infrastructure projects – while his youngest son has devoted his life to a stud farm in one of the must luxurious areas of northern Tehran. A nephew has a key position in the Ministry of Oil, a brother-in-law is a governor of Kerman province, home of the clan, where Rafsanjani himself has stakes in a factory assembling cars in a joint venture with Daewoo. Another son resigned from his post as a director of National Iranian Gas Company to run a unit linking the natural gas suppliers with the auto industry. And so the list goes on – according to Iranian street gossip, all the way to bank accounts in Switzerland, resorts in Goa and smuggling rings.[41] Rafsanjani is a true millionaire mullah: one who epitomises the fusion of bazaari and ulama, of Iranian capital and Shia Islam, that has taken place over the last 25 years.

Another brother-in-law of Rafsanjani, Mohsen Rafiqdoust, stepped down in 1999 from his post as director of the institution that more than any other symbolises the class of millionaire mullahs: Bonyad Mostazafin. Rafiqdoust's own biography reads like an Iranian version of the American dream. A bazaari, his career was kick-started when he was appointed the personal chauffeur of Ayatollah Khomeini; he experienced a meteoric rise through the ranks of the Pasdaran to become its commander, and then continued on to the Bonyad Mostazafin in 1989.[42] Second in size only to the National Iranian Oil Company, the foundation is a pillar of the Iranian economy. Estimated to employ 700,000 workers through its enterprises and subsidiaries, and representing a significant share of the country's GDP on its own, the Bonyad is so vast that, according to Bonyad expert Susan Maloney, Rafiqdoust was on safe ground when he boasted in 1995 that "we touch the life of every Iranian".[43]

The holdings of the Bonyad – exempt from taxes and audits, endowed with preferential access to foreign exchange from the banks, stretching across most economic branches in vertically and horizontally integrated divisions – read like the fantasy of a Rockefeller monopolist. Two-thirds of all bricks, tyres, chemicals and foodstuffs in Iran are produced by the Bonyad. It maintains a strong presence in textiles, tourism, transport and heavy industry; it dominates shipping, hotel chains, domestic aviation, and road and rail construction, and keeps slightly odd assets such as a Disney-style theme park outside Tehran and the Shah's treasure trove of old jewels and carpets. The story of the Bonyad's soft drink operations is an eloquent example of its role in the succession of ruling classes. In the late 1970s, bazaari lemonade dealers suffered under the pressure of Pepsi Cola, which was subsequently handed over to Bonyad Mostazafin after the revolution. Pepsi drinks were relabelled "ZamZam", the logo under which the Bonyad controlled the market without rivals up to 1993, when Coca-Cola made an attempt at intrusion through franchisers. Rafiqdoust then raised the jihad cry of Iranian capital: "God willing, we will soon drive all foreign Coca-Cola plants out of Iran." The nefarious interloper was indeed kicked out by the Foundation of the Oppressed.[44]

The power to muscle out competitors naturally applies to domestic ones as well. Here, the close connections to the Pasdaran are of great advantage. If an independent local entrepreneur challenges the market position of a Bonyad branch, someone may turn up and accuse him of having insulted the Prophet or some imam, and the competitor is simply locked up in jail.[45] Through its networks in the bazaar, however, Bonyad Mostazafin has also assumed the responsibility of being a nursery for millionaire mullah trainees, educating and engaging traditional bazaari in capital accumulation.

And prodigious it is. As the Bonyad straddles the border between state and market, enjoying the divine protection of Al-Faqih, to whom it is solely answerable, and benefiting from the legal vacuum created exclusively for its sake, it is believed to be an extremely profitable enterprise, though no public accounts are available. As such, it appears to have been accepted by the world market. The Bonyad invests extensively in South Asia and the Persian Gulf countries, trades crude oil through a UK subsidiary, and owns companies and operates joint ventures in several other European countries.[46]

The alleged representation of the mostazafin, substantiated by alms and philanthropic construction projects, is, of course, nothing but a fig-leaf for this empire. An array of similar foundations exists as well, maintaining their own clerical-capitalist fiefdoms throughout Iran (one of them, in the holy city of Mashhad, is headed by a family intermarried to Khamene'i's); Bonyad Mostazafin is simply the most munificent. Looking back on the vicissitudes of Iran since the revolution, Susan Maloney concludes: "the robustness of these foundations over the past two decades demonstrates their utility as mechanisms for capital accumulation and reinvestment."[47]

Strategically placed in the border region between public and private sectors, the bonyads stand ready to buy companies sold off by the state. They have been major players on the Tehran Stock Exchange (TSE) since its reactivation, buying and selling assets, and mobilising capital of a quantity few independent private actors can match. Consequently, they have been some of the most ardent advocates of further privatisation. The very first public stock put up for sale on the TSE was a share in Iran Metal Industries, bought by a subsidiary of one of the bonyads, with money allocated to it *by the state* for precisely that purpose.[48] Inbreeding in the millionaire-mullah class is truly endemic, the recycling of assets on the TSE a family affair; the exchange is not structurally autonomous from the state as in "normal" stock markets, but staffed with incumbent government officials and representatives who might very well have family or clan links to intended buyers. Insider trading is known to be the norm. Eighty per cent of the market value of the TSE is owned by the state or the bonyads, with the remaining private actors not-too-distant relatives.[49]

Corruption is rampant in the Islamic Republic. In 1995, in a rare case Reuters called "the trial of the century" in Iran, the brother of Mohsen Rafiqdoust was convicted of embezzling $400 million dollars from a state bank, Bank Saderat.[50] In 2001, the Ministry of Commerce conceded that the smuggler caravans could not possibly bring in huge quantities of goods such as refrigerators and televisions across the borders without government complicity. In 2003, Norway was rocked by a police raid on that country's largest oil company, Statoil, which was alleged to have paid $15 million dollars to Horton Investment, a London-based consulting firm linked to one of Rafsanjani's sons, in order to gain development rights to an oilfield in Khuzestan.[51]

The Economist Intelligence Unit implicitly concedes that such methods are essential for any foreign capitalist wishing to invest in Iran: "The rule of law in Iran is inconsistent and unsatisfactory ... Written agreements offer very little protection for the contracting party. Foreign companies often find that engaging an influential, and experienced, local business partner who also enjoys substantial political patronage is the most effective form of protection."[52]

It has been a routine practice ever since the bazaari infiltrated the Ministry of Commerce for the ministry to issue exclusive import licences to brothers, friends, and business partners; in one case from the late 1990s, some well-connected businessmen reportedly made huge profits on monopoly permits to import black cloth for veils.[53] Opacity is the key: this is the vaulted maze of the bazaar, mosques at its heart, expanded to encompass all of Iran; the smells, colours and noises may be different, but the haggling remains the same. Only the amounts of money in circulation have become astronomical.

PROFITS AND PREMISES

In the Islamic Republic, property and piety are atoms in the molecule of power. After the entry of the bazaari and the ulama into the state apparatus – some stayed behind, of course, to be out there selling and preaching to the people – they have fused to become the millionaire mullahs, or "Agah-zadeh", their sobriquet on the Iranian street, connoting a son of a clergyman who is now a prince.[54] The millionaire mullahs are patriots by virtue of their material interests, for they achieved their position through the expulsion of the comprador bourgeoisie.

One fundamental attribute of a dependent periphery is, however, as some would be quick to point out, undoubtedly still in place.[55] Heavy reliance on the export of one primary product forces Iran to remain embedded in the world market; in this sense, "de-linking" as a route to independence would be catastrophic. It is, on the other hand, questionable how much of a curse dependency on oil exports constitutes in the age of peak oil; moreover, it guarantees up to the very point of exhaustion of the reserves that the national state remains the engine of capital accumulation. And that is precisely where the millionaire mullahs are to be found. They became the ruling class of Iran by *capturing state power* and *thereby* the ownership of the major means of production, including, above all, oil. From this towering citadel they deal with outsiders on their own terms, fundamentally autonomous from the centres of world capitalism, which are now demoted to guests beseeching entrance from the other side of the moat.

Parallels can be drawn with the Soviet Union and Russia. But which one of them? Is the regime of the millionaire mullahs a Stalinist bureaucratic apparatus or a privatised *nomenklatura* mafia?[56] The crucial answer is *both*. The Islamic Republic came into being through a popular revolution which it subsequently destroyed, *and* it put the fortunes of unrestrained accumulation in private pockets *without any rupture in between*. The new millennium has, up to 2006, seen a continuation of the social logic established in the years of the revolution – only now, the millionaire mullahs are also enjoying a financial bonanza.

The numbers supply the evidence, since oil money came onstream. In 1990, aggregate investment equalled 20 per cent of GDP; in 2004, it stood at 31 per cent. In that year, the export of non-oil commodities nearly doubled. While stock exchange indices world-wide were tumbling in 2001–03, the performance of the Tehran Stock Exchange astounded foreign observers; it more than tripled between 2001 and 2005. After negative growth in the 1980s, an average yearly growth of no more than 1.7 per cent in the 1990s (and negative in 1998 again), the Iranian economy took off to 4 per cent growth in 2000, and lingered between 6 and 7 per cent from 2002 to 2005. State representatives have called such growth figures "unprecedented in the Middle East", independent observers choosing the phrase "the envy of the Middle East"; without doubt, it is astounding.[57] Expansion has been led by the manufacturing sector, where a profit miracle has been taking place since the mid-1990s. The expected average rate of nominal profit in manufacturing fell from around 10 per cent in the years before the revolution, to 8 per cent in the mid-1980s, recovered to 12 per cent in the beginning of the 1990s, and settled at a stable *16–19 per cent* between 1995 and 2003, from where the latest data is available.[58] As productivity levels are low, there must be another source for these profits.

Millionaire mullahs may have a bonanza *shukr allah*, but for the working population of Iran, however, that spells winter.

5
The Islamic Republic of Dust

MARTYRS IN THE LABOUR MARKET

The decisive moment in the history of the Islamic Republic, whose consequences would reverberate through the decades, occurred on 22 September 1980. When Saddam Hussein sent his infantry legions and thousands of tanks rolling across the border, Iran was caught unprepared. The revolution had dissipated the royal armed forces and broken up command structures; Iran's arsenals were in disrepair. While Saddam Hussein – whose army at that time was considered formidable – certainly couldn't realise his fantasy of a swift "whirlwind war", large swathes of strategic Iranian territory in the border provinces, including Khuzestan, were initially captured.[1]

To retake their territory and repel the Iraqi Army, the Islamic Republic, weak in arms technology but unmatched in revolutionary zeal, devised a military strategy not seen before. Armies of young men and even boys, clutching bombs in their hands, were dispatched into the mine fields and towards the enemy tanks. As martyrs, the young men supposedly went straight to heaven. They had been equipped with keys strung on necklaces, symbolising their imminent entry into Paradise; recruitment of 13-, 14-, 16-year-old martyrs swept through Iran's schools. The "human waves" of the basiji actually played a significant tactical role in the battlefield, turning the tide of the war; the Shiite cult of martyrdom reached new levels as the original battle of Karbala of 680 was re-enacted along the Iraqi border.[2]

Ayatollah Khomeini spared no efforts to replace the supplies for the struggle against the Yazid of the day. He had already made clear to Iranian women that their particular inspiration should be Fatima, daughter of the Prophet Muhammad, whose greatest act in life was to give birth to Imam Hussein, martyr of martyrs, hero of Karbala. Now, Khomeini began to exhort the pure and modest Fatimas of Iran to procreate at breakneck speed in the service of Allah and the nation; contraception was outlawed, and families producing five or more infants rewarded with a free building plot. The result was a demographic timebomb. While other countries in the region saw a steady demographic transition, Iran's population boomed as never before. In the first half of the 1980s, the yearly growth rate was 3.9 per cent, one of the highest in the world.[3]

Today, the armies of martyrdom do not enter heaven, but the labour market. However, it's getting crowded. Sixty-five per cent of Iran's approximately 70 million citizens are under the age of 25, and since the turn of the millennium this highly educated baby-boom generation has swelled the ranks of wage-labourers year by year. The labour force is forecasted to continue to grow annually by between 800,000 and 1.1 million people (depending on the degree of female participation) to at least 2010. Just to keep the unemployment rate steady, the economy must maintain no less than 8 per cent growth per year. To fully absorb the human tide seems beyond the realm of economic possibilities. Since the late 1990s, the waves of job-seekers are as massive as the population growth rate was in the 1980s, the labour force growing 3–4 per cent yearly. So far, it doesn't add up. Unemployment has been steadily on the increase, from a level of 10 per cent in the 1990s, to between 14 and 16 per cent in the years 2003–05, according to official Iranian estimates. In reality, it is generally believed to be twice as high: roughly 30 per cent.[4]

This man-made demographic development, unique to Iran, weighs heavily on the balance of power between the classes. It has opened up opportunities for unprecedented steps against the living conditions of working people. One drop in the ocean of Iranian unemployment, "Behrooz", tells his story:

I was sacked one year ago from a pump machine factory, because I had quarrelled with the foreman. It was just for him to pick someone else. For those of us who are over 25 years, there is not a chance to get back into the labour market once you've been dismissed. In every employment interview, I am informed that I'm too old. Unemployment is the most severe punishment for a worker. Even in *Kar va Karegar* [the official labour newspaper of the Khane-ye Karegar] we read about daughters of the unemployed who are forced into prostitution to get money to the family.[5]

Permanent employment contracts are rapidly becoming coveted rarities in Iran. Employees are systematically fired and then rehired as, or replaced with, contract workers. The usual extent of a temporary contract is two or three months, and according to established practice, the worker is fired the day before the contract expires, only to be rehired for a new period the day after and so on, in perpetuity. Infamous among Iranian workers is the "blank contract". This document is signed by the worker, whereby he or she relinquishes all rights concerning wages, labour time, holidays or any other work condition to the caprices of the employer: "Capitalists love to hire people under 25 years of age. They make them day-labourers without so much as certificates on the work performed. Every time they employ someone for real, they make them sign the blank contract," says "Jalal", a worker at the assembly line in Iran Khodro. According to official estimates, 50 per cent of the labour force worked for temporary or blank contracts in 2005; the proportion is projected to reach 90 per cent in a few years.[6]

Keeping pace with this general erosion of rudimentary job security, the Islamic Republic has been hollowing out what employers used to regard as the "rigid" post-revolutionary labour law. In February 2000, all companies with five or fewer employees were exempted from the duty to respect labour legislation; in January 2003, all with ten or less were granted the same privilege, and in 2006, government bodies were preparing the next step: effacing all legal rights for workers with temporary contracts. In workplaces thus discharged from legislation – soon to include 90 per cent of the labour force – it is up to the employer to decide, with all the authority of the Islamic state behind him, upon any limit to the working day or duration of a contract. There's no minimum wage, no maternity leave, no compensatory pay in the case of dismissal.[7] This is where the Islamic Republic has brought the mostazafin: to a nation of day-labourers, without a thread of protection.

As related by "Vahid", such is the situation even at the jewel of Iranian industry, Iran Khodro:

Don't think it's an antediluvian factory. It's all the technological rage, everything is getting automated. The only thing moving backwards is our rights. Three-fourths of the workers are hired under temporary contracts with no rights, with half the wage of the permanently employed. For those of us who are lucky enough to have permanent contracts, it is becoming increasingly difficult to raise any demands: the foremen can just pick and choose among young job-seekers. The speed on the line is increased incessantly. Sometimes they increase it gradually, just a little bit, so as to make it hard to notice for us, but every year they make some pompous statement such as: "last year we produced 300,000 cars, this year it'll be 450,000!"

With its 37,000 workers and monumental assembly-line halls, the Iran Khodro factory catches the eye of the traveller on the highway north-westwards through the industrial zone, beneath the sandy mountain crests to the north; it is the single biggest car plant in the

Middle East. Security arrangements are rigorous. "Hussein", another assembly-line worker, adds to the picture of life within the gates:

All international cooperation going on is exclusively among the capitalists themselves. We don't even know if car workers abroad, working for the same multinational companies that come here, know of our existence. Technicians and engineering experts from other countries are escorted to and from the factory, they are forbidden to talk to us ... They force us to work overtime and impose night shifts on us, threatening to dock our wages if we don't accept. We have no time to see our families. Management has resolved it by offering advice from psychologists brought to the factory – as if that would help us get to know our children. Our lives are disintegrating.[8]

Faced with the reserve army of martyrs-turned-labourers, employers in Iran have likewise been emboldened to systematise the most blatant breach of the capital-labour contract: wage stoppage. In the summer of 2005, the International Labour Organisation (ILO) wrote a formal letter of complaint to the Islamic Republic, holding it responsible for the "serious and persistent problems of non-payment of wages, especially in the textile industry". Noting that "the delay in payment of wages often varies from three to nine months and may even stretch to two years", it warned that with no urgent action taken, the country was sliding towards social disaster.[9] Reports to the Majles have claimed that one million workers in the construction sector must engage in regular physical confrontations with their employers to get their weekly or monthly pay.[10]

Workers without protection endure employers who brazenly flout health and safety rules; the already alarming frequency of work accidents has increased further in recent years. According to the Ministry of Social Security, the number of accidents at work was 11 per cent higher in 2004 than the year before.[11] This increase was evident in all kinds of workplaces, for example, the large-scale infrastructure projects pressed forward by the state in the pursuit of technological advancement, such as the huge dams in which Iran takes great pride. In the Karoon 3 Dam project in the south-west, at least 55 workers have died since construction began in 1993, and another 150 have been incapacitated; most have fallen from 70-metre-high scaffoldings into deep shafts. How does management deal with such a record? Allegedly by throwing the accident log book and all the complaint files into the river, on the order of the director.[12] Whether or not that particular story is true, its notoriety is an accurate reflection of the attitude of Iranian capital: any labourer can be cast off. There is an ocean of martyrs to choose from.

OPIATES OF THE IRANIAN PEOPLE

As capital accumulation is nourished by the constant injection of petrodollars into the money supply, Iran's economy is chronically prone to higher than average inflation. In 2004 and 2005, inflation stood at approximately 15 per cent, eating away at already low wages.[13] High inflation, combined with nominal wages pushed downwards if anywhere, have produced a focus of never-ending discussions at family gatherings, in taxis, on shopfloors. To make ends meet, workers must often have two or three jobs. Stories abound of people working in a factory by day, driving a taxi in the evening, working as a security guard overnight, and then walking straight back to the factory floor the next morning. Days are divided not between work and leisure, but between work in one place, and then work somewhere else. The most obvious sign of this national phenomenon is the taxi cab, constantly on the prowl for passengers, offering rides for no price, congesting the streets in every town and city. Iran has accurately been labelled "a nation of cab drivers"; the moonlight drivers include people from what are supposed to be "the middle classes".[14] Others struggle to survive by selling from kiosks and street stalls in their neighbourhoods, or running cross-border smuggling caravans, or taking part in many other twilight businesses.[15] The informal or "service" sector is indeed thriving.

In the spring of 2005, the government set the poverty line at an income of the equivalent of approximately $320 per month. At the same time, it announced a new official minimum wage of $130 per month, or a little more than *a third* of what the state itself considered necessary for survival. However, such arrogance is outstripped by employers, who frequently offer wages as low as $65 per month.

While the Islamic Republic is reputed to have "a comprehensive social protection system" (according to the World Bank's standards), whatever insurances there might be, economic realities erode them.[16] "Maryam" is a secretary at the export department of a Tehran industrial company:

I have the best form of insurance coverage there is in Iran. Yet in case of illness, only the most essential medicines are covered. One of my workmates had to go through cancer surgery, but as the tumour proved benign, no money was paid to her – she was told the insurance covered only life-threatening diseases. And this law stipulating four months' maternity leave with payment is a dead letter. If someone is to be laid off at a company, they always take the mothers first, and in the industry sector, women regularly must sign contracts promising not to get pregnant. If they do get pregnant, they hide it. The best security for women is to prove that they are infertile.[17]

Unless you are connected to the charitable nets of some bonyad, basiji or other Islamic institution, the state is of little comfort in the struggle for survival. The working classes of Iran – including people who *would* be working if there were any jobs – are burdened by a general sense of desperation, individual survival having become the objective overriding all others in the republic.

This very Islamic Republic is thus being buried under an avalanche of social decay, in motion roughly since the mid-1990s. Most noted is the rise in prostitution. During the 1979 revolution, the burnt corpses of prostitutes were paraded through Tehran's streets to chants of "*Allahu Akbar*"; twenty-three years later, in 2002, the Islamic Republic put the number of prostitutes working in Tehran, a city of 15 million people, at 300,000. In the same year, it briefly toyed with the idea of "chastity houses" – that is, brothels run by the police and mullahs – as a way of dealing honourably with the problem.[18]

Such "chastity houses" have been operating clandestinely for a long time. In 1999, Iranian journalist Camelia E. Fard of *Zan* magazine broke the story of how destitute women flock to a cemetery in the holy city of Qom, where theology students buy their services, the transactions sanctified by siqe-contracts. One of the women told Fard that "She had been married to a truck driver who died in an accident a few years ago, leaving her with seven small children and a teenage daughter who had a baby girl of her own. Mehri said she also weaves carpets, but the money is never enough, so three times a week she takes an hour-long bus ride here."[19] A prostitution ring run by Pasdaran officials in northern Iran was reportedly uncovered in April 2005.[20]

But the typical gateway is escape from home: hundreds of thousands of young girls leave their families every year due to unbearable conditions, ending up on the streets of Tehran or some other metropolis, where criminal gangs are ready to "take care" of them. As a generation of girls thus pours out onto the streets, the average age of new prostitutes is falling dramatically; according to some estimates, it stood at 14 in 2004.[21] The extent of the phenomenon makes it impossible to hide and it is a source of deep national shame.

From these "temporary marriages" comes a steady stream of street children, though that is not their only origin. Within minutes, anyone visiting Tehran, or any other Iranian city, will be approached by children demanding money in exchange for cleaning a windscreen, or a shoe shine, or a fortune-telling poem delivered from a canary's beak. But not only street children work; poor families often keep their children at home, for carpet-weaving or other labour-intensive jobs. Children are often supplied by their parents to their employers as extra manpower, a practice particularly prevalent in the brick industry. No reliable official statistic is available, but reports claim that the working children of Iran number in the hundreds of thousands, possibly close to 15 per cent of all Iranian children.[22]

The other side of this everlasting struggle for self-preservation is, predictably, mass escape through drug use. According to the UN World Drug Report for 2005, the Islamic Republic is a leader in per capita addiction to opiates and heroin; with 4 million addicts out of 70 million citizens, it is in a division of its own. Including dealers as well as more occasional users, the official National Centre for Addiction Studies estimates that 20 per cent of the adult population is "somehow involved in drug abuse". Drug consumption is nothing new in Iran: the ingestion of opium balls as a palliative measure is about as Persian, particularly among the elderly in rural areas, as chewing coca is Bolivian or khat Somalian. But the explosion in drug use in the new millennium was set off by two factors: heroin, flowing in from neighbouring Afghanistan in huge quantities at rock-bottom prices, and, even more important, unemployment. A poll conducted by the government in 2005 showed that 80 per cent of Iranians link increasing addiction to soaring unemployment, and the correlation – particularly strong among young people, highly educated but unable to find jobs, and therefore depressed – is identified as the prime factor by most experts. Heroin is the main solace available, the "opiate of the Iranian people".[23]

Iran's suicide statistics are world-leading, human organ trade is on the rise, 1.5 million Iranians were treated for injuries sustained in violent attacks during 2004, while 15 homeless people perish every night on the streets of Tehran.[24] The *internalisation of misery* generates a social implosion of an immensity that the Pahlavi era never approached. The most well-known tragedy of latter-day Iran, the earthquake in Bam and its aftermath, reveals this social misery:

while rescue efforts from the government were – to put it mildly – dilatory, two supplies arrived immediately: methadone for Bam's addicts, and packs of pimps in search of Bam's orphaned girls.[25]

VEILED WORKING WOMEN

The afflictions of the working population of Iran are, of course, not evenly distributed. They are engendered, remoulded and apportioned through the workings of uneven development. However, the uneven development of Iran is, much like the balance of forces on the labour market, more than a national expression of universal laws. It is actively, though not always intentionally, fashioned by the policies of the unique theocracy in charge of the country. This means, first of all, that the primary factor splitting the working population in half relates to *gender*: keeping men and women apart, lest any potentially licentious contact be made between them, has been an obsession of the Islamic Republic from its inception.

The image of an immaculate Muslim woman begins with the enforcement of the veil, to be worn by every female under the jurisdiction of the Republic. The black cloth, preferably in the form of a *chador* that envelops all of the body except the face, was drawn as a curtain straight through the population, separating it into two spheres: family and work. Compelled to dress in what amounted to an extension of the home, women were told by the state to shy away from the labour market; by their actual physical appearance, women were separated from the world of work. In the sharia-based Civil Code, the man was identified as the sole breadwinner, responsible for "providing for the wife"; any work performed by a woman outside the household was to be explicitly approved by her male kin. The effect was, initially, the one intended: there was a mass departure of women from the labour market, their share of the labour force plunging from 19 per cent in 1976 to 9 per cent in 1986.[26]

However, apertures were soon opened in the curtain. The first crack in the image of the Iranian woman as a Fatima, whose sole task was to produce and rear children, appeared when the Islamic Republic abandoned its population policy of the war years. Even the mullahs could no longer deny that the policy was bringing a Malthusian disaster upon the country. In 1989, birth control was legalised and even encouraged by the state, and condom use rose by 140 per cent in one year. The population growth rate stabilised at a healthier 1.5

per cent during the 1990s, and women were relieved from the burden of non-stop pregnancies: from seven births per woman in the early 1980s, the average was three in 2000.[27]

At the same time, the segregation of the sexes showed signs of being a self-defeating policy. If women were all forced to stay at home, who would nurse the girls, treat them and teach them? Who would police the women, serve them in the shops or lead them in prayer? Ironically, in order to preserve the segregation policy, women would have to be allowed to return to the labour market. Specific roles were thus designed for them: female teachers would teach female students, female doctors would treat female patients, female hizbollahis or mullahs would lead female basijis or women's committees in neighbourhood mosques, and so on. Across all the professions where a female presence was found indispensable for upholding both normal social functions and the ban on cross-gender intermingling, women were resurfacing. Indeed, one of the republic's few social achievements was a great expansion and improvement of the educational system, and as a result, female students enrolled on all levels, millions of them taking exams.[28]

The gender curtain was redrawn, this time through the labour market. After the Iran–Iraq War had ended and the reconstruction of Iranian society begun, the share of women in the active workforce rose again, to 12 per cent in 1996. The pattern established was a different one from that in the 1970s, when women had a significant presence in industry; now working women were shifted by the state into more chaste professions. These were first and foremost to be found in the public sector. There, workplaces were large enough to make gender segregation feasible. Male teachers could teach in boys' schools, while in girls' schools, highly educated women, no matter if they happened to be certificated engineers or agronomists, could be dumped. Since the mid-1990s, the public sector job market is thus filled with women. The effect is a degradation of the white-collar professions, as the supply of qualified women rises (only 15 per cent of female university graduates are able to find work corresponding to their education), and wages are depressed. Now even a teacher must find a second job, and sometimes a third.[29]

It was not only the state that tapped the pool of women in need of an income. As industrial development took off in the 1990s, some women were allowed back to the factories. Female supervisors would oversee female workers, which was actually of some benefit to the workers themselves, as they would now be spared sexual harassment by male supervisors. The number of women in the industrial labour force rose from 6 per cent in 1986 to 11 per cent ten years later. However, most women engaged in manufacturing do not go to a factory: they work from home. The image of the Iranian woman as a Fatima, a homemaker supported by her working husband is just that: an image. In reality, a woman at home must *work* within the confines of the family, for the sake of her family's survival. Millions of working Iranian women are thus invisible in the official statistics, as they look after their children while trying to finish orders from their textile manufacturers.[30] "Khadidje" sits on the carpet in her living room in Esfahan, dressed in a light-blue chador, her eight-year old son sleeping by her side:

I used to work at a small workshop for seamstresses nearby. But after two years the owner told us he made no profit from the workshop and would move it to another location. So now I do sewing at home. A human body can endure such work for a maximum of ten years, because you sit in uncomfortable positions and your eyes are constantly strained. Plus it is hard to work at home as your entire life is occupied by labour, and every time someone knocks on the door or the phone rings work is interrupted. You might get angry with the kids.[31]

The small workshops usually found in the textile industry – particularly in rural areas – were the first to be excluded from all labour legislation; for women working at home there has, of course, never been any protection. This is one of the "advantages" of employing women: they are easily exploitable, as their connection to the labour market proper is never more than casual, and officially regarded so by the state. Naturally, this precarious position determines the wages women receive, as related by "Abide" in Saqqez: "Women are a labour force like all others, but we are given no opportunities. I work in the textile industry, going to job at eight in the morning, coming home at six in the evening. Our foreman says that because we are women, we shall only have half of the men's wage. This is the case everywhere in our society: a woman is given half the value of a man, in wages, in inheritance, in the courts ... ."

Another seamstress in Saqqez, "Najibe", adds to the picture of Fatima as doubly burdened:

When women return from work, they are supposed to be responsible for *all* home work – cooking food, washing clothes, cleaning, watching the kids ... But if they utter just a word about being tired, their men ask them with arrogant irony: "What have you done, moved a mountain?" And, of course, the men might vent their frustration on their women physically as well. Here in the Kurdish areas, we suffer from a special honour culture, and it is aggravated in parallel with the rise in unemployment. It is the only "pride" of unemployed men – to control the "honour" of their women. Thus we have a new phenomenon here: a drastic rise in the suicides and suicide attempts by women, young women in particular. The other week, there was a report in the news of a young woman who burnt herself to death. She couldn't stand a life where her man locked her up as soon as he left the house. For how long is the Islamic Republic going to lie about why young women catch fire? No, they don't burn by accident.[32]

Though the female share of the labour force is still creeping upwards – in 2001, it had reached 15.1 per cent – no stratum of the Iranian people suffers from higher unemployment than women with a secondary education, whose rate increased from 20 per cent in 1996 to 42 per cent in 2002.[33] Today, there are actually *more* women than men studying at the universities of Iran, but that is not reflected in the labour market. The structural absence of women, still guarded by the misogynous Republic, is evident in the fact that if they participated at the same rate as their men, the yearly influx to the labour market of Iran would be 1.6 million workers – the same number of workers entering the labour market every year in the US, whose GDP is more than 25 times higher.[34] Such is the mathematics of the female reserve army of Iran, mobilised behind the walls of their homes in a war on the working population.

FACES OF A NOT-SO-UNEVEN DEVELOPMENT

At the apex of capital accumulation in Iran is, of course, the petroleum industry. Of all the ongoing projects in the field, none surpasses the region of Assaluyeh, at the edge of what may be the largest natural gas field in the world, called South Pars. Originally a sleepy area on the Persian Gulf coast, Assaluyeh has been transformed into a closed zone of refineries, warehouses, drilling stations, and factories producing fertilisers, pesticides, synthetic fibres and other petroleum-based products. At its burning heart is a 100-metre-high gas flare, visible far out to sea. A well-advertised source of *amour propre* for the government, the Pars Special Energy Economic Zone has been developed by consortiums that include most non-American petroleum giants, French Total being the major actor. The oil ministry has estimated that sales of gas, oil and other products from the Zone bring in and will continue to yield $11 billion *every year*, this sum projected to some time in the 2030s. Several stages remain before the full potential of the underground deposits, both onshore and offshore, are realised, and construction continues on a round-the-clock basis.

Approximately 70,000 workers work in the zone. Assaluyeh is legendary among Iranians as an El Dorado where easy money can be made. Someone working 24 days straight will on average earn $200 – compared with the monthly poverty line allocation of $320 and the risible "official minimum wage" of $130 – but a skilled welder might make $700. However, working conditions are rumoured to be extremely harsh. For obvious reasons, the site is under heavy security provided by the Iranian Army and independent observations are unavailable, but in late 2005, the Iranian student magazine *Bazr* published an anonymous interview with someone working at Assaluyeh. In this unique document, the man tells *Bazr* how thousands of technicians from Hyundai – who were permitted entry into Iran by Rafsanjani – constantly inspect the area where he works, while road and pier construction are under the direct control of military conscripts and Pasdaran officials. *Bazr* asks the man "Where are the workers' homes?":

Worker: Homes?! We live in barns! There are more than 100 companies in the area, each with their own camp for about 400 workers, located in the desert or near the factories. The camps are surrounded by barbed wire. The pre-fabricated houses are overcrowded, twelve people live in every room, there is not even space for clothes storage. Old people, young, drug addicts, all are put in the same rooms. Many of the young men are raped, but no one dares to say anything. Engineers and administrative staff, however, have nice rooms where three or four of them stay under wholly different conditions. They have their own restaurants. We have to eat in our rooms.

Bazr: What is a work day like?

Worker: At 5 a.m., the sirens go off in the camp. Shortly after, the generators are turned off, and the rooms get so hot so quickly that you have no choice but to leave at once. Even if you're sick, you have to get out. We have an hour to get ready for work, and imagine: there are three or four toilets in every camp, one per hundred workers.

We are in such a hurry that we have to divide the task to get breakfast between us. One goes to get the tea, another gets the bread, the 25-gram pieces of butter and the 25-gram pieces of cheese. The bread has no nutritional value, we call it "photocopy bread". Almost everyone is still hungry after breakfast, unless someone has just returned from vacation with extra bread ...

After breakfast, while the engineers and administrative staff go to their air-conditioned rooms, we are driven out to different sites in the Zone on the back of pick-up trucks. There's all sorts of work to do: you can dig ditches, carry away mud, repair cars, drive trucks, weld pipes, lay pipes in the ditches, and so on.

We start working at 6:10 a.m., continuing straight until noon. The temperature often reaches 50° C, with 60–70 per cent humidity. I'm not joking! If you put the tools in the sun, you'll get burnt if you touch them ...

We work no less than 10 hours a day, but sometimes as many as 12 or even 15 hours. There is also night work; for instance, cement cannot be mixed in the heat of the day. If the supervisor says something must be completed, there is no limit to the working hours, and we cannot object to it. On such occasions, we might have to work 24 hours in a row.

We usually return to the camps just before dark. Everyone is totally covered with dust, it's even hard to recognise your room-mates. We all look like Lawrence of Arabia emerging from a sandstorm! No one has energy left to take a shower, and if we would, the salty water in the few showers keeps getting shut off ... We go home to see our families once every third month.

Bazr: How can the workers endure such conditions?

Worker: By using drugs. According to the managers' own studies, 60 to 70 per cent of the workers in Assaluyeh are addicted. Drugs are distributed like sweets in the camps. As soon as you arrive, there are people offering you drugs. We are on a major drug route from Pakistani Baluchistan to the Gulf States and the Shiraz area. We see the caravans passing by all the time, escorted by army guards on motorcycles ... I was shocked the first night in the camp. Outside every house, there was a group of workers around a fire, smoking opium heated up on iron. Even during work, a welder might take a puff between the pipes. The extent of drug use among the workers defies description ... Some spend all their money on it, drugs have killed their spirit. Thirty-eight bodies were found in the past few months ...

Afghan, Baluchi and local Khuzestani workers do the hardest jobs, but are paid much less than the others. They are day-labourers, called in when the company needs them. They sleep out in the open, next to the pipes. Afghans and Baluchis are forbidden to enter the camps, because they are generally considered to be dirty and carrying lice – but there is lice everywhere in our rooms! ... Often fights break out between workers of different ethnic groups. We are kept divided ...

We have no real employment contracts. Every three 3 months, we are asked to accept blank contracts, but they are really only verbal agreements – they don't even give us a white paper to sign. There is no health insurance, no clinics around, no rules for anything. Our pay is often delayed, sometimes for months, forcing us to borrow money at a high interest rate. They can fire us by raising their eyebrows [that is, at will].

Bazr: How are your workplace safety conditions?

Worker: Non-existent. There are accidents all the time. You risk your life by working in Assaluyeh. When a contractor hires people to build a dirt dam, he tells us frankly: "This job will take 15–20 lives!"[35]

If this gulag-like camp is the apex of Iranian workplace development, the brick mills are its nadir. Brick-makers reside in dusty makeshift barracks. Production continues as long as there is clay to extract from the mine, usually for about six months. Then the workers are dismissed, and those who have no other sources of income head straight to the next brick mill. In the barracks (built by the workers themselves, using bricks made on the spot), ten people might live in a room, sleeping on carpets unrolled over bricks. Water must be bought in shops outside the mill; there is no electricity. At least twelve hours a day, the workers of the mill dig the clay, put it in forms, fire them in the primitive kiln and pile up the finished bricks. The labour supply is infinite and the market closed, so there's not much incitement for modernisation. Everything, except for the supervisor, is enveloped in dust the colour of chalk.[36]

"Kaveh" is a brick-maker in Kurdistan:

All of us working at the brick mills live below the poverty line. In many families, the woman and children have to work side by side with the man. On one day, a man with his wife and one kid might produce 5,000 bricks, but if they are a big family with many kids they might reach 20,000. However, only the man is employed, the women and children are simply attached – it is the man who's on the contract.

Our living situation is intolerable. We have to move twice a year, we can have no normal life. During the season, large camps are pitched along the mills, without any water or hygiene. We must eat inside the barracks. When we put food on the floor, cockroaches might fall down from the ceiling.[37]

BLESSED ARE THE WORKERS

The extreme work conditions highlighted above are not the fate of all workers – the vast majority, of course, at least have permanent residences. But the working class is weighed down in its entirety by the balance of forces developed by the Islamic Republic. An estimated 40 per cent of the population lives under the international poverty line.[38] According to the Iranian Central Bank, more than 50 per cent live below the *government's* designated poverty line for the country.[39]

In May 2005, the state-run newspaper *Iran Daily* published some statistics that illustrate workers' precarious finances:

Figures collected during the past 30 years indicate that per capita income in Iran has declined 120 per cent [!] based on fixed prices. The income-expense deficit for the urban family during March 2003–04 stood at a 3,300,000-million-rials deficit, up from 2,500,000 between March 2002–03 and 2,300,000 rials in 1997. The gap between the rich and the poor has also been rising, increasing by a minimum and maximum of 1.2 and 3 times during March 2003–04.[40]

This development is perhaps nowhere as visible as in the contrast between northern and southern Tehran. In the north, on the slopes of the Elborz mountains, comfortably dressed men and women meander between glossy malls, shady parks and stately villas. The water flowing from the snow-capped mountains above is sparkling clean. Miles to the south, millions are packed in ramshackle houses in narrow, twisting alleys; everything is black, their clothing and their houses, the very air a polluted, choking cloud. By the time it reaches southern Tehran, the water is murky and viscous, and clotted with rubbish.

Whether unemployment is high or low, there is one invariable foundation for this class structure of the Islamic Republic: draconian control over the workplace. In the millionaire mullah's regime of capital accumulation, it is imperative to suppress trade unions, intercept collective agreements, extinguish strikes and, generally, keep Iran free of any autonomous labour organising. To this end, the regime encases the country's workplaces in a special stricture which has been likened to the Arbeitsfront or Sampo of the fascist regimes of the 1930s. The Iranian version imposes a *hadith* that proclaims "to work is like jihad in the service of God" and brands trade unions as "extended operations of imperialism".[41] The Islamic Republic's vision of labour is not *Arbeit macht frei*, but rather submissive work as a *spiritual* effort, remunerated outside any physical boundaries. As noted by Ayatollah Khamene'i (now Al-Faqih), on May Day 1981:

The value of work and the worker in Islam is higher than that in any other materialist ideology. Following the Islamic world view, we view work and the worker to hold divine value, not merely material value. A worker is one who, obeying the command of God, endeavours to develop the earth and its materials ... Thus, the workers are of divine value; and obeying that command is a divine and Islamic duty; it is not merely of a material value ... Differences in expectations and trade demands must not divide the various layers of the population, must not damage the Islamic brotherhood. The atheist ideologies attempt to use these means to define the workers as a class, so separating them from the umma, crushing the unity of the umma.[42]

As evident in this argument, in the formative years of the Republic, true Islam was constituted in negation to "materialist" and "atheist" ideology. In other words, the vision of labour was framed in the confrontation with the democratic undercurrents of the revolution.

Twenty-five years after it vanquished the shora movement, the shora-ye eslami is thus still the glue holding the umma together. In 1983, labour minister Ahmad Tavakolli outlined the principles of this institution:

Islamic attitudes towards consultation are different from the attitudes towards consultation in socialist and Marxist societies. We do not consider it to be correct that the administrative system of a country be based on election from the bottom to the top. That's not the case in our system. We believe in velayat al-faqih, and in fact the velayat [government] is authorised from the top to the bottom.[43]

Every workplace is entitled to a shora-ye eslami. According to labour law, a shora-ye eslami may be established to "protect the legitimate and statutory rights and interests of workers and employers". The main mission of a council is to "propagate and disseminate Islamic culture and to defend the achievements of the Islamic revolution"; the council also has the duty to report any "disturbances and unpleasant incidents".[44] During the confused tug-of-war in the early 1980s, "Islamic Associations" were installed in the workplaces alongside the Islamic councils, their duties overlapping; today, the former have been subsumed under the latter. Thus the original tasks of the "Associations" have been inherited by the councils: "to stop and search those non-workers intending to enter the factory", "to give resolute support to Islamic currents, and to condemn and liquidate entirely the anti-Islamic currents".[45]

A shora-ye eslami services the mosque or praying room of the workplace. It calls for mass prayers, and makes sure there are enough "factory mullahs" in stock. It plasters the workplace walls with posters of the imams or Al-Faqih, paints slogans, and broadcasts prayers or official speeches during work breaks and the lunch hour. Though the councils' zeal has waned considerably since the end of the 1980s, the designated activities of a shora-ye eslami are still to imbue the workplace atmosphere with the presence of the Islamic Republic and to police the workers. All councils are federated to the Khane-ye Karegar – the old headquarters of the shoras, which is officially denominated as the "trade union" of the country.[46]

As the Islamic councils are the only legally-recognised organisations available to the workers, they may sometimes try to use the councils to articulate their demands, but control is tight. "Sina", a welder in Tehran says: "I used to be a representative in the shora-ye eslami in my factory. I raised my voice. After much careful struggle, I managed to get 80 temporary contracts converted into permanent employment contracts. Then the Ministry of Labour kicked me out. Never mind that I knew the Koran and everything else one should know about Islam – they just forbade me from staying in the council."

In calls for election to a shora-ye eslami, issued by the Ministry of Labour, it is stipulated that workers with weak faith or un-Islamic views cannot be candidates. On the poster calling for new elections in his factory, Sina's name appears among the explicitly blacklisted:

Sure, we are allowed to elect representatives. But as soon as the results are known, some officials from the Ministry of Labour come running down to interrogate the representatives: "Can you quote this and that verse in the Koran? How often do you pray? What do you know about Ramadan?" Those who fail the tests are dismissed. In this way, the Ministry controls the "representatives" of the workers and make sure they do not fight for our interests. In my factory, the shora-ye eslami is doing nothing for the workers any more – on the contrary, it assists the managers in robbing us of our rights.[47]

All unions are outlawed. Strikes are still haram and illegal. In large, important factories, or factories experiencing unrest, military units are stationed as patrols, and most factories have armed guards at their entrances.

In 1983, Musavi Ardabili, head of the judiciary at the time, discussed the hierarchy of production in the Islamic Republic: "The management is the brain, the Islamic council the eyes, and the rest are the hands."[48] So it works in Iran, unless, that is, the hands begin to move on their own.

6
Outcry

In January 2004, fifteen hundred construction workers were building a copper-smelting plant in the sweltering desert near the village of Khatonabad, in the southern province of Kerman. The workers had been hired under a joint venture between the state-owned copper-production company and a Chinese corporation. The plant was now nearing completion and the management had promised the workers permanent employment when the plant came online.

The first stages of copper production were set to commence in late January. Just before then, all but 250 of the workers were sacked. The plant was shut down. Workers, joined by their families, blockaded the building, camping in front of it. They demanded that the agreement be honoured and delayed wages paid; they were confronted by the police, but did not relent.

On 24 January, after eight days of strikes and sit-ins, the Security Council of the province dispatched special police forces from Kerman, the provincial capital, to Khatonabad. Circling in helicopters over the plant, the special forces fired rounds of live ammunition into the crowd. Four were declared dead, but according to unofficial figures, seven to fifteen were killed. Up to 300 people were wounded, and at least 80 were arrested and later released – they bore clear indications of torture. Clashes between workers and security forces continued in the area for days.[1]

As word of the carnage in Khatonabad spread throughout Iran, it became a rallying cry for what subsequently developed into a new labour movement. This movement devised a number of ways to circumvent the bans on labour organising. One was to go mountain-climbing. The state and workplace managers may have eyes and ears on the shop-floor, and in the cafés, but their surveillance does not extend to the many mountains and hills around Tehran and other cities, except in the form of Islamic slogans inscribed into the cliffs and hillsides. Hiking is extremely popular in Iran, and hiking clubs are not (at least in most places) illegal. Workers explore these havens: "We don't really think it's that much fun to hike in the mountains.

But it's our only way of meeting outside work! We walk to the first good site and then we sit all day talking", says the chairman of one club in Karrajj, outside Tehran. On the first anniversary of the killings in Khatonabad, an unknown number of "hiking clubs" throughout the country took to the hills, erecting pennants in memory of the victims. Such ceremonies were repeated in 2006.[2]

It's not illegal for citizens of Iran to collect money among themselves for social purposes, though to obtain a formal seal of approval, they might choose to consecrate it with an Islamic name. Hence a collective of workers might set up "The Imam Hussein Fund For the Sick and Disabled" or some such. "Sina", the Tehran welder expelled from his workplace's shora-ye eslami, transferred his activism to such a fund:

It is a pretence for meeting. Workers gather in an assembly and decide to start a fund. They agree upon the mandatory deposit and the sum everyone is eligible to withdraw in cases of need. The point is to spare workers from having to beg the foremen for some extra money if, for instance, a child is sick and needs to see a doctor. Instead, he can go straight to his mate currently handling the fund and demand due payment – it's a form of independence, and it's the mutual trust that makes it work.

Associations of this kind have existed for a long time, but since 2004 they appear to have proliferated with new urgency, and new subversive intent.

A related, more audacious form of organisation is the clandestine workers' committee. Often evolving out of the meetings of the hiking club or the fund, some workers, relying on each other not to disclose any information, form a committee to be active in the workplace. "Arash" works at Toledie Tehran, a major plastics company producing a range of products for export markets in south Asia and eastern Europe. In 2003, severe rationalisations were implemented at his factory:

We have to produce more than double the amount of plastics every day, since they laid off more than a thousand workers. That's why we formed a workers' committee. We used to have a cash fund to help each other, but as the pressure increased we came to the conclusion that something more was needed. It was early 2004. From the beginning, we were a tight-knit group of friends, but we have included more and more people. Those of us who belong to the committee cannot be differentiated from the workforce as a whole. The manager knows we are there, of course, as we distribute our leaflets inside the plant, and as soon as he identifies someone as a member, that person is sacked. We have to be very careful. There are collaborators among us; workers who sold their souls to the management and visit the mosque every day. We know who they are as they receive bonuses and a pat on the back from the foremen; we know more about the collaborators than they know about us.

A workers' committee engages in undercover seditious agitation. How does it evade discovery? "I stick in leaflets at the time-clock or at the entrance to the canteen when nobody is there. When the mates find them and start reading and talking among themselves, I join in with the conversation, read the leaflet with pretended surprise and begin to elaborate on the points ... and so I try to convince them."

Agitation, however, is merely a first step. A workers' committee engages in fleeting moments of very direct action. "Arash" again:

Every day we are obliged to work four hours' overtime. But the payment for these hours is not regulated, differs from time to time and is excluded from the count towards our pensions. We in the committee wrote a letter to the management the other week, demanding that overtime pay be included in the regular wage. We sent one man to hand over the letter at the management's office. They sacked him out of hand. We instantly stopped all production in the factory, and a hundred workers went in to occupy the office, demanding that our mate be reinstated. Management caved in. He was back a couple of days later.[3]

In Saqqez, the city's many seamstresses, who all work either at home or in small workshops, have tried to form an association of their own. "Abide" tells of one workshop in a basement where the supervisor locks in the women early in the morning, only opening up for them to go home late at night. The seamstresses have tried to obtain a licence from the Ministry of Labour to form their association, but the Ministry does not recognise them as workers, and hence won't give them the right even to form a shora-ye eslami. But "Abide" says they will not yield:

We are now some hundred seamstresses who meet just to talk to each other. That's all we want to do, and that's why we demand some real premises. But we don't want to do it illegally. Our men should have no pretext to prevent us from gathering, and the secret police none to harass us. We will take this fight and have our association. Now we have filed an appeal to a court in Tehran, and if we do not succeed there, we will go to the ILO![4]

From early 2004, and in the following two years, clubs, funds, committees and other similar initiatives animated workplaces in more and more parts of Iran. Their most concrete result was a material upsurge in strikes.

STRIKE ACTION TAKES OFF

In January 2004, there was another important strike. In the course of a few months, two men in their twenties had died of strokes at the assembly line when on night-shift at Iran Khodro's plant in Tehran. After the two accidents, exasperation inside the halls reached a tipping point and production was stopped. Striking workers demanded job security, an end to temporary contracts, and overtime pay for night-shift work. The company responded by reinforcing the plant's security troops, called *Herasat*, who were instructed to start taking workers down to the basements for questioning. But the January strike marked the beginning of an enduring radicalisation among sections of the workforce, at the very centre of Iran's industrial progress. "Vahid" belongs to one of several committees:

The only thing we want is the right to try to improve our situation. We fight for the right to go on strike, to form a union, all these basic democratic rights. Everything we do must be kept secret. But we can't just sit twiddling our thumbs, waiting for the Islamic Republic to fall. We must *take* the right to organise, practice it, without waiting for someone's permission. That means we must be ready to sacrifice, as the people did in Khatonabad.[5]

In May 2005, a 30-year old worker at Iran Khodro died in another night-shift accident, the ninth victim since late 2003. Repeated stoppages occurred, while workers' committees circulated harsh indictments against the "killers" who "made contract work the norm". In one committee's leaflet: "We are certain that as long as the cost-cutting measures and subcontracting continue, we will have more such incidents. What does not count at all for the management is the expendable lives of us workers. If we protest, they arrest us in the name of 'saboteurs', or interrogate us on a daily basis."[6]

On 13 December 2005, workers downed their tools again, and security guards marched through the assembly halls to find the instigators; on 8 March 2006, when unexpectedly low bonuses were announced as reward for new records, production in one section was shut down to chants of "workers' unity" and "death to Daneshiyan [a human resources manager]".[7] This time, security forces filmed the workers after pushing them back to the production lines. These are only some of the actions that have erupted at Iran Khodro Tehran, which is now the scene of recurrent confrontations over everything from hazardous conditions to the detainment and dismissal of dissident workers, a number of whom have been freed and reinstated after protests.

In March 2004, teachers entered the fray. A *third* of all teachers in the country heeded the call to strike by a mutineer leader of the Islamic councils (in this case, called "guilds"); 800 schools in Esfahan and 400 in Tehran were shut down on the first day of action. Staff at medical sciences universities joined them, in what was probably the first female-dominated strike action on a mass scale in the history of the Republic. Eighty per cent of Iran's teachers are women. Eighty per cent live below the poverty line and need at least two jobs to survive; hence the focus was on higher wages, including payment of sizeable arrears. The newspaper of the "guilds" was closed down after publishing reports on the strike and the teachers' complaints, and the Ministry of Education refused to make any concessions. Then a new strike broke out in June. This time, the mutineer, Mahmoud Langarudi, and his accomplices were arrested on charges of "agitating" teachers to walk out from schools; apparently, the state thereby laid their particular initiative to rest.[8]

However, teachers have continued to stage protests throughout the country. So have nurses, against the effects of privatisation.[9] One form of action that gained widespread popularity over 2004 and 2005 is to physically confront the mullahs: a workers' collective hires a caravan of buses, drives into Tehran and steps out in front of the Ministry of Labour, the Majles, the presidential office, even the office of Al-Faqih himself. The police generally refrain from attacking the visiting crowds because they're too worried that riots would ignite central Tehran, and officials are somewhat receptive to workers' demands for the same reason. These gatherings have become such a common sight in the capital that news of them sometimes slips through the censorship, as in this report in *Iran Daily*, from 18 October 2005:

More than 100 teachers from Fars and Kermanshah provinces gathered in front of the Parliament on Tuesday to protest their expulsion from work ... Also on Tuesday, some 400 workers from Qazvin province gathered in front of the [M]ajles to object to poor working conditions. The protestors said they have not been paid for 25 months and demanded a meeting with the [M]ajles speaker as well as the chief executive. Some of the protestors have been working for Naznakh Company for eight years now. Workers' representatives said their problems began after the company was handed over to a former deputy minister of industries and mines in 1994 as part of the "privatisation drive".[10]

Slogans might include "Ya marg, ya nan!" ("Death or bread!"), "Mardom ba gheyrat – hemayat, hemayat!" ("Courageous people – support, support!"), and occasionally even "Marg bar estebdad!" (Down with dictatorship!). Chickens from the provinces are coming home to roost. Most disputes, however, occur in occultation. They are hidden from the view of media consumers, workers' collectives, even the most dedicated activists; a permanent blackout on labour actions is the only reliable method to keep the umma united and mute. One hidden case was a strike at a brick mill near Tabriz in the autumn of 2004. Choosing "Kommunard" as his pseudonym, one of the activists describes the strike, an unmistakable pride radiating from his eyes:

The price on the market for one brick had just been raised from 12 to 30 tomans. The piece rate for us, however, remained 3 tomans per brick produced [one dollar is a little less than 1000 tomans]. What about the difference between 3 and 30? Straight into the bosses' pockets! This was a big mill, about 3,000 workers. We decided to set up a shora. Ninety-eight per cent of the workers agreed to strike if the boss refused to accept our demand of a piece rate of 4 tomans per brick. I was one of six elected representatives who approached him, but he rebuffed our demand.

The day before the strike started, all of us, 3,000 workers, gathered in the desert outside the mill. It was like Karbala! Candidates stood up, and a strike committee was elected by show of hands. Since we brick-makers carry our homes on our backs, our strike naturally meant that we occupied the mill. After one week, the army arrived and started threatening us representatives and the others. But no one listened. Strikes may be banned, but in situations like this the law cannot be enforced – 3,000 united workers are strong. The owner goes to the army and complains, and the soldiers come and fire off some threats, but nothing more.

After two weeks there was a new negotiation with the boss. Now he conceded to our demand! As we went back to work, the shora was dissolved, but we elected representatives remained active and stood up against the boss when he delayed our payment.[11]

In a case that due to its longevity attracted some attention, 350 workers of the Kurdistan Textile factory in Sanandajj, capital of Kurdistan province, fought their employers throughout 2004 and

2005. Their chosen weapon of resistance was a shora. A first sit-in strike against mass redundancy plans took place in October 2004, and instantly received support from workers at several other textile, aluminium and plastics factories, as well as from bakers and students in the city. Armed forces laid siege to the factory. After three days, an agreement including only severance pay for those already dismissed was negotiated; the shora representatives were threatened with violent reprisals if they refused to sign.

Strike action was renewed in December. The workers were again attacked by the army and the security services; the elected representatives were arrested and beaten. Yet another strike – this one two months long – ended in November 2005, after management had finally accepted all the workers' demands: an end to arbitrary contracts, safer machines, reduction of dust and noise in the production hall, retroactive payment of wages for the whole strike period, return to the workers' fund of the nearly 20 million tomans pocketed by the management, and more. Throughout the long conflict at Kurdistan Textile, all decisions were taken in regular shora-assemblies.[12]

Shoras – that is, councils including all employees – are not underground operations like workers' committees; they are open units of action formed at advanced stages of collective defiance. The practice is most common in northern Iran. One province stands out in particular.

THE SHORA RESURGENT

In November 1906, 3,000 furious fishermen strode through the streets of Anzali, a port city on the Caspian Sea in the northern province of Gilan; they were heading for the telegraph office and the customs bureau, which they occupied. A Russian merchant was making a fortune from his monopoly concession on all fishing in Anzali; while the workers were paid a pittance, the rich governor was appropriating for himself the catch that was rightfully theirs. The merchant's properties were ransacked. Meanwhile, in the villages of Gilan, peasants were breaking into grain silos, expelling landlords, and thrashing overseers trying to exact taxes; in Gilan's provincial capital, Rasht, a new anjuman accused the established city council of rigged elections and took over the increasingly revolutionary initiative.[13] Gilan was sending shivers down the spine of Iran's affluent classes. The Majles ordered "severe punishment", and, reporting back to the parliament, an officer complained of the unruly province: "People

were attacking lives and property ... And when you ask them 'why
do you do such a thing?' they reply that the government is constitutional. They think constitutionalism means that the rabble takes
charge ... and do as they wish."[14]

When the civil war between Tehran and Tabriz was in full swing in
1908, royal forces slowly made their way through the forests of Gilan
to defeat the rabble once and for all. Suddenly, they were attacked:
"We saw no one, but a hundred bullets rained down on us." In one
of the earliest examples of twentieth-century guerrilla warfare, the
royal forces retreated from Gilan in panic.[15] Twelve years later, the
jangalists emerged from the same forests with a red flag that would
fly over the province – now a socialist republic – for one full year;
51 years later, the Fedaiyan used them as their base for attacking the
gendarmerie post of Siyahkal. But the history of partisan resistance
in this region stretches back even longer: in 1804, invading Russian
forces were shocked by rounds of musketry fire emerging from among
the trees.[16]

Together with its sister-province Mazandaran, Gilan constitutes,
as a British traveller once noted, "another Persia". While the central
and southern plateau's population is pacified by an oppressive heat
and scattered in dusty, isolated villages that are easily controlled
by landowners and ulama, in Gilan to the north, the moist winds
from the Caspian Sea, the intricate, humid jungles and the billowy
mountains provide a material foundation for a different political
economy. For the peasants of the area, there was always the option
of leaving for the forest. Gilan was agriculturally productive,
densely populated, commercialised and industrialised at an early
historical stage.[17]

But it was after the revolution in 1979 that the insubordinate
tradition of Gilan reached its zenith. In March 1980, the shoras of
31 factories *federated* into the Union of Workers' Councils of Gilan.
A body of nearly 30,000 workers, the union confronted Tehran with
a nine-point resolution including demands for official recognition
of shora control over production and distribution, a new budget
to expand and develop production, new labour laws "drawn up by
the genuine representatives of the workers", and "radical change in
production to eliminate dependency on imperialist countries". The
union asked the Fedaiyan for an alliance, but the latter was engrossed
in its own internal turmoil. The Pasdaran crushed the union.[18]

Ever since, the military maintains a highly visible presence in
Gilan. Factories are closely guarded; on the roads, armed soldiers

inspect drivers and passengers at checkpoint after checkpoint. There are no licensed clubs for those who wish to hike in the mountains. But Khuzek Khan, the legendary bearded leader of the radical Rasht Anjuman and later the jangalists, who froze to death in the mountains rather than let Reza Shah's soldiers capture him, is still standing there, as a statue in the central square of Rasht. He looks out over a population which subtly flouts the compulsory dress codes in a manner rare outside the stylish streets of northern Tehran.

In the twenty-first century, the industrial economy of Gilan has been wrecked. Suppose a player in the Republic's corridors of power wants to purchase a public company. It might have respectable assets, employees, and production results, and so it is valuable, and, alas, expensive. To make a tidy profit, the player will do all he can to *run down* the company: devalue assets, dismiss workers, impair business. Then he will make an offer at a bargain price, unrelated to the real economic value of the unit, and, after it's in his hands, do whatever is most profitable, for example, restore some of its productive capacity, asset-strip the company, or sell the land to property speculators.

This scheme was contrived when Rafsanjani first started to talk of privatisation, in 1991. The state declared that overstaffing in public firms makes them unattractive for private investors, and therefore "it is essential that before privatisation of such firms, some changes to their structure be carried out".[19] As the process has gained momentum in the early twenty-first century, hundreds of production units slated for privatisation have thus been run down. Eventually, state officials have had to acknowledge the systematic mismanagement: "several state-controlled factories have been sold to certain people who have failed to run them properly", a government inspector told *Iran Daily* in 2005, adding that "some people have misused insider information".[20]

In Gilan, dozens of medium-sized and large factories have been killed in this way:

The essence of privatisation and neoliberalism is the same all over the world, but the faces are different. Here in Iran, the marauders are mullahs, ayatollahs and members of the Majles who establish their own little papacies. Our experienced industrial companies in Gilan should be performing well, especially considering the construction boom in the country. Instead, they are deliberately brought to bankruptcy. The mullahs do not feel safe in power, they know they might be gone in five years, so they try to make as much money as possible, as quickly as possible. All the consequences are for us to bear, says "Bahram", a steel mechanic and labour activist in Rasht.[21] But the scheme has not been implemented without resistance:

Farshe Gilan is one example. It is a carpet factory that was owned by Bonyad Mostazafin, until it was earmarked for sale to a private capitalist. The 600 workers, the majority of them women, were informed that the factory would be closed, and one day bulldozers came to tear it down. Then the workers sat down, blocked the bulldozers, and stayed on guard in shifts, day and night. They formed a shora. Ten workers were elected to an executive committee; they were people known to be progressive and experienced, and respected by their mates. For three months, Farshe Gilan was run by the shora. The workers administered everything – orders, production, deliveries. Several women were elected to the committee. But in the end, the shora had to surrender the workers' control. The electricity company cut off power, the bank refused to give loans to a company run by workers, no insurance companies would enter contracts. Now the new owner has arrived at the factory. At least production continues, but on a smaller scale.

This happened in 2004, when an estimated thirty Gilani factories were run for various periods of time by shoras. As summed up by "Bahram":

It usually unfolds in the same manner. From the day when bosses start talking about bad results and redundancy, the workers sense what is brewing and start setting up a shora. They choose representatives to lead the fight: "let's block a road, let's march to the provincial authorities, let's occupy the factory." The signal for occupation usually comes when the foremen tell the workforce to go home, "no more wages will be paid." Then the workers stay and produce on their own. But they are separated from other factories, there is no union or coordination, and they do not know how to proceed politically.

Another labour activist, engineer "Muhammad", tells the story of Rasht Electronic, which was privatised and sold to one of Rafsanjani's associates for a price roughly one-sixtieth of the real value:

Just before the sale, the bank suddenly stopped the wage payments. Then the workers assumed control and continued production on their own. One night, however, some henchmen of the old director slipped into the factory, carried out the machines, put them in the rain, and partly destroyed them. When the workers arrived in the morning they were infuriated. A group of them – all committed Islamists – kidnapped the director and beat him to a pulp. The more left-leaning workers disapproved of this impetuous action, arguing that it would only create problems. And police indeed arrived at the factory. At that point, the Islamists, basically loyal to the regime, started to get a little shaky, and at a tense assembly some of them argued that workers should give up control over the factory. The shora Left objected that now was not the time to capitulate. The stand-off was brought to an end by an initiative from some of the left-wing workers: four buses were filled and driven to the Ministry of Labour in Tehran. Cars belonging to the staff at the Ministry were blockaded, and there was obviously some fear of riots, for workers were welcomed into the building. The Ministry immediately made sure eight months of wage arrears were paid.

The story of Rasht Electronic ended in only partial victory: the Rafsanjani associate got his factory after promising that production would continue. One hundred of the original seven hundred workers had been laid off, with unusually high severance pay, as of late 2004. At that time, labour activists held that there was actually space for the formation of genuine workers' councils in Gilan; regime control was less absolute than earlier. However, shora activists had indeed been incarcerated in 2004, shora-run factories isolated, and news of the events suppressed.

Due to the general situation in the province, no information has been obtained on later developments. But most likely, the analysis of "Bahram" is still valid, and not only for Gilan: "Nothing of this occurs because people are socialists. They have no food, no money, no choice! In my block in Rasht, there are fifteen kiosks: unemployed people break holes in the walls of their homes or garages to earn at least some money. Unemployment breeds desperation. That's why people venture into more militant forms of resistance than before."

OUT OF THE PRIVATE BUBBLE

The labour unrest that has engulfed parts of the country since 2004 (its birth generally dated to the Khatonabad massacre) is not one facet of a national uprising, not begotten by torrential rains rapidly melting down the autocratic state. Committees are formed, tools are downed, factories are seized by people who have no specific political ideology. Theirs is simply an outcry, a last-ditch defence of the basic conditions of life, geographically disparate, and, in general, confined to individual workplaces. But that does not mean it is insignificant, or harmless to the Islamic Republic. Just the reverse. The balance of forces between labour and capital is weighed in the sum of the workplaces; every labour action is a perforation in the special structure supposed to keep "the brain" and "the eyes" in absolute control over "the hands" of Iran.

The spread of strikes is the most salient feature of this development. We have only given a few examples here. One could point out the textile workers at the Asia Wool Spinning Company in Kerman, who, unpaid for 14 months, walked out of their factory on 27 July 2005, blocked a highway nearby, and were attacked by security forces. One woman was run over and her leg broken, while another woman, who was pregnant, was kicked and dragged along the road. Or one could visit the Filoor factory near Tehran, scene of repeated disputes and briefly, in early 2005, of workers' control.[22] According to one estimate (all are by necessity approximations), there were 140 strikes in October 2005, followed by 120 in November.[23] Compare this with an estimated 46 cases in the twelve months from March 1998 to March 1999, followed by 41 from May 1999 to May 2000.[24] Or compare it with the "handful" of strikes recorded between 1971 and 1973, or with twenty strikes in 1977.[25] The frequency of strikes since early 2004 appears to be unparalleled in post-Mossadeq *non*-revolutionary Iran, that is, during the ostensible stability of dictatorship.

The current unrest signifies the *externalisation* of misery. Ground down by misery's corrosive internalisation, genuinely sick of the race to a nadir of insecure, miserably paid jobs, narcotic escapes, and self-humiliation under capricious employers, more and more Iranians have reversed their hardships outwards in the form of protests. This reversal, this externalisation, is the fundamental of all labour politics. It is neither necessarily engendered *by* a revolutionary situation, nor does it necessarily *create* one, but *the rise of collective action is replete with potential* for further uprisings. This is especially true in a country where the state is the engine of capital accumulation, for there, labour action tends to focus its anger on the state. There is no abstract, non-personal, self-regulating market ruling Iran with an invisible hand, but rather an extremely visible class of millionaire mullahs interfering personally in all economic activities. For dissatisfied Iranians, there can be no ambiguity about cause.[26] Once they escape from the private bubble of self-blame, or belief in just one more push of individual market performance, Iranians will know whom to hold responsible.

To make the odds of continued calm yet higher for the accumulators of Iran, their fortunes are all too conspicuous to the people. Workers might have been, in absolute terms, worse off in the late 1980s, but now they suffer while painfully aware of how the oil reserves are showering Iranian capital with yet more money. Furthermore, as labour action in a dictatorship based on labour's complete compliance constitutes a political transgression of the first order, *politicisation is already inherent in the action*: striking workers know who is besieging them, and know where to park their buses.

The combination of all these factors – misery of the masses faced with the prosperity of the few, state-run accumulation, anti-labour dictatorship – is incendiary. But class struggle is not an automatic process. However expedient the objective conditions might be, a subjective factor must be added – and this is, of course, where labour activists enter the picture. Their task is to connect these scattered struggles into a self-conscious national movement, ready to challenge directly the regime of the millionaire mullahs.

MAY DAY STRIKES BACK

One way to break through the republic's repression of the struggle is to publish "workers' bulletins". These must be produced surreptitiously, printed in individuals' homes and distributed by hand across workplaces and provinces. Since 2004, a series of such bulletins have appeared, including *Karegar-e Pishro* (*Progressive Worker*), *Karegar-e Andishe* (*Worker's Intellect*), *Laghv-e Kar-e Mozdi* (*Abolish Wage Labour*) and *Shora*. It is rather well-known in the Western world that web logs are a means of uncensored communication favoured by Iranian youth; less well-advertised is the fact that labour activists use them too. Blogs, emails, websites, and radio files make it possible to spread the word to other activists inside – and, increasingly, outside – Iran.

In this sphere, above the surface where the mullahs excise everything they might find offensive, labour activists have introduced the practice of sending each other solidarity statements. When the new official minimum wage was announced in spring 2005, protest petitions were circulated widely, and the demand for $550 as a minimum monthly wage was endorsed by dozens of workers' collectives, from Karrajj to Abadan.[27] This demand developed into a campaign that, coupled with the demand that the government should take responsibility and bring an end to the endemic delays in wage payments, culminated on 16 July 2005, announced as the "Day of Social Welfare and Securities". Mass strikes were coordinated in Bushehr, Yazd and Shushahr; production at Iran Khodro once again came to a halt, some 10,000 factory workers held a strike in Golestan,

17,000 rallied in Ilam, and the holy city of Qom was reduced to chaos when transport workers joined the strike.[28] The event signalled a *national convergence of demands*, as the scattered collectives aired the same grievances: overdue wages, temporary contracts, and no forums for representation.

Some of these points were included in the May Day Resolution of 2004. It was for this Resolution the people of Saqqez were about to manifest their support when they were attacked. Of the forty demonstrators arrested, seven were held in solitary confinement, charged with the felonies of "illicit gathering" and "association with Komele", a Kurdish communist guerrilla group. They came to be known as the "Saqqez Seven". Pending their trials, the state fixed bail fees that were unobtainable for two of the seven: Mohsen Hakimi, a Tehran intellectual (of whom more later), and Mahmoud Salehi, baker and leader of organised labour in Saqqez. Salehi relates what happened: "Families in Saqqez decided to mortgage their houses to obtain the sums for our bail-out. The total value of their houses was enough, so they had to let us go. People came to meet us at the prison with flowers in their hands, and they drove us in a procession through the town, honking, singing, celebrating. It was a show of defiance against the regime."[29]

The case of the Saqqez Seven was picked up by the International Confederation of Free Trade Unions (ICFTU), and became a global trade union *cause célèbre*; perhaps more importantly, information about the case was disseminated by newly formed workers' committees in Tehran and elsewhere. The regime handled the case with crafty care. ICFTU lawyers were, naturally, forbidden to enter the country, and to wear down the determination of the accused and the Saqqez labour community – the mortgaged families in particular – the trial was postponed for months and months.[30]

Eventually, in the autumn of 2005, the seven were tried, one by one, by "revolutionary courts", which now dropped the initial charge, changing it to "convening against national security". During October, verdicts were handed down, one at a time. Mahmoud Salehi was sentenced to five years in prison, to be followed by two years in "internal exile", that is, forced residence in an inaccessible mountain hamlet. Mohsen Hakimi and three others were sentenced to two years in prison, while two were acquitted. More than one year after the original May Day celebration that never was, the fax machines and email accounts of trade union federations across the world, from the headquarters of the ICFTU in Brussels to the Maritime Union of

Australia and Norway's Landsorganisationen, were on stand-by. As soon as the sentences had been announced, the Iranian government was bombarded with protest letters.[31] Salehi himself commented on the verdict: "They claimed we made an illegal party and distributed sweets illicitly, and accused me of shouting communist slogans such as 'workers unite'. What exactly is communist about that? This is a stern warning to the striking workers at Kurdistan Textile [see above], a way of telling them what to expect if they continue. It is a punishment for the protests going on here."[32]

In the meantime, another May Day had passed by. This year, the state had switched tactics. Wary at being saddled with a new group of pugnacious and potentially popular activists, it opted for co-optation: Khane-ye Karegar called for a meeting on May Day 2005 at the Azadi stadium in Tehran. More than 10,000 workers gathered in the western industrial zone near Iran Khodro early in the day. The Pasdaran and the basiji arrived to "escort" the crowd into the stadium, thereby sparking off skirmishes on the highway, responding to stone-throwing with batons and tear gas. After the situation calmed down somewhat, the crowd, now numbering roughly 20,000, marched into the stadium, where loudspeakers greeted them with the announcement that an old acquaintance indeed would show up to deliver a speech: Hashemi Rafsanjani. This effort to canvass support for his ongoing presidential campaign backfired. As told by "Roza Javan" (of whom more later):

People started booing and shouting "the government should leave us alone", "abolish slavery in Iran", "the Majles betrays us and the leaders [of Khane-ye Karegar] support them" and "referendum, referendum [on the constitution of the country], this is what we want". To avoid embarrassing scenes, Rafsanjani's speech was cancelled. Instead, the head of Khane-ye Karegar, Alireza Mahjoub, entered the stage – and started urging people to vote for Rafsanjani! Not a word about workers' rights! Some activists then stormed the podium and pulled down the microphone, while the masses in the stadium simply marched out.[33]

News of the disturbances evaded media censorship. *Iran Daily* quoted a representative of the workers of Ilam, present at the stadium: "Blue-collar workers have no other alternative but to voice their complaints by holding protest rallies. The labour force wants temporary contracts to be revoked and real wages to be declared [sic], but nobody is paying attention."

The scuffle at the stadium was a clear hint of the atmosphere that had gripped the country; an augury of the results of the presidential elections, which would come as such an annoying surprise to the West. More scenes took place during the day. Large areas of the industrial zone in Tehran were closed, as committees at Iran Khodro and other plants had informed their employers beforehand that they had no intention of working on May Day. A speech by one of the Saqqez Seven before a packed audience at Tehran University, a mass picnic by the side of the mountain road north of Tehran, meetings in Tabriz, demonstrations in Kermanshah, and a two-hour strike at an oil refinery in Esfahan were among the other known activities on May Day 2005 – all on a wholly different scale than just a year before.

MORE LESSONS IN SECTARIANISM

Both May Days, 2004 and 2005, were milestones in the pursuit of transforming uncoordinated unrest into a national movement. However, not one, but *two* committees emerged to shoulder the burden. From the May Day activity in spring 2004 evolved the *Komiteye Hamahangi* or "The Co-ordinating Committee to Form Workers' Organisation in Iran". It constituted itself in late May 2005 by publishing the names of, initially, 3,000 workers, who openly proclaimed their intention to establish an organisation informed by issues of class, whatever the Islamic Republic might think of it – a step unthinkable only two years earlier.[34]

But the visions of Komiteye Hamahangi extend far beyond the horizon of a national organisation of labour. Under the leadership of Mohsen Hakimi, one of the Saqqez Seven and a translator of philosophical works who had been brought to Saqqez from his book-lined home in Tehran to give a speech on the occasion, the group has codified a certain interpretation of the revolution of 1979. According to Hakimi:

The major problem during the Shah's reign was the lack of autonomous labour organising, and it is the same today. We have learnt the lessons of the revolution and realised that our most important task is to prepare the ground for workers' councils to take over the country. Next time, no sects, no Fedaiyan, Peykar or Komele shall be allowed to tell the workers what to do, for in whom shall power reside – in the sects or in the workers themselves?

Mahmoud Salehi expresses a similar faith in the council tradition of Iran: "Before the Islamic Revolution, there was a gleam of freedom and the workers established councils forthwith, as they have done at every historical juncture where just a little bit of freedom has appeared. If such a situation would come back, shoras would flourish again."[35]

Not very strangely, the Komiteye Hamahangi activists – many of whom had experienced the revolution first-hand and then stagnated through the decades of political paralysis – have made a fetish of the shora institution which, in the hands of Hakimi, has been petrified into a doctrine of council communism. Falling back on this early twentieth-century strand of western socialism, associated with the names of Anton Pannekoek and Paul Mattick, Hakimi has reached the conclusion that the council is the *only organisation* the workers need. No mediation, transitional steps or organisational apparatus should stand between the workers and their goals. In the programmes of the committee, it is explained thus: "We – workers – establish our own councils. With the power of our councils, any interference by any employer in the fate of production is prevented. Our way is to have our councils take production into our own hands."[36]

To the activists of Komiteye Hamahangi, political parties are anathema. But more crucially, in the light of later events in Iran: trade unions are equally anathema. In council communism, they are considered not only bureaucratic obstacles wasting the energy of shop-floor struggle, but "capitalist organisations" complicit in the trading of labour as a commodity. According to the texts of Komiteye Hamahangi, the trade union is by definition a "bargaining unit", a "mediator between workers and capitalism", just another machine making "profits" on status quo. The only form of organisation permissible is an "anti-capitalist" one, whose activities will be restricted to propaganda, agitation and "support for strikes, workers' control initiatives and the like".[37] Hence Komiteye Hamahangi has declared it of paramount importance to "reveal the dominant resolutions and strategies of 'syndicalism' [that is, trade unionism], 'sectarism' [sic], 'social democracy', 'liberalism' or in a word 'reformism' as a *fundamental obstruction in the way* of the working class struggle."[38]

Here is foretold how relations would soon develop between Komiteye Hamahangi and workers who were actually trying to form trade unions, in contravention of the laws of the Islamic Republic. More lessons on sectarianism were in store for Iranian labour.

In 2005, Hakimi and his network – originally in the lead, on the ground – excelled in reveries about the imminent abolition of all wage labour in Iran, Komiteye Hamahangi's publications littered with paintings of "life without the wage" as a "glimmer of light at the end of a suffocating tunnel – let us come together and burst that tunnel open".[39] The attachment to the realities of Iranian workers – who are either underpaid, about to lose their pay, or unpaid – became ever looser, as Komiteye Hamahangi sermonised that what they really ought to do about wages was to abolish them. The issue of the Islamic Republic and how to deal with it was forgotten, the Iranian predicament read as a naked and pure contradiction, nineteenth-century style, between capital and labour. Thus Komiteye Hamahangi, as we will see later, lost most of its political capital.

Instead, the initiative passed on to the second committee, which originated from a network in Tehran with roots in the Fedaiyan Majority and Tudeh, the two parties that supplied Ayatollah Khomeini's staunchest soldiers on the Left, up to the very moment when he decided to slaughter them. In the 1990s, these remnants teamed up with a supposed pro-labour wing within the Majles, in what proved to be a futile attempt to improve the conditions of working people "from within". Later, in 2003, delegations from the International Labour Organisation (ILO) began to visit Iran to establish formal contact with the Ministry of Labour, and – as the supposed representatives of Iranian workers – Khane-ye Karegar. These initial contacts developed into regular visits from both parties, negotiations over legal issues, and exchange of information.

However, the network, without any illusions left, now railed at the ILO for taking the regime at face value, approving of Khane-ye Karegar as a real workers' organisation, and by-passing all other sources of information about the plight of workers in the country. It called upon the ILO to recognise realities on the ground, and from there, the network took a logical next step by formalising itself into the *Komiteye Peygiri*, or "Follow-up Committee for the Establishment of Free Workers' Organisations in Iran", initially collecting 4,000 names for this aim.

By the time of May Day 2005, Komiteye Peygiri echoed the agenda of the already existing initiatives in the country. Starting with the demand that Iranian workers be allowed freely to form trade unions, the committee now incorporated the elementary principles of the shora institution in its program: "Holding general assemblies during working hours and in the workplace should be recognised. We demand direct participation and intervention of workers' representatives in tripartite meetings and in all matters relating to workers' future. Such representatives should be elected in general assemblies through workers' direct vote."[40]

However, rivalry between the committees was inevitably fuelled by leaden memories of the internecine struggles after the revolution. Peygiri knew how to reciprocate the criticism of Hamahangi; according to "Seper", an ex-Tudeh factory custodian in Tehran:

There is no revolutionary situation in Iran. As Lenin said, two conditions must be met for such a situation to arise: oppressors must be incapable of oppressing any longer, and the oppressed must refuse to be oppressed any more, and neither of these are present in Iran. It's just sheer voluntarism on their [Hamahangi's] part. What we can do is start from where we are, and gradually make the Islamic Republic accept our right to form trade unions. There is no need for dogmatic utopias, no need for underground committees. It would be more useful to petition the ILO and the UN to pressurise the Islamic Republic to change its labour policies.[41]

Whatever the merits of these arguments, it was in fact Komiteye Peygiri that proved to be more in tune with what would become the most articulate and adventurous fight for labour rights in the Islamic Republic to date.

Besides the two Komiteyes, there are still parties on the exiled Left seeking leadership of a socialist mass movement that would rise up against the mullahs, the redemption for which they have been waiting so long. In the early 1980s, the wreckage of the Iranian Left washed ashore in the capitals of western Europe, where they tried to maintain a meaningful existence as opposition to the Islamic regime. They failed, as the process of fragmentation into ever smaller splinter groups and the distance to Iran's political realities only increased.[42] However, internal labour unrest since 2004 has raised hopes, resuscitating the exiled Left, and providing it with causes for demonstrations of solidarity – even cooperative initiatives across the factional barriers – unseen since its arrival in the West.

Naturally, some exile parties have tried to smuggle their agendas into Iran and take credit for the labour movement there; this pertains first and foremost to the "worker-communists". Originally a secession from one of the Maoist tendencies, the Worker-Communist Party is by far the most well-organised, well-informed and vociferous actor on the diaspora scene. Infamous for a rabid hatred of anything Islamic, worker-communists were quick to express solidarity with the Danish newspaper *Jyllands-Posten* in the row over the Muhammad cartoons in early 2006, and regularly to proclaim their support for such measures as banning of the hijab. Now, for the exiled worker-communists, the dawn is nearing in Iran. The mentality of workers is "extremely radical and socialist", making it "unlikely that there is anything to prevent the coming revolution", as a worker-communist leader prophesied in spring 2005. He went on to state that the labour unrest was a product of none but the worker-communists themselves. For they infuse socialism into Iran through a 24-hour satellite channel – "like water being poured over a parched earth" – and among their favourite themes are the mockery of Shia rituals and the denigration of Islam. [43] Nothing could, of course, be further from the truth. The worker-communists – split into two parties in 2004 – do have a tiny presence inside Iran. But they are generally disdained by local labour activists, precisely for their pretensions to ownership. Furthermore, in the eyes of the vast majority of workers who retain their belief in Islam, and who differentiate between true Islam and its distortions by the vile millionaire mullahs, the anti-Islamic harangues of the worker-communists are utterly offensive.

But the worker-communists are of course not alone. As can be gathered from browsing through the websites of the many remaining parties of the Left, few of them have strayed from Marxism-Leninism. The classic characteristics of the Iranian Left are still all there: excessive sectarianism, extreme similarity in approach and equal certitude in the superiority of their own party, and the extravagant application of the aesthetics and terminology of the Marxist-Leninist canon on modern Iranian realities. Not much has changed since the early 1980s, except for the reduced quantity and membership of the groups.

It is an open question whether any of these committees or parties could contribute to the production of an authentic cadre, capable of nurturing the seed through all the many intermediate stages towards a mature labour movement.[44] Conditions conducive to this possibility arose in the early twenty-first century. However, as we will see, they were soon hampered by major new developments. At the same time, the atmosphere did present itself in more indicators than just clear-cut labour action. There were other, strong articulations of the same grievances in Iran. Some of them would remain inaudible, while others, heavily distorted, would profoundly frighten parts of the international community.

7
The Intifada of the Provinces

THE PERSIAN CAT

Look at a map of the Middle East and you will see borders of surreal linearity, devised by someone who obviously unrolled an old map on a table far away and used a ruler to draw straight lines, without considering at all the peoples under the pen. But turn to Iran, and you detect a nation the shape of a burly cat crouched upon the Indian Ocean, its contours rounded and uneven. Iran is no artificial construct at the hands of European imperialists. It has, as the kingdom of Persia, a history longer than most nations; its modern borders have, with only minor changes, been in place for hundreds of years. Here is no mix of peoples that suddenly found themselves confined within borders determined by foreign pens, as in, for example, the patchwork of Iraq or the mosaic of Lebanon.

Nevertheless, every time Iran enters a period of political turmoil, one issue comes to the fore: that of the national minorities. The geography of Iran seems designed for tensions between a centralised government and its fringe peoples. From the edgy viewpoint of Tehran, on the other side of the steppe, the desert, or the mountain chain reside tribes and nations of various languages, customs and beliefs, united only in their desire to live autonomously, undisturbed by decrees from a distant capital.

In modern Iran, the latest tensions between the capital and the far-flung regions have been severely aggravated under regimes of uneven development. When the state-centre drives a process of capital accumulation, investments tend to be propelled into regions that are already relatively developed – prospects for profit are brightest there, and the infrastructure easiest to expand – while the peripheries are left behind, sinking into ever deeper relative deprivation. At the same time, the state tends to forcibly *integrate* the peripheries into a national market of exchange, breaking up whatever pre-capitalist structures are still intact there. As the national minorities are thus simultaneously pauperised *and* drawn into closer interactions with the prospering centre, they tend to become conscious of their position as the outcasts of the nation, and, as soon as there is an opportunity, they rebel.[1] The early twenty-first century has seen no exception to this pattern.

KURDISTAN ABLAZE

One of the Iranian regions left behind is that inhabited by the Kurds, consisting of the province officially known as Kurdistan, plus the parts of western Azerbaijan and Kermanshah that fall within the mountain lands occupied by the Kurdish people, with their distinctive language, customs, and tenacious national identity, since time immemorial. Reza Shah first tried to break the Iranian Kurds on the wheels of uneven development. He subordinated their wild nomad tribes, by confiscating lands and imprisoning clan leaders, and forced them to settle in permanent locations. Their economic self-sufficiency was thus destroyed, while they reaped none of the benefits of the program of "modernisation from above". Here the Kurds' position as a peripheral national minority within the capitalist entity of Iran, dominated by its Persian centre, was constructed. It was subsequently gravely reinforced by Muhammad Reza Shah.[2]

When the central government collapsed in 1979, the Kurds rushed to occupy the ensuing vacuum. They captured military garrisons, seized weapons, formed all kinds of shoras, and mobilised for autonomy. They did not seek an independent nation – there was no reason to secede absolutely from the economic and geopolitical unit of which they were a part – but they demanded a regional parliament for internal affairs, proportional representation in the central government, allocation of development funds, and, of course, cultural rights. But that was far too much for the Islamic Republic to stomach. It was born in Kurdish blood. The first and fiercest battles against internal opposition took place in Kurdish territories, in the inaccessible mountain ranges of Kurdistan. Tens of thousands of *peshmerga*, organised behind the banners of the nationalist Kurdish Democratic Party of Iran (KDPI) and the communist Komele, controlled entire valleys and village areas, holding out for almost a decade, until all aspirations of autonomy were eventually vanquished.

Then the millionaire mullahs could reproduce these contradictions all over again.[3] No major industrial investments have been allocated to Kurdistan. No automobile plants, no oil refineries or huge infrastructure projects provide employment for the working people there; they are supposed to be satisfied with subsistence agriculture, herding, small textile workshops and bakeries. But they are not. There is a permanent surplus of working people. Some find an income in smuggling – the Kurdish border region is notoriously porous – but the most common recourse is migration to other parts of Iran. Together with their illegitimate cousins from other, sometimes even more destitute, minorities, the sons of the Kurdish people constitute a stigmatised subsection within the Iranian proletariat. Kurds are available, particularly in the construction and brick-making sectors, for any employer who wants to avail himself of super-cheap labour. Returning home from such encounters, Kurdish migrant workers bring tales of the fortunes amassed by Persians in the centre.

To add insult to injury, the millionaire mullahs treat the Kurds with cultural and political disdain. Kurds are not allowed to teach or learn the Kurdish language at school. They are excluded from most avenues of educational or political advancement, denied any Kurdish-language media, and are grossly underrepresented in the Majles. At a whim of the government, Kurdish employees may suddenly be made redundant and replaced with ethnic Persians or Pasdaran soldiers considered "in need" of employment.[4] The vast majority of the roughly six million Kurds are Sunni Muslims, superintended by Shia mullahs appointed by Tehran. In some respects, they have enjoyed easier lives than their fellow Kurds in Turkey and Iraq; the Islamic regime has never promoted its ethnic identity as aggressively as the Kemalists or the Baathists. But the incendiary combination of factors assembled under the reign of the millionaire mullahs is present in Kurdistan in even more acute form than in the centre of the country.

This situation was enough to set Kurdistan ablaze on 9 July 2005. On that day, a local Kurdish activist named Shivan Qaderi was approached by Pasdaran soldiers in the street in Mahabad and shot three times. His body was then tied to the back of a truck and dragged through the streets before being handed over, bruised and swollen, to shocked relatives. Fifty years earlier, mobs from Mahabad had occupied the police station, cleared the city of any government presence, and, under the tutelage of the Soviet Army, had proclaimed the mythical Kurdish republic, with demands similar to those raised in the 1979 revolution. After a year's existence, the Kurdish republic was symbolically crucified by Tehran when three of its leaders were hanged in the night in the central square of Mahabad, to be discovered by shocked relatives and inhabitants in the morning.

Now the butchers of Tehran were back to pierce the heart of Kurdish national sensitivity, and Mahabad rose again. Upon learning the news of Qaderi's murder, demonstrators gathered in the central square and stormed the government offices. The house of a mullah loyal to the regime was attacked, and a Pasdaran soldier was lynched.[5]

In a few days, rioting had spread to all the major cities and towns of Iranian Kurdistan, and continued for weeks. Retribution would not be long in coming. On 3 August, yet another demonstration was moving through the city of Saqqez:

People marched arm-in-arm, shouting "Death to Khamene'i" and other chants against the Islamic Republic. They were totally fearless. Some of them threw stones against the army. Then the soldiers started shooting live ammunition into the crowd, killing at least twelve people and injuring many more. But the injured are afraid to go to hospitals, since there are soldiers and basiji there, keeping doctors under supervision and banning them from visiting homes. Therefore we expect more people to die,

narrated Mahmoud Salehi a few days later. Salehi was soon to be among the thousands of Kurdish activists and civilians who were arrested.[6]

The state's response to the uprising was ferocious. According to reports from the province, no less than 100,000 soldiers were deployed to crush the rebellion.[7] One of the two established Kurdish movements, the communist Komele, countered by announcing a one-day general strike and commercial shutdown on 7 August. The entire province was brought to a standstill under Komele's modest demands of withdrawal of the army, respect for the right to protest, release of all recently arrested prisoners, and an international reaction to the regime's crimes. But in the face of the Iranian government's overwhelming power, which literally besieged the region by land and in the air, the unrest abated. Kurdistan once again became a militarised zone, as it had been up until the late 1990s. More than twenty martyrs of the uprising were buried, leaving the province simmering with stifled anger.

The West seemed completely indifferent. The branches of Komele and KDPI in exile – less fragmented than the rest of the Left – attempted to bring some political or at least media attention to the events in Kurdistan, without much success. However, for them a ray of hope emanated from the uprising. As Farhad Shabani, member of the central committee of Komele, pointed out:

Never since 1980 and 1981 have the Kurdish people protested on such a massive scale and been treated with such brutality by the Islamic Republic. The difference is that the militias of Komele are not there to strike back. This time, it is an unprotected civilian population rising up. But it is not necessarily motivated by nationalism. This is being done by workers and unemployed, oppressed people who do not see any future for themselves and their families.[8]

The presence of Komele in Kurdistan had indeed been reduced to a clandestine political, or even cultural, network; neither it nor the KDPI had any peshmerga units at their disposal to be summoned for a new war against the Islamic Republic.[9] That era was over.

However, in the aftermath of the summer uprising, a hitherto unknown organisation suddenly rose up in the valleys of Iranian Kurdistan, engaging angry young Kurds, and leaving both Komele and KDPI in its wake. It did precisely what those two parties had not done: killed Iranian soldiers. In surprise attacks on military outposts, staged from the Iraqi side of the border, dozens fell. The new militants did not conceive of the Kurdish issue as a class struggle, but rather as a nationalist cause. They did start a new war in Kurdistan. However, to put their appearance in the right context – for it occurred under black clouds gathering above Iran – we shall discuss them more later.

BULLDOZING THE ARAB HOMELAND

At around the same time, another powder keg was lit in Iran. In Khuzestan, nearly three million Arabs have suffered their own special version of the fate of the Iranian people. More than 90 per cent of Iran's oil is extracted from Khuzestan; its people live – literally – in the shadow of the oil pumps.

As we have seen, the oil workers of Khuzestan were in the working-class vanguard in the Tudeh era, as well as during the 1979 revolution. Today, the only sign of them being drawn into any labour unrest is under the smoke-screen of sports activities. Oil workers are the precious servant of the millionaire mullahs, purveying to them Iran's oil wealth. Thus the oil workers thereby possess the power to bring down the mullahs as they once did the Shah; as a result, their every step, as evident from Assaluyeh, is monitored by soldiers and government officials. Oil installations are profoundly militarised, the proletariat all but physically shackled, tranquillised with a precisely adjusted mixture of drugs and slightly above average wages.

It is instead the *natives* of Khuzestan – according to whom the true name of the province is Ahwaz – who have become the source of trouble. They have a long history of alienation from the oil installations that have cropped up on their soil. In the Tudeh era, however, they were mobilised against the oil workers, as British interests in the area coaxed Arab clan leaders to attack striking unions; during the 1979 revolution, Arab clashes with the Islamic Republic were of a far less intense nature than those of the Kurds or Turkmen.[10] But since then, the Khuzestan Arabs have suffered calamities. Not only did the Iran–Iraq War scorch the earth of Khuzestan for eight long years, but once its rule of the province was assured, the Islamic Republic began to Persianise it. The rationale is simple: oil reserves cannot be left to Arabs, who are not true Iranians, but backward folk, devoid of the cultural and educational qualities of the heartland Persians. Arabs are potentially disloyal citizens; never mind they feared and fought Saddam as much as anyone else – they are a fifth column, right in the midst of the oil fortunes.

Thus the Arabs have been pushed aside by a military-industrial complex that sprawls across their province. Fertile farmlands are systematically confiscated – some estimates claim 200,000 hectares since 1979 – and allotted to ethnic Persian soldiers and government-trusted agents, on a mission to construct ever more townships and industrial zones of the Assaluyeh type. The elite Al-Quds Brigade of the Pasdaran is permanently garrisoned in Khuzestan, security forces and their families making up an increasing proportion of the local population. For Arabs and their agriculture, there is little space left. Hundreds of thousands have been forcibly displaced, according to the UN, the only compensation being a sum of money one-fortieth the market value of the land; again according to the UN, this is a daily phenomenon in the province. Some are forced to resettle in camps in other parts of the country – such as the "Beheshti" camp (named after a prominent ayatollah) outside Mashhad – while most are concentrated in an expanding ring of shantytowns around the provincial capital of Ahwaz. There, they are squeezed into shacks without electricity, telephones or sewage systems, with social services at a bare minimum.[11]

Neighbours to the fuel of the bonanza, the Arabs of Khuzestan have some of the highest rates of unemployment, illiteracy, child malnutrition and extreme poverty in all of Iran. They are administered by Persian governors and preached to by Persian mullahs, but what hurts the most is the grand larceny of Khuzestan's resources. A bill proposing that a mere *1½ per cent* of the oil revenues should be allocated for local development in Khuzestan has been turned down repeatedly in the Majles. As a constant reminder of how life could be, the slum dwellers can, as a UN envoy observed in July 2005, "see the towers of the oil refineries and the flares and all of that money, which is a lot, and it is going out of the province."[12]

In April 2005, a letter was circulated in the city of Ahwaz, allegedly written by a presidential adviser in Tehran, which spelled out plans for further transfer of the Arab population to other parts of the country, more settlement of Persians into the region, and the renaming of Arab towns and villages in Farsi. On 15 April, an unarmed demonstration in Ahwaz protested against the letter. At least twenty people were shot dead. Crowds from the slums swooped down upon the city centre, rampaging through state banks and buildings. Wearing the emblematic *kouffiyeh*, they proclaimed that this was the beginning of the "Ahwazi intifada". Much like the Israeli Army when dealing with the Palestinians, Pasdaran troops sealed off Ahwaz; they deployed snipers on the roof-tops, cut water supplies to Arab neighbourhoods, torched Arab homes and markets, and ordered hospitals to deny treatment to injured Arab demonstrators. They turned Sunni mosques into temporary prisons, brought in helicopter gunships, and deployed ample amounts of tear gas and live ammunition. The "intifada" continued, and spread to the rest of the province. After one week, Human Rights Watch reported that local sources put the death toll at 50; a little later, the Ahwaz Human Rights Organisation, local partner of Amnesty International, claimed 130 had been killed. On 18 April, the Islamic Republic expelled Al-Jazeera from the country after its coverage of the events – Khuzestan is now cut off from international scrutiny. But Al-Faqih came to Khuzestan. With a retinue of hundreds of Persian Pasdaran families, he staged "Ahwaz Day" as a show of the Islamic Republic's appreciation of the region.[13]

But this hotbed of inequality was not soothed. After some lulls, fresh riots flared in July 2005, and again in January 2006, provoked by rumours of new measures of Persianisation, such as the construction of a wall to separate the industrial zone of Arvand from its Arab surroundings in the Abadan and Khorramshahr areas. Hundreds of Arabs were arrested, activists and relatives of wanted activists taken hostage, and their houses demolished with bulldozers.[14] Then Khuzestan went the same way as Kurdistan. In the autumn of 2005 and spring of 2006, the popular uprising turned into a string of lethal attacks in Khuzestan and even Tehran itself. That, however, took place under the same darkening skies as the armed operations in the far north-west, and we will therefore return to Khuzestan in due course.

MORE TROUBLE FROM THE EDGES

Official demographic data on the various groups inside Iran is neither current nor trustworthy. Ethnic Persians are generally believed to constitute a little more than half of the population. By far the largest minority – about one-fourth – is the Azeris; they are Shiite, Turkish-speaking inhabitants of the densely populated, industrial north. Tabriz is their capital and they have a long history as a revolutionary hotbed with a craving for justice, freedom, and regional autonomy.[15] However, the Azeri north is not underdeveloped in relation to Tehran and other regions of the Persian centre. Millions of Azeris mingle with Persians in Tehran, and they are not excluded from high-ranking positions; on the contrary, Azeris have long been an integral part of the Iranian elite.[16]

Nevertheless, in May 2006, the Azeri north was on fire. After a cartoon in one of the official newspapers portrayed Azeris as cockroaches (or so it was interpreted), hundreds of thousands of Tabriz residents took to the streets in a demonstration against "Persian chauvinism". Riots spread to other cities in Azerbaijan, and dozens of demonstrators were shot dead.[17] Thus the pattern of rebellion witnessed in Kurdistan and Khuzestan seemed to have reached the largest minority – but conditions are fundamentally different. The bulk of those counted as Azeris are well-integrated into Iranian society, and any major uprising on their part would, probably, have to go hand in hand with a generalised *Iranian* uprising.

In the opposite corner, both geographically and figuratively, are the Baluchis. Some 3 per cent of the population, they are, like their Pakistani siblings, sparsely scattered over the limitless barren landscapes of Baluchistan. Theirs is indeed an extreme privation. It is almost as if they were *too* marginal, too remote, too cut off from the routes of Iranian capital accumulation to stand in any relation to the centre at all. The Baluchis are the poorest, and most isolated, of the minorities. Relying on primitive agriculture, smuggling and black market dealing, they move in armed groups that ignore border regulations. Their contact with Tehran is nothing like as intimate as that of the Kurds or the Arabs. However, as the Pakistani Baluchis have engaged in armed confrontation with *their* obtrusive central government, which is robbing them of natural resources in their part of Baluchistan, so have Iranian Baluchis attacked the Iranian Army as well. To these attacks we will come back.

The two minorities that have thus far voiced their discontent most loudly, the Kurds and the Arabs, both *define themselves through their interaction with the Persian centre*. Rather than mice struggling to escape the predations of the cat, they are constituents of the Iranian political entity (to a significant degree, this pertains to the other minorities as well).[18] The similarities of the Kurdish and Arab predicaments and reactions are no coincidence. An indication of this shared fate was the "Congress of Iranian Nationalities" held in London in February 2005 by seven organisations representing Kurds, Arabs, Azeris, Baluchis and Turkmen. There they proclaimed their *unity as Iranian minorities*, beginning their manifesto with the words: "Iran is owned [by] and belongs to all its peoples and nationalities ... We believe the establishment of a federalist system of government on the basis of ethnicity-nationality and geography is the only political mechanism that is enduring, and it [federalism] allows all Iranian nationalities to realise their aspirations and the exercise of self-rule in a framework of a free, united and democratic Iran."

The "summit of minorities" was an event without precedent, followed by mutual solidarity statements and increasing political coordination between the partners. Its target was not Iran as a political entity, but the Islamic Republic; pledging allegiance to the principle of "a united and an integral Iran", the Congress declared that the removal of the "totalitarian" Republic is the first condition for real equality between its citizens.[19] And, as is evident from the popular uprisings of the Kurds and Arabs in 2005, ethnic tensions are but another dimension of the general social contradictions in Iran. Nasser Bani-Assad, the spokesman of the most prominent exile organisation of the Khuzestan Arabs, replicated the logic of this arrangement when, commenting on the 1½ per cent bill, he cited some inflated statistics to declare: "The mullahs' greed will ultimately destroy them, for failure to address the needs of non-Persian minorities – who make up more than 50 per cent of the population – will lead to instability that will shake the foundations of the Islamic Republic."[20]

The minorities are at the edges of uneven development, circling around the central engine of accumulation. Or, simply put: they are the extra, colourful, edges of the wider picture. Their recently heightened visibility has contributed to the illumination of that picture as the one that determines the future of Iran.

8
Reformism's Obituary

THE STILLBORN REFORM MOVEMENT

The sharpening of social contradictions a few years into the new millennium marked the death of the political fashion that swept through Iran in the late 1990s: reformism, embodied in the figure of Muhammad Khatami. As a candidate in the presidential elections of 1997, he offered to depressed Iranians a new message. Now was the time, he proposed, to modernise and rejuvenate the Islamic revolution by breeding a vigorous civil society, side by side with the state. This civil society would be delivered from the very womb of the Islamic Republic by it relaxing some restrictions: a little more freedom of expression, a little less regulation of inter-gender mingling, all nurtured and protected, within an Islamic framework, by a consistent rule of law and a conscientious judiciary. Khatami clothed these ideas with an aura of intellectual sophistication. The dapper, fashion-conscious mullah with an amiable smile won the elections of 1997 by a landslide.

After Khatami's victory, followed by similar successes by his "Second Khordad movement" (named after the date of his victory) in Majles elections, there was indeed a wind of change blowing through the Republic. Publications of various reformist colours mushroomed. Women in some parts of the country began to stretch the boundaries of the Islamic dress code; public debates on the relation between Islam and civic life flourished. It looked like a thaw, but came to a complete halt before anything really had time to defrost. The real power centres of the Islamic Republic nipped reformism in the bud: dissident intellectuals were killed, innumerable newspapers closed down, student dormitories attacked, and, ultimately, the Majles cleared of any candidates supporting anything that could be construed as a reform project.[1] This triumphant campaign was followed closely by the West.

But why did Khatami fail? Why was reformism unable to defend democratic rights against the conservative counteroffensive? In the years of the mini-thaw, which gathered a new wave of accolades from the West to the gallant modernisers of Iran (see below), very few observers managed to identify the Achilles heel of this movement. However, in 2002, Behzad Yaghmaian, in yet another grandiloquent encomium to Iran's "movement for joy", included a rare view of the daily life of working Iranians. Noting that the monopoly held by Khane-ye Karegar on labour "representation" remained undisturbed by Khatami, who never even as much as questioned the Pasdaran's control over the working class, Yaghmaian inferred that

... workers' rights at the point of production, their right to collective and free representation, and the right to challenge their public and private employers were excluded from the discourse of civil society. The official language of rights and participation excluded the wage earners as a specific group with a defined collective interest and rights. A civil society was to be built without the institutionalisation of workers' rights. The narrowness and limits of the official movement for civil society, and the neglect of wage earners and their independent institutions, resulted in the continuation of the old regime of labour at the point of production, *and, ultimately, fear and intimidation in the society at large.* Mohammad Khatami's program of reform and "political development" called for "citizens' participation", "citizens' empowerment" and the "citizens' mastery over their destiny". But "citizens" are a heterogeneous group, with structurally differential social, political, and economic power ... The project of "citizens' empowerment" cannot be realised without the recognition of the social power differentials and the rights of different groups in creating their mediums of collective voice.[2]

If there was any chance of bringing freedom to Iran, Yaghmaian concluded, it rested on the dismantling of Khane-ye Karegar and shora-ye eslami and their replacement with "both ideologically and organisationally independent institutions of wage earners".[3] Here was the battlefield that Khatami never dared to contemplate entering. This was not surprising, for he was a man of the Islamic state. Serving as the Minister of Culture and Islamic Guidance from 1982 to 1992, he was responsible for swathing all cultural life in the monochrome blackness of martyrdom and mourning, every outburst of "atheist" flamboyance obliterated by his staff of censors. It seems that he, towards the end of his incumbency, was afflicted by some remorse, or at least with a will to do good hereafter and be culturally compassionate.

Whatever the personal reasons for his change of mind, Khatami was followed by a generation of Khomeinist puritans who had come to the conclusion that the velayat al-faqih might benefit from some democratic reforms, for these would actually allow people to commit themselves to Islam *voluntarily*. Relaxed ex-hezbollahis, beards now neatly trimmed, were the linchpin of the Second Khordad movement, and they cast their arguments for reform in the moulds of *itjihad*, or reinterpretations of Islamic discourse.[4] Thus the reform project emanated from the interior of the very state apparatus it was supposed to transmute. The reform project didn't leave its grass roots to merge with the state, as reformisms of various shades in the Western world have done: it was an offspring of the state from birth.

The class base was congenial. Reformism was a component of the millionaire mullah nexus. To the millionaire mullahs Khatami consigned the determination of economic policies, his liberally minded core constituencies in the "urban middle classes" were insouciant; their passion was for intellectual and cultural freedom only. No agenda of social or economic justice appeared on Khatami's platform.[5] And that was precisely why it was doomed to fail *even in its restrictedly political-cultural agenda*, for in Iran, the authoritarian system is based in the relations of production: the mullahs ordering the executions of dissidents are the same millionaires who monopolise the oil revenues. One dimension is inseparable from the other.

As the reformist movement had no material base independent of the millionaire mullahs (to the contrary, it was fully entangled in their robes), neither had it any chance to challenge them in their position as guardians of totalitarian morality. The real powers behind the Islamic Republic had no reason to make substantial concessions to the reformist movement, since it did not threaten their authority from the outside; when the mullahs moved to crush it, the movement had no forces to mobilise in its defence. Progeny of the Republic, Khatami and the reformists could not realise their electoral promises of a civil society. The death of their project was inevitable.

PORTRAIT OF A PIONEER

"Roza Javan" is a short, slender woman whose thin arms move in wide gestures as she speaks; sometimes she must stand up to gesticulate freely, as if there was not room in her small body for such vibrancy.

Roza was born the first child of two textile workers in a city somewhere in central Iran. Her family has driven the same car since 1974; now they use a screwdriver instead of an ignition key to start it. When Roza was nine years old, her father was sacked from the factory where he had worked for eight years: "He had refused to go to war, and he was always impertinent and cheeky to the foreman. When he gave him the boot, my father made a lot of noise: 'I will have my job back!' He went to a court in town. The judge offered him a small compensation, but he would accept no money other than his wage – and after half a year of badgering he got his job back. That was too much for the foreman. He quit and left."

When Roza's father came home from work, he used to heap expletives on the company. As it was owned by the state, that meant he cursed the state as well, and that included Ayatollah Khomeini: "When I heard him go on like that I used to tear out papers from my school-books and scrawl *marg bar jomhourie eslami*, death to the Islamic Republic, on them. I put them as leaflets under our neighbours' doors, rang the bells and ran. I was a political being from childhood. The children of the poor of Iran always talk politics, follow the news, try to read papers."

Born in 1981, Roza grew up in the shadow of the Iran–Iraq War. The colour of her childhood was literally black: at the girls' school, everyone was forced to wear chador, with black shoes and bags. Even today, Roza says, she is instinctively drawn to dark clothes rather than colourful ones when entering a shop:

There was no music. Only this imam and that imam, grief in school and grief on television, everywhere the martyrs of the war. "God loves he who mourns" – this was how they raised us! As in a never ending funeral! In school, we always had to pray. My teacher would tell us that if someone knocks on the door while you are at home alone, it might be a man, and therefore you have to be extremely careful. The female voice is so sweet that he might easily be aroused. You must drive your finger deep into the mouth, so that your voice is distorted, and then you can ask *ki-e?*, who's there? Otherwise the man will go wild! And of course they taught us that masturbating is dangerous, it makes you blind. All of this austerity was much more severe in the schools of the poor; middle-class schools were slack in comparison.

Then one day in 1997 appeared Khatami: "He promised that everyone would have more freedom. Freedom to move, freedom to talk. I was sixteen and set on fire. I immediately began agitating for Khatami in school, with such intensity that my friends and I ran into trouble with the local basiji-guys of our age. We all found ourselves having a huge fist-fight in a pit in the neighbourhood."

To be admitted to a university, any Iranian must gain a high grade in an extensive test known as the *concour*. Most students spend a year in preparation for this ordeal, and many make a number of attempts to pass. Roza succeeded at her first try:

At the university, I realised most of the students were from middle-class homes. I compared myself to them and noted that I had invested at least double the efforts to achieve the same results. They had simply bought private lessons, specially adapted to the *concour* – it's a market where you can buy yourself admission! The working class is squeezed out from universities. The only ones where children of workers stand a chance to be admitted are state-run, but as more of these are also privatised, the competition is getting harder there as well.

Though yearning to study social sciences or philosophy, Roza chose chemistry, a discipline with at least some employment prospects. Out of a class of 25, she says, only two were there out of interest in the subject; several of her classmates turned to drugs out of boredom. For Roza Javan, a window was opened by the Internet. She came across web logs where people wrote freely under pseudonyms. The books she had read previously were borrowed from strictly censored libraries; the Web was something entirely fresh and uncontaminated. She encountered feminism, and joined a women's group for impassioned discussions on marriage and legal rights; she kept abreast of the latest political developments and, eyes opened, realised what Khatami's words were worth:

When the first student was killed in the protests of 1999, he said nothing. Those students who had been demonstrating with his picture pressed to their hearts threw it away. When Khatami became president, the situation of poor people did not improve – to the contrary, it worsened. Mine is a generation of unemployed, of junkies, and even if you have a job there's no chance to cover all expenses. Typically, the rent consumes two-thirds of a salary!

Two years into Roza's university studies, debate among the students ceased. Disappointment with Khatami and his unfulfilled promises muffled their voices. Roza kept reading on her own, spending her afternoons in the university library. One day, as she skimmed through a dictionary of political ideologies, she reached "S" and read the entry for socialism. She was astonished: "This was what I had always believed in, without knowing it!" Excited, she searched the Internet for "socialism" in Farsi: the hits were uncountable. Even more excited, Roza sent emails requesting further information to all the

Iranian socialist groups she could find (15, at the time), but only one responded to her questions – an Iranian man living in a Scandinavian country. An intensive correspondence followed, as he advised her about further reading; now she calls him "my mentor".

At home, by her bed, she gingerly lays out the books she has been able to buy: *Capital* in Farsi, Mandel's *Introduction to Marxist Economic Theory*, a bulky volume on the history of the Tudeh party. They are in mint condition:

They were so expensive I don't dare to make any notes in them. I use a notepad instead, and reading Marx is very difficult, so I do what I used to do in chemistry: I set up formulas. When I had first become a socialist, I wanted to get the message out, I wanted all my student mates to know. I touted the books, scribbled slogans in the toilets, pasted a picture of Marx on my folder so it would be clearly visible for anyone passing by in the corridor ... until my mentor told me: "Are you mad? Don't you know that being a socialist carries the death punishment in Iran? Are you not aware that the regime executed thousands of Leftists in the 1980s?" I decided to be more discreet.

In the early months of 2004, word of a planned May Day demonstration in Tehran was circulating. On a blog, Roza had come across some like-minded students in her city and they decided to go. For months, Roza spun a yarn for her parents to get their permission. At the demonstration, "the first communist I met, I fell in love with. I was walking around there in the crowd at the industrial zone, enraptured ... ." Some of her high hopes were, however, quickly dashed. Enrolling in Komiteye Hamahangi, she was challenged by men and their patronising attitudes: "'Who are you, are you a real worker?', they would say. And when I asked about the revolution they would not respond. I would ask 'What do you mean by "abolishing wage labour", what is it supposed to look like in real life? Either one works and gets some money for it, or one works and gets a bag of rice and a chicken – what is it that you want?' They didn't specify."

Roza has some criticism for those she calls "middle-class feminists" as well. When she married her "communist", Roza ensured herself of absolute equality in the marriage contract – equal right to divorce, shared custody in case of divorce, the right for her to travel or work without permission from the husband – but this, she states emphatically, is not all there is to feminist politics: "The middle-class feminists here are only interested in equality with their own men. They don't bother to contact working women, to try find common ground with them, even though they are suffering a much worse oppression. Poor women here are completely dependent on their men and can do nothing if they are raped or beaten. They have no economic safety net whatsoever."

After her encounter with organised feminism and socialism in the Islamic Republic of Iran, Roza took up writing herself. Her computer is now filled with Marxist classics downloaded from the Farsi-language division of the Marxist Internet Archive, as well as her own short stories, essays and commentaries on subjects ranging from the Khatonabad massacre to the merits and demerits of Nobel laureate Shirin Ebadi. No money to buy a printer, her eyes ache from all her onscreen work.

In 2004 and 2005, Roza Javan reached some fame in the virtual networks of the Iranian diaspora and the progressive communities inside the country. She's the webmaster of two sites in Farsi; one feminist, one socialist:[6] "Many students are curious about socialism and enter into intellectual trajectories similar to mine, now that they have no illusions left about reformism. But they are starved, they have no food for their thoughts! They don't know where to turn, there is no organisation capable of reaching out to them, it is difficult to find others of the same mind. Dictatorship means stalemate."

"Brain-drain" is one of the most universally recognised problems of Iran, and the government is anxious to stem the tide of students, numbering in the thousands, who leave the country every year immediately after examinations. Emigration is the most popular route out of the post-reformist deadlock. To Roza, however, it is unthinkable: "As a young girl, my biggest dream was to take off the hijab, put on a short skirt, and run with the wind in my hair. Not even such a small dream can come true in this country. But I will stay. We need a new revolution to get our freedom."

At the time of this writing, in spring 2006, Roza Javan and her husband live somewhere not far from the capital. She runs her two websites, but keeps a low profile, feeling the heat from recent political developments. Her pseudonym alludes to Rosa Luxemburg. *Javan* means young: the young Rosa.

MOVEMENTS BETRAYED

The greatest impact of the brief reform era was an opening – however temporary, however circumscribed – where certain popular movements could move *relatively* freely. Foremost among them were the student and the women's movements. Both were banking on Khatami and his reformists to protect their space, the advertised civil society, and expand it. They were to be profoundly disenchanted.

First to level bitter accusations of betrayal at Khatami was the student movement, which he not only failed to support but publicly denounced as it took to the streets in the summer of 1999. Yet another reformist newspaper had been interdicted; the students protested, and police and basiji vigilantes raided the dormitories of Tehran University, killing and injuring students, who then stepped up their demonstrations in support of freedom of expression. The "reformist" Khatami's reaction was to condemn the *students*. This caused an irreparable rift between the movement and the president.

In 2003, the national student organisation Tahkim Vahdat officially bade farewell to the relics of the Second Khordad movement, and to all attempts to reform the Islamic Republic from within. The new position of Tahkim Vahdat was that theocracy must be scrapped lock, stock and barrel. It subscribed to the idea of a referendum on the constitution of the country as a means to that goal. In the process, it was transformed from a strictly Khatamist organisation to a polyphone organ of student politics, with liberal, constitutionalist and explicitly socialist tones and currents. It had thus travelled all the way from militant Khomeinism in the years of the revolution (when Tahkim Vahdat was the Imam's academic battalion, smoking out the Red ants from their last strongholds during a prolonged university closure) via reformist Khatamism to the quest for a new anti-Islamist radicalism.[7]

The women's movement would soon be searching in the same direction. During the brief period opened up by Khatami's victory, hundreds of NGOs and women's associations established cultural centres, published magazines, and educated women about their rights through websites, seminars and workshops. But in the new millennium the movement found itself at the mercy of a conservative backlash, protected neither by the female reformists in the Majles, nor by Khatami or any other politicians it had thought of as allies. The women's movement departed from the reformist path, and in 2005, it had essentially reached the same position as the student movement: "The obstacles to the progress of women's rights in Iran, these activists have concluded, are not embodied in individual politicians so much as they are inherent in the constitution of the Islamic Republic itself", as Iranian feminist Mahsa Shekarloo noted in an analysis.[8]

On 12 July 2005, a uniquely united women's movement, comprised of ninety groups from Tabriz to Baluchistan, took its new valour to the streets of Tehran, as 2,000 women staged a sit-in in front of the university. Ever since the early 1980s, Tehran University has been the symbolic heart of the Islamic Republic; this is where the highest-ranking government mullahs deliver their homilies on Fridays. And now here were thousands of women sitting in the street, rejecting intimidation from the police surrounding them, singing, chanting, and reading solidarity statements. They called for another constitution and a body of family law whose main source of reference would be not the sharia, but the UN Convention of the Elimination of Discrimination Against Women. No parliamentarians were present.[9] The women's movement was moving forward, without anyone's assistance.

The labour movement, on the other hand, stands out as the one born after the death of reformism. However, it too carried some feelings of betrayal.

As we have noted, the remnants of the Tudeh and the Fedaiyan Majority saw Khatami as a chance to revive the old policies of alliance with clerics; they regarded him as a benefactor of progressive politics.[10] Komiteyeh Peygiri was partly a product of the rejection of that delusion. Among the activists of the workers' committees at Iran Khodro, the distaste for Khatami is acrimonious:

The working class has a tendency to run after others. In the 1990s, the middle classes said Khatami was the big hope for Iran, and workers believed in him. But after a few years we realised he had neither intention nor power to deal with our poverty. He also thought striking is haram. All those in power here know the potentials of independent labour organisations, and therefore they are in complete concord on upholding the ban. And now that we have been striking for our lives at Iran Khodro, no reformists utter a *single word*. It's time to get them off our backs.[11]

Behzad Yaghmaian saw the signs in the late years of the reform period, and prophesied: "Losing control of the movement of wage earners by the House of Labour [Khane-ye Karegar] might result in further collective action and attempts for the creation of independent workers' institutions."[12] The same had happened to the Kurds, who received assurances from Khatami that their situation would be seriously addressed and hence went to the polls in huge numbers; in 2001, the Kurdish deputies of the Majles resigned in protest against his duplicity.[13]

In 2004, reformism suffered its final defeat when all the candidates related to the Second Khordad movement were delisted by the Council of Guardians before the Majles elections in February that year. Tehran journalist "Abide" summed up the collective experience after reform had passed away, in late 2004: "Something new has to come, but we don't know what. The Iranian people have always been unpredictable and explosive – it might overrun the country tomorrow, but it might also wait for another twenty years. The only certain thing is that something has come to an end, and something else must begin."[14]

Behrooz Besadi of *E-temad*, editor of one of the two reformist newspapers still functioning, commented upon the Majles elections:

After the victory of the conservatives and the expulsion of the reform project from the state apparatus, what we will have now is a conflict between, on the one hand, the state in its entirety, and, on the other, the people in its entirety. There is no reflection of popular wishes within the state apparatus any more. Look at us journalists – several of mine have been imprisoned lately – we stand without any protection! Now people have lost all faith in any government or parliament to help them.[15]

The latter diagnosis, however, was patently false. For in 2005, there appeared a politician from the interiors of the Islamic Republic who cared only about the one political dimension that Khatami had never cared about: precisely those popular hopes that Khatami did not touch upon, he would raise high. And just like Khatami, he would do it all within the confines of the edifice of the Islamic Republic.

9
The "Humble" President:
A Man of the People?

THE DUSTMAN VERSUS "AKBAR SHAH"

Of the seven candidates approved to run for president of the Islamic Republic in 2005 (Khatami had served his two permitted terms and was out of the picture), only one drove a 30-year-old Peugeot. He wore a cheap jacket, his shirt collar was unbuttoned, and his black beard neatly combed. He called himself "a dustman of the people". On election day, he lined up in the queue to the polls like any ordinary citizen, and when the press asked him to wave for the crowd after casting his vote, he replied: "The hands of a president are not for waving. They are supposed to work for the people."[1]

Mahmoud Ahmadinejad was born the fourth child of a barber in a village near Tehran; when he was one year old, his family moved to the dingy southern suburbs of the capital, the barber becoming a blacksmith. At university, where he was a brilliant student, Ahmadinejad joined the movement against the Shah, or more specifically, the current committed to the ideas of Khomeini. After the revolution, he rose quickly in the ranks of the Pasdaran. During the Iran–Iraq War, he directed a squadron in the Kermanshah area – within Iranian borders – which specialised in assassinating "enemies of the revolution", that is, Kurdish and Leftist insurgents. He built a reputation as a ruthlessly efficient believer in his cause. When the war was over, he turned to one of the natural trades for men of his kind, the Ministry of Culture and Islamic Guidance, and became, ironically, an adviser to Minister Khatami. In 2003 he was elected mayor of Tehran. His first act in office was to refuse to accept the mayor's salary, and during his two years in the post, he became known as an austere and devout Muslim. He offered interest-free loans to the needy, converted cultural centres to centres for religious improvement, and made a habit of meeting with ordinary local Muslims in informal settings.[2]

And now he was running for president, driving his ancient Peugeot into the same suburbs and villages to meet the poor common folk there, his campaigners distributing CDs showing him at his home *sofreh* – the traditional cloth for dining on the floor – sharing a breakfast of bread, cheese and sweet tea with his family. His battle-cry was "put the oil money back on the people's sofreh." The thrust of Ahmadinejad's campaign was entirely economic. He discoursed on the scourge of unemployment, the fiasco of corrupt privatisation, the danger of a society bitterly dividing into rich and poor. Belittling the reform agenda, he declared that "the country's true problems are unemployment and housing, not what to wear" and promised to "cut the hands off the oil mafia", a metaphor with distinctive connotations of sharia justice. He submitted several concrete pledges to the electorate: if elected, he would effect reallocation of development funds to rural areas, promotion of small workshops, more subsidies and interest-free loans to the needy, health insurance and pensions for women, and expansion of the public sector rather than subcontracting to private companies. For the rich, he had but scorn. He declared that the "thousand families" – a term used for the Pahlavi compradors – were still in control of the country, under a different guise.[3]

For the first time in the history of the Islamic Republic, no candidate scored more than 50 per cent in the first round of a presidential election. In the second, there were two contenders: Mahmoud Ahmadinejad and Ali Akbar Hashemi Rafsanjani. For the former, it was an ideal contest. For the people, the two candidates embodied the social contradictions of the country. Rafsanjani poured millions of dollars into a slick, westernised campaign of airbrushed posters of his beaming face, distributing balloons and badges bearing his name; trucks drove through northern Tehran blaring loud techno music and chic youths were hired to promulgate their new leader's vision. Ahmadinejad derided his opponent as "Akbar Shah", the Bigger Shah. Rafsanjani countered by warning that Ahmadinejad would turn Iran into a Taliban state. Having rebranded himself as a reformist, Rafsanjani now invested all his elite prestige in an attempt to revamp the reform themes and vowed to recreate a democratic atmosphere upon his victory, one which he himself thought was a foregone conclusion. Thus claiming Khatami's mantle, he had nothing to say on equality.[4]

Ahmadinejad humiliated his opponent. He won 62 per cent of the votes, from an overall turnout of 60 per cent. This should have come as no surprise, neither for anyone involved nor for informed spectators, but the reaction of dismay among local and western liberals was one more indicator of how out of touch with Iranian reality were both groups. How could the masses of brick-makers, seamstresses, alms-dependent unemployed be expected to vote for Rafsanjani? No other politician in the history of the Islamic Republic has been the object of such popular loathing, of which the scenes on May Day 2005 were but one small example.

The losers complained of fraud – in fact, Rafsanjani had declared beforehand that if Ahmadinejad won, it could only be as a result of underhanded tactics – and wild allegations were aired of Ahmadinejad bussing in two million (!) Shiites from Pakistan to the poll stations.[5] Though nothing can be excluded in the opaque Islamic Republic, there is a significant distinction between Ahmadinejad mobilising the persuasive power of the basiji-Pasdaran-mosque network on the one hand and outright fraud on the other. Most indicators point to the former as the tool he used.

Fundamentally, the election outcome was, to use the words of editor Behrooz Besadi, a "reflection of popular wishes", of the very state of the Islamic Republic. Distinguished Iran analyst Dilip Hiro notes that it represented "a watershed in the Islamic Republic ... It was the first time in post-revolutionary Iran that the presidential election was decided *on the basis of social class* – with peasants, workers, and the lower-middle class backing Ahmadinejad, and the middle-middle [sic], upper-middle, and upper classes Rafsanjani."[6]

With a twinge of western-liberal self-criticism, *The Economist* acknowledged that Ahmadinejad's landslide was an expression of authentic desires of the Iranian people: "The election result belied the view, especially widespread among Iran's critics in the Bush administration, that Iran's public discourse is essentially a fight between the people, who want freedom, and a repressive state ... In contrast with the pre-revolutionary Iran, the Islamic Republic is a partial democracy, and people let off steam on the polling day."[7]

But was it *freedom*, in any sense *The Economist* conceives the term, for which Iranians had voted? Hardly so. It was for equality. Thus on the western Left, one could hear voices cheering Ahmadinejad as heralding an era of progress in the Middle East. As Tariq Ali, icon of the anti-war movement, wrote in *New Left Review*: "The victory of Ahmadinejad in Iran's presidential elections of 2005 represents the biggest political upset of the new century in the region ... The campaign was sharper in tone and offered a more serious choice of social policy than did the elections of 2004 in the United States, or 2005 in Britain, and saw a higher turnout ... Ahmadinejad's base in the popular classes embeds a greater social sensibility in the new presidency."[8]

So was there truth in the semblance? Was Mahmoud Ahmadinejad actually the ingenuous saviour of the poor people of Iran that he professed to be?

TRAPPED IN THE MULLAHS' WEB

Ahmadinejad's first act in office was to refuse to move to the presidential residence in one of the Shah's old palaces in northern Tehran. He would direct even the highest of dignitaries to the government complexes in the smog-ridden downtown area, at the gates to the southern districts. A few months later, he rejected a $60-million-dollar VIP Airbus previously ordered by Khatami; upon its delivery, he let it be known that a president did not need "such luxuries" and told his transport minister to hand over the plane for ordinary air traffic.[9]

While shunning all signs of opulence, Ahmadinejad initiated his presidency in terms of lay Shia beliefs. His cabinet reportedly wrote a "pact" with the Twelfth Imam, the Mehdi himself, dispatching the Minister of Culture and Islamic Guidance to Jamkaran, near Qom, where there is a holy well, thought to be the ear of the Mehdi. Poor Shiite Iranians have come here for centuries to throw their requests into the well, as the place where they can communicate directly with the Hidden Imam. Unlike any of his predecessors, Ahmadinejad made the doctrine of the second coming of the Mehdi a keynote of his rhetoric, stating that "we should define our economic, cultural and political policies in terms of Imam Mehdi's return."[10] At his international debut, in a speech before the UN General Assembly at its sixtieth anniversary, he intoned: "O mighty Lord. I pray to you to hasten the emergence of your last repository, the promised one, that perfect and pure human being, the one that will fill this world with justice and peace." Afterwards, he confided to a mullah his impression that during that part of his speech, a dazzling light descended on the audience, and not a single person could blink for half a minute. Some rumours claim that the last thing Ahmadinejad did in his position as Tehran's governor was to task the City Council with the construction of a boulevard, wide enough for the Mehdi and his entourage to use as entrance to this world.[11]

This is first-class symbolic politics. Though Ayatollah Khomeini had steered clear of the most superstitious theological speculations (the most famous being his repudiation of the popular belief that his own face could be seen in the moon), Ahmadinejad's image-making is a calculated allusion to Khomeini. The asceticism is a carbon copy of the Imam's lifestyle, as is the solemn show of piety, and, most importantly, the rehabilitation of the mostazafin.

Populism was back on the agenda in the Islamic Republic, thanks to Ahmadinejad. Ervand Abrahamian's analysis applies very well to the newly elected president: "In mobilising the 'common man', populist movements use charismatic figures as well as symbols, imagery and language that have potent value in their popular culture. They promise to raise drastically the standard of living and make their country fully independent of the West."[12]

Ahmadinejad's attempt to replay all the symbolism of the early sansculotte years, his show of the Iranian equivalent of Jacobin purity after Thermidor has been interpreted as a spasm of revolutionary fanaticism, on a par with those in the late 1930s Soviet Union and the late 1960s China.[13] But was there *any* substance to it? There was.

As we have seen, the Pasdaran and its various appendages constitute the arm of the "urban poor" within the state apparatus of the Islamic Republic. It was precisely to this group that Ahmadinejad – the Pasdaran ex-commander, ruthless and dedicated – belonged, and upon taking office, he set out on a special operation to increase its leverage. Literally hundreds of Pasdaran officers were appointed to key positions in the state bureaucracy. Out of 30 new provincial governors, no less then 18 were ex-commanders of Pasdaran, and the cabinet resembled an elite squad of security and intelligence veterans. Among them was Mustafa Pour-Mohammadi, who served as prosecutor in the "revolutionary courts" in the same areas of western Iran where Ahmadinejad led his unit in the 1980s. From his office in the Ministry of Information, Pour-Mohammadi had directed the mass execution of thousands of leftists in the Evin prison in 1988 and the serial murders of dissident intellectuals ten years later. Now he was awarded the post of Minister of the Interior. Ahmadinejad himself was the first president in the mature life of the Islamic Republic who did not don a turban and was neither ayatollah, *hojatoleslam* (a middle-ranking Shiite cleric), or mullah. He was just a simple son of the Pasdaran. In combination with other measures, such as equipping the basiji with more powerful arms, Ahmadinejad thus *enhanced the power of the lumpen barracks* within the state apparatus.[14]

Originally, there was one major economic-political component of Ahmadinejad's operation plan. He intended to use oil revenues as gifts to the faithful poor. Of all his electoral pledges, this seemed sincere: as a means to rekindle the support of the poor for the Islamic Republic, he would put if not all the oil money, then at least some crumbs of it on the people's sofreh. Such ideas floating out from the presidential office were enough to disturb the millionaire mullahs. Their candidate, Rafsanjani, had been outrun by a maverick hezbollahi who sounded like a spectre from those almost forgotten years in the early 1980s, when the hordes of Pasdaran and basiji had the impudence to poke their noses into the business of the bazaar. The Iranian market greeted the new president with distress. The Tehran Stock Exchange index fell 20 per cent between the elections in late June and October; private capital trickled out to investment in the Gulf States.[15]

However, just like in the early 1980s, the capital interests within the state apparatus, only much more powerful this time, would soon demonstrate who was really in the driving seat. When Ahmadinejad proposed a colleague from the Pasdaran barracks to lead the oil ministry, the Majles refused to accept him; after months of negotiations and three nominations from Ahmadinejad, he was forced to install a business-skilled oil technocrat. But most importantly, Al-Faqih himself – again, just as in the power struggle of the early 1980s – intervened to direct the body politic. In a decree in October 2005, Khamene'i gave sweeping new powers to one particular organ: the Expediency Council. Its function is to mediate in conflicts between the president, the Majles and the Council of Guardians – the latter an old bastion of millionaire mullah power, which, since the mass dismissals before the Majles elections in February 2004, has a tight grip on that body as well. Hereafter, the Expediency Council was to be a supreme arbiter of government policy. To lead this empowered Expediency Council, Khamene'i urged the incumbent to stay, namely, Hashemi Rafsanjani. Khamene'i also decided that the novice president was in need of a "tutoring period", and his tutor was to be ... Hashemi Rafsanjani.[16]

Rafsanjani would thus remain the mighty spider in the intricate web of the Islamic Republic. If not publicly, then behind the scenes he would be spinning Iran's major policies with Al-Faqih and the various councils. Popularly elected Ahmadinejad demurred, but had no choice other than to resign himself to his fate. After all, the Pasdaran-basiji-mosque network is forever bound to Al-Faqih, the bonyads, the mullahs and all the other organs by thousands of direct and indirect connections. To take only the Pasdaran, Ahmadinejad's own power base, as an example: its commander-in-chief and spiritual leader is Al-Faqih. Many of the Pasdaran commanders have personal interests in bonyads, and among their highest prioritised tasks is the physical protection of all the leading mullahs. To break loose from the web is not even a hypothetical possibility for the president.

Thus the only concrete attempt at an economic-political offensive – Ahmadinejad's proposition to place millions of petrodollars in an "Imam Reza Love Fund", from which every young couple who married would receive $1000 as a wedding present – was thwarted in late 2005, when the Majles rejected it.[17] In future, there might be new attempts to fulfil parts of Ahmadinejad's plan. If he succeeds in getting some other proposition past the mullahs, it will most likely assume the form of mere crumbs on the sofrehs of families connected to the Pasdaran, basiji or mosque charities. But if not all, then certainly the greater part of the oil revenues will remain a fuel for the capital accumulation of the millionaire mullahs.

No economic redistribution of any significance can be brought about by Ahmadinejad, any more than democratic reforms could have been by Khatami. The laws of the social formation of the Islamic Republic, its state and class structure, have trapped the new president as much as they did his predecessor: since he has no material base independent of the mullahs, he has no chance to challenge them in their capacity as millionaires. The supposedly contradictory dimensions of freedom and equality are, in reality, one, and *Ahmadinejad's pledges of equality will engender as much disappointment as Khatami's of freedom.* This, and of the essence of new presidency, were revealed in early 2006, when a force rose to challenge the entire logic.

THE POWER OF A UNION

On Monday, 9 May 2005, dozens of Tehrani bus drivers were in their office, busy completing the complicated preparations for elections among their co-workers.[18] They were about to form a trade union. Suddenly, hundreds of men stormed into the office, wielding sticks and batons, shouting "Trade unions – the monarchists' hideouts!" and "Death to the hypocrites!" While accompanying security officers sedately filmed their work, men in plainclothes rampaged through the office, tearing up the files and registers, smashing doors and windows, and battering everyone present. A special treatment was reserved for Mansour Ossanlou, the driver considered leader of the union initiative. The men told him they would cut out his tongue if he did not desist from his apostate campaign. To prove their point, they ran a blade over his tongue and face; he was badly injured and needed stitches, his speech thereafter marred with a permanent lisp. The men, it turned out, came from Khane-ye Karegar and the shora-ye eslami of the bus company.

The 17,000 bus drivers of Sherkat-e Vahed, hired for pitiful wages, spend their days manoeuvring overloaded buses through Tehran's murderous traffic and polluted air. In the 1970s, they were organised in a syndicate, but disbanded in 1981 when the Pasdaran jailed all their leaders. In 2004, after being unorganised for more than two decades, the bus drivers tried again. After the outrage in May, 8,000 workers signed up to elect representatives to a general assembly. In defiance of road blockades and other assaults from the regime's forces, the assembly took place on 3 June, hundreds of workers voicing the slogan "Death or the syndicate!" A steering committee of 19 bus drivers was elected, a constitution adopted, and the formation of the *independent* syndicate of Sherkat-e Vahed announced.

After the assembly, Mansour Ossanlou, now elected president of the steering committee, told an Iranian diaspora radio station in Stockholm: "The regime wants to bring us down on our knees. We resist, but we need help from the outside. When people died in the earthquake of Bam, they received a lot of solidarity from other countries – but the agony of the Iranian people did not end there!"[19] Within six months, Ossanlou's prayers of international solidarity would be granted beyond the scope of his imagination.

The bus drivers' demands were humble: recognition of the union, introduction of collective bargaining, wage parity with other public employees (as a first step, a hike of under £1 a day for lunch), two sets of winter and summer uniforms, two pairs of shoes, and an assistant for every driver to ease the stress of driving. The printers of 1910 would have recognised their city. However, for the authorities, the list was unacceptable, the most perfidious idea being that of an independent union. A court ruled that no organ other than the shora-ye eslami, that is, the gang who carried out the attack on 9 May, could represent the bus drivers of Tehran.

On the streets of the capital, there now unfolded a replay of the early 1980s' tug-of-war between workers and the state. Though smaller in scale, it took place in a context where the balance of forces was moving in the opposite direction. In the autumn of 2005, the Sherkat-e Vahed union staged a series of protests. On 7 September, the Tehrani bus drivers – a vast majority of whom had now joined the union – drove with their lights on all day in protest against unpaid wages. On 17 October, they refused to take any fares from passengers. They filed suits in courts, wrote letters to government officials, and publicised their actions on the Web and on their bus windscreens. The state retaliated on 22 December, when agents from the Ministry of Information arrested Mansour Ossanlou and 14 other union members in their homes; their computers were all confiscated.

Three days later, traffic in Tehran reached a new level of chaos as thousands of bus drivers struck. They repelled all attempts to quell their actions, and the impact on the city was such that its mayor, Mohammad Baqer Qalibaf (a senior Pasdaran commander who had performed poorly in the presidential election and had been consoled by Ahmadinejad with the president's former post) agreed to meet the drivers that night. At 11 p.m., some 5,000 rebellious workers marched into the Azadi stadium, chanting "Mansour Ossanlou must be released!" and "Having a union is our absolute right!" The officials at the podium tried to persuade the crowds to greet the mayor with Islamic recitations; they met him with derision. But when one of the arrested unionists was released, he was carried around the stadium on the shoulders of rapturous workers. Mayor Qalibaf promised the bus drivers that the rest of their comrades would be released and instructed the bus company to enter into bargaining with the union.

The bus drivers returned to work, only to find that the bank accounts of active unionists had been frozen. None of the mayor's promises were honoured, and so the union of Sherkat-e Vahed resumed action, first by demonstrating outside Evin prison, where their co-workers were held, then by driving around all day with posters of Ossanlou on their windscreens and lurid banners stating "an independent union must be formed"; few workers have such immediate access to a mass audience. Finally, they announced a general strike on all bus lines in the capital, to take place on 28 January.

This time, the Pasdaran and basiji struck in advance. Mahdiye Salimi, a 12-year-old daughter of one of the 17,000 bus drivers, tells of what happened in her house the night before the strike:

They came when we were asleep. They tore off our quilts and beat us with sticks and kicked us with their boots. They kicked my mum's heart and tried to spray something in the mouth of my younger [two-year-old] sister. All our neighbours were watching and screaming in protest as they took away my younger sister. She began to bleed from her mouth as she fell to the ground, when they pushed her towards their van. The basiji thought we were some seventy or eighty people, but we were only three women and five kids. They even wanted to arrest the guests of our neighbours. They brought us to a cold and dirty prison cell. There, they hit me and mum again, and they beat up kids who were much younger than me.[20]

Yaqob Salimi, the father of the family, who had been hiding during the night, lashed out against the forces of the Islamic Republic, his voice cracking in sobs: "They behave like Israelis! Are we in Palestine? Do we have no rights? Ahmadinejad, who claims to care for ordinary people's rights, should come out and see how they take our families hostage in the middle of the night." [21]

During the early hours before the city awoke, the Pasdaran and basiji swept through neighbourhoods and captured hundreds of bus drivers, their spouses and children. They too were brought to Evin. On state radio, Mayor Qalibaf urged the Islamic forces to eliminate the "illegal organisation" of "counter-revolutionaries" and "saboteurs", and when unrelenting drivers gathered at the depots in the morning to form pickets, they were met with tear gas, batons and threats of live ammunition. Soldiers, outnumbering the workers by two to one, confronted them in all ten transport districts of the capital. Crowds were dispersed, hundreds more arrested, and pickets crossed as conscripts and officers boarded the buses to keep the traffic flowing. The city looked like a war zone, as patrols stalked the streets. By the end of the day, some 1,200 bus drivers and family members – and sympathetic activists from Iran Khodro and metal factories – had been netted and locked up in Evin.

The spokesperson for the Sherkat-e Vahed workers in Ossanlou's absence, Gholamreza Mirzai, went into hiding. He maintained communication with the union members and their families via the Internet and phone, and in early February he wrote them an open letter, which was circulated and republished widely:

Those of us who are still on strike and the wives of our imprisoned comrades are in dire need to meet daily and discuss how to proceed with our actions. Families with their loved ones behind bars are in particular need of such gatherings. But it is impossible. As I cannot meet you, it is my duty to try to reach you through this letter.

Our imprisoned comrades occupy our thoughts more than anything else. The regime wanted to prevent them from speaking out for the right to form a union. They were not to be allowed to participate in the strike and show what a decent life could look like. But we are glad to see that many have joined us, to fill the void left by our imprisoned activists. The newcomers appreciate the union and realise it is more important now than ever ... The wives of our imprisoned comrades have assumed a decisive role, making their voices heard and running the everyday life of their families with minimal resources. They embolden their children, help them with school and try to make up for the absence of their fathers. But they also work for our common cause ...

To our demands, we have now added the release of all our comrades, their reinstatement at work, and the withdrawal of all accusations against them. Do you know any worker of Vahed who does not support these demands? Is there one single worker in this country who does not demand a wage-hike to the level of a decent life? Is there any man or woman who does not want an independent union? Have you heard of any worker who does not support the right to strike in protest against the paltry wages that breed the injustices of our country? Behind our demands, there stand 17,000 Vahed workers and their families. For the sake of our children and our future, we have a duty to persist in all of these demands, without exception. That is why the Vahed union is confronted with such savage measures.

We have had many experiences. We have learned how to hold meetings and build an organisation. Our demands have been adopted by a large majority of the working class. If you only one month ago had never felt the power of an organisation, you have now perceived it in your flesh and blood. They can imprison those of us who are still free. But they can never eliminate the conviction that has taken root in the minds of thousands of comrades.[22]

On 15 February 2006, the ICFTU and its International Transport Workers' Federation coordinated rallies and protests outside Iranian legations world-wide. The AFL-CIO and James P. Hoffa of the US Teamsters Union, transport workers in Thailand and Iraq, subway workers in Stockholm (themselves on strike against the dismissal of their union's leader) and labour activists in Australia under siege by their own anti-union government: all of them and many more united behind the banner of solidarity with the Sherkat-e Vahed workers. On the third anniversary of the global mass demonstrations against the 2003 invasion of Iraq – a deliberate choice of date by the ICFTU – there was an unequalled manifestation of global solidarity with a labour movement in the Middle East. Thousands of protest letters were sent to President Ahmadinejad, and money collected throughout the world for the families of the imprisoned activists.

On the ground in Iran – where solidarity statements were coming even from oil workers in Khuzestan – it was Komiteye Peygiri who maintained close relations with the cadres of the Vahed union. Before his imprisonment, Mansour Ossanlou had been the most prominent leader of Komiteye Peygiri. The activists of Mohsen Hakimi and the other council communists of Komiteye Hamahangi, on the other hand, limited themselves to issuing a few statements, one of which was a condemnation of the global day of action. In that statement, the "anti-wage-labour activists" derided the idea of gathering outside embassies; if the ICFTU was serious, it would have asked "its members, more than 150 million, to walk out of their workplaces for a half hour around the world". Apparently, the Komiteye Hamahangi tried to interpret the demonstration as support for US policies towards Iran: "It means that the ICFTU in the framework of the different sectors of the international bourgeois conflict and in the realm of the current conflict among the bourgeois government of Iran and other bourgeois governments [sic] has wanted the false defence of the demands of workers in Iran be made a pretext in order to support one sector of the bourgeoisie in contrary to another sector."

Ultra-leftist gibberish in this hectoring tone was all of what many ordinary Iranians heard of the Left in 1979: one of the cardinal mistakes of that time.[23] Its repetition in 2006, as it denounced the most awe-inspiring show of global opposition to the labour politics of the Islamic Republic ever recorded, confirmed Komiteye Hamahangi's own self-marginalisation, and further deepened the division of the Iranian labour movement.

In the days after the actions of 15 February 2006, most of the imprisoned bus drivers were quietly released from Evin prison. However, the Ministry of Information ordered the company to keep all the freed workers locked out from the bus depots. In late April, when only Mansour Ossanlou was still in Evin, one of the leading activists of the union told of recent, successful, negotiations with the management:

All but 135 are now back at work. At the last meeting we had with management, on 25 April, they agreed to reinstate 65 workers, probably because they feared renewed disturbances on May Day. I think it is a matter of time before most of the others will be let back as well. But the most active people, like myself, are probably blacklisted forever. We'll have to take up some lousy job like selling vegetables or whatever.

The strike was no defeat for us. The management of the company and the regime have been forced to recognise our existence, and even now, after the mass detentions and lay-offs, 80 per cent of the workforce are still part of the union. We run courses in labour rights, we have strengthened the cohesion of the families, many have quit their addictions to drugs or alcohol through the help of the union. We are not the least dispirited – to the contrary! We had never imagined that people in 70–80 countries all over the world would demonstrate their support for us. The regime has been forced to rethink its actions against us, and on the Internet, we are constantly updated on support from workers in other countries. We will keep hold of these new contacts, since they are very dear to us.[24]

ANOTHER IMPOTENT PRESIDENT

The Sherkat-e Vahed episode was yet more proof that the dichotomy between political freedom and social justice in Iran, mirrored in the two countenances of Khatami and Ahmadinejad, is false. The workers whose tongues are cut for what they say are the same workers who demand a pair of shoes and less than a dollar for lunch. When the people with empty sofrehs take to the streets, the rhetoric of concern for the mostazafin is exposed as a sham, and President Ahmadinejad is revealed as a bellicose commander of the military wing of the state apparatus. Through the Ministry of Information and the structures of the Pasdaran, his government was responsible for the most dramatic attempt to throttle a labour movement since the days of the shoras.

The bus strike being only the most renowned case, labour unrest continued along the same lines in early 2006. If anything distinguished Ahmadinejad's management of the unrest from that of the preceding government, it was precisely the inclination to wave guns, and a stern belief in the need for the supervisory power of shora-ye eslami; the number of Islamic councils in the country will, he declared in 2006, be tripled.[25]

On the crucial issue of labour legislation, Ahmadinejad early on set out his stall, pushing for juridical immunity for all enterprises with 15 or less employees. This choice of policy served to alienate parts of the state apparatus that deal with labour, especially in the leadership of Khane-ye Karegar. Its official newspaper declared the proposal in contravention of "all previous statements made by the president regarding the notion of justice".[26] In an interview on the crackdown on the Vahed workers, which he defended on the grounds that "they have roots in the Shah's regime, they belonged to the Tudeh party then and now to the ICFTU in Belgium [sic]", one of the highest-ranking officials of Khane-ye Karegar, Hassan Sadeghi, claimed that Ahmadinejad didn't even "recognise the legal and lawful labour associations". Rather, the president was determined to "eliminate" them too.[27] Faced with the reality of losing control over the working class and with a labour policy running amok, Khane-ye Karegar has been forced to pretended obstinacy.

A few months into Ahmadinejad's presidency, it was thus obvious that what the poor of Iran would get from their "dustman" was, materially speaking, not much. They would be ruled by a president who resembled themselves in folksiness; indeed, some of their superstitions would be promoted to a status of state religion. Those of their sons who wore the emblems of the Pasdaran or basiji would find their power on the street enhanced, including now the right to exact violence upon homosexuals, adulterers, union organisers and members, unveiled women or others whose behaviours were judged depraved according to the revolutionary Islamic norms re-established by Ahmadinejad.[28]

The president's objective mission and the essence of his rise to power was *the channelling of social contradictions into a course where they would do no harm to the rulers of the Islamic Republic.* But would these crumbs he cast to the masses – arguably, even more insignificant than Khatami's once-proffered civil rights – satisfy them? Would a populism devoid of all substance, save for a few empty symbols, be enough to engineer social peace? Would Ahmadinejad, as we have so far encountered him, pass the test of soothing Iran without real economic redistribution?

No: the enormity of Iran's social contradictions necessitated something more. As the state apparatus had now, through Ahmadinejad's rise to power, been charged with such explosive popular energies, it had to find an object more potent in attracting them. Capital has a tendency to transpose its inner contradictions to higher levels, to repress its contradictions by projecting them onto fields apparently exterior to itself. After the revolution, Iranian capital displayed a true proficiency for this process. To its great fortune, and to Ahmadinejad's rescue, another capital would, in good time, deliver the perfect object for projection. This is the subject of the rest of this book.

10
"Inside Those High Walls": Overtures of War

CENSORED OUT OF SIGHT

Imagine seven young women in their obligatory robes and scarves as they hurry through the sloping alleyways of the city. In their bags, they carry a treasured cargo: British and American novels. They are on their way to a spacious apartment in northern Tehran, the home of their former university teacher in literature, who now offers them the privilege of a private book circle. As the young women and their teacher dive into the marvellous classics, they leave the surface of their tedious lives, swim through the sparkling reefs of literary imagination, and are thoroughly transformed as human beings.

This is the narrative of Azar Nafisi's *Reading Lolita in Tehran*. After its publication in 2003, it stayed on the *New York Times* best-seller list for more than 70 weeks, was translated into more than thirty languages, and acclaimed worldwide as a literary masterpiece. *Reading Lolita* is the memoirs of Nafisi, a professor in literature, stretching from the 1979 revolution to the late 1990s, when she left Iran for the United States. It is a picture of a life under the Islamic Republic, but, more than anything else (or at least, so it claims), it is an homage to the universal power of fiction and imagination. For the most wondrous things happen to the young women as they read and discuss such canonical works as *Lolita*, *The Great Gatsby* and *Pride and Prejudice* in the prison that is the Islamic Republic:

There, in that living room, we rediscovered that we were also living, breathing human beings; and no matter how repressive the state became, no matter how intimidated and frightened we were, like Lolita we tried to escape and create our own little pockets of freedom ... The novels were an escape from reality in the sense that we could marvel at their beauty and perfection, and leave aside our stories about the deans and the university and the morality squads in the streets. There was a certain innocence with which we read these books; we read them apart from our own history and expectations, like Alice running after the White Rabbit and jumping into the hole.[1]

"Against the tyranny of time and politics", the eight initiated members of the sisterhood retreat to their most "private and secret moments", creating a "secret language of our own" in the transport of feeling "absolutely free". The book circle enchants its participants in a "fairy-tale atmosphere".[2] On one level, this is undoubtedly a vision of the universal, placeless, eternal power of literature. Nafisi lectures her students: "'A novel is not an allegory', I said, as the period was about to come to an end. 'It is the sensual experience of another world. If you don't enter that world, hold your breath with the characters and become involved in their destiny, you won't be able to empathize, and empathy is at the heart of the novel. This is how you read a novel: you inhale the experience. So start breathing.'"[3]

On another level, however, *Reading Lolita in Tehran* is a thoroughly concrete, place-bound vision, namely, of a certain desirable position in relation to the reality of life under the Islamic Republic: "Mira began to tell us how she felt as she climbed up the stairs [to Nafisi's apartment] every Thursday morning. She said that step by step she could feel herself gradually leaving reality behind her, leaving the dark, dank cell she lived in to surface for a few hours into open air and sunshine."[4]

This relation to reality – disappearance – presupposes a certain relation to the people who populate it. An act must be performed before the book circle can commence. It takes place in the first pages of the book, where Nafisi describes the house where the reading group soon will immerse itself in the fairy-tale atmosphere. The house faces a hospital:

On "weekends" – Thursdays and Fridays in Iran – the small street was crowded with hospital visitors who came as if for picnic, with sandwiches and children. The neighbour's front yard, his pride and joy, was the main victim of their assaults, especially in summer, when they helped themselves to his beloved roses. We could hear the sound of children shouting, crying and laughing, and, mingled in, their mothers' voices, also shouting, calling out their children's names and threatening them with punishment. Sometimes a child or two would ring our doorbell and run away, repeating their perilous exercise at intervals.

This nuisance, however, is vexing primarily the inhabitants of the first storey of the house. Nafisi's apartment is on the second floor, and there "we could see the upper branches of a generous tree and, in the distance, over the buildings, the Elburz Mountains. The street, the hospital and its visitors *were censored out of sight. We felt their presence only through the disembodied noises emanating from below*."[5]

This is the actual manifesto of Nafisi's vivion. Throughout the rest of the book, after the account of their "assault" on her neighbours' "pride and joy" and "beloved roses" – their offensive victimisation of the inhabitants of the northern house – poor, ordinary Iranians are conspicuously absent. A sordid majority, they are censored out of sight. Characters in or close to the imaginatively insubordinate ring of book readers are invariably authors, literature professors and talented students.

The spellbound members of the book circle even experience a sense of confusing alienation to their surroundings: "The more we withdrew into our sanctuary, the more we became alienated from our day-to-day life. When I walked down the streets, I asked myself, Are these my people, is this my hometown, am I who I am?"[6] But this attitude is a deliberate choice, reconfirmed over and over again: "I have said that we were in that room to protect ourselves from the reality outside. I have also said that this reality imposed itself on us, like a petulant child who would not give his frustrated parents a moment to themselves."[7]

The unending struggle to keep petulant reality at bay is, indeed, the ethical, existential and, in the context, utterly political, project exalted by Nafisi. Among the mentors to be consulted are Henry James, who "kept the war at bay by writing and reading", and Vladimir Nabokov, "who, during the Russian Revolution, would not allow himself to be diverted by the sound of bullets. He kept on writing his solitary poems while he heard the guns and saw the bloody fights from his window."[8]

Again, however, this apparently other-worldly ethics of disappearance is revealed to be connected to the earth, and to a very special part of it. The "emissaries of that forbidden world" (other names include Fitzgerald, Austen, Bellow, Joyce) all happen to be European or American. And the "shadow of another world", one of "'tenderness, brightness and beauty'", attainable for the protagonists only "through fiction", falls from a particular place on earth, the one place where Nafisi herself finds her undisturbed freedom of imagination by the end of the book.[9] That place is the United States.

FREEDOM IN A SHOPPING MALL

In the 2005 film *Syriana*, the camera briefly touches on a conference of "The Committee for the Liberation of Iran", held in Washington, somewhere near the heart of presidential power. The speaker – presumably a neo-conservative, like his audience – does not bellow on about the need for nuking Iran, nor does he fulminate against the cruel mullahs. Instead, he pontificates on the youth of Iran: they are in the majority. They are fed up with the rules of Islam. What they want, he makes clear, is *our* way of life – and we can give it to them. Rarely has so evanescent a movie scene summed up so extensive an intellectual discourse with such accuracy.

As the western gaze focused on Iran during the reform era of the late 1990s, countless articles and books were produced about the country. Interest in Iran reached a height not seen since the feud over Salman Rushdie's *Satanic Verses* and the publication of Betty Mahmoody's best-seller *Not Without My Daughter*. Back then, in the late 1980s, Iran was perceived in the West as a monolithic caliphate of villainy: "this barbarous country", as Ronald Reagan labelled it, or "a belligerent that knows no rules, no morals", as a Republican senator described it.[10] With the ascent of Khatami and the reformist movement, however, a new discourse developed. The Manichaean duality of good and evil was shifted to *inside* the country.

Young Iranians, we were now told, are many in number, instinctively liberal, aching for all things western, and thus pioneering an erosion of clerical dictatorship from within, to be replaced with what will certainly be a pro-American regime. Young Iranians are the forces of good behind the lines of evil.

A crude example of this discourse was a column in the *New York Times* in May 2004 by Nicholas D. Kristof, headlined "Those Friendly Iranians". He begins excitedly: "Finally, I've found a pro-American country. Everywhere I've gone in Iran, with one exception, people have been exceptionally friendly and fulsome in their praise for the United States, and often for President Bush as well." After visiting the "Den of Spies", the old US Embassy in Tehran, Kristof

... stopped to chat with one of the Revolutionary Guards now based in the complex. He was a young man who quickly confessed that his favorite movie is *Titanic*. "If I could manage it, I'd go to America tomorrow," he said wistfully. He paused and added, "To hell with the mullahs."

In the 1960s and 1970s, the U.S. spent millions backing a pro-Western modernizing shah — and the result was an outpouring of venom that led to our diplomats being held hostage. Since then, Iran has been ruled by mullahs who despise everything we stand for — and now people stop me in the bazaar to offer paeans to America as well as George Bush ... Anything American, from blue jeans to 'Baywatch,' is revered. At the bookshops, Hillary Clinton gazes out from three different pirated editions of her autobiography. "It's a best seller, though it's not selling as well as Harry Potter," said Heidar Danesh, a bookseller in Tehran. "The other best-selling authors are John Grisham, Sidney Sheldon, Danielle Steel." Young Iranians keep popping the question, "So how can I get to the U.S.?" ...

Indeed, many Iranians seem convinced that the U.S. military ventures in Afghanistan and Iraq are going great, and they say this with more conviction than your average White House spokesman.[11]

What an extraordinary experience of gratification this must have been for a reporter from the *New York Times*! The run-of-the-mill western dispatch from Iran in the late 1990s or early 2000s was, however, not as overtly tendentious. The focus lay on the manners and tastes of "the youth", for example: "They slice through traffic on their motorbikes, racing each other at breakneck speed while holding their mobile phones. They listen to heavy metal, read Gunter Grass and admire Tom Cruise. They don't go to the mosque the way their parents did, and they have given up on politics."[12]

A fancy place where the liberal libido of the Iranian youth can be studied unveiled is the ski resorts north of Tehran:

... life is more free than in the socially restricted cities, drawing criticism from conservative parts of the establishment. Shemshak, the main resort town a 90-minute drive from Tehran, is known for illegal parties, where young men and women mix without supervision, drink alcohol and use drugs. Shemshak is as far from the traditional image of Iran as you can get. Girls wear hats and ski jackets instead of the regulation scarves and long manteaus ... Here, the talk is of foreign holidays, parties and expensive clothes.

When snowboarders in hip "goatee beards" are reproached by the few moral guardians stationed on the slopes, they simply "disappear down the hillside in a puff of snow, Day-Glo ski pants and Raybans".[13]

Another arena frequented by western journalists seeking encounters with the "real" Iranian youth is one particular supermarket in northern Tehran, called Jaam-e Jam. A correspondent of the main Swedish daily *Dagens Nyheter*, reporting from the elections of 2005, went to Jaam-e Jam to find "a shopping mall in Western style, where hardly anything is wanting; here, you can even buy Coca-Cola, a drink from 'the Great Satan' – the USA – rarely available in Iran. But most of all, this air-conditioned mall is an oasis for romantic appointments between young couples, away from the suffocating Big Brother state that doesn't allow boys and girls to meet."[14]

Freedom in a Coca-Cola shopping mall. Possibly at the same time – did they stumble into each other? – a reporter from the *New Yorker* magazine visited the very same Jaam-e Jam, to find that it "looks like a shopping-mall food court anywhere" and functions as a "gathering spot for fashionable Iranian girls, who come in their skimpiest hijabs". Here, the reporter met Arash, a guide to the mood in the Islamic Republic after – and this is important – "the collapse of the reform movement":

For Arash, who has never been to the United States, being truly modern was all about being American. Born the year after the revolution, he speaks profane but excellent English, littered with slang he has gleaned from contraband hip-hop … Arash told me that he hated living in Iran. "These mullahs fucked up this country. The county is sick right now. I can't live in a sick situation. For that reason, I couldn't vote yesterday [in the presidential elections]. I'd give my life for America, but not for Iran. Because, if I work a lot there, I may achieve something." … The night I met Arash, on the way to a party in the north of Tehran, we'd talked about *8 Mile*, the movie starring Eminem. As he explained the film, "It's about growing up in a place you don't like and working your ass off to get out of it."[15]

No doubt about the origin of solutions for Iran, post-reform.

To introduce one more example, a widely praised essay, "The hope of a new Iran", by Timothy Garton Ash, an exemplary pundit of western liberalism, appeared in the *New York Review of Books* in November 2005. The essay was a summary of the trite themes of the western discourse on Iran. During his two-week visit to the country, Garton Ash noted "a trait, apparently of long pedigree, to which my Iranian interlocutors constantly drew my attention: the contrast between what Iranians say outside and what they say inside those high walls. Double-talk as a way of life."[16] This double-talk is, in Garton Ash's view (and the West's in general), a reflection of the Manichaean duality on a monad level of personal life: evil Islamic Republic outside, good western liberalism inside. A pillar of virtue in public, a profligate consumer in private, or "theocracy vs. techno", as one writer put it.[17] The most glorified fetish-object of the 'liberal', interior, half of the duality is the satellite dish, cited as evidence of the lusting after western life. "They watch satellite television", even though it is "officially prohibited", Garton Ash notes.[18]

Incidentally, the walls behind which he has conducted this research have a certain place in Iranian social geography. Garton Ash "got a taste of life behind the high garden walls of the houses of the middle and upper class, where the hijab immediately comes off ... I was repeatedly told of this generation's hedonism; of wild parties behind the high walls of apartment buildings in prosperous north Tehran, with Western pop music, alcohol, drugs, and sexual play."[19]

In much western male writing on Iran, there is a certain degree of erotic titillation in the omnipresent cliché of "behind the veil". When the BBC's correspondent reported on the thwarted proposal of "chastity brothels" as a method of managing prostitution, he noted: "In many cities, street women ply their trade undeterred. Not all those entering the profession appear to do so out of desperation. For some young women, chicly clad and carrying mobile phones, it appears to be a form of social protest."[20]

Garton Ash fixes his gaze on the young women

... talking on their cell phones or flirting in the parks, the girls' hijabs a diaphanous pink or green, pushed well back to reveal some alluring curls of hair, while their rolled-up jeans deliberately show bare ankles above smart, pointed leather shoes. In the cities, the supposedly figure-concealing long black jackets that were previously required have often been replaced by skimpy, figure-hugging white or pink versions. In a teahouse under the arches of a seventeenth-century brick bridge in Esfahan, I met a beautiful young woman, heavily made up and wearing perfume, who was flaunting a good four inches of bare calf above ankles decorated with costume pearl bracelets.

And in what must have been the unforgettable highlight of his journey through Iran: "Within minutes of my arrival at one such house [a party den in northern Tehran], bikini-clad women were teasingly inviting me to come naked into the swimming pool."[21] You can almost hear him thinking: If only those mullahs would go to hell with their damn restrictions and let us have what they hide behind their walls. If the mullahs have an obsession with keeping men and women separated by the veil, it is mirrored in an obsession among western reporters with penetrating that veil and what's behind it, and to discover a tendency towards all sorts of "sexual play". Arash informed the *New Yorker* reporter that "The enforced sexual repression of the Islamic Republic had spawned a culture of extremes – virginity and arranged marriages on the one hand, sexual libertinism on the other. For young people from Iran's middle and upper classes, promiscuous experimentation was the norm."[22]

There is pornography as well, thanks to the West. The Trojan horse comes in many guises. But since all of these originate in the West (and, largely from the US), these fantasies of what's behind the walls are slightly self-reflective in character. Thus Garton Ash spots a T-shirt in the Tehran bazaar emblazoned with the slogan "Wanted: Meaningless Overnight Relationship". He observes that many of the young "dream of a life in America, sporting baseball caps that say, for example, 'Harward [sic] Engineering School'."[23] "To wear a suit and a tie is a mark of brave nonconformity", he cheers.

This discourse has some unmistakable political implications. Garton Ash learns that young Iranians "have a friendly curiosity about Israel". And oh, quite a few of them "welcomed the invasion of Iraq, hoping it would bring freedom and democracy closer to them".[24]

A BRIDGE FOR BUSH

With the publication of *Reading Lolita in Tehran*, the western discourse on Iran reached a magical moment. Among all the vapid musings of reporters and self-styled experts, here was an artist at work, composing a subtle, sophisticated vision of a tunnel leading out of the Islamic prison.[25] In her book, however, Azar Nafisi elucidated – most clearly in the passage about her house – the fundamental act of this entire discourse, its sine qua non: rendering majority Iran invisible.

To sketch in a liberal force operating behind the lines of the mullahs, Nafisi, Garton Ash and the others sojourn most frequently in one particular spot in the social landscape: northern Tehran. This destination seems to have become the obligatory stop for visiting western journalists and intellectuals. Go north from Meydon-e Enghelab, up along Vali-Asr, leave the rest of the country behind you and meet those cultivated artists and publicists and fashion designers and their loose-living children – especially their children, the "children of the revolution" who worship the western lifestyle. Then go home. You have seen "the hope of a new Iran".

The extent of the censorship going on here, the alienation from "day-to-day life", the departure from the reality of "the dark, dank cell" and its inmates that is repeated by every western observer climbing the stairs to yet another party in northern Tehran is breathtaking. As any traveller with open eyes will comprehend within minutes, Tehran is a city of vendors, taxi drivers, chador-clad mothers, dusty construction workers; a few hours later, such a traveller will see the industrial zones, the shanty-towns, the constantly overloaded buses. If the traveller ventures outside Tehran, he or she will – if not sticking nervously to the few satellites of northern Tehran in other cities – encounter brick-workers, seamstresses, oil workers, Kurds, Arabs, Baluchis, all inhabiting a country under so many scourges, yet so vivacious, so rich in colours and nuances, so socially dynamic that it would take years and encyclopaedias to convey an acceptably accurate picture of it. But if you are a traveller employed in the western production of ideology, you do not have any belief in there being interesting stories among the working majority of Iran, *nor will you see in them any potential for transcending dictatorship.*

Some explicitly spell out this prejudice. Timothy Garton Ash questions whether the Iranian nation by itself, trapped between the two poles of the hedonism of the young and the superstitious dogmatism of the rulers, is "at all susceptible to understanding through reason". Posing as an informed observer, he states: "Industrial workers in Iran have so far shown no signs of organizing themselves, as Poland's did in the Solidarity movement twenty-five years ago." He ignores the fact that his interlocutors represent only a very narrow bank of the social spectrum, or that there are few in Iran who can afford the avenues of "escape", or the goods necessary for little "pockets of freedom"; be they computers, satellite dishes, or spacious apartments.[26]

The product of all this discourse – so unimaginative in its choice of topics – is *a figment of liberal imagination.*[27] Its one footing in Iranian reality is an apartment where the presence of the people below is felt only in disembodied noises. There, at the junction of the younger generations of some families of millionaire mullahs and some families of the intellectual "middle classes", the hack writers of the West have their only chance of finding their "hope of a new Iran". Carrying the West's trauma of the Iranian revolution, they are searching for the Atlantis of the Iranian comprador bourgeoisie. Their quest is for people who like Coca-Cola and Raybans and Tom Cruise, who are "exceptionally friendly and fulsome in their praise for the United States", who "offer paeans to America as well as George Bush"; yes, people who say they'd give their "life for America". Spending some time outside northern Tehran, one cannot but wonder how these westerners manage to find those people. But if one reads their reports in context with the *Index on Economic Freedom*, one discerns a rationale: the banished master wants to come back. He is seeking a way to penetrate those high walls.

The creators of western discourse on Iran – Nafisi, Kristof, Garton Ash et al. – all take care to maintain their innocence; they are not openly war-mongers. It is likely that many of them would oppose a military attack on Iran – even the most cold-hearted visitor would probably soften that position, having met real Iranians in the flesh – but there is objective guilt. Through their particular representation of the country, which overlooks the majority of working Iranians, *they have built the intellectual bridge requisite for a western attack on Iran.* This is the bridge where George W. Bush stood when, in his State of the Union speech in 2006, he looked straight into the camera and called for regime change: "And tonight, let me speak directly to the citizens of Iran: America respects you, and we respect your country. We respect your right to choose your own future and win your own freedom. And our nation hopes one day to be the closest of friends with a free and democratic Iran."[28]

And as the affluent Iranians have proved to be ineffective in opening their country to "friendship" with the West through reform, they just might need a little help from the outside.

Part II

Iran in the World

11
Terror at the Theatre

The city theatre of Tehran is Ta-atre Shahr, a dun-coloured rotunda in the downtown area. Nearby are the university, the central railway station, the libraries, offices, banks and hospitals.

In spring 1987, Chekhov's *The Cherry Orchard* was just about to have its première. The final rehearsal had gone well. I stood in the wings, wearing a white dress that I cherished, waiting nervously for the director to give me a signal. Just as I was to step out on the stage, there was an explosion. The audience screamed, and everyone ran for the exits. I was numb with fear. I sat down, paralysed, until my mum came to my rescue.

The theatre was not hit, but all windows were blown out, and all productions at Ta-atre Shahr were cancelled indefinitely. I never stepped onto that stage.

Later in the year, I began school. Our apartment in the Hafez district of central Tehran was located on a hill; when I left in the morning, I would run backwards waving to my mum at the terrace. For some reason, I would always be late, the iron gate at school already closed. It was heavy as a rock, I thought. I longed for the day when I would be able to open it myself, instead of waiting for the porter to come when I had knocked long enough. He would always give a deep sigh when he opened the gate for me; I would lower my eyes, whispering "forgive me", and run to the school yard for the morning assembly.

I loved Mari jon, my first teacher. She was not exacting and harsh like the others. One grey autumn day, we went to our classroom after morning assembly, as always. Mari jon gave each of us a hug before we entered and sat down, and then we took off our veils, for she allowed us to go bareheaded in class.

Suddenly the sirens were activated. We heard explosion after explosion, drawing nearer. We panicked. Mari jon shouted to us to go into the corridors. I was the last girl to leave the classroom, and just before I stepped out, I turned towards the windows, which had been heavily taped to withstand the blast pressure. With an ear-splitting explosion, the windows were smashed to smithereens, which seemed to fall, as if in slow motion, over the floor. A bomb had detonated in the schoolyard. Even the iron gate fell from its hinges to the ground.

Our school had no air-raid shelter, so all the girls were pressed into one corridor on the ground floor. I sat there, holding my hands over my ears, partly against the blasts, partly against the deafening screeches from the other girls.

Another bomb had hit the yard of the hospital. In the same area, there were also residential complexes, parks I used to play in after school – and the state department for nuclear energy.

The school was shut for two months. Two months of anxiety, as Saddam's bombs fell over our city.

This became our life for three years. I used to stay with my grandparents further north, where it was safer; Saddam was aiming at the government infrastructure in the central districts of the city. I was always worried about my mum, who stayed at home, sleeping on her own.

These are just two short episodes. I was born less than a year after the war with Iraq had begun, and, like most Iranians of my generation, I have an inexhaustible stock of similar memories. The years of war seemed unending.

And now a new generation seems destined to a childhood of terror.

– S. E.

12
Truth or Dare? Iran's Nuclear Programme

THE INVASION OF THE UFOS

It was late 2004 and Tehran was dressed up for a conference. All of the city was clad in odium against America. From every bridge, from every scaffolding around the apartment blocks under construction, above all the major intersections there hung the same image: the Statue of Liberty, a skull under her crown. For weeks, the city's 15 million inhabitants were inundated with the conference theme: "A world without America". Ever since the revolution, the Islamic Republic parades its resistance to imperialism at this time of the year. The last Friday of Ramadan is Al-Quds Day in Iran, when the nation marches in solidarity with the Palestinians, denouncing Israel. As Al-Quds Day approached in 2004, the annual rituals were enacted: state television broadcast the usual intifada videos, fresh mural paintings of Palestinian heroes were uncovered, the authorities distributed blacklists of "Zionist" multinational companies. On the day itself, even in a little town in the Azeri countryside, streets and squares were thronged with schoolchildren displaying handmade placards calling for the liberation of Palestine. In Tehran, a Pasdaran commander told high-school students that "a world without America is a world without oppression, without terror, without invasion, without massacre". The two official events – the conference and the march – coincided, just as in the pavement before the university gates in Tehran are painted the well-trampled flags of the US and Israel.

This year, however, would not be like the others, with its usual surfeit of monotonous anti-imperialist refrains. Indeed, ever since the revolution, the Iranian people had been ordered to shout "*Marg bar Amrika, marg bar Esrail*", year in and year out. During the 1980s, they had truly suffered from foreign aggression, in the longest conventional war of the twentieth century. Their plays and parties had been ruined by alarms and sirens, their sons and brothers lost by the hundreds of thousands in the dugouts and desert fields along the Iraqi border, the water in their fountains coloured red to flow in reverence to these martyrs. Perhaps the deepest scar: their skins had been blistered and their bodies poisoned by Saddam's chemical weapons of mass destruction.[1] When they emerged from this hell, Iranians were weary. They were tired of the marches, of the war drumbeats, of the exhortations against the imperialist aggressors. They wanted to leave behind the fog of war and get on with their lives. By the 1990s, the anti-imperialist chants had lost any significance other than as propaganda for the Islamic state.

But in late 2004, near the Caspian Sea to the north, and near the Iraqi border to the west, people began to notice strange phenomena in the night sky: red flashes lit up the darkness, streaks of green and blue fell slowly to the ground ... and then disappeared. *In chi-e?(What's that?)* No longer thinking in terms of war, Iranians hastily concluded that the county was being invaded by UFOs. Rumours spread in national newspapers; the country was swept by what the Russian newspaper *Pravda* called a "UFO mania". But the mystery was solved by Iranian Air Force commanders, who had once upon a time been trained by the American Air Force and recognised the phenomenon for what it was: American reconnaissance aircraft, surveillance drones, small, pilotless planes designed to gather military information, used in Vietnam and in both Gulf wars as a standard weapon in preparing the ground for massive bombing campaigns.[2] For Iranians, UFO mania gave way to the perception of a more concrete threat.

Iran had been notified of that threat almost three years earlier, in George W. Bush's speech on the "axis of evil", in which he identified Iran as a country in need of "regime change". Immediately after the invasion of Iraq in 2003, the rhetoric had been ratcheted up, western newspapers speculating on Iran as "The Next Flashpoint", "Next Stop Tehran?", "Iran: The Next Target?".[3] To ordinary Iranians, however, it had come across as precisely that – rhetoric – to which they were as indifferent as they were to the rhetoric of their own rulers. This started to change in late 2004 as US and Israeli warnings about Iran grew steadily louder; and after the blast near one of Iran's nuclear plants in early 2005, Iranians began to feel that the threat this time was genuine. The Americans, or the Israelis, could arrive at any moment.

AN ERRATIC PROGRESSION:
THE BIRTH OF IRAN'S NUCLEAR PROGRAMME

Officially, the reason for the threats from the US and Israel had to do with Iran's nuclear programme. Midwife to this programme was the United States itself, when in 1957 it signed an agreement of nuclear cooperation with the Shah. The US impatiently encouraged him to establish a nuclear infrastructure, without any inspections or other control mechanisms, initially providing reactors and laboratories for a research centre at Tehran University. Iran's nuclear reactor went critical in 1967, using uranium supplied by the US and enriched to 93 per cent, that is, to the degree required for atomic bomb construction. American companies, including Westinghouse and General Electric, scrambled to provide equipment and stood to gain billions of dollars. In 1974, the Shah trumpeted Iran's firm ambition to develop a full nuclear fuel cycle, with modern facilities – 22 plants – for milling uranium, enrichment, fuel fabrication, and reprocessing. At the same time, the Shah informed western journalists that "without doubt, and sooner than you think, we will have nuclear arms"; indeed, the US received intelligence on his preparations for proceeding from electricity generation to bomb construction. Yet the US had no qualms about expanding their programme of cooperation, dispatching its top university advisers, and inviting South Africa, Germany, France and other western nations to vie for participation in the construction of the dozens of reactors.[4] Cooperation continued, with the pilot plant located in the searingly hot city of Bushehr, up to the victory of the revolution. Then Ayatollah Khomeini declared atomic bombs a diabolical invention typical of the West and contrary to Islam. All parts of the fuel cycle were included in his condemnation and all contracts were cancelled. The final stages of construction at Bushehr, just before the plant was set to switch on the generators, were scuttled by the Iran–Iraq War. By this time, Washington also had changed its mind. Now its allies were instructed to eschew Iran in all matters nuclear, for, it was assumed, the Iranian regime would inevitably develop the most diminutive part of a nuclear cycle into bombs. Iran's nuclear programme lay dormant through the 1980s.[5]

However, after Khomeini passed away and the Khamene'i-Rafsanjani duo rose to power, the programme was revived. With the US now refusing to communicate with Iran, the regime had to court other prospective patrons, and in the early 1990s China agreed to supply it with research equipment. The US was incensed at the agreement. Within a few years, China had given in to US pressure and cancelled all contracts. Those with Argentina met the same fate. As the US would obviously hound any state it knew had cooperated with Iran, the regime concluded that any nuclear programme would need to be conducted clandestinely. Thus official assistance from the Russian government of Boris Yeltsin was obstructed by the US but continued stealthily, and at some point, the shady network of Pakistani scientist A. Q. Khan was consulted for piecing together some rudimentary nuclear know-how. These dealings, though conducted in secret, were tracked by western intelligence, as were, naturally, the scientific advances publicly declared by the regime.[6]

None the less, there was uproar in the western world when, in 2002, the group Mojahedin-e Khalq revealed the existence of a plant for centrifuge technology in Natanz. In the 1970s, Mojahedin-e Khalq was an Iranian guerrilla movement, the major rival of the Fedaiyan; it espoused a synthesis of Islam and socialism that, at the time of the revolution, seemed relevant to a considerable segment of the population. After it was mangled by the Pasdaran in 1981, the movement regrouped outside the country, degenerated into an authoritarian sect which deified their leader, and specialised in high treason: during the Iran–Iraq War, Mojahedin-e Khalq stood shoulder to shoulder with Saddam's forces in attacking Iran. Now in 2002, representatives of the movement proudly laid at the feet of Iran's arch-enemy documents disclosing a previously unknown nuclear plant.[7]

With such information in western possession, the Islamic Republic had no choice but to confess to the International Atomic Energy Agency (IAEA), that it was in fact conducting a programme for acquiring enrichment technology and other parts of the fuel cycle. This heralded the beginning of the soporific saga of IAEA inspections and round upon round of negotiations, as the western powers sought to finish off Iran's nuclear programme once and for all. No indication of a *weapons* programme had been revealed – the Natanz facility was designed to produce *low-grade* enriched uranium for Bushehr's civil reactors – but the US and the EU used the revelation to conclude that deceitful Iran must be hiding something more lethal.[8] The country must be put in complete nuclear energy quarantine, or it would destroy its enemies with atomic bombs.

A NUCLEAR CONUNDRUM?

In the absence of concrete evidence of nuclear weapons manufacture, central to the western case against Iran was the argument that there can be no reason to develop civil nuclear energy in a country endowed with oil. Scrap your nuclear plans and drill for more oil! Or, as White

House spokesman Ari Fleischer stated, "Our assessment when we look at Iran is that there is no economic gain for a country rich in oil and gas like Iran to build costly indigenous nuclear fuel cycle facilities. Iran flares off more gas every year than the equivalent power that it hopes to produce with these reactors."[9] The argument has been repeated interminably, for example, by columnist Jonathan Freedland of *The Guardian*, who in April 2006 opined that "the Iranians claim that all this work is merely in pursuit of civilian nuclear power. But it's hard to believe that a country drowning in oil is running short of energy."[10]

This fatuous argument borders on the deceptive. At the time of launching its nuclear energy program, the US was "rich" in oil and gas; Britain and Russia likewise exploited their oil and gas reserves while building nuclear power plants. There has never been any contradiction in having oil, gas *and* nuclear sources of energy. Furthermore, taking into account the social formation of the Islamic Republic, there are actually compelling reasons for its rulers to acquire nuclear-generated electricity, as quickly as possible.

Oil, as we have seen, is the fuel for capital accumulation in Iran. However, this only applies to oil *sold on the world market*. From the viewpoint of the millionaire mullahs, oil produced for domestic consumption is simply wasted: it does not yield any export revenues. Thus it is imperative for them to increase the share of national oil production intended for export. So far, even after the oil price began to climb, that share has been distressingly low: of 4.1 million barrels of crude produced per day in 2004, 1.5 million barrels were earmarked for domestic consumption.[11]

The fundamental cause of this relative over-consumption of oil, rising by 10 per cent annually, is the subsidisation of all petroleum products, originally instituted by Ayatollah Khomeini as a benefaction to the mostazafin. These subsidies have been maintained ever since; gasoline and petroleum-product prices are kept well below world market levels, as one of the few measures taken to lessen the financial burdens of Iranian households. One way to decrease consumption and release more oil for export would be to abolish these subsidies. That road, however, is blocked, for it would, as US oil analyst FACTS Inc. put it, "create a major social and political upheaval".[12] *The fragility of Iran's social peace obliges the millionaire mullahs to find other ways to supplant petroleum as a source of domestic energy.*

Natural gas is not a suitable domestic substitute. Oil, not gas, is the real moneymaker; oil exports yield revenues five to six times higher than natural gas exports. Since oil production will begin to flag, for reasons that we address below, there is an urgent need for natural gas to be injected into the oil fields, to force the crude oil to the surface. To this end, gas must be reallocated from popular consumption.[13]

At the same time, the millionaire mullahs are acutely aware that oil bounty is, in reality, not eternal. It will last only as long as there is petroleum in the ground to export. The more Iranians themselves economise with their resources, the longer the bounty will last.[14] In early 2006, Iranian defence minister Mustafa Mohammed Najjar explained that "since fossil fuels are going to run out, we should replace them with nuclear energy." If there is any country that stands to reap "economic gain" from procuring nuclear energy, with which it can light and heat its homes and offices and run its industrial facilities, it is the Islamic Republic of Iran. The proposed nuclear energy programme would release some 200 million barrels of crude oil for export every year, meaning much more money for the millionaire mullahs.[15]

The simplicity of this logic indicates a widespread deceit at the hands of western prosecutors. The energy business itself, well-versed as it is in these kinds of equations, cannot help but vindicate the rationality of Iran's pursuit of civil nuclear energy. As the leading publication *Oil & Gas Journal* explained in an editorial in early 2006: "With its rapidly growing gas-based industries, domestic gas demand stimulated by subsidies and oil-field needs, and fiscal pressures to export as much oil as it can, the Islamic Republic faces large and growing needs for electrical power from nonfossil-fuel energy sources. In fact, it has been studying the nuclear option for decades."[16]

It was with precisely this logic that the US cajoled Iran into nuclear energy research and development in the early 1970s. Washington promoted it to the Shah as the height of capitalist sagacity *after the oil price hikes*, when the production levels on Iranian oil fields were at least a third higher than thus far in the twenty-first century, but at a time, of course, when the capital accumulated in Iran was primarily American.

In a strategy paper on its nuclear cooperation with Iran, President Gerald Ford's administration (in which Donald Rumsfeld was secretary of defence, Dick Cheney chief of staff, and Paul Wolfowitz leading nuclear non-proliferation efforts) wrote in 1975 that Tehran needed to "prepare for the time – about 15 years in future – when Iranian oil production is expected to decline sharply ... [The] introduction of nuclear power will both provide for the growing needs of Iran's economy and free remaining oil reserves for export or conversion to petrochemicals."[17] A lawyer active in the bargaining later testified that "the Iranians were wooed hard with the prospect of nuclear power from trusted US-backed suppliers, with the prospect of the reservation of significant revenues from oil exports for foreign and domestic investment."[18] Iran has abundant domestic supplies of uranium ore, so far unexploited, and it has already diversified by utilising hydro-electric power in the form of huge dam projects which now supply the nation with a fifth of its electricity.[19]

From this it follows that there is no objective ground for the West to *a priori* suspect the mullahs of mendacity. When they claim that the purpose of the nuclear programme is purely civil, when Khamene'i renewed his predecessor's fatwa against atomic bombs, when Mohammad Khatami branded weapons of mass destruction as haram – "inhuman, immoral, illegal and against our basic principles" – and Ahmadinejad reaffirmed the position at his own inauguration, and later, as one expert wrote, went "blue in the face denouncing the immorality of any mass extermination of innocent civilians", all of this could very well be true.[20] The mullahs just might be serious.

That said, however, there is in Iran a thin line between civil and military nuclear capabilities. Such is the case in around forty other countries in the world. There is in nuclear energy an *inherent* potentiality for military application; uranium can always be enriched to higher degrees and warheads assembled.[21] At the end of the day, *any* programme of nuclear energy can be converted into one of bomb manufacturing, much as petrol can be brought from the station to the riot and used in Molotov cocktails. The question is, consequently, not if nuclear weapons *can* be the end-product of Iran's nuclear programme, but *what Iran would do with such weapons*.

For all that can be held against the millionaire mullahs, they cannot be accused of harbouring territorial expansionism. Unlike the truly fascist regimes of the 1930s, Baathist Iraq, or the State of Israel, the Islamic Republic of Iran has never displayed any avarice for its neighbours' lands; there is in its social formation no dynamic of outward aggression. The last time Iran started a war was 1739. In 1980, Iran was the victim of Saddam Hussein's unilateral assault, and even though Ayatollah Khomeini at a later stage chose to continue the war through offensive operations on Iraqi soil, it was Saddam Hussein who imposed on Iran all the atrocious escalations of the war. He brought chemical weapons to the battlefield, began bombarding civilian populations in the cities and sinking tankers in the Gulf, with Iran at the receiving end.[22]

The defensive character of Iran's posture has not changed. Its army is weak. The military procurements in relation to its neighbours in the Gulf are a fraction of the levels maintained by the Shah, in his US-appointed role of regional policeman. In the latter stages of the war with Iraq, the Iranian Navy, Air Force and Army were fractured, and in 2005, Iran still had *fewer* tanks and planes than in 1980.[23] Though its neighbours possess territories that at some point in history belonged to Persia, the Islamic Republic lays no claim to them; indeed, if any recent satrap has been covetous of these spoils of ancient empires, it was the last Shah. Nor is Iran involved in any longstanding sovereignty disputes, such as the ones between India and Pakistan, Israel and Syria, or China and Taiwan. Even the US government's own experts on the military doctrine of the Islamic Republic have acknowledged its defensiveness.[24]

From here, it follows that *if* the mullahs furtively seek to possess nuclear weapons, it is highly unlikely that they will use them to devour others. There remains the possibility that they seek nuclear weapons *for the sake of defensive deterrence*. And reasons here, are blowing in from every quarter. In the east, Pakistan has the nuclear bomb. The Musharraf government – no reliable friend of Iran – is losing control over ever more parts of the country to the Deobandi Wahhabis. Inspired by a vitriolic hatred of Shia Islam, they have been slaughtering civilian Pakistani Shiites for years, just like, more recently, the Wahhabis of Iraq, though without much western attention. They consider the very existence of the Islamic Republic a sacrilege; for Iran, the prospect of an atomic bomb in the hands of the Deobandi Wahhabis is horrifying.[25] To the north, there is the Russian nuclear giant. To the west, there is a hostile entity armed with hundreds of nuclear missiles: the State of Israel.

Even worse, US forces are stationed on the doorstep of the Iranian nation. As we have seen, the US has a history of meddling in Iran for more than sixty years; it has been bent on the destruction of the Islamic Republic since its inception (an ambition reconfirmed with new fervour since 2002), and has recently been struggling to enforce "regime change" in Afghanistan and Iraq. In these occupied neighbours, the US is establishing huge and permanent military resources. The waters of the Persian Gulf are prowled by the powerful Fifth Fleet. To the south, on the peninsula of Qatar, the US Central Command maintains the largest repository of pre-positioned military materiel in the world, in the form of airfields, tent cities, and the command-and-control centres from which was directed the invasion of Iraq. Similar starting-blocks for aggressive warfare – bases for soldiers, sailors, air force personnel and special service squadrons, for fighter jets, vessels, missiles and all other sorts of weapons, *including nuclear warheads*, most likely numbering in the hundreds if not in the thousands – are located in Kuwait, Saudi Arabia, Bahrain, United Arab Emirates and Oman to the south, in Turkey to the north-east, and, further north, in several of the Central Asian republics.[26]

One does not have to be a very paranoid Iranian to come to a conclusion about what is going on. In May 2003, one of the constituents of Khatami's Second Khordad coalition stated: "Previously, America was far away. Now, unfortunately, America is Iran's neighbour in all directions. Liberation of Iraq by America [sic] and considering Washington's long-term objectives make it necessary for Iran to reconsider its foreign and international policies."[27]

Under enemy siege, Iran is thus forced to contemplate methods of strengthening its position. One such method is nuclear weapons – not necessarily building them, but acquiring *the option to do so* within a fairly short period of time. This is an obvious option for a country with a nuclear power infrastructure, and has long been a security strategy for countries such as Germany and Japan.[28]

The Iranian regime knows that none of the nuclear-armed powers intend to disarm. It has seen how non-nuclear Iraq has been flattened by the US, whereas nuclear North Korea has not. It remembers how tens of thousands of its civilians and soldiers were gassed by Saddam Hussein in the worst chemical weapons attacks since the First World War, while the international community studiously ignored Iraq's violation of the Geneva Conventions. Indeed, Iran remembers how the western powers, the US in particular, *condoned* the Iraqi chemical crimes, putting the onus *on Iran*, and *wilfully exported the anthrax and the poison gas components to Saddam* while terrified inhabitants deserted Tehran.[29] Joost R. Hilterman writes: "The young and inexperienced Islamic Republic learned two important lessons from its experience: first, never again allow yourself to be in a position of such strategic vulnerability and second, when you are facing the world's superpower, multilateral treaties and conventions are worthless."[30]

It is up to encircled Iran to defend itself. No other power will come to its protection.[31] Thus the rationality of the pursuit for a "break-out" option – a nuclear infrastructure with latent military potential – is not a product of the paranoid fantasies on the part of the millionaire mullahs. Other rulers of Iran finding themselves in the same situation might well come to similar conclusions. As the US State Department declared in a rare moment of insight in October 2003: "any government – even a secular Western-oriented one – would probably continue the quest for nuclear weapons."[32]

IRAN STRIPPED BARE

When Mojahedin-e Khalq helped the West catch Iran red-handed, the Islamic Republic bowed to its superiors. In an agreement with the EU in October 2003, Iran suspended all its enrichment activities. This was not a binding legal obligation. According to the Non-Proliferation Treaty, of which Iran is a signatory (unlike, for instance, Pakistan and Israel), countries do have a right to enrich uranium within the framework of civil energy programmes. Iran's only misconduct was to hide their programme. The revealed enrichment activities were perfectly legal in themselves, but Iran had failed to *tell* the IAEA about them. Hence it voluntarily suspended its activities as a "confidence-building measure", and attempted to redress past sins by handing over documents chronicling its entire nuclear programme, and submitting to some of the most intrusive and exhaustive inspections in the history of the IAEA. The IAEA was given full access to research centres and premises suspected by the US to have been used for weapons development. Iran allowed the inspectors to take environmental samples, examine requested documents, conduct interviews with Iranian scientists and contractors, and instal tamper-proof seals and surveillance cameras inside the facilities in a show of transparency that Israel and the US, if someone proposed that they should concede to even a cursory investigation, would find risible.[33]

No smoking guns were found. The most damning evidence – traces of highly enriched uranium – was refuted: after assiduous investigations, in late 2005 the IAEA inspectors verified Iran's explanation that the traces were residues from contaminated centrifuges imported from Pakistan.[34] But the West was still not satisfied. Through the IAEA, it continued to question past activities and demand that the suspension be extended to other areas of nuclear research; while the IAEA sometimes praised Iran for unconditional cooperation, it also accused the country of not revealing everything, leading to recurrent crises in Iran's negotiations with the EU.[35] Many in the West argued (most loudly in Washington) that Iran's suspicious behaviour in the past had condemned it to an everlasting state of untrustworthiness.

But Iran did have a good alibi for having been secretive: how could it otherwise have stayed on the nuclear track? The US sabotaged every step taken in the open![36]

Now the US proclaimed that it would be content with nothing less than a *complete cessation* of *all* nuclear-related activities, including a dismantling of already established facilities. The Islamic Republic was damned if it said it had nuclear ambitions, and damned if it said it didn't. No matter what guarantees of maintaining low levels of enrichment the Islamic Republic was prepared to give, and no matter what level of inspection it would accept: every single body of the nuclear programme had to be demolished.

As the US refuses to meet the mullahs face to face, it fell to the EU negotiators to dragoon Iran into this ultimate submission.[37] There evolved the often witnessed division of labour, with the EU as "good cop", sitting at the negotiating table, while the "bad cop" US stands behind with threats of sanctions and "surgical strikes". "My view would be", Richard Armitage of the US State Department explained, "that the incentives of the Europeans only work against the backdrop of the United States being strong and firm on this issue."[38]

Of all that has appeared in the Iranian nuclear saga to the date of this writing, the US-EU demand constitutes the most blatant breach of the Non-Proliferation Treaty. Article IV stipulates an "inalienable right of all the Parties to the Treaty to develop research, production and use of nuclear energy for peaceful purposes without discrimination".[39] Juridical technicalities aside, the demand is irreconcilable with the most basic energy needs of the Islamic regime. The EU has tried to modify the absurdity of its position by offering Iran access to civil nuclear energy *through imports from other countries*, either the EU or Russia; the largesse of the good cop is expressed in such phrases as "easier access to modern technology and supplies in a range of areas".[40]

In other words, the millionaire mullahs have been offered a trade: tentative nuclear independence for permanent dependence on more advanced capitalist countries – like offering a car manufacturer a contract for building horse-drawn carriages. All the instincts of the millionaire mullahs, based as they are on the principle of khod kafai (domestic capitalist self-sufficiency) rise up against the offer: "One should not put one's fate in the hands of others. It would be irrational", as an Iranian foreign ministry spokesman expressed the credo of the Islamic Republic.[41] The millionaire mullahs had envisioned a soon-to-be-realised future where petrodollars would have been transformed into an indigenous nuclear infrastructure, run by cadres of Iranian scientists and engineers, to be used for the generation of *more* petrodollars – and perhaps even export revenues from the sale of nuclear fuel to other Muslim countries. Iran was envisioned as a regional hub not only of car manufacture, but of energy technology.[42] Would they give it all up now, because the EU and the US insisted on it? Of course not. As Mahmoud Ahmadinejad came to office, there appeared to be new motives to stand up against the West (see below), and in August 2005, Iran removed the IAEA seals on the processing lines at the uranium-enrichment facility in Esfahan and resumed production. This signalled the beginning of the breakdown in negotiations between the EU and the Islamic Republic, which was referred to the UN Security Council for "meaningful consequences", a euphemism for UN sanctions backed by the threat of military intervention.[43] Iran was pushed towards the brink.

In the West, the resumption of enrichment activities triggered a frenzy of speculation on how close Iran was to assembling a nuclear weapon: would it be six months? Six years? Did they have it already? Such speculation was, indeed, nothing new. In 1991, the US officially estimated that Iran had "acquired all or virtually all of the components required for the construction of two to three nuclear weapons". In 1993, the CIA believed that "Iran could have nuclear weapons within eight to 10 years." In 1995, US Defence Secretary William Perry said that the Iranian bomb was less than five years away. Israeli Prime Minister Shimon Peres prophesied in 1996 that Iran would have it in four years. In 1998, head of the US Central Command Anthony Zinni predicted that it would be "on track within five years", while in 2000, the CIA was back at its estimation of 1991: Iran might already have it.[44] In late 2005, the US National Intelligence Estimate – a summary of information gathered by all the US intelligence branches – projected that Iran was a decade away from the bomb, while a study from the US Army War College was convinced of "one to four years at most", and Israeli Foreign Minister Silvan Shalom equally sure of "six months".[45]

Slightly less partisan oracles have recognised the scientific basics. Iran's nuclear programme is fundamentally civilian in character. The tens of thousands of centrifuges with industrial enrichment required for bombs manufacturing makes it virtually impossible for Iran to hide any such activities from ongoing IAEA inspections. When Ahmadinejad in April 2006 proclaimed with much fanfare that Iran had joined the "nuclear club" (by successfully enriching uranium to

3.5 per cent), that was a generation away from the 80 or 90 per cent required for weapons construction.[46] Yet US threats against Iran were being voiced at ever higher decibels.

Meanwhile, the US holds sacred its capacity to pulverise the planet several times over, sustaining a defence budget 125 times larger than Iran's, a considerable portion of which is dedicated to the development of a new generation of even more lethal nuclear weapons.[47] The US now enjoys absolute global supremacy in the field: "Today, for the first time in almost 50 years, the United States stands on the verge of attaining nuclear primacy. It will probably soon be possible for the United States to destroy the long-range nuclear arsenals of Russia or China with a first strike."[48]

Destructive capabilities reside not in Iran, but in the US – and, for that matter, in Britain and France, also determined to upgrade their nuclear weapons, and in India, whom the US since early 2006 is actively *helping* to produce more warheads, and in North Korea, and possibly soon in Brazil, where no Treaty or IAEA is in effect, and in China. Finally, there is the State of Israel's nuclear weapons, fully supported by the US, but cloaked in silence.[49]

If the US was ready to deliver all sorts of nuclear technology to Iran less than three decades ago, if the present Iranian government has a reasonable case for acquiring nuclear energy, if its plausible ulterior motive relates to defensive deterrence, if the "break-out" option is still only on the horizon, and if the US has been a foe of the Islamic Republic since its creation, then it follows that nuclear weapons *per se* cannot be the real reason for the threats against Iran. The drones hovering over Iran must be running on some other fuel.

13
Who Commands the Waterfall?

HOW TO AVOID A GLOBAL HEART ATTACK

After the price of crude oil had notched up yet another record in March 2005, and days before the OPEC ministers would gather in Esfahan, George W. Bush, in his simple and unmistakable syntax, succinctly described the situation: "I think if you look at all the statistics, demand is outrunning supply and supplies are getting tight. And that's why you're seeing the price reflected".[1] At about the same time, the US Energy Department was frowning over a new report, entitled *The Peaking of World Oil Production – Impacts, Mitigation and Risk Management*, which didn't mince its words:

The world is fast approaching the inevitable peaking of conventional world oil production ... World oil peaking is going to happen. Only the timing is uncertain ... The development of the US economy and lifestyle has been fundamentally shaped by the availability of abundant, low-cost oil. Oil scarcity and several-fold oil price increases due to world oil production peaking could have dramatic impacts ... The economic loss to the United States could be measured on a trillion-dollar scale.[2]

The problem, however, would not bedevil only the US. As the report noted: "The world has never faced a problem like this", though "the world" here signified something more akin to world capital.[3]

A couple of years into the new millennium, world capital did sense a hazard it had not encountered before. "The time when we could count on cheap oil and even cheaper natural gas is clearly ending", the chairman of Chevron Texaco forecast in February 2005, a prognosis reluctantly reiterated by corporate leaders, market analysts and business press editorials. Headlines began to appear: "The oil pump may be closing", "Is oil heading for $100?", "A crude shock". Economists, geologists and politicians – none were able to dispel the gloom of apocalyptic predictions coming in from the oil fields.[4] While here is not the place for a thorough analysis of the problem, some introductory remarks are in order.

Oil can be divided into two categories. The first is oil situated near the earth's surface. There is no need for onerous efforts to reach down to it and pull it up; a hole in the ground might suffice for the oil to spurt out fountain-like. Then there is oil lying far below the surface. It is not as fluid, rather recalcitrant, even hard as rock; it can be forced above the ground only through massive inputs of human labour and advanced technical equipment. While the former oil is of good, user-friendly quality, the latter might have to be subjected to complicated recovery and refinery processes before it is saleable. Let us thus say that A-oil commands small quantities of labour, while B-oil commands large, including large quantities of dead labour in the form of constant capital. Hence, A-oil will command low value and B-oil high. Ceteris paribus, this will be reflected in market prices: A-oil will be cheap, B-oil expensive.

Naturally, a capitalist corporation will start its operations where oil is within easy reach and earn a good deal of money through rapid extraction. Production soars, pumps work flat-out, markets abound in cheap oil – until the corporation suddenly finds itself standing at a precipice. The A-grade oil supply is depleted, and there is no choice but to grapple with B-grade oil. From now on, the corporation is forced to invest ever more labour and infrastructure *to extract the same amount of oil*. It is not possible to increase production any more; to the contrary, labour and material must be increased to keep production levels *from falling*, and eventually, this becomes impossible. Production is set to irreversibly decline, or in Bush's words, "supplies are getting tight".

The transition from A-grade to B-grade oil, the advent of the precipice, an oil supply's transition from plentiful adolescence to decreasing old age is the turning point in the political economy of oil. It tends to occur when about *half the reserves are gone*. At that point, production reaches a *peak*, from which it can only descend into steadily diminishing supply. The hazard that world capital faces in the new millennium is *the exhaustion of half the reserves of the entire world*: on the other side of the global oil peak looms an endless price rise. Indeed, this has already begun, as oil corporations world-wide spend spiralling sums on technology and production maintenance, as more and more oil countries report national peaks, and as the price of oil hits new records. We are either near or right upon the global oil peak.

This situation is crucial because oil is the single most important commodity in world capitalism. Globally, oil provides for more than 40 per cent of all energy and 95 per cent of all transport fuel; oil is the major component of plastics, as well as asphalt, paints and textiles;

oil is a component in fertilisers, medicines, cosmetics, and tens of thousands of other products. Oil's ubiquity makes it the blood of dead labour, the organic substance throbbing through all the arteries of capital. Hence the unfolding process of change in its value is the potential cause of a global heart attack. If the value of oil increases relative to other products, the rate of profit is put in jeopardy. Surplus value created in the economy must be weighed against and filtered through growing outlays on constant capital. Before the spectre of such a structural imbalance, global capital fears a cataclysm after the next price hike, or the one thereafter.

However, all is not despair. Or, all wouldn't *have* to be despair, for there are still some – a few – countries where oil reserves remain plentiful and productive. As in any given field, there are A-grade and B-grade oil-supplying countries in the world, and A-grade countries are not yet extinct. But here is an annoying inconvenience bequeathed to modern capital. It was grasped by Karl Marx, when in the third volume of *Capital* he postulated one source of energy – steam engines – whose product was expensive in comparison with the other source, a waterfall, where less labour was needed to yield the same amount of energy. The waterfall

... is only at the command of those who have at their disposal particular portions of the earth and its appurtenances. It is by no means within the power of capital to call into existence this natural premise for a greater productivity of labour in the same manner as any capital may transform water into steam. It is found only locally in Nature and, wherever it does not exist, it cannot be established by a definite investment of capital. It is not bound to goods which labour can produce, such as machines and coal, but to specific natural conditions prevailing in certain portions of the land. Those manufacturers who own waterfalls exclude those who do not from using this natural force, because land, and particularly land endowed with water-power, is scarce.

The analogy can be made with oil reserves. Long ago, nature selected certain places where sunshine was captured in the form of fossil fuels, and capital cannot artificially reproduce this heritage. Corporations cannot just set up a laboratory and conjure oil out of tubes. Oil is spatially fixed, embedded in the physical environment, and thus *captive to the conditions in the place*, or, more precisely, to the figures "who have at their disposal" these "particular portions of the earth". The occupation of a spatial location is absolute. Therefore, those "who own waterfalls exclude those who do not", and for the latter, this can be a disturbing situation: "Now let us assume that the waterfalls, along with the land to which they belong, are held by individuals who are regarded as owners of these portions of the earth, i.e., who are landowners. *These owners can prevent the investment of capital in the waterfalls and their exploitation by capital. They can permit or forbid such utilisation.* But a waterfall cannot be created by capital out of itself."[5]

In the age of peak oil, the only chance for global capital to delay thrombosis is to connect to the remaining oil supplies. If this oil is pumped into the circuits of accumulation, a crisis in the rate of profit can be postponed. But this oil would need to be extracted quickly, at maximum capacity, without pause, or, God forbid, dilatory principles of thrift. Will this be the case? *It is up to the owners of the waterfall to decide.* They are in a position to withhold their assets from world capital. They might block investments, render some oil fields fallow, or delay further prospecting, drilling and extraction to a time *they* deem appropriate. For these countries, oil probably constitutes their major asset, and thus they have no urgent reason to give it away to others at a low price; rather, there is every incentive to keep production levels modest, as it will, by raising prices, generate pleasing revenues. *"But hey! We need those waterfalls now!"*, cry the oil-hungry nations.

When *The Economist* devoted a special report to "Oil – How to avoid the next shock" in spring 2005, it identified a possible remedy. In some countries, namely, those in OPEC, there is still oil in the ground – "they have enough oil to pump for most of this century" – and it ought to be transfused at once to the world economy. "Oil supplies will not become constrained until after 2030", *The Economist* echoed the International Energy Agency, "provided the necessary investments are made." Alas, "OPEC has not been investing sufficiently to keep pace with growing demand. As a result, global spare capacity last year dropped to around 1m barrels per day (bpd), close to a 20-year low ... The IMF has recently told OPEC that it must increase global spare capacity to 3m–5m bpd in order to ensure 'the stability of the world order'."

"The biggest obstacle" to the rescue mission is "the fundamental perversity of the oil business. Oil is the only industry in which the best and largest assets (in this case, oil and gas reserves) are not in the hands of the most efficient and best-capitalised firms (the western majors), but of national oil companies."

Even worse, there is, in tandem with the rising needs for unbridled extraction, a rise in what *The Economist* labels "resource nationalism".

Some of the oil producers within OPEC have announced that "foreign firms are mostly unwelcome." Before saving itself, western capital must thus "cope with the rise of resource nationalism, which threatens to choke off access to new oil reserves".[6] So it turns out that "how to avoid the next shock" is really all about political sovereignty over national territories.

THANK HEAVENS FOR IRAN AND CURSE ITS RULERS

In 2002, the petroleum business put the Islamic Republic of Iran as fifth among the oil nations; two years later, it was second. In 2004, the statisticians, field researchers and geological specialists of Iran's oil ministry in Tehran compiled their maps, models and statistical data on newly discovered fields in Khuzestan, added in advances in recovery technology, and reached the conclusion that they had under-estimated their reserves. The minister for oil made an announcement that electrified the global market: previous estimations had given Iran 90 billion barrels in the ground, but recalculations had raised that figure to 133 billion. Saudi Arabia still has more, but Iran – not Iraq – is second. This substantial revision was promptly accepted by the business community, such as in British Petroleum's leading statistical review, and since 2004, Iran is acknowledged as deputy master of the oil empire. Indeed, if one counts the thousand trillion cubic feet of natural gas – equivalent to Iran's oil reserves – the compound sum of the hydrocarbon fortunes of the Islamic Republic is only slightly smaller than Saudi Arabia's. [7]

Certainly, not everyone believes in the revised figures. Doubt has been cast on the substance of the claims. Such is, however, the fate of all official OPEC data, Saudi Arabia's in particular. Even the "oil sceptics", senior among them, Dr Colin Campbell, who usually cuts official reserves data by half, now rank Iran as second.[8] On this crucial matter, there seems to be consensus: Iran is the world's second mightiest cataract. In terms of regions, the Middle East in general and the Persian Gulf countries in particular are, of course, the great falls, home to 62 per cent of known oil reserves (see Figure 3). Matthew Simmons, an oil analyst who served as an adviser to the Bush admin-istration before he wrote his magnum opus on the oil assets of Saudi Arabia, expressed this fundamental condition of world capitalism in memorable terms at a speech in May 2003:

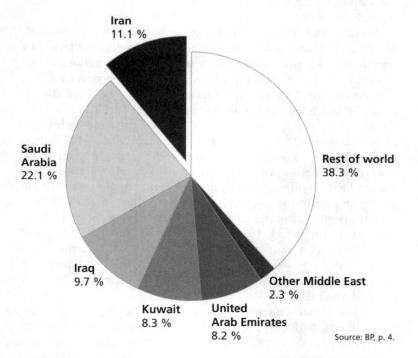

Iran
11.1 %

Saudi
Arabia
22.1 %

Rest of world
38.3 %

Iraq
9.7 %

Other Middle East
2.3 %

Kuwait
8.3 %

United
Arab Emirates
8.2 %

Source: BP, p. 4.

Figure 3 The oil reserves of Iran (2004)

Serious energy planners need to assume non-OPEC supply *is* at a plateau. But thank heavens for the Middle East. The big non-Middle East OPEC producers are also past the peak. Algeria and Libya could probably still grow but they're too small to offset everyone else. And only the Middle East can logically be [expected] to replace declines elsewhere ... Middle East energy is the Promised Land. All roads lead to Rome, and to the future of oil and gas Rome is the Middle East. The Middle East is where we still have abundant reserves. It's still cheap to produce; it's still extremely unexplored. So if the rest of the world is long in the tooth, thank Allah for Mecca.

More precisely, the blessed location is "the golden triangle of the Middle East: if you start at Kirkuk in the north and you draw a line down through the great oil fields of Iran, going down south and come over six or seven hundred miles picking up the great fields of the United Arab Emirates and come back up 800 miles to Kirkuk, virtually every field of any size ... is probably in that basin."[9]

Here, oil is not only still plentiful, but geographically concentrated, of high quality, and within relatively easy reach. Global capital is thus trapped by its growing dependency on a handful of nations in the Persian Gulf, the second most important of which is now Iran.[10]

However, for decades, "the fundamental perversity of the oil business" has ruled the region. In the words of Dick Cheney, then director of Halliburton, at a speech delivered to the London Institute of Petroleum in 1999: "Oil remains fundamentally a government business. While many regions of the world offer great oil opportunities, the Middle East with two thirds of the world's oil and the lowest cost, is still where the prize ultimately lies, but even though companies are anxious for greater access there, progress continues to be slow."[11]

In the beginning of the new millennium, "the biggest obstacle" is thus the territorial fact that (several of) the oil waterfalls lie behind the high walls of *independent political entities*. These entities are regarded as the blood donors of global capital, but they might not do what capital needs them to do. They might write their *own* laws for oil development.

Of today's independent donors, none is as fickle and self-willed as the Islamic Republic. Iran does not pump oil quickly. Before the general strike of late 1978, when the comprador bourgeoisie was still in situ, Iran produced 6 million barrels of oil per day. Since then, daily production has never exceeded 4 million, or to be exact 4.08 million, the average in 2004: that is, no more than *two-thirds* of pre-revolutionary level. The oil-extraction infrastructure is essentially that inherited from the Shah's era, and it is severely dilapidated. Lacking advanced technology, Iran has trouble keeping production levels constant, which is why it needs to inject natural gas into some fields to force up the oil. Consequently, Iran possesses 11.1 per cent of the world's reserves, but sustains only 5.2 per cent of the actual production.[12] This discrepancy *simply must be dealt with* if the effects of the global oil peak are to be abated. On the other hand, this means that Iran, unlike Saudi Arabia, but much like Iraq, is in a state of considerable virginity. It is far from the ceiling of its capacity; indeed, Iran is estimated to be capable of boosting output from today's 4 to at least 7 million barrels per day. The waterfall is waiting to be exploited.[13]

The one prerequisite for actualising the potentialities of Iran is capital investment. To revamp the infrastructure, Iran is in dire need of advanced technology which it cannot supply itself. One obstacle to an inflow of technology worth billions of dollars is the US sanctions – for example, Iran has no access to processes developed by US companies for the liquefaction of natural gas, which is causing serious delays in the development of the South Pars field. However, at least as significant, and perhaps even more so, are the obstacles erected by Iran itself. As we have seen, the millionaire mullahs run a system of "buyback contracts". In this system, the National Iranian Oil Company (NIOC) agrees with a foreign corporation to jointly explore and develop a field. The foreign company deploys its technological services while the NIOC remains in full control of the project. When the contract expires – usually after five to eight years – the Iranian state becomes the sole operator, keeping all revenues from further sales. The only advantage for the foreign firm (after the client has made use of their services and dismissed them) is a fee on the oil extracted, generating a calculated rate of return of 15 per cent.

For foreign capital, these conditions are deeply unsatisfactory. In *Oil & Gas Journal*, two prominent German experts on the Iranian "investment regime", specialising in assisting investors with surveys of the complicated Islamic regulations, bewail the unbearable risks associated with a buyback contract. First of all, the field covered by the contract might never move into production. Second, the corporation has no chance of getting a foothold in the country: "the duration of the investment recovery period of around five years is too short for foreign firms hoping to secure long-term involvement in the Iranian oil and gas sector." Third, the investor is dispossessed of the field as soon as it has been developed: "This makes buyback projects akin to a construction contract but with the important difference that payment is not made until after the contractor has lost possession and control of what is being built." Finally, the oil price may drop to levels lower than forecast in the original contract, or the reserves in the field may turn out to be smaller than expected, so that "the amount of oil available from the project might be insufficient to meet the costs of the project and the agreed return." The foregone conclusion: "buyback contracts cannot offer the fiscal and legal certainty investors require".

Ultimately, this precarious position of foreign oil capital stems from the obnoxious exertion of political power: "The complexity and sluggishness of the decision-making process within NIOC are not always compatible with the need [of foreign capital] to take operational decisions as and when necessary. And if a dispute arises between NIOC and IOC [international oil company], the matter might be taken out of the hands of the disputant by an Islamic court, which could rule that the whole agreement is unlawful."[14]

Global capital – of whatever nationality it might be – cannot be reconciled with this situation. A case in point is Azadegan. One of the most promising of the recent discoveries in Khuzestan and indeed the whole world, Azadegan is a "supergiant" containing some 30–40 billion barrels of oil, though not all of it is reckoned as recoverable. To get this field on track, the Iranian state needs the kind of substantial investment and technological expertise that is available only from major oil companies. The Americans having been excluded beforehand, in February 2004 a Japanese consortium was awarded the contract to develop Azadegan. However, some corporations soon pulled out of the project, and Iran had difficulty finding replacements; Royal Dutch Shell, Total, Statoil and many of the other Big Oil players proved lukewarm. One reason was US pressure to spurn the Islamic Republic. Another was the Iranian provisos: "Many international oil companies may not find the rate of return attractive enough under the revised buyback system."[15] South Pars has faced similar disruptions. In late May 2006, the chief executive of one of the western corporations active in the field, Statoil, commented on the decision to scale down its participation with a general indictment against the investment environment in Iran: "The financial terms, the contract terms, they need to improve generally I think, to attract international oil and gas investors ... for there to be a link between risk and reward."[16]

The oil business is united in its evaluation of Iran's chances of reaching the theoretical capacity of 7 million barrels of oil produced per day. In the words of FACTS Inc., which is frequently consulted by *Oil & Gas Journal*, "Adding 3 million b/d is virtually impossible given the revised buyback system and the way the system is set up ... We believe that this [the current 4 million b/d] is the realistic limit to Iran's capacity *under the present system*". FACTS Inc. concludes that "Iran's success in attracting foreign investment to its oil and gas developments remain tepid."[17] Or, in the words of the US government's Energy Information Administration: "The country is counting on billions of dollars in foreign investment to accomplish this [7 million barrels per day], but this is unlikely to be achieved without a significant change in policy to attract such investment (and possibly a change in relations with the West)."[18]

Thus even if the millionaire mullahs wish that investment would stream into their oil fields, as long as they insist on sticking to the buyback contract scenario, they won't see it coming. The reason for such stubbornness? *Millionaire mullahs don't want foreigners to control their most precious asset.* As deputy oil minister Abar Torkan made clear in 2004:

Many oil sectors, including research, are still incipient in Iran and we hold no licenses. We lag behind other countries in this regard. We must hold licenses in chemical industries, catalysts as well as downstream industries ... The oil industry nationalisation process started in 1953, *but is not complete yet* and we are dependent on foreigners in many sectors, including research and oil engineering. *We must try to become self-sufficient in these areas.*[19]

If ever there was "resource nationalism", this is it. To make matters even worse, Iran is in no rush to satisfy global capital by maximising production levels in its own fields or, by means of persuasion, in that of other OPEC countries – a policy we will soon return to. Tight markets perpetuate the mullahs' feast. An institution at the other end of the oil business, the Association for the Study of Peak Oil, thus assesses the future of the country:

If oil prices rise radically as world shortages bite in earnest in the years ahead, Iran would have ever less incentive to step up production, as higher oil prices would maintain revenue and allow the reserves to be conserved for longer. Much depends on whether or not the foreign companies re-enter the country. They would produce at maximum rate, with the advantage of being able to write off operating expense against taxable income in their home countries, whereas the national company is forced to move more slowly drawing its funds from the national budget on which there are many competing claims. *The slower approach would better serve the long-term national interest.*[20]

Clearly, an antagonistic contradiction is being enacted between the millionaire mullahs and global capital.

WHEN THE OBSTACLE IS REMOVED

To fathom the depth of the contradiction, however, we need to view it in relief against two closely related cases. The first is concerned with the conditions created by the British when Iran's oil fields were in their possession, and the arrangements created subsequent to the coup in 1953, when the original nationalisation was ambushed.

After oil had been discovered in Iran in 1908, Britain lost no time in securing the continuation of a monopoly concession – that is, ownership, exploration, development and marketing – of all known Iranian oil reserves, except for an insignificant few in the north. That concession had been extracted from the docile Shah in 1901, when oil fortunes were still only hypothetical; now, they were materialising before the eyes of the amazed British, and an Anglo-Persian Oil Company was established to take control. The British government itself owned 51 per cent of the shares of this company, collected the lion's share of the profits plus taxes, and furnished its Royal Navy with Iranian oil at a fraction of the market price. Iranians, meanwhile, paid dearly for the oil beneath their feet. The British called all the shots, giving the Iranians no say whatsoever inside the company; they were even forbidden to read the company's books.

In the decades that followed, APOC – later renamed Anglo-Iranian Oil Company (AIOC) – made tremendous profits, 16 per cent of which were paid as a pathetic royalty to the Iranian state. Few Iranians were trained for any skilled jobs.[21] Instead, Khuzestan was swarming with British staff:

The workers lived in a shantytown called Khagazabad, or Paper City, without running water or electricity, let alone such luxuries as iceboxes or fans ... In every crevice hung the foul, sulfurous stench of burning oil – a pungent reminder that every day twenty thousand barrels, or one million tons a year, were being consumed indiscriminately for the functioning of the refinery, and AIOC never paid the government a cent for it. To the management of AIOC in their pressed ecru shirts and air-conditioned offices, the workers were faceless drones ... In the British section of Abadan there were lawns, rose beds, tennis courts, swimming pools and clubs; in Kaghazabad there was nothing – not a tea shop, not a bath, not a single tree.[22]

Water fountains were marked "Not for Iranians", while in the private Persian Clubs uniformed Iranians waited on British executives. Popular discontent with this systematic mortification, accumulated over decades, at last erupted into the nationalisation process. Standing before the UN Security Council in October 1951, Mossadeq explained:

My countrymen lack the bare necessities of existence. Their standard of living is probably one of the lowest in the world. Our greatest natural asset is oil. This should be the source of work and food for the population of Iran. Its exploitation should properly be our national industry, and the revenue from it should go to improve our conditions of life. As now organised, however, the petroleum industry has contributed practically nothing to the well-being of the people or to the technical progress or industrial development of my country. The evidence for that statement is that after fifty years of exploitation by a foreign company, we still do not have enough Iranian technicians and must call in foreign experts.

This was not quite the view of the British. On behalf of world capitalism, British delegate Gladwyn Jebb referred to the confiscation of the AIOC's properties before the same Security Council: "The plain fact is that, by a series of insensate actions, the Iranian Government is causing a great enterprise, the proper functioning of which is of immense benefit not only to the United Kingdom and Iran but to the whole free world, to grind to a stop. Unless this is promptly checked, the whole of the free world will be much poorer and weaker, including the deluded Iranian people themselves."[23]

Iran's "insensate actions" were indeed promptly checked. Within a year after the coup, order was restored to the shores of the Persian Gulf. Formally in the form of a forty-year lease, but effectively nullifying all nationalisation efforts, a new consortium reserved for itself a monopoly on all Iranian oil reserves of any significance. Reflecting the historical shift of power within capitalism, BP's share of the consortium was slimmed down to 40 per cent, while the US corporations were for the first time given an equal share (though in reality, they were now dominant), with Royal Dutch Shell and Compagnie Française de Pétroles splitting the rest. During the rule of this consortium, under the aegis of the Pahlavi state, Iran regained its position as the world's second largest exporter of oil, and the profits accrued to foreigners were once again astronomically high.[24] Then came the revolution.

The second, neighbouring case is Iraq. Before Operation Iraqi Freedom, Iraq's oil profile was remarkably analogous to that of Iran's today. Iraq's was ranked as the second biggest national reservoir, with 11 per cent of the world total. Iraqi oil was considered among the easiest and cheapest to produce, but it lay virtually untapped, for the infrastructure had been terribly degraded by two decades of war and sanctions. Thus the US Energy Information Administration fantasised about 400 billion barrels under the unexplored Iraqi sands; the production capacity was estimated at 8 million barrels per day.[25] In *Forbes* magazine, Paul Klebnikov (who one year later would coin the term "millionaire mullahs") depicted Iraq as "kind of like a Colorado ghost town, abandoned since the silver-mining operation closed down ... only the silver is all still in the ground, and in unbelievable quantities".[26] Iraq was not even remotely integrated into global circuits of capital. But "tomorrow, if America succeeds in toppling the bully-boy of Baghdad, the world could be awash in Iraqi oil", as *The Economist* foresaw, though it didn't mean this literally: "Realistically, experts say, it will take Iraq perhaps five years of hard work, western know-how and big money to turn its oil industry into a serious force again." [27]

Such was the point of departure. What have the occupiers done to Iraq's oil reserves since they seized the country and nabbed Saddam the bully-boy? They may have walked into Iraq without any plan on how to administer the occupied territory, but when they came to the oil fields, they had a detailed blueprint to follow. Commencing in April 2002, the US State Department's "Future of Iraq" group, composed by oil specialists and Iraqi expatriates, had been drawing up plans for how the "coalition of the willing" would deal with Iraq's oil sector. The industry had been state-owned since 1972. From the confidential meetings of the group, it was leaked to the *Financial Times* that Iraq "should be opened to international oil companies as quickly as possible after the war", in order to "establish a conducive business environment to attract investment of oil and gas resources". The means to this goal, championed by the Future of Iraq group, was the institution of a contract system known as "production-sharing agreements", or PSAs. Once Iraq's borders were secured, a swarm of Big Oil senior executives entered the country; under their eminent guidance, the successive authorities that emanated from the US compound in the Green Zone – the Coalition Provisional Authority, the Interim Government, and the Transitional Government – all punctiliously did their part in reshaping the oil industry along the lines of PSAs.[28]

A production-sharing agreement is the antithesis of an Iranian-style buyback contract. Technically, it leaves ownership of the oil reserves in the hands of the state, while the entrusted company extracts them. But the state's role is merely nominal. In practice, a PSA is just another label for a classic form of concession. It bestows upon the company monopoly rights to the development and management of an oil field, *to last for 25–40 years*, during which period the terms of the contract are fixed and cannot be legally altered by the state. Thus the company is free from all politically associated risks. For decades of political development in the host country, it is insulated against any whimsical ideas of additional taxes, regulations, or, worst of all, confiscation. The reserves can be entered into the company's balance sheets as the assets of the company, which is entitled to decide on the rates of their extraction (that is, their depletion) and other production details as it finds best. There is no upper limit on profits. Rising oil prices will translate into rising revenues not for the country where the oil is located, but for the company, and if disputes between the two arise, these will be solved not in the courts of the host country, but in international arbitration tribunals where the company and the state will be regarded as commercial partners with equal claims.[29]

Such is the design of the jemmy used to force open Iraq's treasure-chest. In late 2004, the Interim Government of Iyad Allawi decreed that all fields currently under production should continue to be developed by the public Iraqi National Oil Company (the equivalent of the NIOC) while *all unexploited fields should be rendered the exclusive domain of foreign corporations* through PSAs. Of 80 known oil fields, only 17 were in production at the time of the ordinance, thus granting the remaining 63 *as well as all future discoveries,* possibly containing hundreds of billions of barrels, to private investors.

At one stroke, a minimum of 64 per cent and a maximum of 87 per cent of Iraq's oil reserves were thereby handed over from the Iraqi state to global capital. For Iraq, this means relinquishing public control over the sole economic waterfall the country has in its possession – which today represents 95 per cent of government revenue – for generations to come. A group of progressive NGOs conducting the most detailed investigation of the PSA rip-off to date found that, even with conservative projections of the future oil price, the Iraqi losses of potential revenue will count in the hundreds of billions of dollars. In the opposite column, the oil companies can expect a windfall of profits ranging from *42 to 178 per cent.*[30] Compare this with the lacklustre 15 per cent profit from the Iranian buyback agreements.

These two cases starkly illustrate how capital deals with oil when given a free hand, that is, *when the obstacle of national sovereignty is removed.* In *Oil & Gas Journal,* a policy recommendation can perhaps be read between the lines: "It remains to be seen whether, *in the current political environment,* Iranian oil negotiators can agree to real changes in buyback contracts ... The major drawbacks of investing in the Iranian petroleum industry through buyback agreements as outlined in this analysis make it clear that the buyback scheme *does not present a reasonable alternative* to the concession and PSA schemes used commonly worldwide."[31]

The Big Oil corporations working behind the scenes of the Iraqi oil ministry have indeed declared that the PSA project "should be continued and considered as a 'beachhead' for possible further expansion in the Middle East".[32]

However, it would be too simplistic to regard a possible expansion of the PSA regime to Iran as in the exclusive interest of the corporations. Evidently, they are the ones poised to reap the profits from the direct operations, but their appropriation of Middle East oil reserves corresponds to the objective interests of *oil-consuming global capital as a whole*. In order for the Persian Gulf countries to fulfil their designated role when oil peaks and declines in other regions, they need, according to the Bush-Blair project "US-UK Energy Dialogue", to increase capacity from current 23 million barrels per day to 52 million barrels by 2030. That means *an infrastructure more than doubled in size*, and the US and the UK are in perfect consonance that this requires improved "investment regimes": it's the only way to bring in the necessarily stupendous capitals.[33] Only foreign corporations can be expected to pump at maximum rates, and only limitless profits will induce them to utmost efficiency. No others have the will and the capacity to both increase the flow and protect it.[34]

Independent states thus *need to be replaced as owners and custodians of the waterfalls*. The millionaire mullahs will never allow this to happen. But that is not the only way they can exercise their power.

MORE MISCHIEF

Perish the thought, but the oil producers have the power to close their pumps. If the markets are already strained, and if other producers have no spare capacity that would allow them to compensate for a withdrawal elsewhere (and these are precisely the conditions prevailing in the age of peak oil), the scenario assumes nightmarish proportions. In the words of Cheney's national energy policy report: "U.S. and world exposure to oil supply disruptions increases as the size of strategic and commercial stocks relative to demand declines. This vulnerability is a result of rising global demand, tight supplies, and inadequate efforts to establish or expand stockpiles [that is, by not opening up to foreign investment]."[35]

In Iran's case, the crucial number is 4 million barrels a day. This amount could be taken off the market, without substitutes waiting in the pipes of other suppliers. And the Islamic Republic is not reliable. In April 2002, during the Israeli Operation Defensive Shield, when the massacre in Jenin and the siege of the Church of Nativity took place, President Khatami wrote to the other Gulf countries urging them to agree to a one-month oil embargo against Israel's "main supporters". In the end, it was Saddam Hussein who activated the embargo, unlike Iran, which never carried out its threat: no Iraqi oil left the ports for one month. It was one of the sins for which Saddam was punished less than a year later.[36]

Having not yet put the nightmare scenario into execution, Iran – whose share of the world oil market is of a different order than Saddam's at that time – continues to hint at what they could do. After the referral of Iran to the UN Security Council, economy minister Davoud Danesh-Jaafari warned in early 2006: "Iran is in a very important regional situation, and any disturbance of the economic and political situation of the country could turn the regional situation into a crisis and increase the price of oil higher than the West expects."[37]

Directly addressing the West, Ahmadinejad put it more bluntly: "You need us more than we need you. All of you today need the Iranian nation."[38] This very provocative conceit is grounded in material realities: Iran is even in a position to close the oil spigots of *others*. Iran's geographical position on the northern shore of the Strait of Hormuz, and ownership of three small islands in the south of the Strait, poses another strategic nightmare. By simply firing off a few missiles, Iran could shut down all shipping through the Strait, instantly choking the movement of one-fifth of the world's oil, which passes daily from the Gulf to the global markets through this narrow waterway.[39]

While the Islamic Republic has so far refrained from this drastic tactic – which would incur equally drastic losses of revenue – the Republic has already hurt the West through its self-assured pricing policies. Iran is known as one of the "price hawks" of OPEC, pushing the other members to restrain production and let the oil price rise. Adding to this maddening situation is the fact that the higher the price goes, the more stellar the Iranian revenues, the more capital leaves the western orbit and disappears into the black hole of the Islamic Republic. Cut off from much of the world economy and ruled by self-absorbed accumulators, there is no mechanism guaranteeing that the money paid by oil consumers to Iran is ever recycled into the circuits of global accumulation. It is lost to the pockets of the millionaire mullahs.

Mischievous as the millionaire mullahs are, they have been planning to set up their own oil bourse. Presently, the global marketplaces for oil trading – the most voluminous commodity of world trade – are located in New York and London. But if the oil is extracted from Persian ground, why not *trade* it there as well? Why not bypass intermediate traders, investment banks and the US companies that own the oil bourses? This bold proposition was first mooted in the five-year development plan for Iran presented in 2000; in the summer of 2004, coinciding with the grand upwards revision of Iran's reserves, the government gave it a green light. As of spring 2006, the bourse has yet to be opened, while oil officials in Tehran repeatedly vow that it will do so in a few weeks.[40] Their hope is for the bourse to attract the commodities of the neighbouring Gulf countries, making it – according to the millionaire mullahs – "the main hub for oil deals in the region".[41]

The Iranian bourse is likely to trade oil not in dollars, as on the other two markets, but *in euros*. If Iran succeeded in establishing itself as "the main hub" for the Gulf oil trade, and converted this capitalist artery from dollars to euros, it could spell the end of the global hegemony of the dollar, and, by extension, of the US. Or so it is said, in frenzied debates taking place primarily on the Internet. Some have claimed that Iran's plan to orchestrate a shift to the euro "would flatten the revenues of the American corporations", constituting "an obvious encroachment on U.S. dollar supremacy", even "the ultimate 'nuclear' weapon that can swiftly destroy the financial system underpinning the American Empire". Hence the establishment of an Iranian bourse trading in euros could be a major explanation of US aggression against Iran.[42]

While we cannot go into the complex details of dollar hegemony and its functions, the ideas of the bourse-theorists can be briefly summarised here: if the most important component of world trade was exchanged in euros rather than in dollars, nation states would switch their foreign exchange reserves into euros, selling off billions of dollars in the process. The value of the dollar would plunge. Central banks and investors would no longer be interested in buying dollars, and for the US, hitherto able to run constantly growing trade and budget deficits precisely by selling dollars to the world market, it would be a catastrophe. Consumption levels would nosedive, as would US demand for export products from the rest of the world, possibly precipitating a collapse of the world economy. Saddam Hussein once switched the sales of Iraqi oil from dollars to euros and was duly toppled; now the same fate awaits the Islamic Republic.[43]

Some of this speculation might turn out to be true. In general, however, the notion that Iran is weeks from bringing US capitalism to ruination seems exaggerated. The bourse – if ever activated – would suffer from a number of impediments, most important of which is the sheer scale of the project to attract the bulk of the oil trade from New York and London to Tehran. That it would occur by itself seems improbable: would a whole clan of capitalists, accustomed to the comfort of trading in these two centres of the global economy, one day walk out and move to *Tehran* of all places? The oil consumers, traders, investors and producers of the New York and London bourses will continue to trade in the same way, in the same places and in the same currency, that is, dollars. This structural inertia, known as "path dependency", is similar to that which faces anyone trying to persuade Americans to switch to Celsius, or Europeans to Fahrenheit. The bourses are entrenched in the existing order, and if for some reason the oil markets *were* to decamp, it would not be in response to a clarion call from Iran. The *Index on Economic Freedom* could be a suitable guide for their search for a country that would ensure freedom and security for global capital. It would certainly recommend somewhere other than Iran.[44]

The Iranian oil bourse might attract some operators from neighbouring countries, but its potential to overturn the world economy seems rather slim. Nor does that seem to be Iran's intent. Oil officials have explained that the bourse "means giving Iranians control over oil product dealings" and reducing US "influence over the Islamic Republic's economy".[45] Rather than the harbinger of the demise of US empire, the project should thus be understood as precisely that: mischief from the millionaire mullahs, designed to *consolidate their national regime of accumulation*, with some prospects of incorporating regional circuits of capital. The fundamental menace to global capital, however, stems not from their currency conspiracies, but from their undependable ownership of more than a tenth of the world's oil.

A BOMB FLOATING ON A SEA OF OIL

American capital is in an awkward position regarding Iran. The US government has imposed unilateral sanctions on the Islamic Republic, dating back to 14 November 1979. Since then, the sanctions have never been eased, only tightened, as in the Iran and Libya Sanctions Act of 1995, wherein the Clinton administration stipulated financial punishment of not only American but also *foreign* companies dealing with Iran. The latter proved unenforceable. American citizens, however, were from now on strictly forbidden to trade with Iran or to enter into any commercial contracts regarding the development of Iranian petroleum resources. To their chagrin, US corporations are barred from the theoretical possibility of overcoming Iranian taboos against them and bidding for the country's riches. All is left to their competitors. [46]

From the standpoint of the millionaire mullahs, the American sanctions and reciprocal anti-American policies have encouraged economic relations with others, in particular, Asian countries. China has been moored in the oil and gas fields of Iran through a series of agreements between the two governments; in exchange for Iran exporting crude to China (Iran is China's second largest source of imported oil), Chinese corporations are developing new oil fields and building refineries. As noted earlier, a Japanese consortium, though faltering, has assumed responsibility for the Azadegan supergiant. Together with India and Pakistan, Iran has been planning a mega-pipeline that would funnel liquefied natural gas through the subcontinent. Washington has bemoaned these insolent cooperative projects, arguing that they harm the efforts to isolate the Islamic Republic.[47]

The US has locked itself into a condition of escalating frustration. Iran's resources are ever more badly needed, but the US and thus a major section of global capital are partly self-excluded, partly excommunicated from every contact with them; they can only stand by and watch as some of the fortunes are channelled away to eastern corners of the world market, under the supervision of governments. They yearn for Iran, but they cannot have it. Reconciliation, lifting the sanctions, the full reintegration of Iran into world capitalism all seem out of the question, as long as the Islamic Republic remains the Islamic Republic, and thus frustration is bound to escalate further.

In this contradictory situation, the US has one break-out option: regime change. Indeed, that is the ultimate goal of US policies towards Iran, renewed in the "axis of evil" agenda, but actually in place ever since 1979. The Islamic Revolution was both a slap in the face and an amputation of hands: on a symbolic level, the US was exposed as impotent – most spectacularly in the hostage drama – while on a material level it lost its most important asset in the Persian Gulf.

Pahlavi Iran was the policeman of the Gulf, an "island of stability" in a sea of Arab radicalism, a major procurer of US military products, an important regional market for all kinds of corporations, a petrodollar recycler, and the *second-largest* exporter of oil to the US. In one fell swoop, unprecedented in Middle-Eastern modern history, all of this was eradicated.[48]

As a loss for US power, Iran in 1979 can only be compared with Cuba in 1959 and Vietnam in 1975, but neither of the latter events matches the *strategic magnitude* of losing Iran. Indeed, if the coup against Mossadeq is the primordial trauma of modern Iran, the Islamic Revolution is the equivalent experience for US imperialism in the most crucial region of the world. It forced the US to abandon the Nixon doctrine, according to which US interests in the Persian Gulf were to be protected by the arming of proxies – that is, the Peacock Throne of the Shah, the House of Saud, and the Zionist State of Israel. In its place came the Carter doctrine, whose maxim was announced by President Carter on 23 January 1980: "Any attempts by any outside force to gain control of the Gulf region will be regarded as an assault on the vital interests of the United States of America, and such an assault will be repelled by any means necessary, including military force."[49]

A Rapid Deployment Force was consequently created by Carter, based in Florida, until other bases could be acquired in the Gulf region; three years later, Reagan renamed the force and expanded it into the US Central Command, known under the acronym of Centcom. This signalled the dawn of direct US engagement in the Persian Gulf, the militarisation of the area, the permanent bases and the recurring wars. To this day, the prime operational responsibility of Centcom remains to protect the flow of oil in general and the traffic through the Strait of Hormuz in particular. Commanders regularly restate its *raison d'être* by simply reminding audiences of the unavoidable facts of oil's geographic distribution. Centcom fought the Gulf War in 1991, invaded Afghanistan in 2001, occupied Iraq in 2003. Thus it is no wild exaggeration to say that the world lives in the long shadow of Iran's general strike of 1978.[50]

Ever since, the US has been licking its wounds, striving to negate the Iranian Revolution by reinstalling the comprador bourgeoisie. This was the US's aim when they infiltrated the Iranian Army in 1979 and 1980, assembling hundreds of Iranian agents and hatching plots for the "destabilisation" of the Islamic Republic and its replacement with "a moderate" government. This was the aim when the US buttressed Saddam Hussein's war of aggression, and when the Clinton administration squeezed Iran with new sanctions in conjunction with a fresh "covert action program" to undermine the regime from within.[51] Regime change in Iran is the unbroken thread running through US foreign policy.

All attempts so far have failed, and the Islamic Republic has proved utterly resilient, but *in the age of globalisation and peak oil a change of the Iranian regime becomes exigent.* A nationally-based capitalist class is an anomaly in the age of globalisation, and none is as rich, headstrong and proud in its self-sufficiency as the millionaire mullah class. "Resource nationalism" of the Iranian kind is, in the long run, insufferable for capital in the age of peak oil. If western interests in Iran's oil were strong enough to drive a regime change in 1953, at a time when oil was abundant (when the US and Britain imposed a global boycott on Mossadeq's oil, it had no effect on the market), then how could it not be a burning issue today? The need for the return of an updated, upgraded comprador bourgeoisie has never been as pressing as now. There are structural, objective forces at work against Iran. A different question is whether these forces will actually achieve their goal this time (this depends on the strength of the forces opposing them), but objective they are.

It is in this context that the issue of the Iranian nuclear programme can be properly understood. Nuclear arms, or the capability to produce them when necessary, are the ultimate shield of sovereignty which no one has thus far dared to challenge. A nation possessing neither nuclear arms, nor an alliance with another nation with nuclear arms, be it implicit or explicit, is fair game for an aggressor; this has been proved in a number of cases in modern history.[52] If the Islamic Republic acquired a nuclear capability, it would thus have *a foolproof fortification against regime change by military means.*

Every now and then, the petroleum subtext of the surface preoccupation with weapons of mass destruction in the Middle East is revealed by representatives of Western power. Most famous is perhaps Paul Wolfowitz's reply (before he moved from the Pentagon to the World Bank) to the question of why WMDs in North Korea are grudgingly tolerated while Iraq was invaded: "Let's look at it simply. The most important difference between North Korea and Iraq is that economically, we just had no choice in Iraq. The country swims on a sea of oil."[53]

In another example, Dick Cheney told the annual convention of Veterans of Foreign Wars in August 2002:

Should [Saddam Hussein's] ambitions [to acquire WMDs] be realised, the implications would be enormous for the Middle East and the United States. Armed with an arsenal of these weapons of terror and a seat at the top of ten percent of the world's oil reserves, Saddam Hussein could then be expected to seek domination of the entire Middle East, take control of a great portion of the world's energy supplies, [and] directly threaten America's friends throughout the region.[54]

Iraq's "q" could easily be changed to an "n". In fact, this is happening. When specifying what exactly is the danger with *Iranian* nuclear capability, a tome from the US Army, published in October 2005, was blunt: "Dramatically Higher Oil Prices. A nuclear-ready Iran could be emboldened to manipulate oil prices upward. It might attempt this either by threatening the freedom of the seas (by mining oil transit points as it did in the 1980s, or by threatening to close the Strait of Hormuz), or by using terrorist proxies to threaten the destruction of Saudi and other Gulf state oil facilities and pipelines."

The second danger posed by a nuclear-armed Iran is:

Increased Terrorism Designed to Diminish U.S. Influence. With a nuclear weapons option *acting as a deterrent to the United States and allied action against it*, Iran would likely lend greater support to terrorists operating against Israel, Iraq, Libya, Saudi Arabia, Europe, and the United States. The aim of such support would be to reduce American support for U.S. involvement in the Middle East, for Israel, *and for actions against Iran generally*, and to elevate Iran as an equal to the United States and its allies on all matters relating to the Persian Gulf and related regions.[55]

Distorted terminology, but grains of truth. However much Bush and his acolytes rant about evil Iran threatening the peace of the world, the objective reason is, once again, black and liquid. But it is not the only one.

14
Grooming the Attack Dog

"WHEN IRAN WAS IRAN"

In July 2005, one of the authors of this book, Shora, was returning to her work as a coordinator of the International Solidarity Movement for Palestine; upon her arrival at Tel Aviv's Ben Gurion Airport she was instantly accosted by security guards. After asking her the usual questions and making her wait for five hours, they took her to a room, adorned with pictures of Ariel Sharon and President Moshe Katsav (the latter, incidentally, born in Iran). A man presenting himself as "Sami" entered. Speaking in Persian, he asked Shora about her background in Iran and why she had left for Sweden; when she told him that her mother had been politically active, he demanded to know in what group. A smile lit up his face. "Sami" explained that he used to instruct Savak agents, "those agents that you and your mother feared". After showing her a list of 168 files documenting Shora's activism against the West Bank wall, "Sami" requested her mother's telephone number. He phoned her, insulted her, and threatened to throw her daughter into a cell where no one would ever find her, all this in a manner her mother would find familiar. Once again he explained how he had been a trainer for Savak "*moghe-i ke Iran Iran bud*", "when Iran was Iran".

When Iran was Iran, the Shah delivered oil to Israel, and financed the construction of a pipeline from Eilat to Ashkelon. He had only contempt for the plight of the Palestinians. Israel assisted the Shah in developing missile technology. Most important, and the focal point of their collaboration, the Israeli secret service Mossad reared and trained Savak. In a CIA file discovered upon the seizure of the US embassy in Tehran, the alliance was described thus:

The main purpose of the Israeli relationship with Iran was the development of a pro-Israel and anti-Arab policy on the part of Iranian officials. Mossad has engaged in joint operations with Savak over the years since the late 1950s. Mossad aided Savak activities and supported the Kurds in Iraq. The Israelis also regularly transmitted to the Iranians intelligence reports on Egypt's activities in the Arab countries, trends and developments in Iraq, and communist activities affecting Iran.[1]

The Iranian Revolution was as fierce in its anti-Zionism as in its anti-Americanism. In 1982, the Islamic Republic took a redoubtable revenge when, in the wake of the Israeli invasion of Lebanon, it dispatched Pasdaran legions to the Beka'a Valley to nurture the Hizbollah movement. After expelling the American and French forces from the country, Hizbollah grew into the mightiest guerrilla organisation ever to be active in the Middle East; finally, 18 years later, it forced Israel to leave most of its occupied zone in Lebanon.[2] (A feat of similar proportions was achieved in July 2006 – see the Afterword.) Equally vocal, but less materially forthcoming, has been the support of the Islamic Republic for the Palestinian resistance. And now, a few years into the new millennium, it might be learning how to shake the very foundations of Zionist ascendancy in the region.

AMERICA'S NEW PRIZE FIGHTER

As the Zionist movement fixed its gaze on Palestine, it recognised that the Palestinians identified their very existence with the terraces, fishing ports, citrus and olive groves, the thousand-year-old *suqs*, the beams of sunlight in the alleyways, the crowds around the Al-Aqsa mosque after Friday prayers and all the other attributes of their land. The Zionist movement realised that the only way to make space for a Jewish state was to clear this ancient land of its people through superior physical force. However, it would not be able to muster such a force by its own efforts solely. One of the leaders of the movement, Vladimir Jabotinsky, expressed their need in a famous statement: "Settlement can [only] develop under the protection of a force which is not dependent on the local population, behind an iron wall which they will be powerless to break down." Whether Jabotinsky was also clairvoyant remains unknown, but in the nine-meter-high wall now cutting through the Palestinian landscape, his political vision has certainly been made concrete reality. "Precisely because they are not a mob, but a living nation", nothing less than the supreme physical force of the US-backed State of Israel would suffice to permanently exile the Palestinians.[3]

The first external actor to protect the Zionist settlement was Britain. But it was, of course, the US who brought the compact to perfection. When Nasser emerged as Egypt's Mossadeq, announcing a sweeping programme of nationalisation, and by extension threatening the flow of oil from the Arab states, Israel quickly solved the problem. In three hours in June 1967, it destroyed the Egyptian Air Force. After the Six-Day War, a chastened, weeping Nasser asked his people for forgiveness. Like a coach at a boxing match, the US excitedly realised the talents of the Zionist state; the CIA commended Israel's "destruction of the center of power of the radical Arab Socialist movement, i.e. the Nasser regime". Now the US entered into unflinching alliance with Israel, an alliance that has marked the history of the Middle East ever since.[4] The support of the Zionist state's absolute military superiority over the region would henceforth be a fundamental tenet of US foreign policy. One year after the Six-Day War, Israeli Prime Minister Levi Eshkol boasted: "The value of Israel to the West in this part of the world will, I predict, be out of all proportion to its size. We will be a real bridge between the three continents, and the free world will be very thankful not only if we survive, but if we continue to thrive in secure and guaranteed frontiers [these frontiers were, of course, never defined and still are not]."[5]

In a consummate quid pro quo, the US conferred upon Israel the iron wall of armaments needed against the Palestinians, while Israel kept the Middle East safe for American – capitalist – interests. US aid to Israel increased *tenfold* in 1970, and a decade later, after the loss of Pahlavi in Iran, the stock value of the Zionist state rose even higher. For the US regarded Israel, in the words of Ronald Reagan, as "the only strategic asset in the area that the United States can really rely on" (even Saudi Arabia had earlier betrayed the US and taken part in the 1973 oil embargo).[6] By the late 1970s, Israel was the sole remaining component of the Nixon doctrine, and in February 1981 found itself to be focus of its very own doctrine, as announced by President Ronald Reagan: "Not only do we have a moral commitment, [but] being a country sharing our same ideals, our democratic approach to things, with a combat-experienced military, [Israel] is a force in the Middle East that actually is a benefit to us. *If there were not Israel with that force, we'd have to supply that with our own*, so this isn't just altruism on our part."[7]

Hence Israel as a force had to grow, relentlessly, for its value increased as the imbalance of forces grew more extreme in the Middle East. Under the mantle of Israeli superiority and aggression, any country's attempt at independent management of its resources would risk the same fate as Nasser's; unruly nations, like Syria, would be kept on their knees, and only those conforming to US hegemony, like Jordan and post-Nasserist Egypt, would be left in peace. The logic is as strategically invaluable for the US today as it was in the 1970s or 1980s. Ultimately, it rests on one single platform: Israel's regional monopoly on nuclear arms.[8]

In the early 1950s, Israel began its efforts to acquire the bomb. Nuclear research and development advanced at the Dimona plant in the Naqab Desert (renamed "Negev" in Hebrew). The reactor went critical on the eve of the Six-Day War, and the manufacture of nuclear warheads on assembly lines began in 1968. The following year, the Nixon administration made a mockery of the year-old Non-Proliferation Treaty (NPT) by communicating to the Israeli leadership its full approval of their bomb and ending the international inspections (which had been entirely cosmetic in any case) in the Naqab. However, the parties agreed on maintaining a halo of "ambiguity" around Dimona and its outposts, refraining from publicly divulging Israel's nuclear capability.[9]

This policy of "ambiguity" has persisted over the decades, while the nuclear powers of Israel have expanded. Currently, estimates of its arsenal vary from 200 to 500 nuclear warheads. Israel has various methods of delivery: from the ground, via the "Jericho" missiles, from the air, via its fleet of F-16 and F-15 fighter jets, and from the sea, where three German-made "Dolphin" submarines – one in the Persian Gulf – patrol armed with more than 70 "Harpoon" nuclear warheads.[10]

What has never been left in any ambiguity, however, is Israel's determination to remain the *only* nuclear power in the Middle East. On 7 June 1981, 14 fighter-jets entered Iraq's airspace, continuing undetected for 90 minutes until they reached the Osirak nuclear reactor. There, they hovered overhead for two minutes and then returned home, leaving the insignia of Israeli superiority behind: a huge smoking crater.[11] Osirak had not housed a bomb, nor had it been approaching the nuclear threshold; Saddam Hussein had not, with any certainty, planned a nuclear weapons capability. Iraq had not so much as threatened Israel – to the contrary, it had recently made conciliatory gestures towards the Jewish state.[12] For Israel, *the sheer prospect of any nuclear technology in the hands of another Middle East state is intolerable*. That was the law promulgated in Osirak. Ronald Reagan was said to be "delighted".

Two days after the raid, the government of Israel enunciated what became known as the Begin doctrine: "Under no circumstances would we allow the enemy to develop weapons of mass destruction against our nation; we will defend Israel's citizens, in time, with all the means at our disposal." Ariel Sharon, as minister of defence, later elaborated: "Israel cannot afford the introduction of the nuclear weapon. For us, it is not a question of balance of terror but a question of survival. We shall therefore have to prevent such a threat *at its inception*."[13] Anticipating the concept of pre-emptive warfare, Israel declared its right for "anticipatory self-defence", that is, pre-emptive acts of aggression at times it deemed suitable.

Shlomo Brom, a deputy national security adviser in Israel, ex-director of strategic planning at the general staff, and public interpreter of the Begin doctrine, makes clear that "the immediacy of a WMD threat does not play an important role" for the selection of targets. Rather, bombing nuclear installations in foreign countries is justified at "the point of irreversibility, namely the time in which the proliferator [sic] stops being dependent on external assistance; it controls all the necessary technologies and knowledge; and it cannot be denied these capabilities through pressure over the states and private elements that supply assistance."[14]

IF IRAN HAD THE BOMB

How the Israeli nuclear doctrine applies to Iran is self-evident. "Israel will not allow Iran to be equipped with a nuclear weapon", Ariel Sharon asserted in July 2004. "Israel will on no account permit Iranian reactors – especially the one being built in Bushehr with Russian help – to go critical", defence sources were quoted as saying. "Israel will not be able to accept an Iranian nuclear capability and it must have the capability to defend itself, with all that that implies, and this we are preparing", Defence Minister Shaul Mofaz reaffirmed in January 2006. The mantra has been repeated daily by Zionist leaders up to the present, for example, when Prime Minister Ehud Olmert recently declared to the US Congress that "a nuclear-armed Iran is an intolerable threat to the peace and security of the world. (APPLAUSE) It cannot be permitted to materialise."[15]

Both Israeli and western politicians have repeatedly asserted that Iran will attack Israel as soon as it acquires the bomb, exterminating the Jewish people on their own soil in a nuclear holocaust. Choosing reason and empirical observation rather than scaremongering as tools, one can only reach the conclusion that the thought is preposterous. The risk is nearly zero.

In the most realistic analysis known to us, Ehsaneh I. Sadr methodically dissects the doomsaying of the western states, reminding them, first of all, of the policy that saved them from annihilation during the Cold War: "MAD", or "Mutually Assured Destruction". If two states in enmity both possess nuclear arms, so that state A is capable of destroying state B and vice versa, neither of them will use their bomb, knowing that if they did, they would bring their own annihilation upon themselves. Thus the US and the Soviet Union never attacked one another. Neither did China and the Soviet Union; nor have India and Pakistan. Why, then, would the Islamic Republic drop a (still theoretical) bomb on the State of Israel? It is fully aware that Israel maintains in its nuclear-armed submarines a secure second-strike capability – that is, a capability to retaliate even if a first Iranian missile penetrated Israeli air defences and reached Israeli territory. And side by side with Israel, of course, is the US, with its stand-by capacity to destroy Iran dozens of times over. The US has pledged to strike back immediately if Israel is attacked.[16]

One counter-argument would be that Iran is a "suicidal nation", as it has indeed been described by the Israeli government.[17] The rulers of the Islamic Republic, the argument goes, would gladly give up their lives along with that of their nation for the joy of genocide. Such a diagnosis is based on a flagrant disregard for the most easily observable fact of Iranian society as it has been structured since 1979, namely, that the millionaire mullahs do *everything possible to hang on to power and capital*. Martyrdom is not for them. Heaven they might believe in, but no empirically discernible policies exist that indicate a readiness to sacrifice power, capital or earthly existence for higher ideological or religious goals; in this regard, they are as rational as any other ruling class on earth.

The priority of worldly interests is actually at the heart of the Islamic Republic, where, from the usury of the bonyads down to the prostitution rings of Qom, hardly any taboo of Islam has not been transgressed or a duty not neglected in the pursuit for more power, more capital. The notion of the millionaire mullahs as martyrdom-seeking idealists simply ignores the totality of the Iranian experience. Even if they were driven by religious fervour, and considered the extermination of the Jewish state as their theological duty, the third holiest site of Islam, the Al-Aqsa mosque, would perish with Israel in any successful nuclear strike, as would a major segment of the Palestinian Muslim people.[18] Equally absurd is the idea that the centres of power in Iran, arranged around Al-Faqih, would allow nuclear warheads to fall into the hands of "terrorist organisations" outside the mullahs' control. If any state apparatus is bound to guard its nuclear capacity against freelancers, it is the Iranian one.[19]

The "Israel is threatened with a new Holocaust" spin of 2005 and 2006 is only another variation on a theme, almost as old as Israeli military superiority over the Middle East. The most obvious parallel is the atmosphere before the Six-Day War. At that time, Israeli leaders cried to the western world that Nasser's Egypt threatened "the very existence of the state" with a "final solution", that the Jewish state faced the choice "to live or to perish, to protect the national existence or to forfeit it for all time", and then there were the smoking craters on the Egyptian airfields.[20]

Hence the threat so worrying to Israel, and the US, must, again, be another. And the threat is *the levelling of the imbalance of terror* in the Middle East. As is clear in Sharon's statement above and the other repetitions of the Begin doctrine, Israel will not tolerate a situation of Mutually Assured Destruction. The strategic deadlock MAD tends to foster, the inhibitions against adventurous aggression it imposes on military planners, is precisely what the State of Israel fears. Undeniably, in one sense, this is rooted in a deep fear for the very existence of Israel, as a Zionist state founded on the continuous expulsion of the Palestinian people. In the first public statement admitting to Israel's nuclear capability, Shimon Peres, the father of the nuclear programme, declared in July 1998 that Israel "built a nuclear option, not in order to have a Hiroshima but an Oslo".[21] In translation, this means that the Zionist state amassed the world's fourth or fifth largest arsenal of the deadliest weapons of mass destruction to ensure a balance of forces in the region that permits it to put the occupation of Palestine on a permanent footing. Peres himself has clarified that "acquiring a superior weapons system would mean the possibility of using it for compelling purposes – that is, forcing the other side to accept Israeli political demands." Moshe Sneh, a leading Israeli strategist, has confessed why the idea of an Iranian bomb is so frightening: "I don't want the Israeli–Palestinian negotiations to be held under the shadow of an Iranian nuclear bomb."[22] Or, as stated in an editorial in *Ha'aretz*, Israel's leading liberal newspaper: "At that point" – that is, when Iran possesses enough fissionable material for building a nuclear weapon – "the balance of power in the region will change sharply, to Israel's detriment."[23]

With another nuclear power in the Middle East, Israel would not be able to act as ruthlessly as it has in the last half-century. How could it denigrate states backing the Palestinian people as unworthy of consideration when drawing up borders or dictating "peace accords", if one of them has a nuclear option? How could it casually let off missiles in, for instance, Syria's direction, if its ally Iran has a nuclear bomb? To have such restraint foisted on Israel would shake the very foundations of its power. As Shlomo Brom candidly states: "Preemption and prevention" – regarded by some as unprovoked aggression – "were an important part of the security discourse in Israel since the inception of the state of Israel", the results of that "discourse" being felt every day in the refugee camps scattered across the region.[24]

As for US imperialism in the Middle East, Iran's first strike was the 1979 revolution, which abruptly changed power politics in the region. If Iran were to possess a nuclear capability, that would be its second strike; such a capability would severely curtail the space for Israeli manoeuvres. The attack dog would be muzzled.

A real equalisation of nuclear arsenals in the Middle East is nowhere on the horizon; if Israel and the US were never again to procure so much as a single extra warhead, it would still take Iran decades of technological and economic development to catch up.[25] The relevant measure for Israel and the US is, however, not quantitative. It is Iranian nuclear capability per se that must be pre-empted. Or, as Ariel Sharon stated in July 2004: "We have received here a clear American position that says in other words that Israel must not be touched when it comes to its deterrent capability."[26]

A CONVERGING WALL

Israel is a mastiff straining at its leash, dragging its master forward. It has been sniffing out the most optimistic estimates of Iranian nuclear advancement (according to Israel, Iran has been six months away from an atomic bomb for several years now), delivering crooked intelligence to the US on Tehran's "support for terror". Israel demands more military aid to protect itself and the free world against the Islamic Republic, and has begun, as we will see, preparations for maintaining its position as top dog by killing off Iran singlehandedly. After the destruction of Iraq as a force in the Middle East in 1991, Israel turned its attention to demanding tougher US sanctions against the Islamic Republic, as punishment for its three cardinal sins of "opposing the peace process", "sponsoring terrorism worldwide", and "developing WMDs". Even before the destruction of Iraq as an independent nation state in 2003, Ariel Sharon declared that "as soon as Iraq is dealt with, I will push for Iran to be at the top of the 'to do' list."[27] Ever since, Israel has been pushing for confrontation with Iran. Regime change is as hotly coveted by the State of Israel as it is by the US. It wants the clock turned back to those days "when Iran was Iran".

For the US, however, the autonomy of the Iranian state is part of a malaise that stretches far beyond the borders of historic Palestine. In the two countries under US occupation, that is, Iraq and Afghanistan, Tehran has emerged as the prime alternative locus of power. This has not been achieved through *anti-imperialism*, or any other principled policy: the Islamic Republic has reached its position through insidious Machiavellian plots, immolating the local populations whenever it served its interests. In Afghanistan, Iran was instrumental in the US campaign against the Taliban. Deeply provoked by the Wahhabi madrasa-students' hatred of Shia Muslims, Iran had been a foe of the Taliban regime all through its existence, financing, equipping and training its would-be gravediggers in the Northern Alliance. As the US opted for invasion, Tehran recommended that the Alliance coordinate its operations with the US troops, even assisting it on the ground through special forces. Were it not for Iran, the ground component of Operation Enduring Freedom would not have existed. Ten days after the flight of the Taliban from Kabul, Iran became the first country to reopen its embassy. But for this, in a first change of tune, the US was not happy.

In a strategy soon to be repeated in Iraq, Iran now began to change its cooperation with the occupying forces into an expansion of its own clout in Afghanistan, by supporting the presidency of Hamid Karzai, funnelling hundreds of millions of dollars in aid to his puppet government, and constructing splendid new roads connecting western Herat province to Iran. That province, with a Shiite majority and centuries-old bonds to Persia, is now a satellite territory of Iran, which is one reason why the US is building a new megabase outside the city of Herat, not far from the Iranian border.[28]

In Iraq, a much longer story not to be told in detail here, Iran has similarly supplied crucial sponsorship to the US occupation *and* undermined the Americans' hold over the country.[29] The backbone of the "Iraqi forces" deployed by the US against the Sunni insurgency is the Badr Corps, the armed wing of the Supreme Council of the Islamic Revolution in Iraq, or Sciri. Founded by Iraqi Khomeinists in Iranian exile, having battled in the war against Saddam, Sciri re-entered Iraq under the wings of the US occupation with discipline, combat experience, and absolute allegiance to Tehran. This is the force responsible for the mass mutilations of Sunni civilians uncovered in innumerable ditches, backyards and river banks in central Iraq in 2005 and 2006.

For the Iraqi people, the one hope for national unity and independence lay in the Shiite masses joining the resistance, but there has been one actor throwing a spanner into the works. In 2004, Muqtada as-Sadr's Mehdi movement pointed its Shiite guns against the US troops, putting Iraq at the critical crossroad of united liberation struggle or divide-and-rule occupation. For his offences, Muqtada as-Sadr was ostracised by Iran. Instead, Iran has consistently ordered Sciri and the other Shia party under its influence, Dawa, to counter all insurgent efforts, pilot the Shia population into the political institutions set up by the occupying power, participate in the elections and the government, and gradually wrest power over Iraq into pro- or crypto-Iranian hands. Thus Iran has been instrumental not only in upholding the occupation, but in causing the bloody unravelling of the Iraqi nation. Thanks to Iran, the Wahhabist hatred of Shiites has gained a footing in the country, as the major Shiite parties have in fact acted as the bestial lackeys of the occupation. Ironically, in return, the Sunni insurgency has *objectively* come to the rescue of Iran: thanks to its entrapment of the US Army in the quagmires of the "Sunni Triangle", the prospects of an all-out assault on Iran have been diminished. But as said, the Islamic Republic has never followed principles, either political or moral.

That, however, is not a source of comfort for the US. One country's crass power politics can suffer from collision with another. Since Shia organisations swept through the social and political infrastructures of southern Iraq, it has become, even more than western Afghanistan, satellite Iranian territory. Through the conduit of Sciri, the party of Iraq's equivalent to the Iranian bazaari (Sadr's movement, on the other hand, is clear-cut mostazafin), and the centuries-old ulama networks in the holy cities of Najaf and Karbala, Iran has transmitted its capital into the heartland of southern Iraq. There, the solicitors of the millionaire mullahs have been busy building hotels for the pilgrims, launching infrastructure projects, supplying ample financial and logistic resources, and cutting trade deals between Iraqi and Iranian partners. With the Sciri- and Dawa-dominated government in Baghdad, Tehran has entered a string of agreements: to pump crude Iraqi oil to Iranian refineries and refined products back to Iraq, to expand transport networks between the two countries, to facilitate visas for Iranian businessmen, to loan Iraq $1 billion for the purchase of Iranian products, and so forth. Iran and southern-central Iraq are blending. From base to superstructure, it translates into *a decisive Iranian leverage over its western neighbour*. The millionaire mullahs are extending their social formation, not through *their own* wars of aggression, but rather as viruses travelling on the body of *American* wars of aggression.

For the US, as so many observers have noted, this means losing Iraq with its tenth of the world's oil – immediately upon conquering it – to the bogeyman of the Middle East. As in Afghanistan, and moreover in the Caspian Sea area with its oil and gas resources, the ugly faces of the Islamic Republic show up *from within* the areas supposedly under US mastery. The autonomous ruling class of Iran is pursuing its own interests with surprising success, behind the lines of the US forces encircling their nation.

Thus for US hegemony to prevail in the region, curbing Iran's power is imperative. Ultimately, the Middle East – and, to a lesser degree, Central Asia – can be saved for US and global capital only through a drastic weakening or, preferably, destruction of the Islamic Republic. And so the US has every reason to follow in the tracks of its attack dog. Once again, Israeli and US interests are converging, in the project of erecting an iron wall of supreme physical violence stretching from river to river, from gulf to sea.

15
Real Men Go to Tehran

"EVERYONE WANTS TO GO TO BAGHDAD.
REAL MEN WANT TO GO TO TEHRAN."

Cato's dictum, "Carthage must be destroyed" has been modernised, with the Islamic Republic standing in as the Carthage of our time. The tag "Real men go to Tehran" was revealed to *Newsweek* from the inner circles of American and British war planners in August 2002. Since then, its fame has spread, for over the years, the direction has remained constant: towards a Western war against Iran. The well-oiled war machinery has simply continued to roll eastwards from Baghdad, following the same blueprint. After the fall of Saddam Hussein, the mullahs of Iran have been systematically depicted as striving towards nuclear weapons capability, while delivering arms to "terrorists" in the region and maintaining connections to Al-Qaida. Secretary of State Condoleezza Rice has labelled the Islamic Republic "the central banker for terrorism" – Iran is "something to be loathed" – while Washington has supported Mojahedin and Pahlavi Iranian exiles seeking a triumphant return. Conservative and neocon publications beat the war drums, while mainstream newspapers run full-page ads screaming "Can anyone within the range of Iran's missiles feel safe?", complete with maps of the Eurasian landmass. And finally, sanctions and threats of military measures have been proposed to the UN Security Council, accompanied by accolades praising "the road of diplomacy". With Iraq as a precedent, feelings of déjà vu are justifiable.[1]

But a number of prophecies about the timing of the war against Iran have already been proved false. Writing in March 2005, former UN weapons inspector in Iraq Scott Ritter was certain that there would be a "massive aerial attack against Iran" in June 2005, his sources informing him that time "is seen as the decisive date" in Iran's nuclear development. June 2005 came and went.[2] Some have suggested that the US has been giving false information to the media in a campaign of psychological warfare against Iran. Indeed, the White House methodically plants minatory communiqués in the writings and lectures of its ideologues while President Bush answers questions from reporters with the bland (or ominous) "all options are on the table".[3] While this is clearly meant to put pressure on Iran, it should not be regarded as a hollow threat: the stakes involved, and the record of the Bush administration, rule out any reassuring conclusions.

As the time of writing, in spring 2006, the air is filled as never before with threats and reports of impending strikes. In March, the US National Security Strategy announced "We may face no greater challenge from a single country than from Iran."[4] A few weeks later, celebrated investigative journalist Seymour Hersh published the most compelling account of "The Iran Plans" so far, quoting a senior Pentagon adviser as saying: "This White House believes that the only way to solve the problem is to change the power structure in Iran, and that means war."[5]

It would be unwise to make any predictions here on what a war on Iran would look like, or when it would come, since the equation, where so many variables are in a constant flux, is bound to be constantly recalibrated. The general impression at the moment is that the skies could open any minute; in the most balanced analysis of the war scenarios to date, Paul Rogers surmises that the onset of hostilities would come as a thunderbolt in the night. A key goal would be to take Iran by surprise. Unlike the Iraq invasion, which from the start was a gargantuan ground operation with forces gradually building up along the borders and the whole world watching and marching in protest, Iran would be attacked in a sudden air blitz. The attack would be launched simultaneously from hundreds of launch pads, airfields and bases, carriers, ships and submarines across the globe, possibly more massive than any precedent in military history (see Figure 4).

Operating on intelligence collected by the drones, satellites and teams of special agents sent into Iran over the previous years, planes and missiles would unleash a firestorm over Iran. As Paul Rogers, Seymour Hersh and many others have explained, the attack would, according to the plans, target not only Iran's nuclear facilities, but a nationwide range of factories, research centres, universities, regime institutions, defence installations, arms deposits, missile batteries and Pasdaran and army units. This comprehensive list would be targeted in order to reach the combined objectives of eradicating the nuclear programme, preventing any retaliation or defence from the victim, and opening a chasm under the feet of the regime.[6]

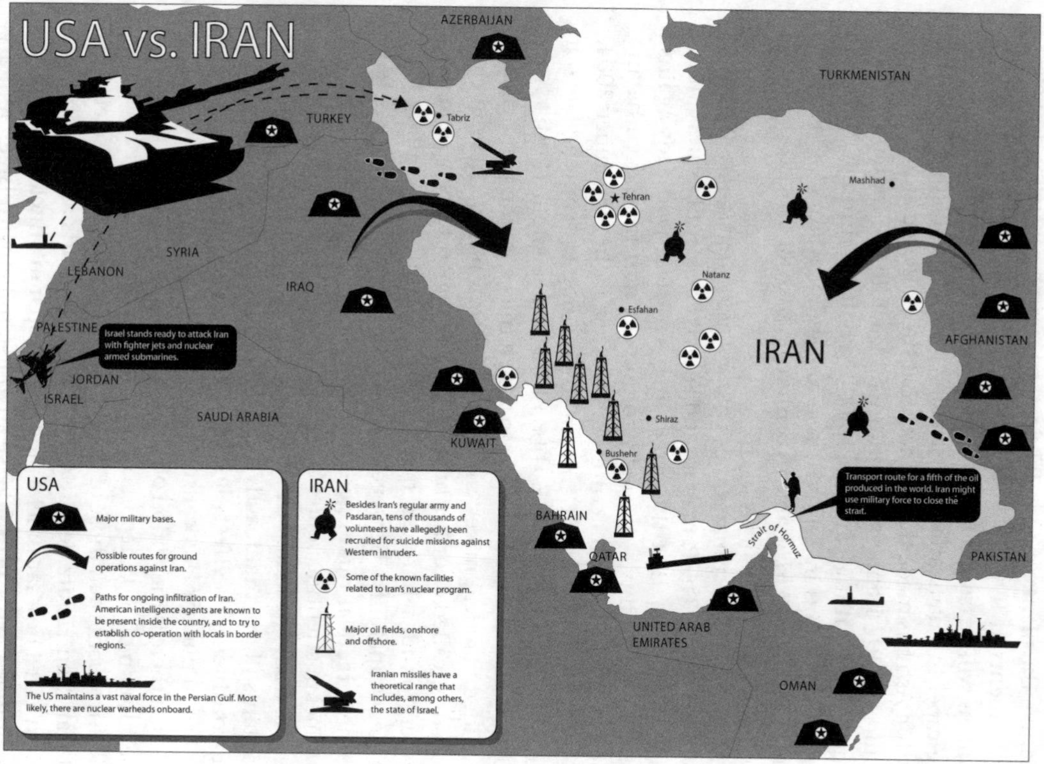

Figure 4 The next battlefield?

Thus, any hour, any day (so is the current mood at this date) Iranians could wake up in an inferno. The targets are all located either in or near population centres. There are the laboratories in Esfahan, the plants outside Tabriz, the research centres and nuclear departments in Tehran ... the guesswork is at full speed: how many civilians will be caught in the flames, without as much as a warning to escape? In a nauseatingly misleading piece of speculation, Timothy Garton Ash has made the estimate that the proposed attack scenario would kill 197 Iranians and injure 533, while the Iranians would avenge with killing "around 10,000" civilians through "massive suicide bombings in Tel Aviv, London and New York". One really must be blinkered to be able to conjure up such statistics concerning the potential killing fields.[7]

More practical estimates speak of *hundreds of thousands* of Iranian civilian victims. The Pentagon, and French President Jacques Chirac, have made clear that the *actual use* of nuclear warheads against Iran is a possibility – allegedly to prevent Iran from even having the *potential* to manufacture such warheads. In November 2004, General John Abizaid of Centcom advised Iran to "contemplate our nuclear capability".[8] The real bombshell in Seymour Hersh's April 2006 revelation was the extent to which the Pentagon planners had included "tactical nukes" in their operation plans. These nuclear weapons, called "bunker busters", are designed to penetrate deep underground, where the Iranians are thought to be hiding their nuclear capability. However, as a united corps of scientists have warned, tactical nukes generate no less radiation than others. A number of scientific bodies have estimated that one to three million people would be killed within weeks of a tactical nuke exploding on Iranian soil, as a radioactive cloud would spread across the Asian subcontinent, its effects lasting for decades.[9] According to these reports, a nuclear Holocaust really could be on the cards.

Then there is the option of unleashing the Zionist attack dog. Since the autumn of 2003, reports of advanced Israeli plans have been even more frequent than those of the US.[10] In December 2005, Israeli chief of staff Dan Halutz declared all diplomatic efforts as stillborn, and when asked how far Israel would go to stop Iran's nuclear ambitions, he quipped, with a confidence anyone familiar with Israeli military personnel can easily imagine: "2,000 kilometres". That is, the distance between Israel and Iran.

Israeli forces have allegedly built a mock-up of the Natanz plant in the Naqab Desert, where they hold exercises on how to "take it out". Pilots, their faces digitally blurred, appear on Israeli television, boasting of their readiness to perform the mission at a moment's notice. To improve their targeting, the Israelis have launched a satellite – incongruously named "Eros" – which enables them to "see people walking in the streets, not to mention cars travelling". In *The Times*, Israeli journalist and former intelligence officer Uzi Mahnaimi first reported of an "initial authorisation" of the operation in March 2005, then claiming that the Israeli Air Force was put on the "highest stage" of readiness in December 2005. He quoted an anonymous source: "It will resemble the destruction of the Egyptian Air Force in three hours in June 1967."[11] Some psychological warfare may be being waged on this front as well, but again, Israel has vested interests in action against Iran.

In July 2004, Moshe Ya'alon, then chief of staff, declared that when it comes to the elimination of the threat from Iran, "we will not rely on others." However, this is – as always – precisely not the case. If Israel attacks Iran, it will use F-15I planes with a combat radius reaching deep into its territory, and bunker-busters penetrating its soil: all recently delivered from the US.[12] Furthermore, with the airspace between Israel and Iran under US control, and with a historically unprecedented degree of military coordination between the two countries, an Israeli attack can only happen at the master's command.

Then there is the scenario that initial air bombardment spirals out of all control. Mahmoud Ahmadinejad has vowed to "cut off the hand of any aggressor" (clearly a favoured metaphor) and representatives of the Iranian armed forces have regularly warned the West with a similar panache.[13] In reality, Iran's military strength is of course miniscule in comparison. None the less, Iran may contemplate some innovative ideas of retaliation – for example, shutting down the Strait of Hormuz with suicide bomber boats, staging sabotage attacks against oil installations in the neighbouring countries, or dispatching the Pasdaran to infiltrate Iraq to ambush US troops. These retaliatory measures might provoke continuous aerial bombardment *and ground operations*.[14] Wars tend to unfold by their own logic. Not even outright occupation should be ruled out.

But all of this has a semblance of madness: would the US really be prepared to ignite such a conflagration? Could it be *so* irrational? In a capitalist society, all tendencies have their counter-tendencies, and the outcome of the dialectic is never known beforehand; this applies to geopolitics as well. The drive to Tehran faces obstacles that might make even real men think twice. With its Shiite arms inside Iraq, Iran has a potential to stab the US in the back in case of war, and with oil markets already tight, the shocks – though temporary – could shatter the American as well as the world economy. One well-aired counter-argument is that the US is too enmeshed in Iraq to be able to fight another war, but this applies primarily to the army; air and naval forces are not as involved. And the drive to Tehran is running on the most powerful of fuels, with a deep underlying material rationale.

However, there has been speculation on war being evaded at the last minute through a "grand bargain". One day, the leaders of Washington and Tehran could shake hands and announce to a startled world that their differences have been resolved: Tehran promising to scrap its nuclear infrastructure, Washington to respect Iran's sovereignty, the historic accord including a road map on how the Iranian economy would be opened to American corporations. And no, not even this scenario can be excluded, at the time of writing. However, this possibility goes against the grain of any developments since the Islamic Revolution, in fact would signal its nullification, and would require a *complete reformation of the power structure of the millionaire mullahs*. So, if they are to be integrated into the global circuits of capital under US patronage, as any petit-nation bourgeoisie, they must first be clobbered.

Only two things are known with any certainty. One: the antagonistic contradiction between the ruling classes of the West and Iran will be resolved somehow in the coming years. Two: this contradiction has already been taking a heavy toll on social life *inside Iran*.

16
A People Caught in the Crossfire

THE EVER-CHANGING WAR

In 1907, just as democracy under the anjumans was beginning to flourish, the British and Russian governments carved up Iran between themselves: the British zone in the south, the Russian in the north. The purpose of the Anglo-Russian Convention was, of course, to ensure control over the country's rich resources, but one barricade had to be removed. That was the democratic revolution. "We are neither minors who need guardians, nor lunatics who need a trustee!", a constitutionalist newspaper reacted to the conspiracy. The two great powers now moved in concert to undermine the achievements of the constitutionalists, of whom they had never been fond. "Persia was being allowed to drift towards anarchy", the British chargé d'affaires wrote in the summer of 1908, declaring that neither Britain nor Russia would tolerate the proliferation of the anjumans. The Majles was ordered to show more respect for the Shah.[1]

This was the immediate background to the royalist counter-revolution in 1908. When the mojahedin and anjuman militants rushed to defend the beleaguered Majles, one of its leaders declared the battle lost beforehand and urged surrender, arguing that "the foreigners believe that the anjumans have taken excessive steps and have removed power from the hands of the Majles and that is why there is such chaos."[2] The contradiction had been there all the time. In the very first months of the first Majles, its delegates had stopped the Shah from accepting a new major loan from Britain and Russia and thus increase the country's debt. They also stopped him from selling commercial monopolies for a pittance to foreigners; henceforth, all such deals had to be approved by the Majles. One of the very first bulletins of the Tabriz anjuman was addressed to European consulates, announcing that all loans and commercial agreements between the Shah and the western powers would be considered null and void.[3]

In the civil war that engulfed the country in 1908, the British and Russian governments worked closely with the Shah. They advised him to write a new constitution where anjumans, freedom of the press,

and popular representation in the Majles would be countermanded.
The response was a radicalisation of the anjuman movement, both in
depth and breadth. In Tabriz, elections were held more frequently, and
provinces outside the control of the royalist forces, such as Esfahan,
Mashhad and Gilan, saw the accession of new local councils. They all
threatened the long-standing commercial interests of the two great
powers, who had just entered an agreement on their insurance.

With encouragement from London, Russia moved armed forces into
northern Iran. In April 1909, they entered Tabriz, and the continuing
revolutionary activities in the region – as in Anzali, where the workers
attacked the Russian merchant who had monopolised fishing –
provided them with ample reasons to stay. The British, meanwhile,
encountered difficulties in the south. Oil had been discovered in
Khuzestan the previous year, and the trade routes and British staff
caravans were constantly pillaged by the tribes inhabiting the region.
In 1910, London issued an ultimatum to the second constitutional
government in Tehran: if safety was not restored for business in the
south, Britain would fill the zone with its own troops.[4]

As the snare tightened around Iran, with Russian forces coming
in from the north and British from the south, revolutionary activity
increased. Mass demonstrations in Tehran protested against the
coordinated assault, and when Russia expanded its occupation in
1911, the streets were filled with armed residents. American constitutionalist Morgan Shuster noted that the anjumans, having played "a
heroic part in Persia's struggle towards free institutions" now "sprang
vigorously into action the moment that their ideas were threatened".
All over the country, European goods and services were boycotted.
People used candles instead of imported lamp oil, shunned Belgian
trams, smashed shop windows displaying Russian commodities, and
boycotted "unclean" British banks.[5]

However, by December 1911, Russian troops were only hours from
Tehran. To avoid occupation of the capital, the Majles dissolved.
Martial law was declared; all anjumans and independent newspapers
were ordered to discontinue. In the north, Russia gave the revolution
a death-blow, stating that "in this case true humanity requires
cruelty. The whole population of Tabriz must be held responsible
and punished."[6] In that city, all councils were liquidated, schools
were shut down, and hundreds of residents and anjuman activists
massacred. The cities of Gilan suffered a similar fate. In the south,
the British authorities temporarily solved their security problems
by employing gullible tribal leaders to quell the unrest, until the

outbreak of the First World War impelled the British to put the region under formal occupation. Together, the two allies coerced the new Iranian cabinet to recognise the Anglo-Russian Convention. Not only was Iranian democracy put to sleep, but the nation was now independent in name only.[7]

With the death of the Constitutional Revolution, the social life of modern Iran was imbued with a fundamental contradiction, which would be seen again and again. By the end of the First World War, revolutionary Russia had renounced all its concessions, cancelled all debts, and begun to support the social movements of northern Iran; from the south, however, the British secured monopoly control over the military, the government and the economy, making southern Iran a de facto protectorate. Popular democratic and guerrilla movements in Azerbaijan and Gilan challenged the occupation *and* the proprietary classes of Iran. Accordingly, the British applauded Reza Shah's rise to power. Rather than holding on to the country as a colony, a situation which was considered unworkable due to the massive popular resistance, the British backed the Shah's suppression of the jangalists and other rebellious movements. British direct control receded to the oil enclaves in Khuzestan.[8]

Then the United States entered the picture. During the Second World War, the US mission assumed control over the whole purview of government activities, from finances and trade to the gendarmerie and the internal security services. It was under US guidance that the autonomous republics of Mahabad and Azerbaijan were quashed, while in the south, Britain tried to curb the growth of the Tudeh party by arming tribal leaders and setting up a right-wing party advocating the return to Islam. At this time, Iran was still extremely underdeveloped. The peasantry's state of health was one of the worst in the world, and not a single city had a modern water system. Nevertheless, the Americans in charge of the Iranian body politic refused to encourage the growth of domestic industry. All their development plans emphasised the technical measures required to increase the production of wool and raw cotton, intended for export markets in the West. Any other industrialisation would be left to the vagaries of privatisation: "Fundamentally the profit motive must be present if efficiency and quality of management and production are to be achieved."[9]

But the Iranian people would not acquiesce to this treatment. That was why Muhammad Mossadeq was elected, in a prototype of parliamentarian democracy. At the pinnacle of Mossadeq's career, after nationalisation, the US ambassador reported that he had "the backing of 95 to 98 per cent of the people of this country".[10] That second spring was again terminated through a conspiracy among two imperialist powers, though the reconquering of Iran required less effort this time than in 1907–11. Afterwards, Mossadeq told his judges: "My only crime is that I nationalised the Iranian oil industry and removed from this land the network of colonialism and the political and economic influence of the greatest empire on earth."[11]

Despotism was the main attribute of the reign of Muhammad Reza Shah, who was held in highest esteem by the West. Hence the general strike and the shora movement were, as we have seen, passionately anti-imperialist. For them, as for the anjumans, for the jangalists, for the Mossadeq supporters and all the other progressive, democratic forces of the preceding decades, foreign masters had to be ejected in order that Iranians become "our own masters".

And how did imperialism react this time? By declaring war on the Islamic Republic. It is delusional to believe this war was for the sake of Iranian democracy. The US opposed the revolution from its outset, before the true character of the new order had been determined. During the US embassy occupation, American and British warships patrolled in the Persian Gulf (as they had done during the oil nationalisation crisis some three decades earlier) and the Carter administration contemplated a combined naval and air assault. But when Saddam Hussein came up with his own invasion plans, the US chose to tacitly encourage him instead, providing him with intelligence on Iranian military capabilities before he struck.

Thus began not only the longest conventional war, but an eight-year-long American engagement with the Iraqi side. In 1981, Washington began to pass on intelligence about Tehran's tactical planning and high-resolution reconnaissance photographs revealing Iranian troop movements to Saddam Hussein, who used them to strike exactly where it hurt the Iranians most. In 1982, the Reagan administration began to give direct financial aid to Iraq, first in the form of agricultural export credits, then through agreements of cooperation on energy, health, telecommunications and other areas, in effect saving the country from economic collapse. In 1983, Reagan signed a directive stating that Iraq's defeat in the war would be "contrary to U.S. interests"; in 1984, he removed Iraq from the list of nations "supporting international terrorism" and added Iran; in 1987, he banned the import of petroleum or any other products from the Islamic Republic. Helicopters were shipped to the Iraqi Air

Force, which was offered assistance by the US Air Force generals in its bombing campaigns.

Finally, in the autumn of 1987, the US engaged in direct combat by sending 22 vessels with 15,000 men aboard – the largest US fleet in action since the Vietnam War – to fight alongside Iraq in the "tanker war" in the Persian Gulf, initiated by Saddam Hussein. The fleet sank the bulk of the Iranian Navy, destroyed oil platforms, and on 3 July 1987, weeks before the end of the war, shot down a civilian airbus. Two hundred and ninety passengers fell from the sky into the waters of the Gulf, among them a woman who was found with her child clutched to her breast even after death. The tragedy was yet another trauma for the Iranian nation; back in the US, the men who fired the missiles were awarded combat action ribbons.[12]

But the Islamic Republic survived. Never faltering through the eight-year-long war, standing up against the combined forces of Iraq, its Arab allies and the US, it broke the pattern of the preceding eighty years. *Iran won the battle for independence, but lost the one for democracy*, and the outcomes were interrelated. With the Islamic Republic emerging from the Iran–Iraq War unbroken as a non-imperialist state, the so far rectilinear contradiction – foreign influence on the one hand, domestic democracy on the other – assumed a new shape. From now on, the dimensions of the mastering of Iran would be tortuously criss-crossed.

AS AN IRANIAN, I WILL RESIST

Hostility to foreign plans to control their country is deeply anchored in the Iranian popular mindset. After the revolution, however, the unceasing material tensions with imperialism have been turned by the Islamic Republic into a rod for punishing groups pushing for democratic reforms. When Ayatollah Khomeini banned strikes as haram, his argument was straightforward and, in a way, cogent. The "citadel of Islam" was in danger because of "the war imposed by the United States and Iraq", increased production was a matter of national survival – and workers on strike would undermine the war effort. According to one estimate, in 1983 there were 80 independent shoras still functioning in Iran; within a year, they were all gone. Ammunition from the front was instrumental in the mowing down of the councils. Workers had a national and religious duty to donate their labour to the war effort, which meant submitting unconditionally to the decisions of the Islamic management in the workplaces. All disruptions were condemned as sabotage.[13]

Saddam Hussein's western-backed aggression initially aroused the patriotic sentiments of the Iranian people, who streamed westwards to defend the borders; even the radical Left, such as the Fedaiyan Minority, dispatched brigades to the battlefield. But the Minority, and other enemies of the Islamic Republic, soon left the front after realising that the Republic had transformed the defence effort into an "anti-people's" war.[14] Indeed, the new rulers had quickly grasped the power of the rod. A similar dynamic has been observed in many wars and revolutions, but in Iran, at the crossroads between extreme dissolution of power through revolutionary organs and a history of exceptional foreign infringements on all sorts of political rights, this dynamic took on a special intensity. All opponents to the Islamic order were as a matter of routine branded as traitors and imperialist-Zionist agents.

When Saddam Hussein offered Iran a truce in 1982, after nearly all the Iraqi troops had been pushed back to the border, Ayatollah Khomeini baulked at the opportunity for peace. He preferred to send his forces to "liberate Karbala" by conducting offensive operations on Iraqi soil. Without the war, the Islamic Republic would lose its most effective weapon against the working class, the ethnic minorities, the leftist guerrillas and all the other opposition groups on the home front.[15]

Exactly the same logic has been mobilised by Mahmoud Ahmadinejad. In the 2005 election campaign, taking place under the threatening skies of a nuclear conflict, he swore to pursue a hard line against the West. Against liberal Iranians who argued for *rapprochement* with the US, he invoked the history no one had forgotten:

When the world formed a united front to fight Iran [during the war with Iraq], our oil could not sell on the international markets and our economy was paralysed, the nation did not extend its hand [to outsiders] for help. Now that we have managed to build the infrastructure [for nuclear energy] and the country has progressed, we do not need to accept any imposed relationship with America. The US severed its ties with the Islamic Republic to harm the Iranian nation and so do the [Iranians] who favour resumption of the ties with the US.[16]

Though empirical data on the subject is unavailable, it seems likely that Ahmadinejad's cocky posture against foreign powers trying to impose their interests on Iran (the second essential component of populism, as defined by Abrahamian) was as important for attracting the electorate as his talk of social justice.

But unlike the latter, the promised policy of pride and resistance on the issue of the nuclear programme has been implemented excessively by President Ahmadinejad. There is a certain social dynamic directing and energising this choice of policy. Again, ironically, we turn to *Oil & Gas Journal* for a rare western insight into what is happening in Iran:

International mischief by Iran nearly always has roots in domestic politics, which from outside the country can be perplexing. In this case, though, Ahmadinejad's desperation is clear enough. As the failure of his reformist predecessor shows, his position lacks power. Supreme Spiritual Leader Ayatollah Ali Khamenei and his cronies run Iran. Ahmadinejad won last year's presidential election partly by promising to help Iran's poor and partly by not being associated with reformists with whom Iranians had lost hope. Ahmadinejad thus presides with little authority over a growing and restive population that largely detests the oppressive theocracy. It's a population that hoped for change through elections but didn't get it and that hasn't been able to effect change in the streets, though not for lack of trying ... So Ahmadinejad injudiciously vents outward, threatening Israel and flouting the West.[17]

With millionaire mullahs blocking any implementation of social reforms, the *inner social contradictions of their country had to be projected outwards*, and to the mullahs' good fortune, the West delivered the perfect object for that projection: a crusade against Iran, lacking all justification in the eyes of its people. The millionaire mullahs have fared well in making nuclear persistence a *popular* project. While no data is available on this subject either, practically all reporters and observers have noted a nearly unanimous support for the nuclear programme, across all ideological boundaries.[18] For the western demands on Iran to forsake its nuclear programme strike all the chords of historic Iranian experience: "Are we minors who need guardians?" Are we an insensate people who do not deserve our own national industry? Should *America* dictate our economic needs? Hell, no! And, as in the very physics of nuclear energy, there is a slippery slope in this popular position. As reported by a BBC correspondent in October 2004: "'Why should the US, Britain and Israel all have nuclear weapons and not us?' asks student Saida Hussein. It is a frequently repeated reaction, but Saida says she is willing to fight for Iran's rights if it comes to war."[19] Threatening Iran is a gift to the millionaire mullahs. For the first time since Saddam Hussein's aggression, they can appeal to both their people's national pride and their fear, and portray themselves as underdogs. So Al-Faqih preaches:

The Islamic Republic of Iran, because of supporting the oppressed and confronting oppressors, is being attacked by the global tyrants. They [America] are trying, in a real but nonmilitary confrontation, through every possible means, to deny the talented Iranian nation of progress and deprive it of existence ... America is like one of the big heads of a seven-headed dragon. The brains directing it are zionist and non-zionist capitalists who brought Bush to power to meet their own interests.[20]

And so President Ahmadinejad responds to the EU's demand that Iran scrap its uranium enrichment programme: "It is an insult to the Iranian nation ... They have talked to us ... as if the Iranian nation was suffering from backwardness, [as if it] was 100 years ago and our country was their colony."[21]

There is a similar political economy to the conspiracy theories and anti-Semitic diatribes that made Ahmadinejad a pariah of the West in late 2005. The Iranian people have experienced more conspiracies, remote control and disguised foreign manipulation than most. The western practices of buying newspapers, mullahs, mobs and other Iranian subjects to impersonate in the roles suiting the West's interests for the moment – one day they would star as bloodthirsty Tudeh activists, the next day obsequious citizens grovelling before the Shah – culminated in the coup of 1953. Afterwards, the head of the CIA's Iran desk remarked: "In Iran you can get a crowd that's fearsome. Or you can get a friendly crowd. Or you can get something in between. Or one can turn into the other."[22] Before the coup, there had been, to name but one example, the machinations of the Russian and British embassies during the Constitutional Revolution; afterwards came the era of Savak and the CIA's undercover control of the streets and the prisons.

As many analysts have noted, this history has naturally left a predisposition for paranoia in the Iranian political psyche.[23] Who really *is* this person, what are the interests he or she serves, where is the foreigner with the big wallet? Among the general experiences of domination, this sense of paranoia has proved invaluable for the Islamic Republic, whose rulers have used it to slander and indict opponents. Ordinary Iranians still have a propensity to see hidden actors behind the scenes of daily politics (including ideas about the mullahs really being US or British puppets), and in combination with the memory of manipulations from Israel, this paranoia can be readily exploited by an astute Islamic politician.

That was precisely what Ahmadinejad tried to do a few months into his shaky presidency. On Al-Quds Day in 2005, at a conference whose theme was "A world without Zionism", Ahmadinejad quoted Khomeini: "as the Imam said, Israel must be wiped off the map". The announcement was received with apoplexy in the western world: newspapers were filled with reports on Iranians trampling Israeli flags, as western leaders attempted to outdo each other in describing their disgust with the president's statement. Analysts generally believed that Ahmadinejad had not expected the world to listen to his words, and would not repeat his assertion. He did the exact opposite: he raised the volume. When the UN Security Council condemned his talk of wiping Israel off the map as "unacceptable", Ahmadinejad responded that the UN's condemnation had been "dictated by the zionist entity in order to ignore the crimes of the zionists and to twist the facts"; when the publication of caricatures of the prophet Mohammed caused chaos in Denmark and the West, he declared that the Zionists were behind their publication in a plot to cover up failures in Palestine. And then came the ultimate provocation. The Holocaust, Ahmadinejad stated, is a myth invented to justify the occupation of Palestine.[24]

During late 2005 and early 2006, utterances of this kind became a theatrical part of nearly every presidential performance. The louder the outcry from the West, the more adamant and outlandish were his statements. When the EU threatened to impose sanctions because of his denial of the Holocaust, Ahmadinejad called for a "scientific" conference on the Nazi Holocaust to expose the sham.

One of the reasons for his theatrical pronouncements was, most likely, to solicit support among lay Shia masses by using images of the conspiracy mentality, and of the Islamic Republic as standing up against the West on behalf of the downtrodden Muslims. A second purpose was probably to prove the anti-Israeli and anti-American credentials of Iran which had fallen into disrepute because of its collaborationist policies in Iraq. The degree to which these two goals were met is not known. But there is no doubt that the third and most important objective was achieved: escalation of the conflict with the West.[25]

As a result of his demagoguery, the governments of Israel and the US have labelled Ahmadinejad the "new Hitler", a position always open for the latest enemy of the West. The *Washington Post* called the president a "certifiable lunatic", Israeli Prime Minister Ehud Olmert branded him a "psychopath of the worst kind", and all the mainstream media used the word "extremist".[26] But that brought him little harm; after all, even Mossadeq had been portrayed as "probably a lunatic" (*Newsweek*), "obsessed with one xenophobic idea" (the *Observer*), "whose fanaticism bordered on the mental" (British Foreign Secretary Herbert Morrison).[27] In spring 2006, the demonisation campaign resorted to shameless forgery, such as the widely published story that Iran was preparing to force its 30,000 Jews (who have one permanent representative in the Majles and are guaranteed constitutional protection) to wear yellow badges. But the association with Nazism was not entirely far-fetched, for Ahmadinejad persisted in speaking about how the Jews are humiliating the German nation for a crime it has not committed, in words difficult to distinguish from those of Germany's own extreme right. The exchange of gifts between the Islamic Republic and Western imperialism had, in a sense, become mutual. Anti-Semitic statements that could be associated with Nazism were the perfect ideological pretence for the crusade against Iran.

The rulers of the Islamic Republic see this situation as an opportunity to *galvanise patriotic support for the regime* and *clamp down on all social and political opposition as treason*. It is the Republic's oldest trick. Thus in the latter part of 2005, Ahmadinejad used threats from the West to increase the general militarisation of Iran. One of his Pasdaran fellows, the current Commander Yahya Rahim Safavi, had already at the time of the 2003 Iraq invasion announced that the American war to dominate Islamic culture made Pasdaran's cultural mission a top defence priority.[28] Now the Pasdaran has taken full advantage of the heightened tension, and while their worst apprehensions have thus far not been fulfilled, Ahmadinejad has indeed used his power to step up repression. Journalism, Internet traffic, philosophers and student activists have been among the victims of attacks, carried out under the pretext of thwarting Western schemes for infiltration.[29] And the West is indeed assisting.

The financial support of Iranian dissidents perceived as pro-Western has been a US policy ever since the revolution. In later years, however, in line with neo-conservative advocacy of the strategy, funds have been sharply increased. In January 2006, after the bus drivers' strike, Washington finally discovered the *trade unions*, whom it quickly decided to support and assist "much as Ronald Reagan did with the trade union organisation Solidarity in Poland in the early 1980s".[30]

On 15 February 2006, senior US State Department official Elizabeth Cheney (daughter of the vice-president), made an "emergency request" to Congress for a *sevenfold* increase in funding. Seventy-five million dollars would now support supposed agents of regime change in "non-governmental bodies that promote democracy, human rights and trade unionism".[31]

For some, this was the kiss of death. Mansour Ossanlou, the imprisoned leader of the Vahed workers, was officially accused of "maintaining relations with and receiving financial support from a foreign power". That was, of course, an attempt to frame him (unless the global labour movement is to be counted as "a foreign power"), but the announcement that the US intended to fund Iranian trade unionists was, again, perfect circumstantial evidence for the prosecutors. In a capital where the bus drivers' actions were put under media blackout, *this* particular news was wired everywhere: the US is trying to meddle in Iranian affairs through unions and strikes.[32]

On 6 May 2006, the appeal court in the province of Kurdistan actually rescinded the harsh sentences meted out to the Saqqez Seven; this climbdown was perceived to be the result of the two-year-long campaign for their cause. One month later, however, they were all ordered to return to the court and face a new charge: "collusion to act against the internal and external security of the country".[33]

The crocodile tears for the labour movement of Iran showed bourgeois politics at its most revolting hypocrisy. In Sweden, one could see at the time of the bus strike a leading liberal politician, Fredrik Malm, known for his hatred towards Iran and Islam, displaying heartfelt solidarity with Iranian workers. From both a proletarian and an Iranian standpoint, all such gestures are of course to be rejected.

There is in this regard one major difference between America's focus on Iranian trade unions and on Poland's in the 1980s. The latter had not had democratic endeavours crushed repeatedly by western powers. Radio Free Europe and a host of similar media channels are trying to repeat their Cold War success by beaming western values into Iran, thereby delivering the most efficient ammunition to the Islamic Republic.[34] When Radio Israel was first to broadcast the violent basiji attack on the 2006 International Women's Day demonstration, those very Iranian feminists found themselves struggling against accusations of being "Western agents".[35] Solidarity and imperialism are forever irreconcilable antitheses.

Thus there circulated in the spring of 2006 a petition among NGOs and dissidents in Iranian cyberspace, where the signatories pledged never to touch the money of the "merchants of blood and oil": "The independent Iranian opposition deems it indecent and politically immoral to accept any aid (financial or otherwise) from the United States or any other government and condemns such aid as a clear insult to the Iranian people."[36] A similar case was made even by the West's universal heroine of human rights in Iran, Shirin Ebadi, who argued in a *New York Times* editorial in early 2005 that Iranian civil society was being strangled by the US's divisive policy of funding with one hand, while warmongering with the other.[37]

From the view of the millionaire mullahs, however, considering that the social unrest of recent years has become more difficult to control, the political climate of foreign intrusion is ideal. If some elder millionaire mullahs initially viewed Ahmadinejad with anguish, they ganged up with him as soon as his presidency was stripped of any social substance that might threaten their position. Ahmadinejad's empty populism and militarisation of Iran, framed in the discourse of defence against western imperialism, proved to be the best available recipe for managing the social crisis; not only harmless to the millionaire mullahs, but a *propitious modulation of their power formula*. With material interests contradictory to those of the US, they had no trouble accepting Ahmadinejad's taunts against the West. Indeed, these were coordinated with the other centres of power within the state, verified by Al-Faqih and echoed by other leading mullahs. As for the nuclear programme, the president has never been in charge of the decision-making. It is subject to a consensual process among the most dominant ringleaders, including, in particular, Hashemi Rafsanjani and his Expediency Council.[38]

The nuclear programme has thus been primed with the social dynamite of today's Iran. At the time of writing, this makes it extremely difficult for the Islamic Republic to back down from confrontation with the West and comply with its demands. The Republic's management of this crisis – projecting domestic unrest outwards, converting foreign aggression to internal repression – has, to date, resulted in a precarious equilibrium. Soon, this brinkmanship might be taken one step too far and bring on an attack from the West. In their own way, the mullahs in that case will have contributed to the attack.

However, not even a war would necessarily be detrimental to the government of Islamic Republic. For the history of imperialist aggression has marked the Iranian people with one more predisposition, as expressed by one of the leaders of the bus workers' strike: "We don't deal with these political issues of nuclear projects and threats from the West. We are a trade union. But, as an Iranian, I can only say that our people has a right to nuclear power, just as we have the right to form trade unions. And as an Iranian, I will resist the enemy if he attacks."[39]

THE POTENTIAL CARVE-UP

In non-partisan analyses of the different war scenarios, it is acknowledged that the Iranian people will put up a fierce resistance. It is expected that they would rally behind the Islamic Republic, as the force leading the defence of the nation. This could, for the first time in decades, generate a huge surge in popular support for the regime.[40] The threadbare, senile discourse of the Islamic Republic, which is preached to nearly empty mosques at Friday prayers in recent years, could all of a sudden find itself reinvigorated. Indeed, the Karbala template has proved its worth before: martyrs may line up again for sacrifice.

The patriotic identification with Iran as an integral, indivisible, independent entity is generally thought to be more deeply rooted than in, say, Iraq, for the Persian cat has been perched between the Caspian Sean and the Gulf for millennia. This implies that resistance could be *even fiercer and more popular* than what has occurred in Iraq, where confessional and tribal identities have impeded national unity. However, on Iran's fringes, there are parts that the US may try to break off. The *national minorities* could be lured into collaboration with an invading West. Their identification with the central government and the nation at large could prove to be tenuous. This strategy is already being pursued by the US. According to a steady trickle of reports from the border areas and the US intelligence community in 2005 and 2006, agents have been busy reconnoitring the political terrain, flirting with potential partners, and recruiting local scouts for joint penetration into the Iranian heartland and establishment of a covert infrastructure of safe houses, front companies and weapons caches.[41] Two areas are mentioned frequently: Kurdistan and Khuzestan.

After the uprising in the summer of 2005, a previously unknown Kurdish guerrilla group began staging daring attacks against Iranian Army and Pasdaran border outposts. No fewer than 120 Iranian soldiers were reported to have been "martyred" by the mysterious group during autumn 2005 and spring 2006.[42] Young Kurds were leaving their villages and towns to join the guerrillas in the mountains, clearly representing the continuation of the civil uprising with other means: Iranian Kurds were using bullets again. However, unlike KDPI and Komele, the two organisations that fought the forces of the Islamic Republic in the 1980s, this one did not emerge from radical politics in Iran. It called itself *Pejak*, or the Kurdistan Free Life Party. It was a new, Iranian branch of the revitalised PKK movement, whose roots are in *Turkish* Kurdistan, up to now the only field for its struggle for autonomy. But the PKK's operational base is located in Iraqi Kurdistan, and so are Pejak's camps and staging posts. They were bombed repeatedly by Iran in early 2006.[43] In addition, Iraqi Kurdistan is also the one corner of the Middle East that is saturated with western intelligence personnel – including those from Mossad.

At the time of writing, there was no evidence of Pejak actively cooperating with western armed forces or security services. In the spring of 2006, however, Pejak posted on its website an open letter to "the rulers of Iran" containing a thinly veiled threat:

As you know, the US and the West have begun to connect with the Iranian opposition, and as everyone knows, oppressed people will use any road to reach freedom. So ask yourself why the opposition is searching for solutions in the US and the West ... Sirs, use your reason and start giving us our rights before others do it ... If you want to evade the destiny of Yugoslavia and Iraq, and show that you really do care about the country, then give the minorities their rights and gather them behind you, without any trickery.[44]

This development was mirrored in Khuzestan. After the Ahwazi intifada, bombs exploded in the provincial capital. In June 2005, just before the presidential election, four explosions within 24 hours killed seven people in Ahwaz. In January 2006 a state bank and a governmental headquarters for natural resources were ripped apart by planted devices on the very same day that Ahmadinejad was scheduled to visit the city; at least eight people were killed. Though the bombers' identity remained a mystery, the Islamic Republic had, of course, no doubts: "Traces of the occupiers of Iraq are evident in the Ahwaz events. They should take responsibility in this regard", ran the statement of Ahmadinejad after he had cancelled his trip to Ahwaz.[45]

In March 2006, anonymous rebels stopped a convoy of governors and high clerics on a remote road in Baluchistan, ordered them out of their vehicles and killed all 21 of them. Iran's new national police chief (a relative of Ahmadinejad) announced that "we have information that the bandits had meetings with British intelligence services". An interior ministry spokesman further explained that "we do not consider this to be a limited regional incident. It is related to the plans that the enemy [that is, the US and Britain] is launching in the bandits' area."[46]

This time these analyses *could be correct*. Just as in the north, across the border from Khuzestan there are areas swarming with CIA and MI6 agents, with obvious interest in stirring turmoil in Iran and attaining the resources required for covert operations; the same holds true for Baluchistan. There is of course *no proof*. But the fact that the Americans and their allies are present in the border regions and seeking ways into the country provides Tehran with tangible material reasons for their accusations of "foreign agents" and "foreign interference".

Kurdistan and Khuzestan are militarised as never before, with war games and military exercises taking place regularly, tanks rolling back and forth over the restive regions. At one such Pasdaran-basiji show of force in Khuzestan in December 2005, commanders said the exercise was needed to "maintain unity, and prepare the basiji forces to combat any threat against the Islamic revolution".[47] According to Yahya Rahim Safavi, the Pasdaran commander: "Domestic and foreign enemies are worried by [evidence of] unity and steadfastness inside the country and try to create ethnic strife in various regions, especially in the border regions, using excuses such as underdevelopment."[48] Underdevelopment: an invented *excuse* for intervention, without footing in Iran's own reality? Fundamentally, it is, as we have seen, nothing but the reverse side of the very uneven development that produces the riches of Tehran. There is, of course, a real risk that the West, for its own purposes, is or will be manipulating the region. The darkest prospect is the US making Khuzestan a second Kuwait: an extremely oil-rich enclave of docile allies. This has been the topic of much speculation on the Internet.[49]

But it does not have to go that far. The damage caused by *any* systematic manipulation of the minorities would be severe, as one of the most important ingredients in Iran's mixture of discontent would be isolated and placed *in contradiction to the majority population*. The minorities' political struggles would be barred from entering into further combinations and synergies with those of the majority, as they have done in all other periods of political transition in Iran.

Worst of all is the spectre of the US carving up the Persian cat. So far, secessionist currents have enjoyed only negligible support, but they could be given a major impetus if the US were to knock on the doors of the minorities, saying: give us a hand in toppling the mullahs, and we will give you mini-states of your own. The prospect is very tempting. Already, disastrously, steps have been taken in this direction. On 30 May 2006, a delegation from the Congress of Iranian Nationalities went to the site of their potential political suicide: the US Senate.[50]

17
Thoughts on a Country of Contradictions

HERE TO STAY

From early 2004, after the bullets had ploughed into the crowd of workers outside the Khatonabad copper plant, an embryonic labour movement was suddenly budding across Iran. The country under the dictatorship of the millionaire mullahs appeared to be a frozen landscape, but in the tiny cracks and crevices beginning to appear, the workers acted to defend their living. In the coming two years, a movement developed which was virtually nationwide in scope; not in the shape of one big union or party, but as strengthening networks of dissent in action.

Unlike the reformist movement of the late 1990s, this one emerged from outside the state apparatus of the Islamic Republic. It was a clarion call for independent, collective struggle for decent lives. After two years of development, it seemed that the call had attracted the attention of other groups in Iranian society as well. Students disillusioned by the experience of reformism were beckoned by the labour movement to try again, as evident in exchanges in the wake of the bus drivers' strike, and the demand for the right to form independent workers' organisations travelled as a catchword across the country and its dissident circles.[1]

The new labour movement was developing as the skies filled with drones and the airwaves with threats from the West. This situation was deliberately exploited by the Islamic Republic against workers' protests, but in autumn 2006, the movement still had refused to fall victim to the stratagem. After 25 years, it was too easy for Iranians to see through the Islamic Republic: "People are used to these kinds of games. We have always been subjected to threats from America, but it does not change our resolve to fight for our rights, now that workers have found their own way", was a typical statement by activists in spring 2006.[2]

The bus drivers' strike took place at the same time as the West's threats were sounding at an ever-higher pitch. May Day 2006 saw another example of workers drawing attention to the more immediate problems of everyday life despite the ominous beat of the war drums.

The government had invited workers from all over the country to the Khane-ye Karegar march in Tehran, in what was supposed to be a show of a nation demanding, as the most important facet of life, nuclear energy. Estimates of the number of demonstrators marching through the capital varied from 20,000 to 100,000. From the podiums, they were exhorted to chant "Nuclear energy is our obvious right!", "Woe! Imam Hussein has been killed!" and other slogans related to the government's international conflicts. However, these slogans quickly petered out, to be replaced with forceful chants of "Employment is our obvious right!", "Organisation is our obvious right!", "Today is a day of mourning, because the Iranian workers are mourning!", "Jailed workers must be freed!", "Workers' representatives must come from amid workers!", and even, alluding to the recent French upheaval against revisions in the labour code: "Look at France, do something for us!". The tumult of the previous year, with scuffles around the microphones, was repeated, forcing security forces to intervene. Workers from Bushehr had brought large drums to drown out the speeches, while the contingent from Qom led the demonstration with a banner saying "End slavery".[3] The most recent trend was rising rank-and-file radicalism inside the Khane-ye Karegar itself; demands for separation from the state were sounded as never before.

At the time of writing, it seems that labour unrest in Iran has come to stay, to grow, and to ripen.

A CALCULATED MADNESS

When George W. Bush hints at attacking Iran, is he mad? If the answer is yes, then only because the underlying motives are mad, for he, and the members of his coven of neo-conservatives, are not alone in their yearning for confrontation. In the 2004 US presidential race, the Democratic candidate Senator John Kerry decried Bush's foreign policy as too *soft* on Iran, stating in his election platform that "a nuclear-armed Iran is an unacceptable risk to us and our allies" and vowing that "we will insure that, under all circumstances, Israel retains its qualitative edge."[4] Kerry's Democratic colleague, Senator Hillary Clinton, running a not-yet-declared race for the White House, denounced Bush in January 2006 for not having released some of the troops mired in Iraq to prepare them for the more urgent task in Iran: "We lost critical time in dealing with Iran because the White House chose to downplay the threats ... Let's be clear about the threat we face. A nuclear Iran is a danger to Israel, to its neighbours and beyond."[5] Other leading Democrats have been equally or even more hawkish, as have leading Labour party figures in Israel.[6]

Sometimes, if only rarely, the oily fuel surfaces in the reports. In April 2006, Seymour Hersh quoted a high-ranking diplomat in Vienna with insight into the transatlantic war discussions: "This is much more than a nuclear issue. That's just a rallying point, and there is still time to fix it. But the Administration believes it cannot be fixed unless they control the hearts and minds of Iran. The real issue is who is going to control the Middle East and its oil in the next ten years."[7]

What looks like madness is truly the product of the calculating machine, that counts barrels of oil, and stocks and shares, but not the lives of Iranians.

THE PLANET'S BEST HOPE

In moral terms, there is no gainsaying Iran's right to a nuclear capability. As the British magazine New Statesman put it: "Given that Israel is the region's only nuclear power – and also spends more than twice as much on defence as its five closest neighbours combined – a conciliator from Mars might conclude that the planet's best hope is to allow Iran to get the bomb, even to give it a helping hand. Only one thing is worse than a balance of terror: an imbalance of terror."[8]

In the current world order, some states are considered worthy of nuclear possession while others are not, the criterion being American assent. This is not a moral measure but its opposite: licence based on pure power. Thus the countries deemed responsible enough to possess the bomb are those with a glorious past or present – Russia, China, France – and/or luxuriate in military alliances with the US – Britain, Israel, India, Pakistan. All of them are in compliance with the universal power of American and global capital. But, again, these countries' possession of nuclear weapons has nothing to do with *moral entitlements*. Rather, the current nuclear order is one of apartheid, and it gives every incentive to states facing threats from the privileged bullies to acquire the bomb. Muhamad ElBaradei, director of the IAEA, has himself declared that "we must abandon the unworkable notion that it is morally reprehensible for some countries to pursue weapons of mass destruction yet morally acceptable for others to rely on them for security – and indeed to continue to refine their capacities and postulate plans for their use."[9]

The only reasonable justification for acquiring nuclear-weapons capability is for use as a defensive deterrent against foreign attack. Today, Iran holds to that position. No other state on earth is living under such presages of unprovoked assault from the most powerful nation in history. If ever there was a case for nuclear deterrence, this is it.

But the current nuclear order is morally bankrupt, as is manifest in the use of the Non-Proliferation Treaty as *carte blanche* for aggression from nuclear powers – possibly even *nuclear aggression* – against states accused of "proliferation". The future of disarmament hinges upon breaking away from this paradigm. It must be replaced with one where the nuclear-weapons powers bear the moral responsibility for reducing the threat.[10] Iran itself has come up with a promising suggestion: a nuclear-free zone in the Middle East – first of all, complete dismantling of Israel's nuclear arsenal, and complete withdrawal of all US nuclear weapons from the region. The proposal enjoys the support of a range of Arab states, but the US has, of course, rebuffed it.[11] There is also a political reason not to resist Iran's possession of a nuclear deterrent. Unlike the threat of war or sanctions against Iran, a nuclear capability would not diminish the prospects of a democratic revolution.[12]

WELLS

The democratic tradition of Iran, however transient its appearances in history, provides a glimpse into the depths of the concept of democracy. In this regard, the anjumans and the shoras eclipse any democratic experiments that have taken place on US soil. Iran and its wells are, in other words, superior to the US as a source of democratic inspiration for humankind.

PSYCHOSIS

Of all the rationales given for attacking Iran, the most ridiculous is this: bomb the Iranians and they will shake off the mullahs. This belief is touted by the most cocksure neo-conservatives. A defence official explained to Seymour Hersh that the Bush administration's planning of an attack "was premised on the belief that 'a sustained bombing campaign in Iran will humiliate the religious leadership and lead the public to rise up and overthrow the government'".[13] This belief, in turn, is premised on the false impression that there is a hugely populous middle class in Iran just waiting to throw themselves into the arms of the West, and that the moment will come "the minute the aura of invincibility which the mullahs enjoy is shattered", as a US government consultant put it.[14] This blurring of reality with one's own hallucinations is psychosis.

EMANCIPATION

Of the roughly three dozen US military interventions after the Second World War, not one has produced a stable democracy. Think of Guatemala, Lebanon, South Vietnam, Nicaragua, Grenada, Somalia, Afghanistan ... [15] In the meantime, the labour movement has time and time again demonstrated its capacity as a protagonist in the overthrow of tyrants: from South Korea to South Africa, from El Salvador to Poland, from Brazil to Nigeria ... [16] Hence the emancipation of Iran must be the act of Iranians themselves, or in other words: either Iran will be liberated by its working class, or it will not be liberated at all.

In the historical landscape of every country, there is a wellspring of popular democracy that can nurture democratic structures. From other parts of the Middle East, one could mention the *lijan shabiya* or popular committees of Palestine, the *naqabat muhannia* or professional unions of Iraq, the *shuras* or councils of Kurdistan. These are the fountains of indigenous democracy, the alternatives to synthetic institutions imposed from the outside by aircraft carriers or merchant ships; indeed, these alternatives present the only hope for a truly democratic Middle East. With such a profusion of this resource, the Iranian people should be left to construct functional pumps on its own.

PROTECTING A DYNAMIC IRAN

While Afghanistan and Iraq were, politically speaking, dormant at the time of US attack, Iran is vibrant with political commotion. In comparison with these two recent casualties of imperialism, Iran is, furthermore, a highly advanced, compactly layered, class society. It is with the dynamic structure of this society that US aggression will, and indeed already does, interfere and interact. If the worst scenarios come true, much of that dynamic will simply be destroyed, for faced with massive aggression, the demands of a decent, ordinary life – a permanent contract, a wage paid in time, two pairs of shoes

– become trifles to be put aside; under a nuclear cloud, class politics is irrelevant. If a nuclear attack does take place, it will bury the democratic tradition of Iran six feet under. Launched under the pretext of bringing democracy to Iran it would desecrate the concept of democracy.

What is at stake here is not only the future of Iran. The victory of the Islamic current of the Iranian revolution was the "big bang" of Islamic politics. It gave an immensely strong stimulus to other projects of Islamism in the Middle East, both Shia and Sunni – but Khomeini's revolution was built on the bones of another, deeper one. Had that revolution prevailed, the political winds of the last decades in the Middle East and the Muslim world at large would probably have blown in an entirely different direction. Here, we are back at the contra-factual questions as vertiginous as those that can be posed on the interwar period in Europe.

But Iran retains the potential to turn the tide. If the fundamental failure of Islamism to enfranchise the mostazafin were to be exposed through a domestic transformation, originating from the experience of the last three decades, the effects would once again fan out across the region. Hence the threats of a war against Iran prove – once again – how utterly destructive the western domination of the Middle East is on an ideological level. That domination is by far the most powerful cause of reaction and stagnation in the region.

As for the Iranian labour movement, it has already exposed the lie of the united umma, which is revealed to be split in classes. Thus, the labour movement has also contributed to the exposition of the lie, so cherished in the West, of a clash of civilisations, of "One Muslim World" with an insane hatred against everyone in the West. Thus when more than 10,000 striking bus drivers in Tehran were beaten and harassed, no photos and few reports appeared in the western media; but when 400 state-employed Pasdaran members demonstrated outside the Danish embassy in Tehran in protest against the Muhammad cartoons at exactly the same time, the images were ubiquitous.[17] Fortunately, important sections of the global labour movement, including in the West, knew how to respond to the strike action, thereby highlighting how the world is *really* divided.

DILEMMAS AND DIVISIONS UNDER THE ROCKET FLARES

If the US, or Israel, or some other combination of western armies enters Iran, should progressive forces line up with the Islamic

Republic in defence? Here, we see the same dilemma progressives were faced with in 1978–79, but in a more complicated form. For in situations of *direct military control*, of invasion and occupation, the choice of repelling the home-grown oppressors in one's own country tends to be politically impossible.[18] In the Middle East, these are the lessons from countries that have suffered military occupation: in Palestine, Lebanon and Iraq, the option of desisting from all cooperation with Islamic resistance simply is not viable. Hamas and Jihad, Hizbollah, the Sadr movement and the Sunni resistance actually engage in *securing the premise for all political progress*, that is, freedom from occupation. No Palestinian leftist will advocate a strategy of denouncing Hamas and Jihad; on the contrary, all secular armed resistance groups in the West Bank and the Gaza Strip have entered into tactical cooperation with their brigades, while at the same time maintaining their own agendas for domestic politics. The very experience of life under military occupation – one that has not applied to Iran for half a century – makes such strategies of cooperation intuitively incontrovertible. In addition, recent events in Palestine and Iraq, the latter in particular, have proved the extreme danger and destructiveness of infighting under conditions of military occupation. An occupied people *must unite against the enemy*.

The difference in the case of western troops on Iranian soil, or hovering permanently in its airspace, would of course be that the Islamic resistance would be waged by a state apparatus that has *been in power for decades*. Its record would put Iran's secular forces in a totally puzzling predicament that the Palestinians, Lebanese and Iraqis have been spared: fight together with the domestic oppressors? Fight both them and the foreign ones at the same time? Fight alongside the armed forces of the Islamic Republic, in operational alliances, while building resistance structures with independent leaderships and social programmes to vie for the souls of the struggling nation?

Luckily, as of spring 2006, all this is speculation. Hopefully, the conflict between Iran and the West will somehow be defused, and the Iranians will be left to construct their own road to freedom and justice. But for all eventualities, some certainties can be stated:

- Iranian control over Iranian resources is of paramount importance for Iranian social progress. In this regard, the actual achievements of the revolution must be defended.
- The Iranian working class has learnt that a national bourgeoisie is not much better than a comprador one, if it is better at all.

Otherwise stated: anti-imperialism is a necessary condition of emancipatory politics in the periphery, but it is never sufficient; the moment imperialism is defeated, a thousand new issues arise.

- In the case of a military attack against Iran, the restitution of the Islamic Republic can never be a goal; only the restitution of sovereignty can. The ongoing victimisation of Iran must not tempt an anti-war movement in the West and other parts of the world to fall into the trap of minimising the defects of the Islamic Republic, for these are terrible.[19] Under all conditions, solidarity should be directed to none other than the masses of ordinary, working Iranians.

An invasion of Iran would bring on not a winter, but a lava stream scorching the country. How it would affect the seeds and wellsprings of democracy, if they survive at all, one cannot know. But one thing is for certain. Unlike the B-52s, F-16s and bunker-busting bombs that fall from the sky, the democracy of labour grows from below.

Afterword

In the summer of 2006, long-standing tensions between Israel and the Lebanese-based Hizbollah erupted along the Israel-Lebanon border, plunging the area into war for 34 days. The spark that lit this conflagration was an audacious operation on 12 July 2006, dubbed "Truthful Promise", in which a Hizbollah command crossed the border into Israel, captured two Israeli soldiers and killed another six in the ensuing battles. Hizbollah hoped to use the captured Israeli soldiers as bargaining chips to secure the release of Lebanese prisoners in Israeli jails. However, Israel's response was not to engage in "indirect negotiations", as the secretary-general of Hizbollah Sayyed Hassan Nasrallah called for, but to launch an all-out military assault on the Lebanese nation in general and the Hizbollah movement in particular. Israel's stated goal was the complete eradication of Hizbollah as a viable force. This goal was fully embraced by the Bush administration, which stood by Israel in its war against "evil" and blocked all diplomatic initiatives to bring about a quick cease-fire. It was time to get the job done.

But Israel did not fare well. The war soon turned out to be "the most unsuccessful we have ever had", in the words of Israeli historian Ze'ev Sternhell.[1] The overall goal of eliminating Hizbollah was never within reach, and as this became obvious, Israel replaced it with a series of more modest aims, such as pushing all enemy combatants to the north of the Litani River, killing Nasrallah or destroying Hizbollah's missile stockpiles – but none of these objectives was achieved. On the contrary, Hizbollah defeated the Israeli Defence Forces on the tactical battlefield.

One key to this astounding victory, besides Hizbollah's motivation, knowledge of the terrain, and weaponry, was the neutralisation of one of their rival's most formidable weapons: the Israeli-built Merkava tank, which has a reputation as the most impenetrably armoured model in the world. As the Merkavas advanced into Lebanese territory to rout Hizbollah, small teams of resistance fighters would suddenly pop out of their hidden bunkers – and disable the tanks. In one of many astonished reports about Hizbollah's performance published in the western media during the war, *The Times* wrote:

Individual Hezbollah fighters carry the shoulder-fired RPG29, a more advanced version of the RPG7 beloved of guerrilla groups since the 1960s. It has a dual-purpose warhead. "The first punches through the armour and the second is aimed at the personnel," Elias Hanna, a retired Lebanese general, said. Hezbollah's ability to knock out Merkava tanks has frustrated the traditional Israeli military doctrine of rapid armoured thrusts deep into enemy territory.[2]

The traditional Israeli military doctrine was thus found wanting. No significant Hizbollah strongholds were conquered in this brief war; the IDF was kept at bay near the border.

This outcome brought unprecedented anxiety and panic to the Zionist entity, which was shaken to its very core. In the midst of the fighting, one Israeli journalist, Shlomo Ganur, told Al-Jazeera: "Israel cannot allow anyone to undermine its military capability; it cannot, as a state, as a people, or as an entity in this region, have its prestige challenged." But this is exactly what happened. After the war, in one typical comment in *Ha'aretz*, Reuven Pedatzur wrote:

This is not a mere military defeat. This is a strategic failure whose far-reaching implications are still not clear. And like the boxer who took the blow, we are still lying dazed on the ground, trying to understand what happened to us. Just like the Six-Day War led to a strategic change in the Middle East and established Israel's status as the regional power, the second Lebanon war may bring about the opposite. The IDF's failure is eroding our national security's most important asset – the belligerent image of this country, led by a vast, strong and advanced army capable of dealing our enemies a decisive blow if they even try to bother us … In Damascus, Gaza, Tehran and Cairo, too, people are looking with amazement at the IDF that could not bring a tiny guerrilla organization (1,500 fighters according to the military intelligence chief, and a few thousand according to other sources) to its knees for more than a month, the IDF that was defeated and paid a heavy price in most of its battles in southern Lebanon.[3]

Another party to this game watched the results with increasing uneasiness and frustration: the Bush administration. That, in turn, heightened fears in Israel. David B. Rivkin Jr and Lee A Casey wrote in *Ha'aretz*:

Israeli leaders ought to worry more about a different scenario, one in which American policymakers, analyzing the Israel Defence Forces' failure to defeat Hezbollah after 30 days effort, lose their faith in Israel's ability to "get the job done" on issues of shared strategic interest. Should the IDF lose its aura of invincibility in American eyes, Israel's perceived value as an ally could decline sharply … The hard truth is that Israel must appear to be, and be, a winner in order to remain a valuable strategic partner for the United States ... Israel's inability to defeat Hezbollah, at least at the tactical and operational level, makes it look less like a valuable ally and more like a liability. Any conclusion of the current conflict on terms that leave Hezbollah unbowed would further undercut the West's credibility, and would squander much of the deterrent effect of Israel's past military successes from 1948 to the present.[4]

In other words: Hizbollah threatened to tear apart the whole strategic map of the Middle East.

Behind this confrontation lurked Iran. Israel routinely explained every setback during the war by pointing to Tehran. The lethal "dual-purpose" anti-tank missiles were traced to Iranian suppliers, as was the communication equipment used by Hizbollah to eavesdrop on Israeli military radio. Ze'ev Schiff, a semi-official military analyst, early in the war reported that

... well-placed sources in Israel argue that Iran is behind the decision to attack Israel [sic] and that Tehran influenced the timing of the Hezbollah attack in which two soldiers were abducted last Wednesday. Iran is Hezbollah's main arms supplier, including long-range rockets and missiles of the kind that struck an Israeli destroyer ... on Friday night. This in addition to massive transfers of cash ... Some [Iranian] advisers, all members of the Revolutionary Guard, remain [on Lebanese soil]. These are mainly responsible for instruction in the use of long-range rockets, the operation of Iranian-made unmanned aerial vehicles and also in planning and combat operations training.[5]

Israeli Prime Minister Ehud Olmert agreed with this analysis, declaring that "our enemy is not Hezbollah, but Iran, which employs Hezbollah as its agent".

The idea of a proxy war waged by Iran against Israel was readily adopted by much of the western media and political establishment – but it was disputed by experts on the Hizbollah movement. Though once a creation of Pasdaran, Hizbollah has since completely detached itself from Iran, evolving into a strictly Lebanese national movement. There is no evidence that it takes any orders from Tehran. Iranian cash represents, even by the highest estimates, a fraction of Hizbollah's funds, and rumours of Iranian presence on the battlefield were never verified, but vehemently denied by Sayyed Hassan Nasrallah. The only material link that could be discerned (and was likewise acknowledged by Nasrallah) was arms supplies: some of Hizbollah's weapons were indeed from Iran. And considering the impact of these weapons, that seemed to be enough to label Hizbollah yet another party to the "axis of evil".

Thus the outcome of the war between Israel and Hizbollah had immediate bearings on the tensions between Iran and the West. However, Iran was part of the picture even *before* the outbreak of conflict. In the later weeks of the war, the western media revealed that Israel had been planning for confrontation with Hizbollah for more than a year, waiting patiently for a pretext to put it in motion. "Of all of Israel's wars since 1948, this was the one for which Israel was most prepared", Gerald Steinberg, professor of political science at Bar-Ilan University, told the *San Francisco Chronicle*.[6] In another revealing article, Seymour Hersh detailed how the Israeli preparations were coordinated with the Bush administration:

> President Bush and Vice-President Dick Cheney were convinced, current and former intelligence and diplomatic officials told me, that a successful Israeli Air Force bombing campaign against Hezbollah's heavily fortified underground-missile and command-and-control complexes in Lebanon could ease Israel's security concerns and also serve as a prelude to a potential American preemptive attack to destroy Iran's nuclear installations, some of which are also buried deep underground.

The US strategic interest in such a war was twofold. First, Hizbollah was perceived as a "fifth column" of the Iranian military forces, stationed on Lebanese soil and ready to respond to any attack on Iran by pummelling Israel with missiles. Therefore, the US's road to Tehran needed to be cleared of the Hizbollah obstacle. Second, south Lebanon would serve as a testing ground. Hersh again:

> "The big question for our Air Force was how to hit a series of hard targets in Iran successfully," the former senior intelligence official said. "Who is the closest ally of the U.S. Air Force in its planning? It's not Congo – it's Israel. Everybody knows that Iranian engineers have been advising Hezbollah on tunnels and underground gun emplacements." ... The Israeli plan, according to the former senior intelligence official, was "the mirror image of what the United States has been planning for Iran." ... Cheney's point, the former senior intelligence official said, was "What if the Israelis execute their part of this first, and it's really successful? It'd be great. We can learn what to do in Iran by watching what the Israelis do in Lebanon."[7]

So what did they learn? The experience seems contradictory. On the one hand, the fact that tiny Hizbollah vanquished mighty Israel signalled that a war against Iran, with its recently refined guerrilla tactics, could prove to be a disaster of unimaginable strategic proportions. On the other hand, the strength of the resistance reinforced one basic US perception of the Middle East: western, US and Israeli interests in the region will never be secured until Iran undergoes regime change. As the time of writing, the drive towards regime change seems dominant. After a lull, the thinly veiled threats and the odds against a coming showdown are once again running high.

On the other front, inside Iran, violent confrontations occurred in the shadow of the war in Lebanon. Armed forces attacked striking carpet workers in the northern province of Mazandaran. A union leader in Kermanshah was imprisoned after several strikes in the western city. Security agents ransacked the homes of Iran Khodro workers in Tehran, just after they had ended a successful 40-day hunger strike against wage cuts, while reports of rapidly falling support for Ahmadinejad's handling of domestic issues (though not for his foreign policies) surfaced in the international media. On 12 October, international news agencies quoted Alireza Mahjoub, secretary-general of Khane-ye Karegar: "Close to 200,000 workers in 500 factories have not received any salary for months. Some of these workers have been waiting for their wages for about 50 months."

Stockholm, late September 2006.

Notes

PREFACE

1. Ali Akbar Dareini: "Conflicting Stories Given for Iran Blast", *The Guardian*, 16 February 2005 <www.guardian.co.uk>.
2. The original report can be read in Farsi (and, of course, in Swedish) at <www.arbetaren.se/tema>.

1 MAY DAY IN THE CHILDREN'S PARK

1. The account of the Saqqez events is based on visits to the city and interviews with numerous participants, including those who stood trial for the demonstration.

2 AFTER SPRING COMES WINTER

1. Afary, pp. 63–78. The account of the constitutional revolution is based on Afary. For an insightful overview of the earlier history of Persia/Iran, see Keddie.
2. Afary, pp. 89–115.
3. Quoted in ibid., pp. 105–106.
4. Quoted in ibid., p. 170.
5. Ibid., pp. 280–82.
6. See Dailami.
7. Keddie, pp. 73–104.
8. After meeting Nazi dignitaries in Tehran, one of Reza Shah's newspapers declared: "The cardinal goal of the German nation is to attain its past glories by promoting national pride, creating a hatred of foreigners, and preventing Jews and foreigners from embezzlement and treason. Our goals are certainly the same." Quoted in Kinzer, p. 45.
9. Ibid., pp. 110–12; Moghadam (1996), pp. 69–71; Behrooz (2000), pp. 4–6, 144–5.
10. Moghadam (1996), p. 71.
11. Kinzer, pp. 144–87.
12. The CIA's postmortem quoted in ibid., p. 188.
13. Behrooz (2000), pp. 4–16; Kinzer, p. 179.
14. Bayat (1987), pp. 59–65; Moghadam (1996), pp. 73–80; Parsa, pp. 141–2.
15. Quotations from Parsa, p. 143.
16. Quoted in Kurzman, p. 14. Cf. Sasan Fayazmanesh: "Iran and the 'Experts'", *Znet*, 25 July 2005, <www.zmag.org>.
17. Parsa, pp. 144–6; Bayat (1987), pp. 79–80.
18. Bayat (1987), p. 82. On the Esfahan steel strike, see Parsa, pp. 148–9.

19. Parsa, pp. 157–64; Bayat (1987), pp. 80–81; cf. Kurzman, pp. 78–9.
20. Bayat (1987), p. 91.
21. Ibid., pp. 92–5; Parsa, pp. 151–3.
22. Parsa, pp. 268–9.
23. Bayat (1987), p. 111.
24. Ibid., pp. 109–12.
25. Bayat (1987), pp. 138–40; Goodey, pp. 6–8; Rahnema, pp. 82–3.
26. Bayat (1987), p. 8.
27. E.g. Azad; Goodey; Moghadam (1988); Rahnema; Moghadam (1996); Parsa, pp. 267–75; Moaddel, pp. 231–41; Poya, pp. 125–8.
28. Goodey, p. 5.
29. Bayat (1987), pp. 121–3.
30. Quoted in ibid., p. 126.
31. Poya, pp. 126–8.
32. Bayat (1987), pp. 107–24; Moghadam (1988), pp. 198–9. For a discussion of the crucial inclusion of technical staff in the shoras, see Rahnema.
33. Bayat (1987), p. 125.
34. Ibid., p. 123.
35. Ibid., p. 111–12.
36. Moghadam (1988), p. 196.
37. Bayat (1997), pp. 53–5, 89–91. There is a most striking similarity between the shora-ye mahallat and the *lejna shabiye*, or "popular committees", of the next mass uprising to occur in the Middle East: the first intifada. The best account of the lejna shabiye available in English is Robinson.
38. For the komitehs, squatters and unemployed, see Bayat (1997), pp. 51–67, 122–6; for the peasants, see Azad; Behrooz (2000), 108–11; Parsa, pp. 260–62; Koohi-Kamali, pp. 181–2.
39. Moghadam (1988), p. 185.
40. Quoted in Parsa, pp. 161–2.
41. Bayat (1997), pp. 90–91; Parsa, pp. 293–4. Taleqani died a natural death.
42. Bayat (1997), pp. 123–5; Parsa, pp. 163, 271.
43. Rahnema, pp. 83–9; Bayat (1987), pp. 88–91.
44. For a close study of the Fedaiyan, see Behrooz (2000), pp. 48–70, 105–20.
45. On these events, see Parsa, pp. 237–47; Behrooz (2000), pp. 68–9.
46. Behrooz (2000), p. 105. Behrooz tells the story of how five guerrilla teams from different factions, after the armed resistance against the Islamic Republic had begun in late 1981 and early 1982, were fighting the same enemy forces in the very same mountains – and refusing to establish even a tactical coordination among themselves. The outcome was a foregone conclusion. Ibid., p. 162.
47. Ibid., pp. 159–62.
48. Goodey, p. 8; Behrooz (2000), pp. 150–52; cf. Bayat (1987), pp. 148, 194. On the Fedaiyan's early shoraism, see Azad, pp. 17–18.
49. Behrooz (2000), pp. 162–63; Bayat (1987), pp. 146–48.
50. Behrooz (2000), p. 154. As Behrooz (2000) shows, the Left parties remained based on students and the intelligentsia, and never really

found a foothold in the working class, ibid., pp. 153–8; cf. Mirsepassi, pp. 240–44.

51. Quoted in Parsa, p. 270.
52. Quoted in Azad, p. 19.
53. Quoted in Moaddel, p. 236.
54. Parsa, p. 272; Bayat (1987), p. 115; cf. Rahnema, pp. 72–3, 84–5.
55. Quoted in Bayat (1987), p. 109; cf. p. 88.
56. Azad, pp. 19–20; Moghadam (1996), p 87.
57. Bayat (1987), pp. 131–9, 151–2, 186–9; Moghadam (1988), pp. 202–206; Parsa, pp. 273–5.
58. Quoted in Parsa, p. 273. Cf Bayat (1987), p. 132.
59. Bayat (1987), pp. 107–15, 157; Moghadam (1988), pp. 201–205.
60. Quoted in Parsa, p. 249.
61. Bayat (1987), pp. 157–8.
62. Interview.
63. Bayat (1997), pp. 71, 91–5, 127–8.
64. Interview.
65. Interview.

3   THE SWORD THAT CHOPPED OFF AMERICA'S HAND

1. See Parsa. Though new accounts of the revolution are published nearly every year, Parsa's study remains the most penetrating.
2. Ibid., p. 2; Halliday (1988), pp. 35–6. The numbers on participation rates from Kurzman, pp. viiii–viii. For an appraisal of the psychological importance of the guerrilla struggle in 1970s, however, see Behrooz (2004), pp. 202–203.
3. Keddie, p. 232; Bayat (1987), pp. 93–5.
4. Parsa, p. 153.
5. Quoted in Parsa, pp. 157, 162.
6. Keddie, pp. 148–65; Amid & Hadjikhani, pp. 23–30.
7. Keddie, pp. 158–64; Ehteshami (1995), pp. 82–5.
8. Bayat (1987), pp. 80–81.
9. See Parsa, pp. 148–64. Italics added.
10. Ibid., p. 166.
11. Hiro, pp. 2–4; Moaddel, pp. 105–107; Parsa, p. 92.
12. Hiro, pp. 4–7; Afary, pp. 50–59; Moaddel, pp. 113–16.
13. Quoted in Moaddel, p. 120.
14. Ibid., pp. 118–21; Parsa, pp. 102–106, 118.
15. Keddie, p. 30; Moaddel, pp. 108, 116–18; Hiro, pp. 7, 11.
16. Keddie, p. 225; Parsa, pp. 108–25.
17. Parsa, pp. 201–205, 210–18; Mirsepassi, pp. 233–4; Behrooz (2000), pp. 136–7.
18. Parsa, pp. 215–19; Abrahamian (1991), pp. 113–15.
19. Quoted in Moaddel, p. 146.
20. Quotations from Saad-Ghorayeb, pp. 59–60. One insightful analysis of velayat al-faqih and Khomeinism in general is Abrahamian (1991).

21. This process is analysed in detail in Parsa, pp. 201–19; Moaddel, pp. 130–63. While Parsa stresses the "vacuum theory" – that the mosques assumed their role because there was no other infrastructure – Moaddel explicitly rejects it and lays all emphasis on the superior, inherent revolutionary potential and strength of Shia discourse. These two factors should not, however, be regarded as mutually exclusive, but rather as complementary.
22. Keddie, pp. 241–5; Bayat (1997), p. 94.
23. Moaddel, p. 201.
24. Hiro, pp. 8–17; Parsa, p. 216.
25. Ehteshami (1995), p. 207; see further pp. 82–7, 207–208; Moaddel, p. 261.
26. Parsa, pp. 275–7; Hiro, pp. 13–16; Moaddel, pp. 224, 244–53; Ehteshami (1995), pp. 86–90; Abrahamian (1991), pp. 115–17.
27. Ehteshami (1995), p. 124.
28. Bayat (1997), pp. 39–51, 99; Khomeini quotations from Abrahamian (1991), p. 114.
29. Bayat (1997), p. 56; Parsa, p. 298
30. Parsa, pp. 277–83; Moaddel, pp. 234–7; Farhi, pp. 104–105. On the consumer cooperatives, see Bayat (1997), pp. 52–3, 96–8.
31. Quoted in Hiro, p. 18.
32. Cf. Halliday (1988), p. 41; Moaddel, p. 254.
33. Abrahamian (1991), p. 118.
34. Parsa, pp. 296–8.
35. Moghadam (1987), pp. 12–13.
36. Quotation from Alavi, pp. 46–7.
37. Quotations from Behrooz (2000), p. 127; Moghadam (1987), p. 23.
38. Quotation from Behrooz (2000), p. 115.
39. Ibid., pp. 150–52.
40. Ibid., p. 126. However, it should be remembered that the groups that actually participated in the construction of the new state apparatus did not belong to the Left, but to the liberal movement, which occupied posts in early cabinets and even produced the two first presidents of the Islamic Republic (Mehdi Bazargan and Abolhasan Bani-Sadr). No Left groups were so close to Islamic power, and no liberals opposed it with the kind of resistance that the radical Left eventually did. Cf. Matin-Asgari, p. 48; Mirsepassi, p. 246.
41. Behrooz (2000), pp. 104, 112–13; Moghadam (1987), pp. 19–20.
42. See, e.g., Halliday (2004), pp. 30–33; Mirsepassi, pp. 237–8; Behrooz (2000), pp. 137–8.
43. Moghadam (1988), pp. 205–206; Rahnema, p. 85.
44. E.g., Halliday (1987), p. 37.

4 THE MILLIONAIRE MULLAH BONANZA

1. On the event, see Hiro, pp. 184–9; Kizner, p. 49.
2. For basics on the petroleum assets of Iran, see Energy Information Administration: "Iran Country Analysis Brief" <www.eia.doe.gov/emeu/cabs/iran.html>. Edition used here: March 2005. See further below.

3. See Ehteshami (1995), pp. 79–81, 93–6, 115–19.
4. Energy Information Administration: "OPEC Revenues Fact Sheet" <www.eia.doe.gov/cabs/OPEC-Revenues/OPEC.html> (accessed 14 January 2006).
5. Alizadeh (2003), p. 272.
6. E.g., Badiei & Bina, p. 1.
7. Jalali-Naini, pp. 96–97, 104; Dadkhah, p. 87.
8. Jahangir Amuzegar: "Iran's Stabilization Fund: A Misnomer", *Middle East Economic Survey*, Vol. XLVII, No. 47, 21 November 2005 <www.mees.com>.
9. Cf. Ehteshami (1995), pp. 78–81, 120; Ghorashi, pp. 80–82.
10. Ehteshami (1995), p. 212.
11. Amid & Hadjikhani, pp. 53–9; cf. Ehteshami (1995), pp. 210–14. On the sanctions, see Fayazmanesh.
12. Amid & Hadjikhani, pp. 49–51, 67; Ehteshami (1995), pp. 92–93, 210–214. After the revolution, the share of capital goods in Iranian imports actually increased somewhat, while that of consumer goods decreased; the latter being a function partly of the destruction of comprador consumer patterns, partly of protection of Iranian consumer goods industries. See Amid & Hadjikhani, p. 49.
13. Khajehpour, pp. 103–104. This was expressed in a remarkable increase in the share of non-oil exports: in 1979, non-oil products represented less than 10 per cent of Iranian export, in 1999 more than 50 per cent; Amid & Hadjikhani, p. 55. This, however, has changed since then, due to the rising value of oil exports.
14. CIA: "The World Economic Factbook: Iran" <www.cia.gov.cia/publications/factbook> (accessed 16 January 2006).
15. *Iran Daily*: "Auto Projects Under Review", 8 November 2004 <www.iran-daily.com>.
16. *Persian Journal*: "Iran Khodro exports top $115m", 18 December 2005; *Persian Journal*: "Iran Khodro to ship Samand cars to Russia", 5 January 2006; *Persian Journal*: "Iran Khodro eyes world market", 10 January 2006; *Persian Journal*: "Iran Ranks 11th Among World Automobile Makers", 28 February 2003, all <www.iranian.ws>; Nicholas Birch: "Iran's rich and well-connected favour economic status quo", *Daily Star*, 12 August 2003 <www.dailystar.com.lb>; Amid & Hadjikhani, pp. 80–81.
17. *Payvand*: "Iran: Foreign investments in industry exceeds $5 billion in third development plan", 26 June 2005 <www.payvand.com/news>; Jahangir Amuzegar: "Iran's Stabilization Fund: A Misnomer", *Middle East Economic Survey*, Vol. XLVII, No. 47, 21 November 2005 <www.mees.com>.
18. *Iran Daily*: "Challenges to Economic Takeoff", 19 December 2004 <www.iran-daily.com>. Cf. Amid & Hadjikhani, p. 92.
19. Amid & Hadjikhani, p. 80.
20. Ibid., pp. 66–7, 80–81.
21. *Iran Daily*: "Improving Productivity", 25 August 2005 <www.iran-daily.com>.
22. Interviews with carpet weavers; *Iran Daily*: "Giving Textiles a Bigger Share", 15 January 2005 <www.iran-daily.com>. On the amount of smuggling, see Amid & Hadjikhani, p. 50, and below.

23. Visits to homes of seamstresses and weavers in Kurdistan and Esfahan.
24. Visits to clay mills in Azerbaijan and Tehran.
25. Salehi-Esfahani, p. 136. On uneven development under the Shah, see e.g. Moghadam (1988), pp. 189–92.
26. Amid & Hadjikhani, p. 3.
27. Quotations from Khajehpour, p. 95; Hiro, p. 199.
28. Quotations from Abrahamian (1991), p. 119; Ehteshami (1995), p. 101.
29. Ehteshami (1995), pp. 101–110; Khajehpour, pp. 96–8; Keddie, pp. 263–5.
30. Ehteshami (1995), pp. 215, 220; cf. pp. 114, 123, 208–209.
31. Alizadeh (2003); Dadkhah, pp. 90–91; Keddie, p. 265.
32. Amid & Hadjikhani, pp. 48, 61, 76; *Iran Daily*: "Automakers Blamed for Sluggish Car Imports", 21 September 2004 <www.iran-daily.com>.
33. Amid & Hadjikhani, pp. 36–43; *Iran Daily*: "Auto Ambitions", 23 September 2004 <www.iran-daily.com>.
34. Heritage Foundation: "2006 Index on Economic Freedom, Country: Iran", <www.heritage.org/research/features/index/> (accessed 10 April 2006).
35. Quoted in ibid.
36. *Payvand*: "Iran: Foreign investments in industry exceeds $5 billion"; Kambiz Foroohar: "Rafsanjanis Are Iran's Power Brokers for Investors", *Bloomberg*, 21 April 2006 <www.bloomberg.com>; *Iran Daily*: "Auto Projects Under Review"; Energy Information Administration: "Iran Country Analysis Brief" <www.eia.doe.gov/emeu/cabs/iran.html> (edition used here: March 2005).
37. Hiro, p. 205; Heritage Foundation: "2006 Index ... Iran"; Dadkhah, p. 94.
38. Heritage Foundation: "2006 Index ... Iran". Cf. Zangeneh, p. 129.
39. "Freedom"-rankings are within brackets: Russia (122), India (121), China (111), Argentina (107), Turkey (85), Thailand (71), Saudi Arabia (62) and Singapore (1). Of course, there are many countries whose GDPs in absolute numbers are smaller than Iran's and growing faster.
40. Paul Klebnikov: "Millionaire Mullahs", 21 July 2003, *Forbes* <www.forbes.com>.
41. Ibid.; Kambiz Foroohar: "Rafsanjanis Are Iran's Power Brokers".
42. Maloney, pp. 153–9.
43. Quoted in ibid., p. 153. The estimates of the share of GDP vary between 1.5 per cent and 10 per cent, ibid., p. 155.
44. Ibid., pp. 156–64.
45. Alizadeh (2003), p. 279.
46. Maloney, pp. 150–61. The Foundation added "Janbazan", "those who sacrifice themselves", to its name in 1989, but is still known in the Iranian street under the original name of Bonyad Mostazafin.
47. Ibid., p. 160.
48. Ibid., pp. 165–6; Alizadeh (2003), p. 278.
49. Dadkhah, pp. 89, 96–101; Jalali-Naini, pp. 109–110; Alizadeh, p. 278.
50. Reuters, *Brief on Iran*, No. 201, "Brother of Powerful Iranian in Fraud Case", 29 June 1995 <www.iran-e-azad.org/english/boi/002010630.95>.

51. Maloney, p. 162; Amid & Hadjikhani, p. 61; Kambiz Foroohar: "Rafsanjanis Are Iran's Power Brokers". Two weeks after the Statoil raid, its three top executives resigned, though none has been charged with any wrongdoing.
52. Quoted in Heritage Foundation: "2006 Index ... Iran".
53. Amid & Hadjikhani, p. 61.
54. Alavi, p. 148.
55. Ehteshami (1995), p. 206.
56. Cf. Maloney, pp. 146–7.
57. *Payvand*: "Iran's economy grew by average of six per cent in past three years", 15 July 2004 <www.payvand.com>; Dan De Luce: "Banking on Prosperity", *The Guardian*, 5 April 2004 <www.guardian.co.uk>.
58. Figures from Jalali-Naini, pp. 94–9; Alizadeh (2003), p. 269; Khajehpour, pp. 95–6, 111; Zangeneh, pp. 113–14; Myles Neligan: "Iran: Economy in transition", *BBC News Online*, 13 February 2004 <http://news.bbc.co.uk>; The World Bank Group: "Country Brief: Iran", March 2004 /September 2005 <www.worldbank.org>; CIA: "The World Economic Factbook: Iran". Not only industry became highly profitable from the mid-1990s onwards; trade and services also did. See Jalali-Naini, p. 99. For more rosy depictions of profitability in Iranian capitalism, based on interviews with industrialists, see Amid & Hadjikhani, pp. 130–34.

5   THE ISLAMIC REPUBLIC OF DUST

1. For an extremely graphic account of the war, see Fisk, pp. 181–360.
2. For accounts of this phenomenon, see ibid., pp. 247–50, 283–5; Reuter, pp. 33–51; Davis, pp. 45–53.
3. Hakimian; Hiro, p. 18; Khajehpour, p. 96.
4. Salehi-Esfahani, pp. 117, 140–41; Alizadeh (2003), p. 270; Jalali-Naini, pp. 91–2; Zangeneh, pp. 109–110; CIA: "The World Economic Factbook: Iran" <www.cia.gov.cia/publications/factbook> (accessed 16 January 2006).
5. Interview.
6. Interviews; ICFTU, p. 312; *Workers in Iran*, No. 1, 21 April 2005; *Workers in Iran*, No. 5, 8 July 2005, both <www.kargaran.org/_main-eng.htm>.
7. Yaghamaian, pp. 173–4; ICTU, p. 312.
8. Interviews.
9. International Labour Conference, 93rd Session, 2005: "Report of the ILO Committee of Experts of Workers Situation in Iran", republished in *Workers in Iran*, No. 6, 12 August 2005.
10. Shahram Rafizadeh: "More Worker Protests in Future", *Rooz Online*, 15 November 2005 <http://roozonline.com/english>.
11. The Persian year spans from 20 March to 20 March, creating a certain overlap with the Western calendar. Here, Persian years are converted to their closest Western equivalents, with an unavoidable element of distortion.
12. *Workers in Iran*, No. 4, 10 June 2005.
13. Jalali-Naini, pp. 105–106, 112; Zangeneh, pp. 114–16; Alizadeh (2003), p. 270; CIA: "World Economic Factbook: Iran".

14. Yaghamaian, p. 157; cf. Salehi-Esfahani, p. 133.
15. Cf. Khajehpour, p. 113.
16. The World Bank Group: "Country Brief: Iran", September 2005 <www.worldbank.org>.
17. Interview.
18. Nazila Fathi: "To Regulate Prostitution, Iran Ponders Brothels", 28 August 2002 <www.newyorktimes.com>.
19. Camelia E. Fard: "Unveiled Threats", *Village Voice*, 28 April 2001 <www.villagevoice.com>.
20. *Iran Focus*: "Child prostitution ring run by Revolutionary Guards officers uncovered in Iran", 11 April 2005 <www.iranfocus.com>.
21. Interviews with journalists in Iran. Cf. Alavi, p. 158; Chris De Bellaigue: "Teenage girls fall prey to Tehran's gangs", *The Independent*, 13 November 2000 <www.independent.com>.
22. IRIN: "Iran: Focus on child labour", 31 May 2004 <www.payvand.com/news>; *Workers in Iran*, No. 8, 14 October 2005; *Iran Focus*: "14 percent of children in Iran forced to work", 31 December 2004.
23. Karl Vick: "Opiates of the Iranian People", *Washington Post*, 23 September 2005 <www.washingtonpost.com>.
24. Yaghmaian, p. 170; Basmenji, pp. 313, 58; *Iran Focus*: "15 homeless persons die in Iran capital every night", 7 December 2005.
25. Vick: "Opiates of the Iranian People"; Alavi, pp. 249–265.
26. Poya, pp. 61–73; Moghissi & Rahnema, p. 287; Alizadeh & Harper, p. 183.
27. Poya, pp. 99–100; Salehi-Esfahani, pp. 122–3.
28. Alizadeh & Harper, p. 194; Moghissi & Rahnema, p. 286; Poya, pp. 67, 82; Salehi-Esfahani, pp. 125–7.
29. Poya, p. 87; Alizadeh & Harper, pp. 186, 184–6; Salehi-Esfahani, pp. 127, 131.
30. Poya, pp. 83–9; Alizadeh & Harper, p. 84; ICFTU, p. 314.
31. Interview.
32. Interviews.
33. Center for Women's Studies, University of Tehran: "Gender Dimensions of Labor Market and Employment Patterns in the IRI (2004)" <http://cws.ut.ac.ir> (accessed 12 April 2006).
34. Salehi-Esfahani, pp. 138, 141.
35. Excerpts translated from Bazr: "Inja Assaluyeh ast: tah-e jahanam! Inja labkhandi bar labi nemibini!" ("This is Assalyeh: the bottom of hell! Here, no one is smiling!"), *Bazr*, No. 6, Aban 1384 (November 2005) <www.bazr84.com> (accessed 20 April 2006).
36. Visits to brick mills in Kurdistan and southern Tehran.
37. Interview.
38. CIA: "World Economic Factbook: Iran".
39. *Der Spiegel*: "Wave of Strikes Shakes Tehran", *Spiegel Online*, 12 April 2006 <www.spiegel.de/international>.
40. *Iran Daily*: "Stock Market Spurs Economic Growth", 29 May 2005 <www.iran-daily.com>.
41. Comparison made by Moghissi & Rahnema, p. 290; quotations from Bayat (1987), pp. 184–5. In their analysis of the Islamic councils, Moghissi

and Rahnema even claim that "no other type of state, including fascist regimes, has ever succeeded in establishing and employing such diverse apparatuses of control over a deliberately weakened civil society", p. 292
42. Quoted in Bayat (1987), p. 185. Cf. Parsa, p. 273.
43. Quoted in Bayat (1987), p. 193.
44. Quotations from Moghissi & Rahnema, p. 291; ICFTU, p. 311; *Workers in Iran*, No. 13, 7 February 2006.
45. Quotations in Bayat (1987), p. 188.
46. Ibid., pp. 187, 189; interviews.
47. Interview.
48. Quotation in Bayat (1987), p. 187.

6   OUTCRY

1. ICFTU, pp. 312–13; interviews.
2. Interviews.
3. Interview.
4. Interview.
5. Interview.
6. Quoted in *Workers in Iran*, No. 4, 10 June 2005 <www.kargaran.org/_main-eng.htm>.
7. *Etehad-e Chap*: "Strike and Protest at Iran Khodro" <www.etehadchap.org/irankhodro3.html> (accessed 2 April 2006).
8. ICFTU, p. 314; Alavi, pp. 205, 323.
9. International Alliance in Support of Workers in Iran: "Nurses Protest Against the Denial of Their Demands", 22 January 2005 <www.workers-iran.org/nurses>.
10. *Iran Daily*: "Teachers Protest Work Conditions, Workers Demand 25-month Arrears", 18 October 2005 <www.iran-daily.com>.
11. Interview.
12. ICFTU, pp. 314–315; *Workers in Iran*, No. 9, 11 November 2005; *Workers in Iran*, No. 10, 28 November 2005.
13. Afary, pp. 155–164.
14. Quoted in ibid., p. 173. The continuation of the report is indicative of the class contradictions of the Constitutional Revolution: "Alas, a hundred times alas, I wish the day we thought of [constitutionalism] and planned its foundation a plague had emerged and killed us all so we would not see such results from our actions."
15. The battle is retold in ibid., pp. 172–74.
16. Ibid., p. 155.
17. See ibid., pp. 154–6; Keddie, p. 2.
18. Azad, pp. 21–2; Moghadam (1988), p. 202. Assef Bayat claims that "Shomali" and "Azeri" workers, i.e., with origins in Gilan, Mazandaran and Azerbaijan, were at the forefront of shora organising in Tehran and displayed more progressive, democratic attitudes during the years of the revolution than workers originating from, for instance, the conservative Yazd area. Bayat (1987), pp. 43–5. This pattern appears to persist, as the Shomali and Azeri workers are clearly overrepresented in the progressive labour networks of Tehran today.

19. Economic Affairs Secretariat 1991, quoted in Ehteshami (1995), p. 104.
20. *Iran Daily*: "Corruption Undermining Privatization Process", 29 October 2005. Cf. Maloney, p. 165; Amid & Hadjikhani, p. 75.
21. Interview. There is an interesting precedent to this *aprés nous, la déluge-* mentality in the way governors taxed the economy mercilessly in the nineteenth century: "they were not sure they could hold their posts and hence were not concerned to leave the peasants enough to maintain fertility, investment, and productivity", Keddie, p. 25.
22. *Workers in Iran*, No. 1, 21 April 2005; *Workers in Iran*, No. 6, 12 August 2005; *Workers in Iran*, No. 7, 2 September 2005.
23. *Iran Focus*: "More than 290 political protests in Iran in past month", 1 November 2005 <www.iranfocus.com>; *Iran Focus*: "420 political protests in Iran in past month", 30 November 2005.
24. Yaghmaian, p. 173; Yusef Abkhun & Sohrab Yekta: "The labour movement in Iran: A year of increasing protest", *Iran Bulletin*, May 2000 <www.iran-bulletin.org/labour>.
25. Parsa, pp. 142–4.
26. This analysis is adapted from Parsa, pp. 13–15. In this regard as well, there is a striking continuity with the Pahlavi era.
27. *Workers in Iran*, No. 1, 21 April 2005.
28. *Iran Focus*: "Labour discontent, protests spread across Iran" 18 July 2005; *Der Spiegel*: "Wave of Strikes Shakes Tehran", *Spiegel Online*, 12 April 2006 <www.spiegel.de/international>.
29. Interview.
30. Interviews; cf. ICFTU, pp. 313–14.
31. Some of them were published in *Workers in Iran*, No. 10, 28 November 2005.
32. Interview.
33. Interview. Cf. *Iran Focus*: "Rafsanjani prevented from speaking on May Day in Iran", 1 May 2005; *Workers in Iran*, No. 2, 11 May 2005.
34. The proclamation is included in *Against the Wage*, No. 1, 17 June 2005 <www.againstthewage.com>.
35. Interviews.
36. *Against the Wage*, No. 1, 17 June 2005.
37. See *Against the Wage*, No. 2, 19 August 2005.
38. Ibid., italics added.
39. Ibid.
40. The May Day Resolution of Komiteye Peyigiri, published in *Workers in Iran*, No. 2, 11 May 2005.
41. Interview.
42. Cf. Behrooz, p. 164; Moghissi & Rahnema, p. 296.
43. Asqar Karimi: "Fundamental developments in the labour movement in Iran", 24 April 2005 <www.wpiran.org>.
44. See Behrooz, i.e., pp. 42, 140–42.

7 THE INTIFADA OF THE PROVINCES

1. Cf. Parsa, pp. 19–21; Koohi-Kamali, pp. 157–62, 258; Keddie, pp. 155–6.

2. Koohi-Kamali, pp. 24–43.
3. Ibid., pp. 171–89; cf. Parsa, pp. 258–60.
4. Koohi-Kamali, pp. 213–15. Koohi-Kamali's examples are taken from the special dossier on the situation of Iranian Kurds presented by UNESCO in 2002.
5. Morad Shirin: "Iranian Kurds revolt in response to state murder of a youth", *Pishtaaz*, 1 August 2005 <www.pishtaaz.com>; *Iran Press Service*: "Unrests continue in Iran's minority-dominated provinces", 6 August 2005 <www.iran-press-service.com>; Human Rights Watch: "Iran: Security Forces Kill Kurdish Protestors", 11 August 2005 <www.hrw.org>. On the Mahabad republic, see Koohi-Kamali, pp. 89–125.
6. Interview.
7. Michael Howard: "Iran sends in troops to crush border unrest", *The Guardian*, 5 August 2005 <www.guardian.co.uk>.
8. Interview.
9. On Komele and KDPI, their development and differences, see Koohi-Kamali, pp. 174–89, 210–12.
10. Cf. Moghadam (1996), p. 72; Parsa, p. 262.
11. IRIN: "Iran: Interview with Human Rights Special Rapporteur on Adequate Housing, Miloon Kothari", 9 August 2005 <www.irinnews.org>; British Ahwazi Friendship Society (BAFS): "Reports: Ahwazi Fact File, Forced Migration and Land Confiscation, Economic Marginalisation" <www.ahwaz.org.uk/reports.html> (accessed 20 January 2006).
12. IRIN: "Iran: Interview with Human Rights Special Rapporteur"; BAFS: "Iran: Parliamentary Think Tank Warns of Ethnic Unrest", 5 January 2006.
13. BAFS: "Iran's 'Bloody Friday' massacre in Ahwaz", 16 April 2005; BAFS: "At least 23 dead in Ahwaz unrest", 18 April 2005; BAFS: "Ahwaz Intifada intensifies", 24 April 2005; BAFS: "A tragic week in the history of Ahwaz", 24 April 2005; Amnesty International: "Khuzestan, Iran: Amnesty International calls for an end to the cycle of violence in Khuzestan and investigation into the root causes of recent unrest", 20 April 2005 <www.amnesty.org/news>; Human Rights Watch: "Iran: Reports of Ethnic Violence Suppressed", 11 May 2005.
14. BAFS: "Iran: 30 arrested and four killed as Ahwaz unrest continues", 27 July 2005; BAFS: "Iran prepares for ethnic cleansing the Arvand Free Zone", 26 January 2006; Amnesty International: "Iran: Need for restraint as anniversary of unrest in Khuzestan approaches", 13 April 2006.
15. For instance, the Kurdish republic of Mahabad in 1946 had an Azeri counterpart. See Keddie, pp. 111–12.
16. See e.g., ibid., p. 314; Koohi-Kamali, p. 157.
17. Navid Ahmadi: "Growing Unrest in Azerbaijan", *Rooz Online*, 29 May 2006 <www.roozonline.com>; Nazila Fathi: "Ethnic Tensions Over Cartoon Set Off Riots in Northwest Iran", *New York Times*, 29 May 2006 <www.nytimes.com>.
18. Cf. Koohi-Kamali, pp. 214–15.
19. See <www.iranfederal.org/eng>. The seven organisations of the Congress were: Komele, Kurdish Democratic Party of Iran, Democratic Solidarity Party of Ahwaz, Federal Democratic Movement of Azerbaijan, Baluchistan

United Front, Baluchistan People's Party, and Organisation for Defense of the Rights of Turkmen People.
20. Quoted in BAFS: "Iran: Parliamentary Think Tank Warns of Ethnic Unrest", 5 January 2006.

8   REFORMISM'S OBITUARY

1. For profiles of the triumphant conservatives, see Farhad Khosrokhavar: "The New Conservatives Take a Turn", and Morad Saghafi: "The New Landscape of Iranian Politics", both in *Middle East Report*, No. 233, Winter 2004 <www.merip.org>.
2. Yaghmaian, p. 146. Italics added.
3. Ibid., p. 147.
4. Cf. Moghissi & Rahnema, p. 297. Khatami's career is sketched in Hiro, pp. 171–5. A good overview of the reform period is Keddie, pp. 269–311.
5. Sohrab Behdad: "Khatami and his 'Reformist' Economic (Non-)Agenda", *Middle East Report Online*, 21 May 2001 <www.merip.org>. Behdad writes of Khatami's submission of the budget to the Majles in 1999: "His statement to parliament was more like a literary essay on social alienation and political empowerment than a budget representation." A positive interpretation of this is intellectual sophistication verging on eccentricity; a negative is cowardice.
6. The acclaimed account of Iranian cyberspace, the blogosphere in particular, is Alavi. In it there is, typically, no mention of the Left-leaning galaxy in that space. For further critique of Alavi, see below.
7. *Middle East Report*: "'Our Letter to Khatami Was a Farewell': An Interview with Saeed Razavi-Faqih", *Middle East Report Online*, 15 July 2003; cf. Alavi, pp. 137–41, 301, 321.
8. Mahsa Shekarloo: "Iranian Women Take on the Constitution", *Middle East Report Online*, 21 July 2005.
9. Ibid.
10. Cf. Moghissi & Rahnema, p. 295.
11. Interview.
12. Yaghmaian, p. 175.
13. Koohi-Kamali, pp. 212–15.
14. Interview.
15. Interview.

9   THE "HUMBLE" PRESIDENT: A MAN OF THE PEOPLE?

1. Jason Burke: "Meet the West's worst nightmare", *The Observer*, 15 January 2006 <www.guardian.co.uk>; Basmenji, pp. 280–81; Hiro, p. 372.
2. Hiro, pp. 375–6; Burke: "Meet the West's worst nightmare"; Stanley Reed & Babak Pirouz: "Election Aftershock In Corporate Iran", *Business Week*, 11 July 2005 <www.businessweek.com>.
3. Basmenji, pp. 281–7; Hiro, pp. 373–4; Ardeshir Mehrdad & Mehdi Kia: "New conservatives, regime crisis and political perspectives in Iran", *Iran Bulletin*, July 2005 <www.iran-bulletin.org>; Robert Tait: "Hardline Iran

hails a devout working class hero", *The Guardian*, 21 June 2005 <www.
guardian.co.uk>; Doug Lorimer: "Iran: A vote against neoliberalism",
Green Left Weekly, 6 July 2005 <www.greenleft.org.au>.
4. Basmenji, pp. 284–90; Hiro, pp. 371, 376.
5. For the fraud hypothesis, see Basmenji, pp. 285–95; Ahmad Sadri: "Exact
opposite of paranoia", *Iranian.com*, 30 June 2005 <www.iranian.com>.
6. Hiro, p. 375, italics added.
7. Quoted in ibid., p. 374.
8. Ali, pp. 15–16.
9. Hiro, p. 376; AFP: "I'll be no VIP jetsetter: Ahmadinejad", 3 December
2005 <http://news.yahoo.com>.
10. *Iran Press Service*: "Iran government urging the hidden imam to help",
21 October 2005 <www.iran-press-service.com>; Scott Peterson: "Waiting
for the rapture in Iran", *Christian Science Monitor*, 21 December 2005
<www.csmonitor.com>; Richard Eernsberger Jr.: "Religion Versus Reality",
Newsweek, 12 December 2005.
11. Peterson: "Waiting for the rapture in Iran".
12. Abrahamian (1991), p. 106.
13. Fred Halliday: "Iran's revolutionary spasm", *Open Democracy*, 1 July 2005
<www.opendemocracy.net>.
14. Human Rights Watch, pp. 1–10; UPI: "Iran's President purges bureaucracy",
Iran Focus, 5 December 2005 <www.iranfocus.com>; *Iran Focus*: "Iran gives
heavy arms to para-military vigilantes", 16 October 2005.
15. Mehrdad & Kia: "New conservatives, regime crisis and political
perspectives in Iran"; Reed & Pirouz: "Election Aftershock In Corporate
Iran"; Zvi Bar'el: "A tutor for the president", *Ha'aretz*, 2 November 2005
<www.haaretz.com>.
16. Bar'el: "A tutor for the president"; Laura Secor: "Fugitives", *New Yorker*,
21 November 2005; cf. Hiro, p. 376.
17. Eernsberger Jr.: "Religion Versus Reality".
18. The account of the Sherkat-e Vahed episode is based on a number of
interviews with activists inside and outside Iran, and reports from the
conflict including: Safa Haeri: "Leaders of Tehran Bus Company Arrested,
the Union Dissolved", *Iran Press Service*, 24 December 2005; Iranian
Workers Solidarity Network: "Around 3000 Vahed Bus Company workers
end their strike after most leaders are released", 29 December 2005 <www.
pishtaaz.com>; Workers' Liberty: "Tehran Bus Workers challenge the
authorities in Iran", 7 January 2006 <www.workersliberty.org>; *Iran Press
Service*: "Hundreds of Workers and Drivers Arrested, Strike Banned", 29
January 2006; Shahram Rafizadeh: "Strikes Follow Police Arrests", *Rooz
Online*, 30 January 2006 <www.roozonline.com>; International Transport
Workers' Federation: "Tehran Bus Dispute – Background" <www.iftglobal.
org > (accessed 2 February 2006); Workers' Fund: "Campaign to Support
Workers Fund Iran" <www.workersfund.org> (accessed 2 April 2006);
National Union of Public and General Employees: "World calls on Iran to
release jailed strikers", 2 February 2006 <www.nupge.ca/news>; *Etehad-e
Chap*: "Urgent call for international solidarity with Tehran bus workers",
28 January 2006 <www.etehadchap.org>; *Payvand*: "February 15: Day of
Action for Imprisoned Iranian Bus Drivers", 10 February 2006, Teamsters:

"Hoffa Calls in Iranian President to Release Bus Drivers", 10 January 2006 <www.teamster.org>; various reports on Labor Start <www.laborstart. org>.

19. Radio Hambastegi, June 2005, broadcast in the Stockholm area.
20. Radio Avayeashena: Interview with Mahdiye Salimi, 12 April 2006 <www. avayashena.com>.
21. Radio Avayeashena: Interview with Yaqob Salimi, 28 January 2006 <www. avayashena.com>.
22. Letter obtained from Gholamreza Mirzai. It was published in, among other publications, *Dagens Nyheter*, Sweden's major daily newspaper.
23. See Behrooz (2000), pp. 141–2.
24. Interview.
25. *Der Spiegel*: "Wave of Strikes Shakes Tehran", *Spiegel Online*, 12 April 2006 <www.spiegel.de/international>; Kamel Nazer Yasin: "Iran: Labor discontent a potential distraction for government", *Eurasia*, 2 May 2006 <www.eurasianet.org>.
26. Kar va Karegar: "Paradoxical", quoted in *Iran Daily*: "Persian Press Watch", 23 August 2005 <www.iran-daily.com>.
27. Barbad Kaveh: "Elimination of Labor Associations", *Rooz Online*, 7 February 2006. Cf. Sadeghi's rhetoric in *Iran Daily*: "Workers may strike", *Iran Daily*, 19 July 2005.
28. See, e.g., Mehdi Khalaji: "Tehran renews war on culture", 26 November 2005 <www.iran-press-service.com>.

10 "INSIDE THOSE HIGH WALLS": OVERTURES OF WAR

1. Nafisi, pp. 25, 38.
2. Ibid., pp. 6, 21, 28, 57.
3. Ibid., p. 111.
4. Ibid., p. 57.
5. Ibid., p. 8, italics added.
6. Ibid., p. 74.
7. Ibid., p. 59.
8. Ibid., pp. 213, 18–19.
9. Ibid., pp. 39, 57, 32. Cf. pp. 106–107, where intelligence among Iranians is measured in their familiarity with New York.
10. Quoted in Fisk, pp. 270–71. The senator was John Warner, former secretary of the US Navy.
11. Nicholas D. Kristof: "Those Friendly Iranians", *New York Times*, 5 May 2004 <www.nytimes.com>. To bring home his point one more time, Kristof rounds off: "Oh, that one instance when I was treated inhospitably? ... a group of people two tables away went out of their way to be rude, yelling at me for being an American propagandist. So I finally encountered hostility in Iran — from a table full of young Europeans."
12. Dan De Luce: "Anger grows among children of Iran's 25-year-old revolution", *The Guardian*, 9 February 2004 <www.guardian.co.uk>.
13. Angus McDowall: "Drink, Drugs and Sex on the Slopes: The Secret World of Iranian Youth", *The Independent*, 8 May 2004 <www.independent. com>.

14. Michael Winiarski: "Irans unga skeptiska till valet", *Dagens Nyheter*, 21 June 2005.
15. Laura Secor: "Fugitives", *New Yorker*, 21 November 2005 <www.newyorker.com>.
16. Timothy Garton Ash: "Soldiers of the Hidden Imam", *New York Review of Books*, 3 November 2005.
17. Basmenji, p. 39.
18. Cf. Yaghmaian: "Defiant, jubilant, beautiful, and modern, these were the children of MTV and satellite dishes, computer games, rock & roll, techno music, and all that was forbidden", p. 100. Cf. e.g., Basmenji, pp. 51–2.
19. Garton Ash: "Soldiers of the Hidden Imam".
20. Jim Muir: "Iran 'brothel' plan rejected", *BBC News Online*, 27 July 2002 <http://news.bbc.co.uk>.
21. Garton Ash: "Soldiers of the Hidden Imam".
22. Secor: "Fugitives".
23. [*sic*] in original.
24. Garton Ash: "Soldiers of the Hidden Imam".
25. To be fair, Nafisi also includes the trite ideas of the signs of dawning freedom: the popularity of *Baywatch*, "showing a little hair from under our scarves, insinuating a little color into the drab uniformity of our appearances, growing our nails"; women's "scarves are more colourful and their robes much shorter; they wear makeup now and walk freely with men who are not their brothers, fathers or husbands", pp. 67, 26, 341. In this discourse, the struggle over Iran often appears as a struggle over women's adornments, reviving that old fantasy of the West liberating the women of the Orient: cosmetics defeat the veil. The belief that the dictatorship of the Islamic Republic would in fact crumble if women use make-up or wear colourful scarves is about as naïve an idea as Khomeini's belief that the best way to defeat imperialism is for women to wear the chador.
26. It is worth noting that the liberal discourse has permeated progressive accounts of today's Iran as well. A Left movement on the run from the category of class has applied its own interpretation of identity politics to life in the Islamic Republic. One example is Janet Afary and Kevin B. Anderson's remarkable study *Foucault and the Iranian Revolution*. In this, they reveal how Foucault, as correspondent for *Corriere della Sera*, followed the revolution to the point of unreserved enthusiasm for the Islamist, anti-modernist, anti-democratic current, supposing the revolution to be of intrinsic political value for humanity (unlike those Marxists who reached the same conclusion from a distorted logic of anti-imperialism, while postulating Islamism as a necessary evil). Foucault showed complete disregard for the popular, democratic undercurrents of the revolution. The authors themselves, however, end their book by singling out a "new democratic movement" consisting of "journalists, lawyers, fashion designers, actresses and film directors, college students" and so on; the most powerful of the movement's indicators being *fashion*: "Young secular women, in contrast to their parents' generation, Leftist

radicals who abhorred bourgeois decadence, express their defiance of the morality police by wearing makeup, streaking their hair in vibrant colors (the bit they can show from under their colorful scarves). Before the eyes of the clerics and police authorities on the streets, they claim the public arenas with elegant capes in creative designs that meet the minimum requirement of the morality police, but are nowhere near the drab black veils recommended by them." As indeed any visitor to Iran will notice, this fashion disappears from sight as soon as one leaves northern Tehran and heads off for other parts of the metropolis, never mind the provinces.

27. Another example is the acclaimed study of the Iranian blogosphere, Nasrin Alavi's *We Are Iran*. Here, the heroes of the Constitutional Revolution are two *American* individuals, a sign of freedom the arrival of Valentine's Day to northern Tehran; "Iranian bloggers review ... forbidden fruits of Western culture with a unique passion"; "Iran's new generation no longer sees political radicalism as the way forward", etc.: Alavi, pp. 40–42, 18–20, 329, 226, 319. Typically, the book includes dozens of pictures of dissident journalists, of well-dressed youngsters having fun, of people shopping, parachuting, skiing, playing rock music, picnicking, reading, dancing, visiting trade expos, visiting coffee shops, visiting vets with pets, and *one single picture of a person performing labour*: a dentist. The reviewer in *Persian Journal* wrote: "As another Iranian blogger, who does not appear in the book, points out, the vast majority of Iranians do not have access to the web. As in most countries, Iranian bloggers 'represent the views of a very limited demographic group – affluent and otherwise privileged individuals'. I liked reading the blogs in this book, but I want to know the views of the majority of Iranians without blogs": Amir Amirani: "Book review: 'We Are Iran' by Nasrin Alavi", *Persian Journal*, 10 November 2005 <www.iranian.ws>.

28. The White House: "President Bush Delivers State of the Union Address", 31 January 2006 <www.whitehouse.gov>. Cf. Guy Dinmore: "Bush 'calling for Iran regime change'", *Financial Times*, 1 Febraury 2006 <www.ft.com>.

12 TRUTH OR DARE? IRAN'S NUCLEAR PROGRAM

1. On the effects of Saddam's chemical warfare, see Fisk, pp. 257–62.
2. Dafna Linzer: "U.S. Uses Drones to Probe Iran For Arms", *Washington Post*, 13 February 2005 <www.washingtonpost.com>; Richard Sale/UPI: "USAF playing cat and mouse game over Iran", *World Peace Herald*, 26 January 2005 <www.wphereald.com>.
3. *Newsweek*, 30 June 2003; *The Guardian*, 26 May 2003 <www.guardian.co.uk>; *Sunday Herald*, 25 July 2004 <www.sundayherald.com>.
4. CSIS, pp. 20–24; IISS, pp. 9–11; Dafna Linzer: "Past Arguments Don't Square With Current Iran Policy", *Washington Post*, 27 March 2005; Abrahamian (2004), p. 137.
5. IISS, pp. 9–12.
6. Ibid., pp. 12–16, 57; CSIS, pp. 26–31.

7. On the current state of Mojahedin-e Khalq and its relations to the US, see Howard, pp. 191–204; Neda Bolourchi: "Friendly fire and the US in Iran", *Asia Times*, 18 November 2005 <www.atimes.com>.
8. IISS, pp. 10–16, 43–51.
9. Quoted in Howard, p. 98.
10. Jonathan Freedland: "The problem is: Iran does pose a threat in every way Iraq did not", *The Guardian*, 26 April 2006.
11. Energy Information Administration: "Iran Country Analysis Brief", March 2005 <www.eia.doe.gov/emeu/cabs/iran.html>.
12. Judy R. Clark: "Gas use at issue in Iran as oil production sags", *Oil & Gas Journal*, 9 May 2005.
13. Ibid. Cf. Sam Fletcher: "Middle East grows as oil consumer, product exporter", *Oil & Gas Journal*, 7 February 2005.
14. Brendan O'Neill: "Let Iran have the bomb", *The Guardian*, 31 March 2006.
15. Howard, p. 98.
16. *Oil & Gas Journal*: "Iranian desperation", 23 January 2006.
17. Linzer: "Past Arguments Don't Square With Current Iran Policy". One of the signatories to this strategy paper was Secretary of State Henry Kissinger. In 9 March 2005, he wrote a piece in the *Washington Post* where he declared that "for a major oil producer such as Iran, nuclear energy is a wasteful use of resources." Asked about his change of mind by the *Post*'s own reporter Dafna Linzer, he replied: "They were an allied country, and this was a commercial transaction. We didn't address the question of them one day moving toward nuclear weapons", ibid.
18. Donald Weadon quoted in William O. Beeman: "U.S. instigated Iran's nuclear policy in the '70s", *Providence Journal*, 20 February 2006 <www.projo.com>. Cf. CSIS, pp. 20–21.
19. Rogers (2006 b), p. 5.
20. Quotations from Howard, pp. 92–3; Juan Cole: "Fishing for a pretext in Iran", *Truthdig*, 13 March 2006 <www.truthdig.com>.
21. Conn Hallinan: "Nuclear Proliferation: A Gathering Storm", *Foreign Policy in Focus*, 2 February 2006 <www.fpif.org>; David Krieger: "Iran, International Law and Nuclear Disarmament", *The Transnational Foundation for Peace and Future Research*, 28 March 2006 <www.transnational.org>.
22. Ali M Ansari: "A reality check on the 'Persian menace'", *New Statesman*, 14 February 2005.
23. Stephen Zunes: "The U.S. and Iran: Democracy, Terrorism, and Nuclear Weapons", *Foreign Policy in Focus*, 31 August 2005.
24. Ward, pp. 560–61, 574.
25. Mokhtari, p. 211; Ehteshami (2004), p. 188. On the wahhabi slaughter campaigns in Pakistan, see International Crisis Group.
26. Johnson, pp. 240–53; Rogers (2006b), p. 6.
27. Quoted in Ehteshami (2004), p. 181.
28. Cf. IISS, p. 26, 111.
29. Ibid., p. 70; Polk, pp. 132–3; Afrasiabi & Kibaroglu, pp. 257, 265; Joost R. Hilterman: "Iran's Nuclear Posture and the Scars of War", *Middle East Report Online*, 18 January 2005 <www.merip.org>.
30. Hilterman: "Iran's Nuclear Posture".

31. Cf. Ehteshami (2004), p. 193.
32. Steven R. Weisman: "U.S. Takes Softer Tone on Iran, Once in the 'Axis of Evil'", *New York Times*, 29 October 2003 <www.nytimes.com>.
33. Afrasiabi & Kibaroglu, p. 258, 265; IISS, pp. 16–20, 64–5; Hiro, pp. 282–9.
34. Dafna Linzer: "No Proof Found of Iran Arms Program", *Washington Post*, 23 August 2005.
35. E.g., Ewen MacAskill: "Hope of saving Iranian nuclear deal is fading", *The Guardian*, 30 July 2004; Simon Tisdall: "Diplomacy sidelined as US targets Iran", *The Guardian*, 10 August 2004 <www.guardian.co.uk>; David Rennie: "US out to sabotage Iran's atom bomb programme", *Daily Telegraph*, 9 August 2004 <www.telegraph.co.uk>; Scott Peterson: "What's next in Iranian nuclear saga?", *Christian Science Monitor*, 16 September 2004 <www.csmonitor.com>; Robin Wright: "Europe to negotiate with Iran over weapon development", *The State*, 17 October 2004 <www. thestate.com>.
36. See IISS, pp. 16–30.
37. See ibid., pp. 25–7, 46.
38. David E Sanger: "A 'Good-Cop, Bad-Cop' Approach on Iran", *New York Times*, 21 November 2004. Cf. Noah Barkin: "Europe, U.S. in Good-Cop, Bad-Cop Roles with Iran", *Reuters*, 20 January 2005 <www.news.yahoo. com>.
39. Department for Disarmament Affairs, United Nations: "The Treaty on the Non-Proliferation of Nuclear Weapons (NPT)" <www.un.org/events/ npt2005/npttreaty.html> (accessed 15 May 2006).
40. IISS, pp. 20, 26.
41. *Al-Jazeera*: "Iran rejects nuclear handover call", 3 October 2004 <http:// english.aljazeera.net>. Cf. Judith Ingram/AP: "Tehran calls for nuclear facility in Iran", *The State*, 28 March 2006.
42. Afrasiabi & Kibaroglu, p. 255.
43. One version, written from an American standpoint, of these events is found in CSIS, pp. 44–9.
44. Quotations from ibid., pp. 72–4.
45. Dafna Linzer: "Iran Is Judged 10 Years From Nuclear Bomb", *Washington Post*, 2 August 2005; Sokolski, p. 5.; *Herald Sun*: "Iran 'six months' from nuclear bomb", 28 October 2005 <www.heraldsun.news.com>.
46. See, e.g., IISS, pp. 53–7, 11–112. IISS has itself rightly been accused for partisan American leanings in the build-up to the Iraq invasion, see Kaveh L. Afrasiabi: "Building a case, any case, against Iran", *Asia Times*, 14 September 2005 <www.atimes.com>.
47. Johnson, p. 64; Hallinan: "Nuclear Proliferation"; Simon Tisdall: "An exercise in bravado", *The Guardian*, 5 April 2006; Andrew Buncombe: "US nuclear upgrade may violate test ban", *The Independent*, 8 February 2005 <www.independent.co.uk>.
48. Keir A. Liber & Daryl G.Press: "The Rise of U.S. Nuclear Primacy", *Foreign Affairs*, February 2006 <www.foreignaffairs.org>.
49. E.g., Tony Benn: "Atomic hypocrisy", *The Guardian*, 30 November 2005; Conn Hallinan: "India, Iran, & the United States", *Foreign Policy in Focus*, 19 October 2005; David Krieger: "India, Iran and U.S. nuclear hypocrisy",

Transnational Foundation for Peace and Future Research, 29 March 2006; Michael T. Klare: "Ending Nonproliferation", *The Nation*, 3 April 2006; Howard, p. 110.

13   WHO COMMANDS THE WATERFALL?

1. John W. Schoen: "OPEC says it has lost control of oil prices", *MSNBC*, 16 March 2005 <www.msnbc.msn.com>.
2. Adam Porter: "US report acknowledges peak-oil threat", *Al-Jazeera*, 9 March 2005 <http://english.aljazeera.net>.
3. The literature on peak oil is growing exponentially. For introductions, see, e.g., Campbell & Laherrère; Roberts; Goodstein; McKillop & Newman. A Marxist theory of peak oil and its place in today's imperialism is outlined in Malm.
4. Quotation from *The Economist*: "Oil in troubled waters – A survey of oil", 30 April 2005. *Business Week*: "The oil spigot may be closing", 12 November 2001 <www.businessweek.com>; Dan Ackman: "Is oil heading for $100?", *Forbes*, 19 October 2004 <www.forbes.com>; Paul Krugman: "A crude shock", *New York Times*, 14 May 2004 <www.nytimes.com>.
5. Marx, pp. 443.
6. *The Economist*: "Oil in troubled waters".
7. BP (2003), p. 4; BP (2005), p. 4; AFP: "Iran claims number-two position for world oil reserves", *Channel News Asia*, 4 July 2004 <www.channelnewsasia.com>; *Iran Daily*: "Oil – A Security Link for Middle East", 20 October 2004 <www.iran-daily.com>; Dale Allen Pfeiffer: "Target Iran", 24 August 2004, *From the Wilderness* <www.fromthewilderness.com>; Brendan Murray: "Bush Leverage With Russia, Iran, China Falls as Oil Prices Rise", *Bloomberg*, 1 May 2006 <www.bloomberg.com>; Michael T. Klare: "Oil, Geopolitics, and the Coming War With Iran", *TomDispatch*, 11 April 2005 <www.tomdispatch.com>. Cf. Klare (2004), p. 110.
8. Mansour Kashfi: "Lack of data casts doubt on Iranian reserves hike", *Oil & Gas Journal*, 1 November 2004; A.M. Samsam Bakhtiari: "Middle Eastern Reserves", *ASPO Newsletter*, No. 63, March 2006 <www.peakoil.net>. On the real and imagined reserves of Saudi Arabia, see Simmons.
9. Matthew Simmons Transcript: "Revealing Statements from a Bush Insider about Peak Oil and Natural Gas Depletion", *From the Wilderness*, 12 June 2003.
10. See, e.g., "FACTS: Middle East production capacity to continue climb", *Oil & Gas Journal*, 4 April 2005.
11. Excerpts from the speech published in Kjell Aleklett: "Dick Cheney, Peak Oil and the Final Count Down", The Association for the Study of Peak Oil, 12 May 2004 <www.peakoil.net>.
12. Energy Information Administration: "Iran Country Analysis Brief", March 2005 <www.eia.doe.gov/emeu/cabs/iran.html>; Simmons, p. 299; Klare (2004), pp. 106–107; BP (2005), pp. 4–6.
13. Pfeiffer: "Target Iran"; Klare: "Oil, Geopolitics, and the Coming War With Iran".

14. Alexander Brexendorff & Christian Ule: "Changes bring new attention to Iranian buyback contracts", *Oil & Gas Journal*, 1 November 2004.
15. Sam Fletcher: "US pressure disrupts Iran's S. Azadegan development", *Oil & Gas Journal*, 20 September 2004.
16. Reuters: "Iran oil terms do not lure investment: Statoil", *Iran Focus*, 24 May 2006 <www.iranfocus.com>; cf. Energy Information Administration: "Iran Country Analysis Brief".
17. Judy R. Clark: "Gas use at issue in Iran as oil production sags", *Oil & Gas Journal*, 9 May 2005, italics added.
18. Energy Information Administration: "Iran Country Analysis Brief".
19. *Iran Daily*: "Oil – A Security Link for Middle East", 20 October 2004, italics added.
20. Association for the Study of Peak Oil: "Country Assessment – Iran", *ASPO Newsletter*, No. 32, August 2003 <www.asponews.org>, italics added.
21. Kinzer, pp. 49–51, 68; Keddie, p. 123; Hiro, p. 193.
22. Manucher Farmanfarmaian, director of Iran's petroleum institute after 1949, quoted in Kinzer, p. 67.
23. Quotations in ibid., pp. 121–3.
24. Keddie, pp. 13–132, 137–9, 165.
25. James A. Paul: "Oil in Iraq: the Heart of the Crisis", *Global Policy Forum*, December 2002 <www.globalpolicy.org>.
26. Paul Klebnikov: "Hitting OPEC by way of Baghdad", *Forbes*, 28 October 2002 <www.forbes.com>.
27. *The Economist*: "Don't mention the O-word", 14 September 2002. Cf. Klare (2004), pp. 93–105.
28. Platform, pp. 4–5, 16–17; cf. Klare (2004), pp. 99–100.
29. Platform, pp. 4, 9–16, 24–6.
30. Ibid., pp. 4–5, 17–26.
31. Brexendorff & Ule: "Changes bring new attention to Iranian buyback contracts", italics added.
32. The International Tax & Investment Centre, quoted in Platform, p. 14.
33. UK Foreign Office quoted in ibid., p. 8; cf. NEPD, p. 5; Klare (2004), p. 79.
34. Klare (2004), p. 82.
35. NEPD, p. 16.
36. Howard, p. 48; Caroline Langie: "Oil Experts Say War with Iraq Wouldn't be War for Oil", US Department of State, 19 December 2002 <http://usinfo.state.gov>.
37. AFP: "Iran says not scared of Security Council, warns on oil prices", *Yahoo News*, 15 January 2006 <http://news.yahoo.com>.
38. Robert Tait: "Iran issues stark warning on oil price", *The Guardian*, 16 January 2006 <www.guardian.co.uk>. Cf. AFP/Reuters: "Back off or suffer oil shock: Tehran", *The Australian*, 7 March 2005 <www.theaustralian.news.com>.
39. See, e.g., Klare (2004), pp. 107–108.
40. Terry Macalister: "Iran takes on west's control of oil trading", *The Guardian*, 16 June 2004; Islamic Republic of Iran Broadcasting: "Iran's oil stock exchange, next week", *Energy Bulletin*, 26 April 2006 <www.energybulletin.net>. On the origin of the idea, see Chris Cook: "Iran

– Perception and Reality", *Asia Times*, 14 February 2006 <www.asiatimes. com>.

41. Hossein Talebi of NOIC, quoted in *Iran Mania News*: "Oil bourse closer to reality", 28 December 2004 <www.iranmania.com>.

42. Elias Akleh: "The Iranian Threat: The Bomb or the Euro?", *Information Clearing House*, 24 March 2005 <www.informationclearinghouse.info>; William Clark: "The Real Reasons Why Iran is the Next Target: The Emerging Euro-denominated International Oil Marker", *Global Research*, 27 October 2004 <www.globalresearch.ca>; Krassimir Petrov: "The Proposed Iranian Oil Bourse", *Energy Bulletin*, 18 January 2006. Cf. Toni Straka: "Killing the dollar in Iran", *Asia Times*, 26 August 2005.

43. See the above references; Looney, pp. 26–9; Ed Blanche: "Iran takes on US – but at what cost?", *The Middle East*, March 2006; Richard Heinberg: "Onward to Iran", *MuseLetter*, 7 March 2005 <www.MuseLetter.com>; Cóilín Nunan: "Trading oil in euros – does it matter?", *Energy Bulletin*, 30 January 2006. A theory of dollar hegemony is outlined in Malm.

44. Looney, pp. 32–4; Jerome Paris: "Let me kill off once and for all the Iranian oil bourse story", *Daily Kos*, 24 February 2006 <www.dailykos.com>; F. William Engdahl: "Why Iran's Oil Bourse Can't Break the Buck", *Energy Bulletin*, 13 March 2006; Howard LaFranchi: "Iran's oil gambit – and potential affront to the US", *Christian Science Monitor*, 30 August 2005 <www.csmonitor.com>; James D. Hamilton: "Strange ideas about the Iranian oil bourse", *Econbrowser*, 22 January 2006 <www.econbrowser. com>.

45. Quotations from *Iran Daily*: "Oil – A Security Link for Middle East"; AP: "Analysts skeptical of Iran oil plan", *Persian Journal*, 5 May 2006 <www. iranian.ws>.

46. Fayazmanesh, pp. 230–35.

47. Robin Wright: "Iran's New Alliance With China Could Cost U.S. Leverage", *Washington Post*, 17 November 2004 <www.washingtonpost. com>; Antoaneta Bezlova: "China-Iran tango threatens US leverage", *Asia Times*, 30 November 2004 <www.asiatimes.com>; Reuters: "Iran seeks to sign key oil deal with China by Jan", *MSNBC*, 17 December 2005 <www. msnbc.com>; *Oil & Gas Journal*: "Talks continue for Pakistan-Iran pipeline megaproject", 10 January 2005; Neil Ford: "Tehran puts the cat among the pigeons", *The Middle East*, March 2006; Klare (2004), pp. 169–71.

48. Cf. Abrahamian (2004), pp. 98–9.

49. Quoted in Johnson, p. 223. Cf. Aruri, pp. 23–4.

50. Klare (2001), pp. 28, 53–62; Klare (2004), pp. 1–6, 43–7, 71–2. It has even been suggested that the occupation of Iraq was an attempt to acquire a substitute for lost Iran: a client state with all the functions once exercised by Pahlavi Iran. Ehteshami (2004), pp. 189–90.

51. Hiro, pp. 250–52, 266–7. On the American intrigues against Iran uncovered through the seizure of the Tehran embassy, see also Fisk, pp. 138–9, 159.

52. See the analysis in Randal Mark: "Nonproliferation: From Noble Lie to Pretext for War", *Liberty Forum*, 15 March 2006 <www.libertyforum. org>.

53. George Wright: "Wolfowitz: Iraq War was About Oil", *The Guardian*, 4 June 2003.

54. Quoted in Klare (2003), p. 172. Cf., e.g., RAND, p. 9.

55. Sokolski, p. 2.

14   GROOMING THE ATTACK DOG

1. Quoted in Fisk, pp. 156–7. Cf. Cooley, pp. 80–81, 84, 118–22; Fayazmanesh, p. 227.

2. On the relations between the Islamic Republic and Hizbollah (analysed primarily on an ideological level), see Saad-Ghorayeb.

3. Quoted in Finkelstein, p. 17.

4. Aruri, pp. 18–20, Nitzan & Bichler, pp. 241–4; quotation from Finkelstein, p. 143.

5. Quoted in Aruri, p. 20.

6. Quoted in ibid., p. 39; numbers from ibid., p. 37.

7. Quoted in ibid., p. 39, italics added.

8. For American appreciation of this monopoly, see, e.g., Sokolski, p. 12.

9. Hersh, pp. 179, 209–11. Recently revealed is the extent of British collaboration in the build-up of Israel's nuclear arsenal, see Meirion Jones: "Britain's dirty secret", *New Statesman*, 13 March 2006.

10. Israel's possession of nuclear submarines, and American collaboration in deploying them, were disclosed days after Israel bombed Syria in October 2003. Peter Beaumont and Conal Urquhart: "Israel deploys nuclear arms in submarines", *Observer*, 12 October 2003 <www.observer.co.uk>.

11. Cooley, pp. 159–62; Hersh, pp. 8–10; Sadr, p. 60.

12. Brom, p. 140.

13. Quotations from ibid., pp. 137–8.

14. Ibid., pp. 140, 139.

15. Uzi Mahnaimi & Peter Conradi: "Israel Targets Iran Nuclear Plant", *The Times*, 18 July 2004 <www.timesonline.co.uk>; AP: "Talk of military action in Iran standoff", *USA Today*, 21 January 2006 <www.usatoday.com>; *Ha'aretz*: "Prime Minister Ehud Olmert's Address before Congress", 24 May 2006 <www.haaretz.com>.

16. Sadr, p. 63; Julian Borger: "Bush commits US to defence of Israel in face of Iran threat", *The Guardian*, 24 January 2006 <www.guardian.co.uk>. Of course, many others have emphasised the applications of MAD to the Iran issue, e.g., Peter Preston: "A nuclear Iran is not the problem", *The Guardian*, 7 February 2005 <www.guardian.co.uk>.

17. Uzi Mahnaimi & Peter Conradi: "Israel Targets Iran Nuclear Plant", *The Times*, 18 July 2004 <www.timesonline.co.uk>. Cf., e.g., Timmermann; Reuel Marc Gerecht: "To Bomb, or Not to Bomb", *Weekly Standard*, Vol. 11, No. 30, 24 April 2006 <www.weeklystandard.com.>

18. Sadr, p. 65.

19. Ibid., pp. 65–6; cf. Rai, pp. 29–31.

20. Abba Eban quoted in Finkelstein, p. 130.

21. IsraelWire: "Peres Admits to Israeli Nuclear Capability", *Global Security*, 14 July 1998 <www.globalsecurity.org> (accessed 2 May 2006).

22. Quotations from David Hirst: "If one side in a conflict goes nuclear, the other is bound to follow suit", *The Guardian*, 4 April 2006 <www.guardian.co.uk>.
23. *Ha'aretz*: "Sanctions on Iran", 10 August 2005 <www.haaretz.com>.
24. Brom, p. 133.
25. Sadr, pp. 68–9.
26. *World Tribune*: "CFR to Bush: Stop Israeli strike on Iran's nuke sites", 30 July 2004 <www.WorldTribune.com>.
27. Stephen Zunes: "The United States, Israel and the Possible Attack on Iran", *Foreign Policy in Focus*, 28 April 2006 <www.fpif.org>; Kurt Nimmo: "Sharon Tries to Pawn Off Fake Photos of Iran's 'Nuclear Installations'", *Counterpunch*, 13 April 2005 <www.counterpunch.org>; Howard, pp. 54–6; Fayazmanesh, pp. 227–30; Sharon quoted in Brom, p. 155.
28. Howard, pp. 69–74; Hiro, pp. 279–81; Ehteshami (2004), p. 187; Abrahamian (2004), p. 96.
29. The analysis of Iran in Iraq is based on Taremi; Ehteshami (2004); newspaper reports.

15   "REAL MEN" GO TO TEHRAN

1. Cf., e.g., Tom Engelhardt: "Connecting the Dots, Bush-Style", *TomDispatch*, 19 March 2006 <www.tomdispatch.com>; Conn Halliman: "Targeting Tehran", *Foreign Policy in Focus*, 25 January 2006 <www.fpif.org>; Joseph Cirincione: "Fool me twice", *Foreign Policy*, 27 March 2006 <www.foreignpolicy.com>; Robert Skidelsky: "The Madness of Bombing Iran", *Iran Press Service*, 26 April 2006 <www.iran-press-service.com>.
2. Sasan Fayazmanesh: "Iran and the 'Experts'", *Znet*, 25 July 2005 <www.zmag.org>. Scott Ritter tried to save his face by twisting the definitions of war: Scott Ritter: "The US war with Iran has already begun", *Al-Jazeera*, 21 June 2005 <http://english.aljazeera.net>. The year before, in August 2004, Simon Tisdall of *The Guardian*, a very well-informed commentator, wrote: "The US charge sheet against Iran is lengthening almost by the day, presaging destabilising confrontations this autumn and maybe a pre-election October surprise"; "Diplomacy sidelined as US targets Iran", *The Guardian*, 10 August 2004 <www.guardian.co.uk>. Rumours of attacks before the elections were rampant on the Internet.
3. E.g. *Financial Times*: "US debates military strikes on 'nuclear Iran'", 16 September 2004 <http://news.ft.com>; John Barry & Dan Ephron: "War-Gaming the Mullahs", *Newsweek*, 27 September 2004; Reuters: "Bush Won't Rule Out Action Against Iran Over Nukes", *Yahoo News*, 17 January 2005 <http://news.yahoo.com>.
4. This view was, according to polls, shared by a majority of Americans in early 2006, regarding Iran even as a bigger threat than Al-Qaida. Jim Lobe/IPS: "Polls: Anti-Iran Propaganda Working", *Antiwar.com*, 10 February 2006 <www.antiwar.com>.
5. Seymour M. Hersh: "The Iran Plans", *New Yorker*, 10 April 2006 <www.newyorker.com>. The day before, the *Washington Post* had run its own story of the plans: Peter Baker, Dafna Linzer & Thomas E. Ricks: "U.S.

Is Studying Military Strike Options on Iran", *Washington Post*, 9 April 2006 <www.washingtonpost.com>. Cf. e.g. *Der Spiegel*: "Is Washington Preparing a Military Strike?", *Spiegel Online*, 31 December 2005 <www.spiegel.de/international>; Philip Sherwell: "US prepares military blitz against Iran's nuclear sites", *The Telegraph*, 12 February 2006 <www.telegraph.co.uk>.

6. Rogers (2006b), pp. 7–9; Seymour M. Hersh: "The Iran Plans", *New Yorker*, 10 April 2006 <www.newyorker.com>.

7. Timothy Garton Ash: "The tragedy that followed Hillary Clinton's bombing of Iran in 2009", *The Guardian*, 20 April 2006 <www.guardian.co.uk>.

8. AFP/AP: "Don't mess with the US, Tehran told", *The Australian*, 30 November 2004 <www.theaustralian.news.com.au>. Cf. Philip Giraldi: "Deep background", *American Conservative*, 1 August 2005 <www.amconmag.com>. Already in early 2002, a secret Pentagon report to Congress on its "Nuclear Posture Review" picked Iran as one of seven countries that could be targeted with nukes "in the event of surprising military developments". Quoted in Gareth Porter/IPS: "Analysts: Fear of US Drove Iran's Nuclear Policy", *Antiwar.com*, 8 February 2006 <www.antiwar.com>. Referring to Iran, Chirac, speaking on board a French nuclear submarine, said: "The leaders of states who use terrorist means against us, as well as those who would consider using, in one way or another, weapons of mass destruction, must understand that they would lay themselves open to a firm and adapted response on our part. This response could be a conventional one. It could be of a different kind." Quoted in Conn Hallinan: "Nuclear Proliferation: A Gathering Storm", *Foreign Policy in Focus*, 2 February 2006 <www.fpif.org>.

9. See, e.g., Matthew Rothschild: "The Human Costs of Bombing Iran", *The Progressive*, 11 April 2006 <http://progressive.org>; Union of Concerned Scientists: "Animation: The Nuclear Bunker Buster", <www.ucsusa.org> (accessed 25 May 2006).

10. E.g., *Ha'aretz*: "Report: IDF planning to attack nuclear sites in Iran", 12 October 2003 <www.haaretz.com>; Uzi Mahnaimi & Peter Conradi: "Israel Targets Iran Nuclear Plant", *The Times*, 18 July 2004 <www.timesonline.co.uk>; Laura King: "Israel May Have Iran in Its Sights", *Los Angeles Times*, 22 October 2004 <www.latimes.com>; Amir Oren: "Israeli joker in the Iranian poker game", *Ha'aretz*, 23 January 2005 <www.haaretz.com>; Anne Penketh: "Israel refuses to rule out attack on Iran", *The Independent*. 27 January 2005 <www.independent.co.uk>.

11. AP: "Halutz: Diplomacy unlikely to curb Iran's nuclear plans", *Ha'aretz*, 5 December 2005 <www.haaretz.com>; Uzi Mahnaimi: "Revealed: Israel plans strike on Iranian nuclear plant", *The Times*, 13 March 2005; Uzi Mahnaimi & Sarah Baxter: "Israel readies forces for strike on nuclear Iran", *The Times*, 11 December 2005 <www.timesonline.co.uk>; Uri Avnery: "Lebanon and the Avaricious Superpower", *Antiwar*, 10 March 2005 <www.antiwar.com>; Ora Koren: "Quality of new Israeli spy satellite photos said 'excellent'", *Ha'aretz*, 30 April 2006 <www.haaretz.com>.

12. Aluf Benn: "U.S. to sell Israel 5,000 smart bombs", *Ha'aretz*, 21 September 2004; Aluf Benn: "Pentagon proposes sale of 100 bunker-busting bombs

to Israel", *Ha'aretz*, 27 April 2005 <www.haaretz.com>; Rogers (2006a), p. 263. For a more "pessimistic" evaluation of the Israeli strike capabilities vis-à-vis Iran, see Brom, pp. 148–52.
13. David Fickling: "Iran 'will cut off hands of aggressors'", *The Guardian*, 18 April 2006 <www.guardian.co.uk>.
14. See, e.g., Kaveh L. Afrasiabi: "How Iran will fight back", *Asia Times*, 16 December 2004 <www.atimes.com>.

16   A PEOPLE CAUGHT IN THE CROSSFIRE

1. Afary, pp. 131–9.
2. Quoted in ibid., p. 140.
3. Ibid., pp. 63, 216.
4. Ibid., pp. 218–27, 285–305.
5. Ibid., pp. 307, 329–32.
6. The tsarist gazette *Novoye Vremya*, quoted in ibid., p. 337.
7. Ibid., pp. 335–9.
8. Keddie, pp. 73–85.
9. Ibid., pp. 109–23. Quotation from ibid., p. 122.
10. Quoted in Kinzer, p. 98.
11. Quoted in ibid., p. 193.
12. Hiro, pp. 219, 229–31, 248–57; Polk, pp. 131–3; Fisk, pp. 262, 272–3, 305–308.
13. Moaddel, p. 237; Moghadam (1988), pp. 197, 203.
14. Behrooz, p. 112.
15. See, e.g., Hiro, p. 220.
16. Quoted in Doug Lorimer: "Iran: A vote against neoliberalism", *Green Left Weekly*, 6 July 2005 <www.greenleft.org>. Cf. Basmenji, pp. 282–4. Cf. Robin Wright: "Iran Gets New President Amid Tensions With the West", *Washington Post*, 4 August 2005 <www.washingtonpost.com>.
17. "Iranian Desperation", *Oil & Gas Journal* (editorial), 23 January 2006.
18. See, e.g., Afrasiabi & Kibaroglu; Mokhtari.
19. Frances Harrison: "Iranians unite over nuclear row", *BBC News*, 20 October 2004 <www.bbc.co.uk>. Cf., e.g., Robert Tait: "Bells ring out on day of rejoicing and patriotic pride", *The Guardian*, 13 April 2006 <www.guardian.co.uk>.
20. Quoted in Nasser Karmimi/AP: "Iran, Syria dismiss Bush's accusations that they sponsor terror", *San Francisco Chronicle*, 3 February 2005 <www.sfgate.com>.
21. "Iran has new proposal as IAEA meets on N-row", *Jang Group/The International News*, 10 August 2005 <www.jang.com.pk/thenews>.
22. Quoted in Kinzer, p. 178. See further ibid., e.g., pp. 5–8, 136–9, 150–65, 177–82.
23. E.g., Behrooz, pp. 138–9; Kinzer, pp. 214–15; Halliday (2004), p. 29; Abrahamian (1991), p. 118; Robert Tait: "Blaming the British", *The Guardian*, 1 March 2006 <www.guardian.co.uk>. An essay whose analysis itself shows traces of this way of thinking is Mokhtari, pp. 215–26.

24. Some of the clippings from the tumult: Mary Jordan & Karl Vick: "World Leaders Condemn Iranian's Call to Wipe Israel 'Off the Map'", *Washington Post*, 28 October 2005 <www.washingtonpost.com>; *BBC News*: "Iran leader defends Israel remark", 28 October 2005 <www.bbc. co.uk>; UPI: "Iran blasts Security Council condemnation", *Washington Times*, 29 October 2005 <www.washtimes.com>; Scott Peterson: "Iranian leader eyes key constituency: young people", *Christian Science Monitor*, 28 October 2005 <www.csmonitor.org>; John Daniszewski: "Pressure to Isolate Iran Gathers Steam", *Los Angeles Times*, 16 December 2005 <www.latimes.com>; *Ha'aretz*: "EU: Iran president's Holocaust remarks may result in sanctions", 16 December 2005 <www.haaretz.com>; Simon Tisdall: "Ahmadinejad on Israel: global danger or political infighting?", *The Guardian*, 20 December 2005 <www.guardian.co.uk>. Juan Cole, whose knowledge of Farsi is undoubtedly superior to most Western media, has claimed that an accurate translation of Ahmadinejad's original statement would have been: "the occupation regime must vanish"; Juan Cole: "Fishing for a pretext in Iran", *Truthdig*, 13 March 2006 <www. truthdig.com>. Notably, Israel has claimed that Iran is an alarming threat because "it wants to destroy Israel" for many years. See, e.g., Abrahamian (2004), p. 105.

25. Reuters: "Iran president doubts Holocaust, suggests Israel move to Europe", *Ha'aretz*, December 2005; AP: "Iran president urges 'active' Muslim approach to Palestinians", *Ha'aretz*, 13 December 2005; AP: "Iran plans conference on 'scientific aspect' of the Holocaust", *Ha'aretz*, 16 January 2006; AP: "Iran pres.: The 'real Holocaust' is now, against Palestinians, Iraqis", *Ha'aretz*, 12 February 2006 <www.haaretz.com>; Yasmin Mather: "Deliberate mistake?", *Iranian.com*, 4 November 2005 <www.iranian.com>.

26. Charles Krauthammer: "In Iran, Arming for Armageddon", *Washington Post*, 16 December 2005 <www.washingtonpost.com>; *Ha'aretz*: "Olmert: Ahmadinejad is 'psychopath' who 'speaks like Hitler'", 29 April 2006 <www.haaretz.com>. Cf. Seymour M. Hersh: "The Iran Plans", *New Yorker*, 10 April 2006 <www.newyorker.com>.

27. Quotations from Kinzer, pp. 120, 95, 113; cf. pp. 128–33.

28. Quoted in Ward, p. 564.

29. Mehrdad Sheibani: "Dangerous Game", *Rooz Online*, 5 May 2006 <www. roozonline.com>. On the apprehensions, see, e.g., Robert Tait: "Iranian reformists fear era of repression", *The Guardian*, 22 July 2005 <www. guardian.co.uk>.

30. Sarah Baxter: "Bush urged to stir rebellion within Iran", *The Times*, 12 February 2006 <www.timesonline.com>. The US Department of State had already noticed the May Day events in 2004 and 2005 and the teachers' strikes. U.S. Department of State: "Iran: Voices Struggling To Be Heard", 3 November 2005 <www.state.gov>. Cf. Jim Lobe: "Hawks Plan 'Peaceful' Regime Change in Iran", *Antiwar.com*, 22 December 2004, <www.antiwar. com>; Alec Russell: "US encourages Iran's reformers to rise against the rule of clerics", *Daily Telegraph*, 4 February 2005, <www.telegraph.co.uk>.

31. Ewen MacAskill & Julian Borger: "Bush plans huge propaganda campaign in Iran", *The Guardian*, 16 February 2006 <www.guardian.co.uk>.

32. Maryam Kashani: "Hunger-Striking Workers Forced to Confess", *Rooz Online*, 6 February 2006; Bahram Rafiee: "Bus Workers Go On Strike in Prison", *Rooz Online*, 5 February 2006 <www.roozonline.com>.

33. International Alliance in Support of Workers in Iran (IASWI): "Congratulations to All Our Fellows around the World on the Repeal of Prison Sentences Against the Saqqez Labour Activists!", 6 May 2006; IASWI: "Saqqez Labour Leaders Back to Court Again!", 6 June 2006 <www. workers-iran.org>.

34. This was actually noted in *The American Conservative* of all magazines: Scott McConnell: "Mission Improbable", *American Conservative*, 27 May 2006 <www.amconmag.com>.

35. Mehdi Kia: "Iranian People Between Islamic State Octopus and Imperialist Vulture", *Iran Press Service*, 25 March 2006 <www.iran-press-service.com>. Cf. Abrahamian (2004), pp. 141–2. Abrahamian also mentions – and here it's difficult not to feel queasy – a neo-conservative memorial service in 2003 for the mass executions of up to 10,000 Leftist prisoners in Iran in 1988. It seems this was the best equivalent to the Halabja massacre (which the US of course originally also approved of) they could find in the history of the Islamic Republic, ibid., p. 106f. On the charges against the feminist movement, see Mahsa Shekarloo: "Iranian Women Take on the Constitution", *Middle East Report Online*, 21 July 2005 <www.merip. org>.

36. Hussein Bagerzadeh: "The US Wants to Reach to the Iranian People. But Whom Should They Talk To?", *Iran Press Service*, 7 April 2006 <www. iran-press-service.com>.

37. Shirin Ebadi & Hadi Ghaemi: "The Human Rights Case Against Attacking Iran", *New York Times*, 8 February 2006 <www.nytimes.com>.

38. Afrasiabi & Kibaroglu, p. 262; Ehteshami, p 182; Arang Keshavarzian: "The Bush Administration and Iran's New President", *Foreign Policy in Focus*, 10 August 2005 <www.fpif.org>.

39. Interview.

40. See, e.g., Roger (2006b).

41. Richard Sale/UPI: "USAF playing cat and mouse game over Iran", *World Peace Herald*, 26 January 2005 <www.wphereald.com>; Seymour M. Hersh: "The Coming Wars – What the Pentagon can now do in secret", *New Yorker*, 17 January 2005; ibid.: "The Iran Plans", *New Yorker*, 10 April 2006 <www.newyorker.com>; Simon Tisdall: "Drumbeat sounds familiar", *The Guardian*, 7 March 2006 <www.guardian.co.uk>.

42. E.g., Simon Tisdall: "US encouraged by Tehran's enemy within", *The Guardian*, 31 March 2006 <www.guardian.co.uk>.

43. "Iraq accuses Iran of border violations", *Al-Jazeera*, 3 May 2006 <http:// english.aljazeera.net>.

44. Pejak/Rojhilat: "Name-i be sahebe ekhtiaran-e mellat-e Iran" (Letter to the rulers of the Iranian people), *Rojhilat – The Kurdish Observer*, 21 April 2006 <www.rojhilat.org>.

45. Robert Tait: "Bombs kill eight in city due to host Iranian leader", *The Guardian*, 25 January 2006 <www.guardian.co.uk>; "Iran blames UK for bombs – reports", *CNN*, 16 October 2005 <www.cnn.com>.

46. Robert Tait: "Iran links Britain to ,
    18 March 2006 <www.guardian.co
47. "Iran's military stages war games ne
    2005 <www.iranfocus.com>.
48. "Military chief says Iran prepared fo
    December 2005 <www.iranfocus.co
49. E.g., Hossein Bagher Zadeh: "The
    Press Service, 21 April 2006 <www.ii
    "Annexing Khuzestan: Battle-plans fc
    2 January 2006 <www.informationcle
50. "Iranian democracy conference to cc
    Kurdish Media, 29 May 2006 <www.Ku

17 THOUGHTS ON A COUNTRY OF CONTRADICTIONS

1. Interviews with student activists in Tehran.
2. Interviews with labour activists in northern Iran.
3. Interviews; Iranian Workers Solidarity Network: "Report on the Labour House's May Day rally in Tehran", <www.iwsn.org> (accessed 25 May 2006); Navid Ahmadi: "Workers: Address Our Problems Instead of Nuclear Energy", Rooz Online, 3 May 2006; Shervin Shareie: "Nuclear Power Overshadows Workers Issues", Rooz Online, 3 May 2006 <www.roozonline.com>.
4. Stephen Zunes: "Democratic Party Platform Turns Toward the War Party", Antiwar.com, 10 August 2004 <www.antiwar.com>; Edward Luttwak: "John Kerry will make his adoring anti-war groupies look like fools", Daily Telegraph, 24 October 2004 <www.telegraph.co.uk>.
5. John O'Neil: "Hillary Clinton Says White House Has Mishandled Iran", New York Times, 19 January 2006 <www.nytimes.com>.
6. Cf. Stephen Zunes: "The United States, Israel and the Possible Attack on Iran", Foreign Policy in Focus, 28 April 2006 <www.fpif.org>; Brom, p. 146.
7. Seymour M. Hersh: "The Iran Plans", New Yorker, 10 April 2006 <www.newyorker.com>.
8. "Will the US now attack Tehran?", New Statesman (leader), 27 September 2004.
9. Muhamad ElBaradei: "Saving Ourselves From Self-Destruction", New York Times, 12 February 2004 <www.nytimes.com>. Cf. Gareth Porter/ IPS: "Analysts: Fear of US Drove Iran's Nuclear Policy", Antiwar.com, 8 February 2006 <www.antiwar.com>.
10. Cf. Richard Falk & David Krieger: "The Non-Proliferation Treaty is failing: What now?", The Transnational Foundation for Peace and Future Research, 29 March 2006 <www.transnational.org>; Brendan O' Neill: "Let Iran have the bomb", The Guardian, 31 March 2006 <www.guardian.co.uk>; Randal Mark: "Nonproliferation: From Noble Lie to Pretext for War", Liberty Forum, 15 March 2006 <www.libertyforum.org>.
11. Stephen Zunes: "The United States, Israel and the Possible Attack on Iran", Foreign Policy in Focus, 28 April 2006 <www.fpif.org>.

sh: "The Iran Plans", *New Yorker*, 10 April 2006 <www.
m>.

.*A*. Hersh: "The Coming Wars – What the Pentagon can now
·cret", *New Yorker*, 17 January 2005 <www.newyorker.com>.

.*k*, p. 187.

Moody, p. 206.

This was pointed out by Nick Cohen: "Why striking bus drivers in Tehran
are the real defenders of Muslim rights", *The Guardian*, 12 February 2006
<www.guardian.co.uk>.

18. Cf. the distinction of Moaddel, pp. 255–6.
19. The power of that temptation can be detected in, e.g., Abrahamian (2004),
pp. 134–6; Ali.

AFTERWORD

1. Ze'ev Sternhell: "The most unsuccessful war", *Ha'aretz*, 2 August 2006,
   <www.haaretz.com>.
2. Nicholas Blandford, Daniel McGrory, Stephen Farrell: "Tactics that have
   kept the Middle East's most powerful army at bay", *The Times*, 10 August
   2006, <www.timesonline.co.uk>.
3. Reuven Pedatzur: "The Day After – How We Suffered a Knockout",
   Ha'aretz, 16 August 2006, <www.haaretz.com>.
4. David B. Rivkin Jr and Lee A Casey: "Israel must win", *Ha'aretz*, 11 August
   2006, <www.haaretz.com>.
5. Ze'ev Schiff: "Tehran's role is extensive", *Ha'aretz*, 16 August 2006, <www.
   haaretz.com>.
6. Matthew Kalman: "Israel set war plan more than a years ago", *San
   Francisco Chronicle*, 21 July 2006, <www.sfgate.com>.
7. Seymour M. Hersh: "Watching Lebanon", *New Yorker*, 14 August 2006,
   <www.newyorker.com>.

Bibliography

Abrahamian, Ervand (1991): "Khomeini: Fundamentalist or Populist?", New Left Review, No. 1/186, March-April 1991, pp. 102–119.

Abrahamian, Ervand (2004): "Empire Strikes Back: Iran in U.S. Sights", pp. 93–156 in Abrahamian, Ervand; Cumings, Bruce & Ma'oz, Moshe: *Inventing the Axis of Evil – The Truth About North Korea, Iran, and Syria*, New York/London, The New Press.

Afary, Janet (1996): *The Iranian Constitutional Revolution, 1906–1911 – Grassroots Democracy, Social Democracy, & the Origins of Feminism*, New York, Columbia University Press.

Afary, Janet & Anderson, Kevin B. (2005): *Foucault and the Iranian Revolution – Gender and the Seductions of Islamism*, Chicago/London, University of Chicago Press.

Afrasiabi, Kaveh & Kibaroglu, Mustafa (2005): "Negotiating Iran's Nuclear Populism", Brown Journal of World Affairs, Vol. XII, No. 1, Summer/Fall 2005, pp. 255–268.

Alavi, Nasrin (2005): *We Are Iran*, London, Portobello Books.

Ali, Tariq (2006): "Mid-Point in the Middle East?", New Left Review, No. 2/38, March–April 2006, pp. 5–19.

Alizadeh, Parvin (ed) (2000): *The Economy of Iran – Dilemmas of an Islamic State*, London/New York, I.B. Tauris.

Alizadeh, Parvin (2003): "Iran's Quandary: Economic Reforms and the 'Structural Trap'", Brown Journal of World Affairs, Vol. IX, No. 2, Winter/Spring 2003, pp. 267–281.

Alizadeh, Parvin & Harper, Barry (2003): "The feminization of the labour force in Iran", pp. 180–196 in Mohammadi.

Amid, Javad & Hadjikhani, Amjad (2005): *Trade, Industrialization, and the Firm in Iran – The Impact of Government Policy on Business*, London/New York, I.B. Tauris.

Aruri, Naseer H. (2003): *Dishonest Broker – The U.S. Role in Israel and Palestine*, Cambridge, South End Press.

Azad, Shahrzad (1980): "Workers' and Peasants' Councils in Iran", Monthly Review, October 1980, pp. 14–14–29.

Badiei, Sousan & Bina, Cyrus (2002): "Oil and Rentier State: Iran's Capital Formation, 1960–1997", Topics in Middle Eastern & North African Economics: Proceeding of the Middle East Economic, www.sba.luc.edu (accessed 2005–12–21).

Basmenji, Kaveh (2005): *Tehran Blues – How Iranian Youth Rebelled Against Iran's Founding Fathers*, London, Saqi.

Bayat, Assef (1987): *Workers and Revolution in Iran – A Third World Experience of Workers' Control*, London/New Jersey, Zed Books.

Bayat, Assef (1997): *Street Politics – Poor People's Movements in Iran*, New York, Columbia University Press.

Behrooz, Maziar (2000): *Rebels With a Cause – The Failure of the Left in Iran*, London/New York, I.B. Tauris.

Behrooz, Maziar (2004): "The Iranian Revolution and the Legacy of the Guerrilla Movement", pp. 189–203 in Cronin.

Brom, Shlomo (2005): "Is the Begin Doctrine Still a Viable Option for Israel?", pp. 133–158 in Sokolski & Clawson.

Campbell, Colin J. & Laherrère, Jean H. (1998): "The End of Cheap Oil", Scientific American, March.

Cole, Juan; Katzman, Kenneth; Sadjadpour, Karim & Takyeh, Ray (2005): "A Shia Crescent: What Fallout for the United States?", Middle East Policy, Vol. XII, No. 4, Winter 2005, pp. 1–27.

Cooley, John K. (2005): An Alliance Against Babylon – The U.S., Israel, and Iraq, London/Ann Arbor, Pluto Press.

Cronin, Stephanie (ed) (2004): Reformers and Revolutionaries in Modern Iran – New Perspectives on the Iranian Left, London/New York, Routledge.

CSIS [Center for Strategic and International Studies] (2006): Iranian Nuclear Weapons? – The Uncertain Nature of Iran's Nuclear Programs, CSIS [download available at www.csis.org].

Dadkhah, Kamran M. (2003): "Iran and the global finance markets", pp. 86–106 in Mohammadi.

Dailiami, Pezhmann (2004): "The First Congress of Peoples of the East and the Iranian Soviet Republic of Gilan, 1920–21", pp. 85–107 in Cronin.

Davies, Joyce M. (2003): Martyrs – Innocence, Vengeance, and Despair in the Middle East, New York/Hampshire, Palgrave MacMillan.

Ehteshami, Anoushiravan (1995): After Khomeini – The Iranian Second Republic, London/New York, Routledge.

Ehteshami, Anoushiravan (2004): "Iran's International Posture After the Fall of Baghdad", Middle East Journal, Vol. 58, No. 2, Spring 2004, pp. 179–194.

Farhi, Farideh (1989): "Class Struggles, the State, and Revolution in Iran", pp. 90–113 in Berch Berberoglu (ed): Power and Stability in the Middle East, London, Zed Books.

Fayazmanesh, Sasan (2003): "The Politics of the U.S. Economic Sanctions against Iran", Review of Radical Political Economics, Vol. 35, No. 3, Summer 2003, pp. 221–240.

Finkelstein, Norman G. (2001): Image and Reality of the Israel-Palestine Conflict, London/New York, Verso.

Fisk, Robert (2005): The Great War for Civilisation – The Conquest of the Middle East, London, Fourth Estate/HarperCollins.

Ghorashi, G. Reza (2003): "Economic globalization and the prospects for democracy in Iran", pp. 77–85 in Mohammadi.

Goodstein, David (2004): Out of Gas – The End of the Age of Oil, New York/London, Norton.

Goodey, Chris (1980): "Workers' Councils in Iranian Factories", MERIP Reports, No. 88, June 1980, pp. 5–9.

Hakimian, Hassan (2000): "Population Dynamics in Post-Revolutionary Iran: A Re-examination of Evidence", pp. 177–203 in Alizadeh (ed).

Halliday, Fred (1987): "The Iranian Revolution and Its Implications", New Left Review, No. 1/166, November–December 1987, pp. 29–37.

Halliday, Fred (1988): "The Iranian Revolution: Uneven Development and Religious Populism", pp. 31–63 in Fred Halliday & Hamza Alavi (eds): State and Ideology in the Middle East and Pakistan, Basingstoke, MacMillan.

Halliday, Fred (2004): "The Iranian Left in international perspective", pp. 19–36 in Cronin.

Hersh, Seymour M. (1991): *The Samson Option – Israel, America and the Bomb*, London/Boston, Faber and Faber.

Hiro, Dilip (2006): *Iran Today*, London, Politico's.

Howard, Roger (2004): *Iran in Crisis? – Nuclear ambitions and the American response*, London/New York, Zed Books.

Human Rights Watch (2005): *Ministers of Murder – Iran's New Security Cabinet*, HRW [download available at http://hrw.org].

ICFTU [International Confederation of Free Trade Unions] (2005): *Annual Survey of Violations of Trade Union Rights 2005*, ICFTU [download available at www.icftu.org].

International Crisis Group (2005): *The State of Sectarianism in Pakistan*, ICG [download available at www.crisisgroup.org].

ISS [The International Institute for Strategic Studies] (2005): *Iran's Strategic Weapons Programmes – A Net Assessment*, Oxford/New York, Routledge.

Jalali-Naini, Ahmad R. (2005): "Capital Accumulation and Economic Growth in Iran: Past Experiences and Future Prospects", Iranian Studies, Vol. 38, No. 1, March 2005, pp. 91–117.

Johnson, Chalmers (2004): *The Sorrows of Empire – Militarism, Secrecy, and the End of the Republic*, New York, Metropolitan/Henry Holt.

Keddie, Nikki R. (2003): *Modern Iran – Roots and Results of Revolution*, New Haven/London, Yale University Press.

Khajehpour, Bijan (2001): "Iran's Economy: Twenty Years after the Islamic Revolution", pp. 93–122 in John L. Esposito & R.K. Ramazani (eds): *Iran at the Crossroads*, New York, Palgrave.

Kinzer, Stephen (2003): *All the Shah's Men – An American Coup and the Roots of Middle East Terror*, New Jersey, Wiley.

Klare, Michael T. (2001): *Resource Wars – The New Landscape of Global Conflict*, New York, Henry Holt.

Klare, Michael T. (2003): "Blood for Oil – The Bush-Cheney Energy Strategy", pp. 166–185 in Panitch, Leon & Leys, Colin (eds): *Socialist Register 2004 – The New Imperial Challenge*, London, Merlin Press.

Klare, Michael T. (2004): *Blood and Oil – The Dangers and Consequences of America's Growing Petroleum Dependency*, New York, Metropolitan/Henry Holt.

Koohi-Kamali (2003): *The Political Development of the Kurds in Iran*, Hampshire/New York, Palgrave Macmillan.

Kurzman, Charles (2004): *The Unthinkable Revolution in Iran*, Cambridge/London, Harvard University Press.

Looney, Robert (2004): "Petroeuros: A Threat to U.S. Interest in the Gulf?", Middle East Policy, Vol. XI, No. 1, Spring 2004, pp. 26–37.

Malm, Andreas (2004): *När kapitalet tar till vapen – Om imperialism i vår tid* [Capital at war – On imperialism in our time], Stockholm, Agora.

Maloney, Suzanne (2000): "Agents or Obstacles? – Parastatal Foundations and Challenges for Iranian Development", pp. 145–176 in Alizadeh (ed).

Marx, Karl (1959): *Capital Vol. III – The Process of Capitalist Production as a Whole*, Institute of Marxism-Leninism [download from www.marxists.org.].

Matin-Asgari, Afshin (2004): "From social democracy to social democracy: the twentieth-century odyssey of the Iranian Left", pp. 37–64 in Cronin.

McKillop, Andrew & Newman, Sheila (2005): *The Final Energy Crisis*, London/ Ann Arbor, Pluto Press.

Mirsepassi, Ali (2004): "The Tragedy of the Iranian Left", pp. 229–249 in Cronin.

Moaddel, Mansour (1993): *Class, Politics, and Ideology in the Iranian Revolution*, New York, Columbia University Press.

Moghadam, Val (1987): "Socialism or Anti-Imperialism? The Left and Revolution in Iran", New Left Review, No 1/166, November–December 1987, pp. 5–28.

Moghadam, Valentine M. (1988): "Industrialization Strategy and Labour's Response: The Case of the Workers' Councils in Iran", pp. 182–209 in Roger Southall (ed): *Trade Unions and the New Industrialisation of the Third World*, London, Zed Books

Moghadam, Valentine (1996): "Making History, but Not of Their Own Choosing: Workers and the Labor Movement in Iran", pp. 65–97 in Ellis Jay Goldberg (ed): *The Social History of Labor in the Middle East*, Boulder, Westview Press.

Moghissi, Haideh & Rahnema, Saeed (2004): "The Working Class and the Islamic State in Iran", pp. 280–301 in Cronin.

Mohammadi, Ali (ed) (2003): *Iran Encountering Globalization – Problems and Prospects*, London/New York, Routledge.

Mokhtari, Fariborz (2005): "No One Will Scratch My Back: Iranian Security Perceptions in Historical Context", Middle East Journal, Vol. 59, No. 2, Spring 2005, pp. 209–229.

Moody, Kim (1997): *Workers in a Lean World – Unions in the International Economy*, London/New York, Verso.

Nafisi, Azar (2004): *Reading Lolita in Tehran – A Memoir in Books*, London/New York, Fourth Estate/HarperCollins.

Nitzan, Jonathan & Bichler, Shimshon (2002): *The Global Political Economy of Israel*, London/Sterling, Pluto Press.

Parsa, Misagh (1989): *Social Origins of the Iranian Revolution*, New Brunswick/ London, Rutgers University Press.

Platform [IPS, War on Want, Global Policy Forum, Oil Change, NEF] (2005): *Crude Designs – The Rip-Off of Iraq's Oil Wealth*, Platform [download available from www.platformlondon.org].

Polk, William R. (2005): *Understanding Iraq – The Whole Sweep of Iraqi History, from Genghis Khan's Mongols to the Ottoman Turks to the British Mandate to the American Occupation*, New York, HarperCollins.

Poya, Maryam (1999): *Women, Work and Islamism – Ideology and Resistance in Iran*, London/New York, Zed Books.

Rahnema, Saeed (1992): "Work Councils in Iran: The Illusion of Worker Control", Economic and Industrial Democracy, Vol. 13.

Rai, Milan (2003): *Regime Unchanged – Why The War on Iraq Changed Nothing*, London/Sterling, Pluto Press.

Reuter, Christoph (2004): *My Life Is a Weapon – A Modern History of Suicide Bombing*, New Jersey, Princeton University Press.

Roberts, Paul (2005): *The End of Oil – On the Edge of a Perilous New World*, Boston/New York, Houghton Mifflin.

Robinson, Glenn E. (1997): *Building a Palestinian State – The Incomplete Revolution*, Bloomington & Indianapolis, Indiana University Press.

Rogers, Paul (2006a): *A War Too Far – Iraq, Iran and the New American Century*, London/Ann Arbor, Pluto Press.

Rogers, Paul (2006b): *Iran – Consequences of a War*, Oxford Research University Group [download available at www.oxfordresearchgroup.org.uk].

Saad-Ghorayeb, Amal (2002): *Hizbu'llah – Politics and Religion*, London/Sterling, Pluto Press.

Sadr, Ehsaneh I. (2005): "The Impact of Iran's Nuclearization on Israel", Middle East Policy, Vol. XII. No. 2, Summer 2005, pp. 58–72.

Salehi-Esfahani, Djavad (2005): "Human Resources in Iran: Potentials and Challenges", Iranian Studies, Vol. 38, No. 1, March 2005, pp. 117–147.

Simmons, Matthew R. (2005): *Twilight in the Desert – The Coming Saudi Oil Shock and the World Economy*, New Jersey, Wiley.

Sokolski, Henry (2005): "Getting Ready for a Nuclear-Ready Iran – Report of the NPEC Working Group", pp. 1–20 in Sokolski & Clawson.

Sokolski, Henry & Clawson, Patrick (eds.) (2005): *Getting Ready for a Nuclear-Ready Iran*, Strategic Studies Institute [download available at www. strategicinstitute.army.mil].

Taremi, Kamran (2005): "Iranian Foreign Policy Towards Occupied Iraq, 2003–05", Middle East Policy, Vol. XII, No. 4, Winter 2005, pp. 28–47.

Timmerman, Kenneth R. (2005): "The Day after Iran Gets the Bomb", pp. 113–129 in Sokolski & Clawson.

Ward, Steven R. (2005): "The Continuing Evolution of Iran's Military Doctrine", Middle East Journal, Vol. 59, No. 4, Autumn 2005, pp. 559–576.

Yaghmaian, Behzad (2002): *Social Change in Iran – An Eyewitness Account of Dissent, Defiance, and New Movements for Rights*, New York, State University of New York Press.

Zanganeh, Hamid (2003): "The Iranian economy and the globalization process", pp. 107–134 in Mohammadi.

Index

bus drivers, strike and union
    initiative, xvi, 116–122, 200–1,
    207, 212
Bush, George W., xvi
    alleged popularity of in Iran, 127,
        132
    on Iran, xvii, 133, 140, 179,
        185–6, 208
    on oil prices, 152–3
    and war between Hizbollah and
        Israel, 218
Bushehr, 83, 141–2, 178, 208
buy-back contracts, 48, 159–61,
    164–5

capital accumulation
    in the Islamic Republic, 40–1,
        50–3, 58, 64, 68, 82–3, 91, 99,
        116, 143, 169
    and oil, 152–6, 167
    in Pahlavi Iran, 26–9
Carter, Jimmy, 11, 171, 194
Caspian Sea, 77–8, 140, 184, 203
Caterpillar, 11, 14, 27
censorship, 12, 75, 83, 85, 101, 104,
    125–6, 131
Central Command, US, 146, 150,
    171
chador, 3, 61, 103, 131
"chastity houses", 59, 130
chemical weapons, 139, 145–7
Cheney, Dick, 144, 158, 166, 172–3,
    218
child labour, 60, 67
China, 25, 42, 44, 71, 114, 141,
    146, 151, 170, 179, 209
CIA, 9, 150, 174, 176, 198, 205
Clinton, Hillary, 128, 208
Coca-Cola, 50, 128–9, 132
comprador bourgeoisie, 26–9, 33–9,
    43, 45–6, 49, 52, 111, 132, 158,
    171–2, 214
Congress of Iranian Nationalities,
    99, 206
conspiracy theories, 3, 198–9
Constitutional Revolution
    (1907–11), 5–8, 28, 77–8,
    191–3, 198
construction sector, 44–5, 50, 57,
    79, 93

corruption, 51–2
council communism, 87, 121
Council of Guardians, 34, 109, 115
coup of 1908, 7
coup of 1953, 9–10, 22, 161–3, 171,
    198

dam construction projects, 44, 57,
    67, 145
delayed wages, 7, 57, 71, 77, 80–1,
    83–4, 117–18, 211, 219
demographic policies, of the Islamic
    Republic, 54–5
dependency, on advanced capitalist
    countries, 14, 26–7, 34, 42,
    44–5, 52, 78, 149, 161
drugs, 60, 65–6, 95, 104, 121, 128,
    130

Ebadi, Shirin, 106, 202
The Economist, 112, 155, 164
    Economist Intelligence Unit, 47, 52
elections
    to Majles in 1906, 5
    to Majles in 1984, 34
    to Majles in 2004, 109, 115
    presidential in 1997, 100
    presidential in 2005, 85–6,
        110–12, 115, 118, 196–7, 204
embassy occupation, 1979, 22, 174,
    194
Esfahan, 11, 15, 24, 63, 75, 86, 130,
    150–2, 188, 192
EU, 142, 148–50, 198–9
Evin prison, 24, 114, 118–21
Expediency Council, 115, 202

Al-Faqih, 33–6, 45, 48, 50, 68, 69,
    75, 97, 115–16, 179–80, 198,
    202
Fatima, 54, 61, 63
Fedaiyan
    armed struggle and ideology of,
        17–18, 30, 78, 142
    in 1979 revolution, 17–18, 78
    on shora movement, 20
    Majority, 20, 37–8, 88, 108
    Minority, 37–8, 196
feminism, 104–7, 201

taunted by Ahmadinejad, 197,
199–200
threatening and planning attack
on Iran, xvii, 140, 181–2,
188–9, 212

Jangalist movement, 8, 17, 78–9,
193–4
Japan, 147, 160, 170
Javan, Roza, 85, 102–6
joint ventures, 43, 47, 49–51, 71
journalists, xvi, 49, 59, 109, 128,
131, 141, 186, 189, 200

Karbala, 32, 54, 76, 183, 196, 203
Karrajj, 72, 83
KDPI, Kurdish Democratic Party of
Iran, 92, 94–5, 204
Kerman, 49, 71, 82
Kermanshah, 75, 86, 92, 110, 219
Khamene'i, Ayatollah Ali
and Ahmadinejad, 115–16, 202
in Khuzestan, 97
on labour, 68
and millionaire mullahs, 50–1,
197
and nuclear programme, 145, 198
protests against, 75, 94
and Rafsanjani, 45, 115, 141
succeeding Khomeini, 45
Khan, Khuzek, 8, 79
Khane-ye Karegar, 16–17, 24, 55,
70, 85, 88, 101, 108, 117,
122–3, 208, 219
Khatami, Mohammad, 100–11, 113,
116, 122–3, 127, 145, 147, 167
Khatonabad massacre, 71–2, 74, 81,
106, 207
khod kafai, 42, 149
Khomeini, Ayatollah
and bazaari, 33–4
demographic policies of, 54
on economic policies, 42, 45
in Iran–Iraq War, 145, 196
and Israel, 199
as leader of 1979 revolution, 12,
22, 25–7, 31–3, 37, 212
and Left, 37–8, 88
on nuclear weapons, 141

and Pasdaran, 23
and populism, 35, 113–14, 143
and Shah's regime, 30–1
and shora movement and strikes,
21–3, 37, 145
theological ideas of, 31–2
Khuzestan
Arab minority of, 95–8
armed struggle in, 203–5
and Iran–Iraq War, 54, 96
militarisation of, 205
oil in, 9, 51, 156, 160–2, 192–3
oil workers of, 11–12, 16, 21, 27,
40, 66, 95, 120
popular uprising (2005), 97–8
underdevelopment in, 95–7, 99,
205
Klebnikov, Paul, 49, 163
Komele, 84, 86, 92–5, 204
komitehs, 15–16, 32
Komiteye Hamahangi, 86–9, 105,
121
Komiteye Peygiri, 88–9, 108, 120–1
Koran, 22, 31–2, 40, 70
Kristof, Nicholas D., 127, 133
Kurdistan
autonomy struggles, 92–3
Fedaiyan Minority in, 38
labour struggles in, 76–7, 85, 201
peasant shoras in, 16
popular uprising (2005), 93–5
underdevelopment, 92–3
(see also Pejak, Saqqez)
Kurds, 32–6, 99, 108, 132, 174, 204
Kuwait, 147, 205

labour laws, 56, 63, 69, 78, 122
Lebanon, 91, 175, 211, 213, 215–19
Left
in 1979 revolution, 17–20, 30–1,
36–9, 86, 89, 121
in exile, 89–90, 94
in Gilan shora, 80–1
and Iran–Iraq War, 196
on Islamic Republic as disguised
comprador, 45–6
Lenin, 18, 89

MAD, Mutually Assured
Destruction, 179–80

Donachunt@hotmail.com

Neil mcdonald   Irish Independent

Ronald me beauty   Irish Times

Ronall me Greafer

Rmacreere@Irish-times.e

RmcGreevy@Irish-times.ie

GW00361463

Summary
and
Practice

with answers

Paul Hogan
St Wilfrid's C of E High School, Blackburn

Barbara Job
Christleton County High School, Chester

T

Text © Paul Hogan, Barbara Job 2004
Original illustrations © Nelson Thornes Ltd 2002

The right of Paul Hogan and Barbara Job to be identified as authors of this work has been asserted by them in accordance with the Copyright, Designs and Patents Act 1988.

All rights reserved. No part of this publication may be reproduced or transmitted in any form or by any means, electronic or mechanical, including photocopy, recording or any information storage and retrieval system, without permission in writing from the publisher or under licence from the Copyright Licensing Agency Limited of 90 Tottenham Court Road, London W1T 4LP.

Any person who commits any unauthorised act in relation to this publication may be liable to criminal prosecution and civil claims for damages.

Published in 2004 by:
Nelson Thornes Ltd
Delta Place
27 Bath Road
CHELTENHAM
GL53 7TH
United Kingdom

04   05   06   07   08   /   11   10   9   8   7   6   5   4   3

A catalogue record for this book is available from the British Library.

ISBN 0 7487 9034 9

Page make-up by Tech Set Ltd

Printed and bound in Spain by Graficas Estella

Acknowledgements
The publishers thank the following for permission to reproduce copyright material:
Leslie Garland Picture Library 80; Collections/Brian Shuel 68; Martyn Chillmaid 112, 145, 147.
Thanks to Graham Newman, Chief Marker for Key Stage 3 Mathematics, for the Practice Examination Questions and Test Tips and for his invaluable contributions at review.

Contents

How to use this book

This book has been carefully designed to help you to prepare for the National Key Stage 3 Tests that all students do in Year 9.

You will take the tests at one of four 'tiers'; Tier 3–5, Tier 4–6, Tier 5–7 or Tier 6–8. The numbers in these tiers are the National Curriculum levels. They are an indication of the difficulty of the work.

This book will help you to revise and give you practice for all of the tiers. You need to know which tier you are aiming for before you start using the book.

The book covers the National Curriculum in 13 short clear topics. On the next page, you can see how the book has been designed to help you study and practise your Maths. You should read this carefully before you start to use the book.

There are lots of Practice Questions. These are like the questions that you will get on the maths tests. One of the best ways to revise maths is to do lots of practice questions and check your answers.

When answering the questions you can write your answers in the spaces or write them on a sheet of paper. Your teacher will tell you which method to use.

The answers to all the questions are given at the back of the book.

Don't just copy the answers out. That won't help you learn! Try the questions and then check your answers. You can learn a lot by checking your own answers and looking to see where you may have lost marks, so that you can do better next time.

We hope you will find this book very helpful in preparing yourself for the tests.

Paul Hogan
Barbara Job

There are 13 topics in this book. Each one starts with work that **everyone needs to know**.

If you are doing Tier 6–8 or Tier 5–7 you may feel that you don't need to do any of the early part of each chapter. It is still a good idea to read it and do the Test Yourself and Practice Questions to make sure that you understand everything!

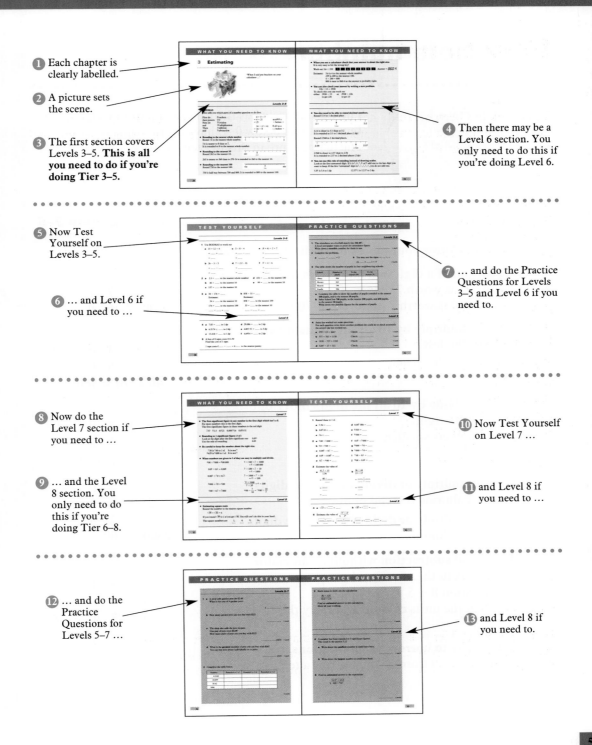

1 Each chapter is clearly labelled.

2 A picture sets the scene.

3 The first section covers Levels 3–5. **This is all you need to do if you're doing Tier 3–5.**

4 Then there may be a Level 6 section. You only need to do this if you're doing Level 6.

5 Now Test Yourself on Levels 3–5.

6 … and Level 6 if you need to …

7 … and do the Practice Questions for Levels 3–5 and Level 6 if you need to.

8 Now do the Level 7 section if you need to …

9 … and the Level 8 section. You only need to do this if you're doing Tier 6–8.

10 Now Test Yourself on Level 7 …

11 and Level 8 if you need to …

12 … and do the Practice Questions for Levels 5–7 …

13 and Level 8 if you need to.

1 Whole numbers

The Celsius scale has the freezing point of water at 0 °C.
Temperatures below 0 °C have minus signs in front.
The temperature in this freezer is −10 °C.

Levels 3–5

- **You need to know your tables up to the 10 times table.**

- **The position of a digit in a number is important.**
  The 7 in 571 is worth 7 tens = 70
  The 7 in 4760 is worth 7 hundreds = 700

Th	H	T	U
	5	7	1
4	7	6	0

- **When you multiply by 10 all the digits move one column to the left.**
  The number gets bigger.

H	T	U
	4	6
4	6	0

  46 × 10 = 460

- **When you divide by 10 all the digits move one column to the right.**
  The number gets smaller.

H	T	U
5	8	0
	5	8

  580 ÷ 10 = 58

- **When you multiply or divide by 100 the digits move two columns instead of one.**

- **When you multiply or divide by 1000 the digits move three columns.**

Th	H	T	U
2	3	0	0
		2	3

  2300 ÷ 100 = 23

- **Addition and subtraction without a calculator**
  Put the digits in the correct columns.
  In this question 8 + 5 = 13
  Put the 3 in the units column and carry the 1.

H	T	U
	2	4	8
+		2	5
	2	7	3
			1

- **You may have to borrow in subtractions.**
  You cannot take 9 from 6. You borrow a ten to give
  16 − 9 = 7

H	T	U
	2	²3̶	¹6
−		1	9
	2	1	7

- **Multiplication without a calculator**
  Multiply by the units digit first.
  Put 0 in the units column before multiplying by the tens digit.
  Add the two parts.

$$\begin{array}{r} 1\ 2\ 3 \\ \times\ \ \ 3\ 2 \\ \hline 2\ 4\ 6 \\ 3\ 6\ 9\ 0 \\ \hline 3\ 9\ 3\ 6 \\ 1 \end{array}$$

- **Division without a calculator**
  In this question start by working out the 13 times table.
  $31 \div 13 = 2$ with 5 to carry because
  $2 \times 13 = 26$ and $31 - 26 = 5$
  Then $52 \div 13 = 4$ because $4 \times 13 = 52$

$$13\overline{)3\ 1^5 2}\ \ \ ^{2\ 4}$$

$1 \times 13 = 13$
$2 \times 13 = 26$
$3 \times 13 = 39$
$4 \times 13 = 52$

- **Negative numbers have a minus sign in front of them.**
  This thermometer shows a temperature of $-5\,°C$
  $-10\,°C$ is lower than $-5\,°C$.
  $5\,°C$ is higher than $-5\,°C$.

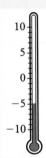

- **Use a thermometer scale to help you add and subtract.**
  To work out $-5 + 8$ start at -5 and move up 8.
  You get to 3   so $-5 + 8 = 3$
  To work out $-5 - 2$ start at -5 and move down 2.
  You get to -7 so $-5 - 2 = -7$

Level 6

- **Adding and subtracting with negative numbers.**
  $6 - -3 = 6 + 3 = 9$ $- -$ becomes $+$
  $7 + -2 = 7 - 2 = 5$ $+ -$ becomes $-$
  $-4 - -5 = -4 + 5 = 1$
  $-2 + -6 = -2 - 6 = -8$

- **Multiplying and dividing with negative numbers.**
  $+ \times + = +$ $- \times - = +$ Two signs the same give $+$
  $+ \times - = -$ $- \times + = -$ Two different signs give $-$
  The same rules work for division.
  $+4 \times +3 = +12$ $-4 \times -6 = +24$ $+12 \div +6 = +2$ $-24 \div -6 = +4$
  $+5 \times -2 = -10$ $-10 \times +3 = -30$ $+20 \div -5 = -4$ $-16 \div +2 = -8$

- **5^3 means $5 \times 5 \times 5$. The power 3 tells you how many 5s to multiply together.**

- **A power of 2 is called square.**
  10^2 means 10×10
  You say this as 'ten squared'.

- **A power of 3 is called cube.**
  10^3 means $10 \times 10 \times 10$
  You say this as 'ten cubed'.

Levels 3–5

1 The value of

Th	H	T	U
5	1	3	8

   a the 3 is ......

   b the 1 is ......

2 **a** $4 \times 7 =$ ......   **b** $6 \times 9 =$ ......   **c** $8 \times$ ...... $= 24$

3 **a** $26 \times 10 =$ ......   **b** $41 \times 100 =$ ......   **c** $53 \times$ ...... $= 530$

4 **a** $360 \div 10 =$ ......   **b** $8000 \div 100 =$ ......   **c** $4860 \div$ ...... $= 486$

5

a
```
   260
 + 123
 ─────
```

b
```
   187
 +  35
 ─────
```

c
```
   174
 −  51
 ─────
```

d
```
   509
 −  46
 ─────
```

6

a
```
   237
 ×  25
 ─────
 ─────
```

b $14\overline{)322}$
$1 \times 14 =$
$2 \times 14 =$
$3 \times 14 =$

7 Put these numbers in order $12, -4, -6, 5, 0$

Start with the smallest   ...... , ... , ... , ... , ...

8 The temperature is $-2\,°C$. It rises $5\,°C$. The new temperature is ...... °C.

Level 6

9 **a** $4 - {-6} =$ ......   **d** $20 \div -4 =$ ......   **g** $-5 \times$ ...... $= 15$

   b $-8 - 3 =$ ......   **e** $18 - {-2} =$ ......   **h** $-36 \div$ ...... $= -6$

   c $-4 \times -7 =$ ......   **f** $-6 + -12 =$ ......   **i** ...... $\div -10 = -5$

Levels 3–5

1 Here are some number cards.

| 4 | 2 | 3 | 5 |

   a Write down the **smallest** number that can be made with these cards.

.... 1 mark

   b Write down the **largest** number that can be made with these cards.

.... 1 mark

   c Which extra card is needed to make a number **ten** times bigger than **4235**?

.... 1 mark

2 a A shop sells CDs for **£13** each.
        Find the cost of **25 CDs**.
        Show your working.

Cost of 25 CDs is £ .... 2 marks

   b The shop also sells packs of video tapes for **£18**.
        What is the greatest number of packs of video tapes that could be bought
        with **£300**?
        Show your working.

.... packs 2 marks

3 **a** Write down the **temperature** shown by the arrow.

.... °C   1 mark

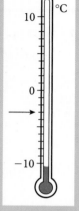

b Draw an arrow on the scale to show a temperature of **8 °C.**

1 mark

c A temperature of **4 °C** went down **6 °C.**
What is the temperature now?

.... °C   1 mark

Level 6

4 −5, −4, −3, −2, −1, 0, 1, 2, 3, 4, 5

Choose a number from the list above which will give

a the **lowest** possible answer

−4 − .... = ...   1 mark

b the **highest** possible answer

−4 − .... = ...   1 mark

In each case also work out the answer.

5 Substitute the values $a = 15, b = -2$ into the formula and work out the value of T:

$$T = \frac{4a}{b}$$

$T = $ ....   1 mark

- **When you multiply by a number between 0 and 1 the answer will be smaller than the number you started with.**

  $200 \times 0.5 = 100$ 100 is less than 200

  $300 \times \frac{2}{3} = 200$ 200 is less than 300

- **When you divide by a number between 0 and 1 the answer will be larger than the number you started with.**

  $200 \div 0.5 = 400$ 400 is more than 200

  $300 \div \frac{2}{3} = 450$ 450 is more than 300

- **Use the bracket keys (( )) on your calculator to help you work out complicated problems.**

  To work out $\dfrac{246 - 157}{4.3 \times 9.1}$ put brackets around the top and bottom. Key in

  (2 4 6 − 1 5 7) ÷ (4 . 3 × 9 . 1) =

  to get 2.27 to 2 dp.

- **The opposite of 'square' is 'square root'.**
  $\sqrt{25} = 5$ because $5 \times 5 = 25$
  -5×-5 is also 25 so $\sqrt{25}$ can be 5 or -5.
  $\sqrt{25} = \pm 5$. There are two answers.

- **The opposite of 'cube' is 'cube root'.**
  You write the cube root as $\sqrt[3]{}$
  $\sqrt[3]{8} = 2$ because $2 \times 2 \times 2 = 8$

- **Power rules**
  When you multiply, add the powers.
  When you divide, subtract the powers.
  With brackets, multiply the powers.

  $a^3 \times a^5 = a^{3+5} = a^8$
  $b^7 \div b^4 = b^{7-4} = b^3$
  $(c^4)^5 = c^{4 \times 5} = c^{20}$

  $2^x \times 2^y = 2^{x+y}$
  $3^p \div 3^q = 3^{p-q}$
  $(x^3)^m = x^{3m}$

- **Negative powers**
  When you get a negative power it always means divide,
  2^{-3} means divide by 2^3.

  So $2^{-3} = 1 \div 2^3 = \dfrac{1}{2^3} = \dfrac{1}{8}$ and $10^{-4} = \dfrac{1}{10^4} = \dfrac{1}{10\,000}$

- **Any number can be written as a number between 1 and 10 multiplied by a power of 10.** This is called standard form. To write 67 000 in standard form, the number between 1 and 10 is 6.7. You need to multiply 6.7 by 10 four times to get 67 000.

  So $67\,000 = 6.7 \times 10^4$

  $$\overset{1\ 2\ 3\ 4}{\frown\frown\frown\frown}$$
  $6.7\,0\,0\,0.$

  To write 0.000 024 6 in standard form, the number between 1 and 10 is 2.46 You need to divide by 10 five times to get to 0.000 024 6.

  To show you have to divide, put a minus sign in the power.

  $$\overset{5\ 4\ 3\ 2\ 1}{\frown\frown\frown\frown\frown}$$
  $0.0\,0\,0\,0\,2.4\,6$

  So $0.000\,024\,6 = 2.46 \times 10^{-5}$

- **You use these rules to change numbers in standard form back to ordinary numbers.**

  $7.13 \times 10^6 = 7\,130\,000$

  $$\overset{1\ 2\ 3\ 4\ 5\ 6}{\frown\frown\frown\frown\frown\frown}$$
  $7.1\,3\,0\,0\,0\,0.$

  $4.02 \times 10^{-3} = 0.004\,02$

  $$\overset{3\ 2\ 1}{\frown\frown\frown}$$
  $0.0\,0\,4.0\,2$

- Most calculators have an **EXP** or **EE** key.
  You can use this key to enter numbers in standard form.

  For 7.13×10^6 key in **7** **.** **1** **3** **EXP** **6**

  The calculator display will look like 7.13×10^{06}

  Use the **+/−** key to enter negative powers.

  For 4.02×10^{-3} key in **4** **.** **0** **2** **EXP** **+/−** **3**

  The calculator display will look like 4.02×10^{-03}

- **Never write the calculator display as your answer.**

  6.5×10^{-04} must be written 6.5×10^{-4} with the 10 shown full size.

  To work out $(3.9 \times 10^4) \div (1.3 \times 10^{-6})$ key in

  3 **.** **9** **EXP** **4** **÷** **1** **.** **3** **EXP** **+/−** **6** **=**

  to get $3. \times 10^{10}$. You must write this as 3×10^{10}.

1 Fill in the space with $\times$ or $\div$

    a 60 ...... 0.2 = 300   **c** 260 ...... 0.4 = 104

    b 50 ...... 0.3 = 15   **d** 150 ...... 0.1 = 1500

2 Write down the calculator keys you would press to work out

    a $\dfrac{4.86 \times 1.63}{4.37 + 1.94}$ ....

    b $\dfrac{4.2 + 3.6^2}{4.91 - 2.87}$ ....

3 **a** $25^2 = $ ....   **c** $\sqrt[3]{27} = $ ....

    b the square root of 81 is ......   **d** the cube root of ...... is 4

4 **a** $p^5 \times p^4 = $ ....   **c** $(r^3)^7 = $ ....

    b $m^{12} \div m^7 = $ .... = ...   **d** $4^{-3} = $ .... = ...

5 Write these numbers in standard form

    a 0.005 = ...   **b** 12 million = ...

6 Write these as ordinary numbers

    a $2.81 \times 10^5 = $ ....   **b** $8.3 \times 10^{-7} = $ ....

7 Write down the calculator keys you would press to work out

    $(4.2 \times 10^6) \div (2.1 \times 10^{-4})$ ....

    ....

Levels 5–7

1 Write numbers into each of the empty boxes so that each problem will work out correctly.

a | 821 | − | 647 | = | ☐

d | 182 | ÷ | 7 | = | ☐

b | ☐ | × | ☐ | × | 5 | = | 40

e | ☐ | − | ☐ | = | 31

c | 1400 | ÷ | ☐ | = | 14

f | 37 | × | 9 | = | ☐

6 marks

2 Sean makes large wax candles that are sold for **£27** each.

a Sean sells **34** candles.
How much does he get for the **34** candles?
Show all your working clearly.

£ .... *2 marks*

b Sean packs **12** candles in a box.
He has **200** candles.
How many full boxes can he pack with the **200** candles?
Show all your working.

.... boxes *2 marks*

3 $K = \dfrac{14.2p}{q - r}$

Use your calculator to find K when $p = 37.4$, $q = 80.4$, $r = 13.53$

$K =$ .... *1 mark*

4 The table shows information about the local taxes raised in four towns.

Town	Taxes	Population
A	£86 850 000	347 400
B	£119 945 000	521 500
C	£98 784 000	403 200
D	£170 977 500	670 500

a Which town had the lowest tax per person? .... 1 mark

b Which town had the highest tax per person? .... 1 mark

Level 8

5 Light travels at the speed of 9.46×10^{12} km/year.

The time it takes for light to reach Earth from the edge of the known universe is 15 000 000 000 years.

a Write the number 15 000 000 000 in standard form.

.... 1 mark

b Calculate the distance in kilometres from the edge of the known universe to Earth. Give your answer in standard form.

.... 2 marks

6 In the United States a centillion is 10^{303}.
In the United Kingdom a centillion is 10^{600}.
How many times bigger is a United Kingdom centillion than a United States centillion?

.... 2 marks

2   Fractions, decimals and percentages

You would never see a price like this!

- **An amount of money which has both pounds and pence must have 2 decimal places.**
  £6.43 is £6 and 43 pence.

- **Your calculator sometimes only gives 1 decimal place.**
  If you work out £30 ÷ 4 on your calculator
  your display will look like this:
  You must write the answer as £7.50

  | 7.5 |

- **The position of a digit after a decimal point is important.**
  The value of the 3 is 3 tenths or $\frac{3}{10}$.
  The value of the 8 is 8 hundredths or $\frac{8}{100}$.

U	.	t	h
4	.	3	8

- **Adding and subtracting decimals without a calculator.**
  Put the digits in the correct columns.
  In this question 7 + 6 = **13**
  Put the **3** in the 't' column and carry the **1**.

	T	U	.	t	h
	3	5	.	7	4
+	1	2	.	6	
	4	8	.	3	4
				1	

- **You may have to borrow in subtractions.**
  You cannot take 8 from 2 in the 't' column.
  You borrow one from the 'U' column to give 12 − 8 = 4

	T	U	.	t	h
	3	⁴5̷	.	¹2	7
−	1	3	.	8	5
	2	1	.	4	2

- **Always make sure the decimal points go underneath each other.**

- **When you multiply by 10 all the digits move one column to the left.**
  The number gets bigger.

  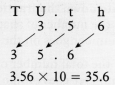

  $$3.56 \times 10 = 35.6$$

- **When you divide by 10 all the digits move one column to the right.**
  The number gets smaller.

  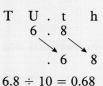

  $$6.8 \div 10 = 0.68$$

- **When you multiply or divide by 100 the digits move two columns instead of one.**

H	T	U	.	t	h
5	9	6	.		
			5	. 9	6

  $$596 \div 100 = 5.96$$

- **When you multiply or divide by 1000 the digits move three columns.**

H	T	U	.	t	h
		0	.	5	1
5	1	0	.	0	0

  $$0.51 \times 1000 = 510$$

- **Multiplying decimals without a calculator.**
  Start with the **4**.
  The $_2$ and the $_1$ are carries.
  Put 0 in the right hand column before multiplying by the **2**
  The $_1$ is a carry.
  Now add the two parts together.
  Make sure you don't add the carries.

  $$
  \begin{array}{r}
  1\,2\,.\,6\,3 \\
  \times \quad\quad 2\,4 \\
  \hline
  5\,{}_2 0\,.\,{}_1 5\,2 \\
  2\,{}_1 5\,2\,.\,6\,0 \\
  \hline
  3\,0\,3\,.\,1\,2 \\
  \end{array}
  $$

- **Dividing decimals without a calculator.**
  $7 \div 5 = 1$ with **2** to carry
  $24 \div 5 = 4$ with **4** to carry
  $41 \div 5 = 8$ with **1** to carry
  Add a **zero**
  $10 \div 5 = 2$

  $$5)\overline{7\,{}^2 4\,.\,{}^4 1\,{}^1 0} \quad = 14.82$$

- **To write down the fraction shaded**
  Count the number of shaded sections.
  This number goes on the top of the fraction.

  Count the total number of equal sections.
  This number goes on the bottom of the fraction.

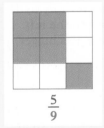

$$\frac{5}{9}$$

- **Different fractions can show the same amount.**

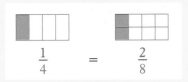

$$\frac{1}{4} \quad = \quad \frac{2}{8}$$

$\frac{1}{4}$ and $\frac{2}{8}$ are equivalent fractions

- **Cancelling fractions**

$$\frac{9}{12} \xrightarrow{\div 3}_{\div 3} \frac{3}{4}$$

$$\frac{75}{300} \xrightarrow{\div 25}_{\div 25} \frac{3}{12} \xrightarrow{\div 3}_{\div 3} \frac{1}{4}$$

- **To find a fraction of an amount multiply by the top number and divide by the bottom number.**

  So $\frac{3}{5}$ of 400 g = 240 g

  $400 \times 3 = 1200$
  $1200 \div 5 = 240$

- **A percentage is a fraction where the bottom number is 100.**
  This circle has **100** equal sections.
  There are **15** shaded sections.

  The fraction shaded is $\frac{15}{100}$

  This is the same as **15%**

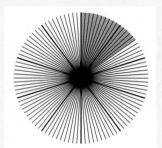

- $\frac{1}{10} = 10\%$ $\frac{1}{5} = 20\%$ $\frac{1}{4} = 25\%$ $\frac{1}{2} = 50\%$
  $\frac{7}{10} = 70\%$ $\frac{2}{5} = 40\%$ $\frac{3}{4} = 75\%$

- **To find a percentage of an amount multiply by the percentage and divide by 100.**

  So **65%** of £800 = £520

  $800 \times 65 = 52\,000$
  $52\,000 \div 100 = 520$

- **To put decimals in order of size**
  Look at the number before the decimal point first.

  26.415 is smaller than 40.1 because 26 is smaller than 40

  If the numbers before the decimal point are the same, look at the first number after the decimal point.

  6.372 is smaller than 6.43 because 3 is smaller than 4

  Sometimes you need to look at the second number after the decimal point.

  7.208 is smaller than 7.261 because 0 is smaller than 6

  Carry on like this. Look at one decimal place at a time.

- **To change a fraction to a decimal divide the top number by the bottom number.**

  $$\frac{7}{8} = 7 \div 8 = 0.875$$

- **To change a percentage to a fraction put it over 100.** Then you can get to a decimal by dividing if you need to.

  $$23\% = \frac{23}{100} = 0.23$$

- **To put a mixture of fractions, percentages and decimals in order, change them all to decimals first.** Remember to change them back at the end.

- **To change a decimal to a percentage multiply it by 100. To turn this into a fraction put it over 100.**

  $$0.31 = 0.31 \times 100\%$$
  $$= 31\%$$
  $$0.31 = 31\% = \frac{31}{100}$$

- You should be able to use the $\boxed{a^b/_c}$ key on your calculator to help you do fractions.

- **To write one number as a fraction of another number.**
  Make sure the units are the same.
  Put the first number on top of the second number.

  Use the $\boxed{a^b/_c}$ key to see if your fraction will cancel.

  To write 45 as a fraction of 180.

  Start with $\frac{45}{180}$. Key in $\boxed{4}$ $\boxed{5}$ $\boxed{a^b/_c}$ $\boxed{1}$ $\boxed{8}$ $\boxed{0}$ $\boxed{=}$
  to get $\frac{1}{4}$ which is the simplest form of the fraction.

- **To write one number as a percentage of another number**

  Write the numbers as a fraction.
  Change the fraction to a percentage by multiplying by 100.
  To write 26 as a percentage of 40

  Start with $\dfrac{26}{40} = \dfrac{26}{40} \times 100\% = 65\%$

- **Finding percentage change**

  The value of a car decreases from £10 000 to £8500 in one year.
  Find the percentage decrease.

  $\text{Percentage decrease} = \dfrac{\text{actual decrease}}{\text{original amount}} \times 100 = \dfrac{1500}{10\,000} \times 100 = 15\%$

- **Ratio can be used to compare two quantities.**

  There are 2 red counters   The ratio   red : blue
  and 4 blue counters   is   2 : 4

  You can simplify this because 2 goes into both numbers
     red : blue = 1 : 2

- **Ratio can also be used to show how a quantity is divided up.**

  To divide £70 in the ratio 2 : 3

  Find the total number of parts by
  adding the numbers in the ratio.   2 + 3 = 5 parts

  Find the value of one part.   £70 ÷ 5 = £14
  Work out the value of each share.   £14 × 2 = £28
                                                    £14 × 3 = £42

- **Scales on maps are often given as a ratio of the form 1 : n**

  Any ratio can be changed to this form.
  Divide both of the numbers in the ratio by the first number

  $2 : 3 = \dfrac{2}{2} : \dfrac{3}{2} = 1 : 1.5$

- **Sometimes ratios are given in the form n : 1**

  This time divide both numbers by the second number

  $3 : 8 = \dfrac{3}{8} : \dfrac{8}{8} = 0.375 : 1$

- **Adding fractions**
  If the bottom numbers are the same add the top two numbers. $\frac{2}{7} + \frac{3}{7} = \frac{5}{7}$
  If the bottom numbers are the different make them the same. $\frac{2}{3} + \frac{1}{5}$

  3 and 5 both go into 15.

  Now you can add $\frac{2}{3} + \frac{1}{5} = \frac{10}{15} + \frac{3}{15} = \frac{13}{15}$

- **Subtracting fractions**
  This works just like adding fractions. $\frac{2}{3} - \frac{5}{12} = \frac{8}{12} - \frac{5}{12} = \frac{3}{12} = \frac{1}{4}$

- **Multiplying fractions**
  Multiply the two top numbers and
  multiply the two bottom numbers. $\frac{2}{3} \times \frac{3}{8} = \frac{6}{24} = \frac{1}{4}$
  Change any mixed numbers to improper fractions. $2\frac{1}{2} \times \frac{3}{8} = \frac{5}{2} \times \frac{3}{8} = \frac{15}{16}$

- **Dividing fractions**
  Turn the second fraction over and then multiply. $\frac{2}{3} \div 1\frac{3}{5} = \frac{2}{3} \div \frac{8}{5} = \frac{2}{3} \times \frac{5}{8} = \frac{10}{24} = \frac{5}{12}$

- **Powers of fractions**
  $\left(\frac{3}{5}\right)^2$ means $\frac{3}{5} \times \frac{3}{5}$ so $\left(\frac{3}{5}\right)^2 = \frac{3^2}{5^2} = \frac{9}{25}$

- **Ordering fractions**
  Think about moving along a number line to compare fractions.

 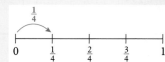 $\frac{1}{3}$ is bigger than $\frac{1}{4}$

  You can also think about moving back from the other end

  $\frac{1}{7}$ is smaller than $\frac{1}{6}$ so $\frac{1}{7}$ is a smaller step back from 1.

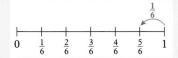  $\frac{6}{7}$ is bigger than $\frac{5}{6}$

  Another way to order fractions is to change them $\frac{3}{8}, \frac{5}{12}, \frac{1}{3}$
  so that they all have the same bottom number. $\frac{9}{24}, \frac{10}{24}, \frac{8}{24}$

  Now you can write the fractions in order. $\frac{1}{3}, \frac{3}{8}, \frac{5}{12}$

Levels 3–5

1 **a** 2.14
        + 1.79

    b 12.76
        − 8.58

    c 2.53
        × 24

    d
    $5\overline{)8.95}$

2 **a** $\frac{5}{8}$ of £224 = £ ....

    ...... ÷ ...... = ...

    ...... × ...... = ...

    b 72% of 900 g = ... g

    ...... ÷ ...... = ...

    ...... × ...... = ...

3 **a** Colour in 25%

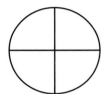

    b Colour in $\frac{3}{4}$

Level 6

4

Fraction	$\frac{1}{2}$	......	......	$\frac{3}{4}$	......	......
Decimal	......	0.25	......	......	0.6	......
Percentage	......	......	20%	......	......	81%

5 **a** 16 as a fraction of 40

    is $\dfrac{\text{.......}}{\text{......}} = \dfrac{\text{.......}}{\text{......}}$

    b 35p as a percentage of £2.50

    = 35p as a percentage of ......p $= \dfrac{\text{.......}}{\text{......}} \times 100\%$

    = ...%

6 Share £180 in the ratio 2 : 3 : 4

    Total number of parts = ...

    Value of 1 part = ... ÷ ...... = £ ......

    Value of each share

    2 × ...... = £ .... × ...... = £ .... × ...... = £ ......

7 a $\frac{2}{5} + \frac{1}{5} = \frac{\cdots\cdots}{\cdots\cdots}$

c $\frac{5}{7} - \frac{2}{7} = \frac{\cdots\cdots}{\cdots\cdots}$

b $\frac{2}{3} + \frac{3}{4} = \frac{\cdots\cdots}{\cdots\cdots} + \frac{\cdots\cdots}{\cdots\cdots}$

$= \frac{\cdots\cdots}{\cdots\cdots} = \cdots\cdots$

d $\frac{8}{9} - \frac{2}{3} = \frac{\cdots\cdots}{\cdots\cdots} - \frac{\cdots\cdots}{\cdots\cdots}$

$= \frac{\cdots\cdots}{\cdots\cdots}$

8 a $\frac{2}{7} \times \frac{3}{5} = \frac{\cdots\cdots}{\cdots\cdots}$

d $\frac{3}{4} \div \frac{1}{8} = \frac{\cdots\cdots}{\cdots\cdots} \times \frac{\cdots\cdots}{\cdots\cdots}$

b $\frac{3}{4} \times \frac{8}{9} = \frac{\cdots\cdots}{\cdots\cdots}$

$= \frac{\cdots\cdots}{\cdots\cdots}$

$= \frac{\cdots\cdots}{\cdots\cdots}$

$= \cdots\cdots$

c $2\frac{1}{3} \times 1\frac{1}{2} = \frac{\cdots\cdots}{\cdots\cdots} \times \frac{\cdots\cdots}{\cdots\cdots}$

$= \frac{\cdots\cdots}{\cdots\cdots}$

$= \cdots\cdots$

e $2\frac{1}{2} \div 1\frac{1}{3} = \frac{\cdots\cdots}{\cdots\cdots} \div \frac{\cdots\cdots}{\cdots\cdots}$

$= \frac{\cdots\cdots}{\cdots\cdots} \times \frac{\cdots\cdots}{\cdots\cdots}$

$= \frac{\cdots\cdots}{\cdots\cdots}$

$= \cdots\cdots$

9 Write these fractions in order starting with the smallest

$$\frac{1}{2}, \qquad \frac{7}{15}, \qquad \frac{3}{5}$$

$\frac{1}{2} = \frac{\cdots\cdots}{\cdots\cdots}$ $\qquad$ $\frac{7}{15} = \frac{\cdots\cdots}{\cdots\cdots}$ $\qquad$ $\frac{3}{5} = \frac{\cdots\cdots}{\cdots\cdots}$

$\frac{\cdots\cdots}{\cdots\cdots},$ $\qquad$ $\frac{\cdots\cdots}{\cdots\cdots},$ $\qquad$ $\frac{\cdots\cdots}{\cdots\cdots}$

Levels 3–5

1 Kathy and Neil each have 16 counters.

a Kathy uses **half** her counters for a game.
   How many counters does Kathy use?

.... 1 mark

b Neil uses 4 counters for his game.
   What **fraction** of his counters did Neil use?

.... 1 mark

c **How many** counters does Kathy have left?

.... 1 mark

d **How many** counters does Neil have left?

.... 1 mark

2 Here are the ingredients for a Greek meal.
   The table shows the quantities needed for 6 people.

6 people	9 people
Cloves of garlic: 2	Cloves of garlic: ......
Chick peas: 4 ounces	Chick peas: ...... ounces
Tablespoons olive oil: 4	Tablespoons olive oil: ......
Paste: 5 fluid ounces	Paste: ...... fluid ounces

Complete the table to show the quantities needed for 9 people.

2 marks

3 a What **fraction** of the diagram is shaded?

.... 1 mark

b What **percentage** of the diagram is shaded?

.... 1 mark

c Shade $\frac{2}{3}$ of the second diagram.

1 mark

4 Kevin has bought a computer game from his uncle.
His uncle asks him for weekly payments which are either **5% of £30** or $\frac{2}{5}$ **of £4**.

a Work out 5% of £30.   £ .... 1 mark

b Work out $\frac{2}{5}$ of £4.   £ .... 1 mark

c Which is the least amount that Kevin
will need to pay per week?   £ .... 1 mark

Level 6

5 To make a shade of orange paint, **2 parts red** is mixed with **3 parts yellow**.
12 litres of **yellow** paint are to be mixed with red paint to make some orange paint.

a How many litres of **red** paint are needed?

.... litres of red paint   2 marks

b What is the total quantity of **orange** paint made?

.... litres of orange paint   1 mark

Level 7

- **To increase an amount by a given fraction or percentage**
  Work out the fraction or percentage. Add it on to the original amount.

  Increase £400 by 5%   5% of £400 = £20   New amount = £420

- **To decrease an amount by a given fraction or percentage**
  Work out the fraction or percentage. Take it away from the original amount.

  Reduce 375 g by $\frac{2}{15}$ $\frac{2}{15}$ of 375 g = 50 g   New amount = 325 g

- **You may be given harder fraction questions.**
  $3\frac{1}{3} - 1\frac{3}{4} = \frac{10}{3} - \frac{7}{4} = \frac{40}{12} - \frac{21}{12} = \frac{19}{12} = 1\frac{7}{12}$

Level 8

- **You may have to increase or decrease the amount more than once.**
  £100 is invested. Each year 6% is added as interest.
  Find the balance after 3 years.

Year 1	Interest = 6% of £100 = £6	New balance = £106
Year 2	Interest = 6% of £106 = £6.36	New balance = £112.36
Year 3	Interest = 6% of £112.36 = £6.74	New balance = £119.10

- **You may be given the final amount and how it has been changed. You will have to find the original amount.**
  A coat is reduced by **15%** in a sale. The sale price is £61.20
  Find the original price.
  The sale price is 100% − **15%** = 85% of the original price.
  So 1% of the original price = £61.20 ÷ 85 = £0.72
  100% of the original price = £0.72 × 100 = £72

- **Sometimes changes are given as fractions.**
  $\frac{5}{12}$ of a number is 45.
  Find the number.
  $\frac{5}{12}$ is 45 so $\frac{1}{12}$ is 45 ÷ 5 = 9.
  So $\frac{12}{12} = 9 \times 12 = 108$

- **Recurring decimals are exact fractions.**
  $0.\dot{1} = \frac{1}{9}, 0.\dot{2} = \frac{2}{9}, 0.\dot{3} = \frac{3}{9} = \frac{1}{3}$ and so on.

---

1 Increase   **a** 650 g by 20%   **b** £460 by $\frac{2}{5}$

   a 20% of ...... = ...

      New amount = ... g

   b ...... of ...... = ...

      New amount = £ ......

2 Decrease   **a** 370 cm by 15%   **b** 2400 kg by $\frac{3}{8}$

   a ...... of ...... = ... cm

      New amount = ... cm

   b ...... of ...... = ... kg

      New amount = ... kg

3 VAT at 17.5% is added to a bill of £60. Find the total.

17.5% of ...... = £ ......   Total bill = £ ......

---

4 Asha buys a car for £8600. The value of the car decreases by 15% every year. How much is the car worth after 3 years?

     Year 1   Loss = 15% of ...... = £ ......   New value = £ ......

     Year 2   Loss = ... of ...... = £ ......   New value = £ ......

     Year 3   Loss = ... of ...... = £ ......   New value = £ ......

5 The population of Plumley village has increased by 7% since 1990. It is now 2568. What was the population in 1990?

New population = 100% + ... = ... % of the 1990 population

So 1% of 1990 population = ... ÷ ...... = ...

100% of 1990 population = ... × 100 = ...

6 Every year a firm increases its workforce by $\frac{3}{17}$.
This year the firm will take on 420 people.
How many people work for the firm at the moment.

$\frac{3}{17}$ is ...... so $\frac{......}{......}$ is .... Number of people now is ...... × ...... = ...

---

1 Complete these calculations.

a .... $\times 150 = 54$

b $5.4 \div$ .... $= 54$

c $675 \times$ .... $= 54$

3 marks

2 A cake is divided into four pieces.

The first three pieces are: $\frac{1}{2}$ of the cake
$\frac{1}{4}$ of the cake
$\frac{1}{8}$ of the cake

a What **fraction** of the cake is the fourth piece? .... 1 mark

b Each $\frac{1}{16}$ of the cake has a mass of **20 g**.
What is the mass of the piece which is $\frac{1}{4}$ of the cake? .... g 2 marks

3 There are **295** pupils in Year 8 and Year 9 at a school.

	Year 8	Year 9
Boys	60	90
Girls	75	70

a What **percentage** of these pupils are in **Year 9**? ....% 2 marks

b Write the **ratio** of boys to girls in the form 1 : *n*

Ratio of boys to girls is 1 : ...... 2 marks

4   Simon keeps $\frac{3}{8}$ of his money in his piggy bank and spends the rest.

   a   What **fraction** of his money does he spend?   .... 1 mark

   b   What **percentage** of his money does he spend?   .... % 1 mark

   c   He has £24 to start with.
   How much does he **save**?   £ .... 1 mark

Level 8

5   The value of a computer is expected to fall by 20% every year.

   a   What is the value of a computer which is 2 years old,
   if it had a value of £800 when new?

   £ .... 2 marks

   b   A different computer has a value of £704
   when it is 2 years old.
   What was its value when it was new?   £ .... 2 marks

   c   What single decimal number could you multiply
   the original value of a computer by, to find its value

   (i)   after 2 years?   ....

   (ii)   after *n* years?   .... 2 marks

   d   A new computer is advertised with a price of £1500.
   What will its value be after 4 years?

   £ .... 2 marks

   e   How many years will it take for the value of
   any computer to fall by more than half of its
   original value   .... years   2 marks

3   Estimating

'When I said put brackets on your calculator …'

● **BODMAS**
This tells you which parts of a number question to do first.

First do	**B**rackets
then powers	**O**f
Next do	**D**ivision
and	**M**ultiplication
Then	**A**ddition
and	**S**ubtraction

$4 + 3 \times 7$
$= 4 + 21$ BOD**MA**S
$= 25$ $\times$ before $+$

$16 \div (2 + 6)$ BO**D**MAS
$= 16 \div 8$ ( ) before $\div$
$= 2$

● **Rounding to the nearest whole number**
Round 7.6 to the nearest whole number.

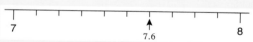

7.6 is nearer to 8 than to 7.
It is rounded to 8 to the nearest whole number.

● **Rounding to the nearest 10**
Round 263 to the nearest 10.

263 is nearer to 260 than to 270. It is rounded to 260 to the nearest 10.

● **Rounding to the nearest 100**
Round 750 to the nearest 100.

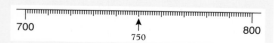

750 is half way between 700 and 800. It is rounded to 800 to the nearest 100.

- **When you use a calculator check that your answer is about the right size.**
  It is very easy to hit the wrong key!

  Work out 3.6 × 239   **3** **.** **6** **×** **2** **3** **9** **=**   Answer = *860.4*

  Estimate: 3.6 is 4 to the nearest whole number.
  239 is 200 to the nearest 100.
  4 × 200 = 800
  800 is near to 860.4 so the answer is probably right.

- **You can also check your answer by writing a new problem.**
  You use the inverse operation.
      226 × 13 = 2938
  To check this you can work out
  either   2938 ÷ 13   or   2938 ÷ 226
        to get 226   to get 13

- **You also need to be able to round decimal numbers.**
  Round 3.14 to 1 decimal place

  3.14 is closer to 3.1 than to 3.2
  It is rounded to 3.1 to 1 decimal place (1 dp)

  Round 2.568 to 2 decimal places.

  2.568 is closer to 2.57 than to 2.56
  It is rounded to 2.57 to 2 decimal places (2 dp)

- **You can use this rule of rounding instead of drawing scales.**
  Look at the first unwanted digit. If it is 5, 6, 7, 8 or 9 add one to the last digit you want to keep. If the first 'unwanted' digit is 0, 1, 2, 3, 4, you do not add one.

  5.38 is 5.4 to 1 dp   12.5731 is 12.57 to 2 dp.

1 Use BODMAS to work out

   a $15 + 12 \div 4$ **c** $3 \times 8 - 4$ **e** $(8 + 6) \div 2 + 7$

      $= \ldots\ldots + \ldots\ldots$ $= \ldots\ldots - \ldots\ldots$ $= \ldots\ldots\ldots\ldots\ldots$

      $= \ldots\ldots$ $= \ldots\ldots$ $= \ldots\ldots\ldots\ldots\ldots = \ldots\ldots$

   b $26 - 3 \times 5$ **d** $7 \times (12 - 8)$ **f** $3^2 + 4 \times 6$

      $= \ldots\ldots - \ldots\ldots$ $= \ldots\ldots\ldots\ldots\ldots$ $= \ldots\ldots\ldots\ldots\ldots$

      $= \ldots\ldots$ $= \ldots\ldots$ $= \ldots\ldots$

2 **a** $2.3 = \ldots\ldots$ to the nearest whole number   **d** $434 = \ldots\ldots$ to the nearest 100

   b $46 = \ldots\ldots$ to the nearest 10   **e** $99 = \ldots\ldots$ to the nearest 10

   c $137 = \ldots\ldots$ to the nearest 10

3 **a** $34 \times 176 = \ldots\ldots$ **b** $858 \div 33 = \ldots\ldots$

      Estimate: Estimate:

        $34 = \ldots\ldots$ to the nearest 10 $858 = \ldots\ldots$ to the nearest 100

      $176 = \ldots\ldots$ to the nearest 100 $33 = \ldots\ldots$ to the nearest 10

      $\ldots\ldots \times \ldots\ldots = \ldots\ldots$ $\ldots\ldots \div \ldots\ldots = \ldots\ldots$

4 **a** $7.85 = \ldots\ldots$ to 1 dp   **d** $29.086 = \ldots\ldots$ to 2 dp

   b $6.3174 = \ldots\ldots$ to 2 dp   **e** $4.857\,31 = \ldots\ldots$ to 3 dp

   c $13.418 = \ldots\ldots$ to 1 dp   **f** $4.6954 = \ldots\ldots$ to 2 dp

5 A box of 8 tapes costs £11.50
     Find the cost of 1 tape.

   1 tape costs £. . . . . . $\div$ . . . . = £. . . . . . to the nearest penny

1 The attendance at a football match was **346 487**.
A local newspaper wants to print the attendance figure.
Write down a **sensible** number for them to use. .... 1 mark

2 Complete the problems.

    a .... ÷ .... = 5

    b You may use the signs +, −, ×, ÷

       24 ...... 3 ...... 1 = 9 2 marks

3 Give two **different** pairs of numbers.

    .... × .... = 72

    .... × .... = 72 2 marks

4 Complete the problems.

    a 3 × .... + ... = 33

    b (45 − ....) × .... = 90 2 marks

5 Put brackets in the calculations to make the answer given.

    a 3 + 6 + 2 × 4 = 17

    b 6 + 4 + 2 × 3 = 36 2 marks

6 Mark needs 31 litres of paint.
The paint is sold in 5-litre tins.
How many tins of paint should he buy?

   .... 2 marks

7 480 counters are to be put into packets of 50 each for sale.
How many packets will there be to sell?

   .... 2 marks

8 The table shows the number of pupils in four neighbouring schools.

School	Number of pupils	To the nearest 100	To the nearest 10
Olney	884		
Mesnes	662		
Heaton	788		
Pendle	906		

4 marks

a Complete the table to show the number of pupils rounded to the nearest **100** pupils, and to the nearest **10** pupils.

b Salus School has **700** pupils, to the nearest **100** pupils, and **650** pupils, to the nearest **10** pupils.
Write down two possible figures for the number of pupils.

.... and ....

2 marks

9 Anita has worked out some questions.
For each question write down another problem she could do to check accurately the answer she has worked out.

a $359 \times 13 = 4667$ Check: ....   1 mark

b $377 + 761 = 1138$ Check: ....   1 mark

c $1830 - 727 = 1103$ Check: ....   1 mark

d $5287 \div 17 = 311$ Check: ....   1 mark

10 Barry has to put 65p into a machine to get a gift.
The machine will take the following coins:

5p, 10p, 20p, 50p   No change is given.

The table shows the number of each coin put in the machine in one day

Coin	5 p	10 p	20 p	50 p
Number of coins	21	43	26	27

How many gifts were sold on that day?   ....   3 marks

- **The first significant figure in any number is the first digit which isn't a 0.**
  For most numbers this is the first digit.
  The first significant figure in these numbers is the red digit

  257   81.5   0.621   0.000 316   0.020 31

- **Rounding to 1 significant figure (1 sf)**
  Look at the digit after the first significant one   0.064
  Use the rule of rounding.   0.06

- **Be careful to keep the number about the right size.**

  738 is 700 to 1 sf.   It is not 7
  4629 is 5000 to 1 sf. It is not 5

- **When numbers are given to 1 sf they are easy to multiply and divide.**

  $400 \times 2000 = 800\,000$ $4 \times 100 \times 2 \times 1000$
  $\qquad\qquad\qquad\qquad = 8 \times 100\,000$

  $0.03 \times 0.2 = 0.006$ $3 \div 100 \times 2 \div 10$
  $\qquad\qquad\qquad\qquad = 6 \div 1000$

  $0.003 \times 70 = 0.21$ $3 \div 1000 \times 7 \times 10$
  $\qquad\qquad\qquad\qquad = 21 \div 100$

  $8000 \div 20 = 400$ $\dfrac{^{4}\cancel{8} \times 100\cancel{0}}{\cancel{2} \times \cancel{1}0} = 4 \times 100$

  $600 \div 0.3 = 2000$ $600 \div \dfrac{3}{10} = {}^{2}\cancel{6}00 \times \dfrac{10}{\cancel{3}}$

- **Estimating fractions.**
  When you estimate the answer to a question that involves a fraction
  there is often a better way than just estimating by rounding to 1 sf

  Look at this question. $\dfrac{65.8 \times 52.4}{44}$

  Rounding each number to 1 sf gives $\dfrac{70 \times 50}{40} = \dfrac{3500}{40} = 87.5$

  The actual answer is 78.4 to 3 sf

This time start by rounding all the numbers to the nearest whole number.

$$\frac{66 \times 52}{44} = \frac{66 \times 52}{11 \times 4}$$

Now you need to spot that the 44 can be split as 11×4.

$$= \frac{66}{11} \times \frac{52}{4}$$

This means that you can cancel the fraction like this.

$$= 6 \times 13$$

78 is a much better approximation than 87.5

$$= 78$$

Sometimes you have to round so that you can cancel the fraction. Look at this question.

$$\frac{47.4 \times 79.7}{7.8 \times 9.9}$$

Round the numbers in the denominator to the nearest whole number.

$$\frac{47.4 \times 79.7}{8 \times 9}$$

Now look at the numbers in the numerator and round them to multiples of the numbers in the denominator.

$$\frac{48 \times 81}{8 \times 9} = \frac{48}{8} \times \frac{81}{9}$$

$$= 6 \times 9$$

This is close to the actual answer of 53.2 to 3 sf.

$$= 54$$

Level 8

- **Estimating square roots**
  Round the number to the nearest square number

  $$\sqrt{39} \simeq \sqrt{36} = 6$$

If you round $\sqrt{39}$ to 1 sf you get $\sqrt{40}$. You still can't do this in your head.

The square numbers are

1,	4,	9,	16,	25,	...
1×1	2×2	3×3	4×4	5×5	

1 Round these to 1 sf.

    a $3.94 = \ldots\ldots$

    b $0.0718 = \ldots\ldots$

    c $26 = \ldots\ldots$

    d $0.007\ 006 = \ldots\ldots$

    e $6503 = \ldots\ldots$

    f $9500 = \ldots\ldots$

2 **a** $500 \times 1000 = \ldots\ldots$

    b $60 \times 400 = \ldots\ldots$

    c $0.003 \times 0.1 = \ldots\ldots$

    d $0.06 \times 0.007 = \ldots\ldots$

    e $0.2 \times 400 = \ldots\ldots$

    f $0.03 \times 5000 = \ldots\ldots$

    g $9000 \div 30 = \ldots\ldots$

    h $1000 \div 50 = \ldots\ldots$

    i $700 \div 0.1 = \ldots\ldots$

    j $900 \div 0.03 = \ldots\ldots$

3 Estimate the value of

    a $\dfrac{47.7 \times 35.2}{42}$

      $= \dfrac{48 \times \ldots\ldots}{6 \times \ldots\ldots}$

      $= \dfrac{\ldots\ldots}{\ldots\ldots} \times \dfrac{\ldots\ldots}{\ldots\ldots}$

      $= \ldots\ldots \times \ldots\ldots$

      $= \ldots\ldots$

    b $\dfrac{28.6 \times 43.8}{4.8 \times 7.1}$

      $= \dfrac{\ldots\ldots \times \ldots\ldots}{\ldots\ldots \times \ldots\ldots}$

      $= \dfrac{\ldots\ldots}{\ldots\ldots} \times \dfrac{\ldots\ldots}{\ldots\ldots}$

      $= \ldots\ldots \times \ldots\ldots$

      $= \ldots\ldots$

4 **a** $\sqrt{17} \simeq \sqrt{\ldots\ldots} = \ldots\ldots$

    b $\sqrt{87} \simeq \sqrt{\ldots\ldots} = \ldots\ldots$

5 Estimate the value of

$$\sqrt{\dfrac{5^2 \times 62}{2^4}}$$

$$= \sqrt{\dfrac{\ldots\ldots \times \ldots\ldots}{\ldots\ldots}} \simeq \sqrt{\dfrac{\ldots\ldots \times \ldots\ldots}{\ldots\ldots}} = \sqrt{\ldots\ldots \times \ldots\ldots} = \sqrt{\ldots\ldots} = \ldots\ldots$$

Levels 5–7

1 **a** A shop sells garden pots for **£2.45**
What is the cost of 4 garden pots?

£ .... 1 mark

b How many garden pots can you buy with **£12**?

.... 1 mark

c The shop also sells the pots in pairs.
One pair of pots costs **£4.49**
How many pairs of pots can you buy with **£12**?

.... pairs   1 mark

d What is the **greatest** number of pots you can buy with **£16**?
You can buy pots either individually or in pairs.

.... pots   1 mark

2 Complete the table below.

Number	Rounded to 1 sf	Rounded to 2 sf	Rounded to 3 sf
0.5182			
10.099			
58.42			
3486			

4 marks

3 Mark wants to work out the calculation

$$\frac{81 \times 155}{42.4 \times 2.4}$$

Find an **estimated** answer to this calculation.
Show all your working.

.... 2 marks

Level 8

4 A number has been rounded to 3 significant figures.
The result is the answer 5.12

   a Write down the **smallest** number it could have been.

.... 1 mark

   b Write down the **largest** number it could have been.

.... 1 mark

5 Find an **estimated** answer to the expression:

$$\sqrt{\frac{12.2^3 \times 14.3}{440 \times 9.6^2}}$$

.... 2 marks

4   Patterns and sequences

This number pattern is special.
The dots always form a square.

Levels 3–5

- **The square numbers are 1, 4, 9, 16, 25, ...**
  You can draw them as square dot patterns.

  $1 \times 1 = 1$ $2 \times 2 = 4$ $3 \times 3 = 9$ $4 \times 4 = 16$ $5 \times 5 = 25$

- **The triangle numbers are 1, 3, 6, 10, 15, ...**
  You can draw them as triangular dot patterns.

  1 $1 + 2 = 3$ $1 + 2 + 3 = 6$ $1 + 2 + 3 + 4 = 10$ $1 + 2 + 3 + 4 + 5 = 15$

- **The odd numbers are 1, 3, 5, 7, 9, ...**

- **The even numbers are 2, 4, 6, 8, 10, ...**
  These are the numbers in the 2 times table.

- **The multiples of 3 are the 3 times table 3, 6, 9, 12, 15,...**
  The multiples of 5 are the 5 times table 5, 10, 15, 20, 25, ...

- **A number that divides exactly into another number is called a factor.**

  To find the factors of 12
  look at all the pairs of numbers that
  multiply to give 12.
  The factors of 12 are 1, 2, 3, 4, 6, 12

  $12 = 1 \times 12$
  $12 = 2 \times 6$
  $12 = 3 \times 4$

- **Prime numbers have exactly two factors, themselves and 1.**

  $19 = 1 \times 19$ No other two numbers multiply to give 19.
  So 19 is a prime number.

- **The prime numbers are 2, 3, 5, 7, 11, 13, 17, 19, 23, 29, ...**

  2 is the first prime number. It is the only even prime number.
  1 is not a prime number.

- **The cube numbers are 1, 8, 27, 64, 125, ...**

  $1 \times 1 \times 1 = 1$, $2 \times 2 \times 2 = 8$, $3 \times 3 \times 3 = 27$, $4 \times 4 \times 4 = 64$, $5 \times 5 \times 5 = 125$, ...

- **Square rooting is the opposite of squaring.**

  9 squared $= 9^2 = 9 \times 9 = 81$
  Square root of 81 $= \sqrt{81} = 9$

Level 6

- **A number sequence is a list of numbers that follows a rule.**
  Each number in a sequence is called a term.

- **To find the rule for a sequence**
  Look at how to get from one term to the next

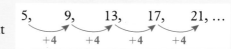

$$5, \qquad 9, \qquad 13, \qquad 17, \qquad 21, ...$$
$$+4 \qquad +4 \qquad +4 \qquad +4$$

  The rule for this sequence is add 4.
  The 2nd term is $5 + 1$ lot of 4
  The 3rd term is $5 + 2$ lots of 4
  The 20th term is $5 + 19$ lots of 4
  The nth term is $5 + (n - 1)$ lots of 4

TEST YOURSELF

1 Look at these numbers. Write down

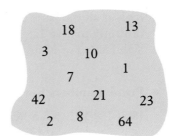

    a the multiples of 7   ....

    b the prime numbers   ....

    c the triangle numbers   ....

    d the cube numbers   ....

2 a Write down the first ten multiples of 4.

....

    b Write down the first ten multiples of 9.

....

    c Write down the number that appears in both lists. ....

3 a 7th square number = ...   **c** 1000 = ...th cube number

    b 6th cube number = ...   **d** 196 = ...th square number

4 Look at this sequence   3,   8,   13,   18,   23, ...

                               ....

    a The rule is ....

    b The 2nd term is 3 + 1 lot of ....

    c the 50th term is ...... + ...

    d The nth term is ....

1 Mrs Kay wants **32** desks in her classroom.
She can put them in **4** rows,
with **8** desks in each row.

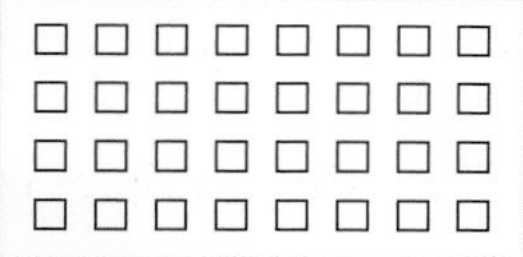

a Draw a diagram to show a **different**
way that Mrs Kay can arrange the
32 desks. She must have the same
number of desks in each row.

1 mark

b Mrs Kay would like to put **6** desks in each row, with the same number of
desks in each row.
Explain why Mrs Kay **cannot** arrange the **32** desks in this way.

.... 1 mark

2 The diagram shows a pattern made out of **black** and **white** tiles.
The diagram is **6** tiles long.

a Continue the diagram so it becomes **10** tiles long. 1 mark

The table shows the details of the tiles used.

Length of pattern (tiles)	1	2	3	4	5	6
Number of white tiles	3	5	8	10	13	15
Number of black tiles	0	1	1	2	2	3

The rule for finding the number of white tiles for a length of an
even number of tiles is

Number of white tiles = Length $\div$ 2 $\times$ 5

b How many **white tiles** are there in a pattern of length **22 tiles**?

.... 1 mark

c Complete the rule to show the number of **white tiles** for a length of an
odd number of tiles:

Number of white tiles = ...

1 mark

3 Melissa arranges some marbles to make a series of patterns.

The number of marbles in each shape is **1, 3, 6**.
To make the next pattern an extra row is added at the bottom.

a Write down the number of marbles in each of the next three patterns.

.... , ... , ...   1 mark

Melissa chooses 5 marbles, but cannot make any shape out of 5 marbles.
She cannot make any shape out of 7 marbles either.
The numbers **5** and **7** are **prime** numbers

b Write down **two** other numbers which are **prime** numbers.   .... , ...

1 mark

c Melissa thinks that **15** is also a **prime** number.
Explain why she is **wrong**.

.... 1 mark

Level 6

4 A series of patterns is made out of **grey** and **red** counters.

Pattern number 1   Pattern number 2   Pattern number 3   Pattern number 4

a How many **grey** and **red** counters will there be in pattern number **6**?

.... grey counters .... red counters   1 mark

b How many **grey** and **red** counters will there be in pattern number **15**?

.... grey counters .... red counters   1 mark

c T = total number of grey and red counters in a pattern, N = pattern number.
Use symbols to write down an equation connecting T and N.

.... 1 mark

- **To find a formula for a sequence look at the differences between the terms.**

- **If those differences are the same, find the formula like this.**

  The rule is $+3$.

  You need to $+1$ to each multiple of 3
  to get the terms of the sequence.
  The formula for the nth term is $3n + 1$.

  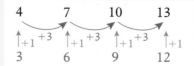

- **If these differences are not the same, look at the second differences.**

  If the second differences are the same the formula for the nth term will contain n^2.
  The number in front of the n^2 is half the second difference.

  The second differences are $+4$.
  The formula will start $2n^2$.

  Write down the sequence for $2n^2$.
  Write down what you need to add to
  each of these to get the terms of the
  sequence.
  Use the above method to find the
  formula for this new sequence.

  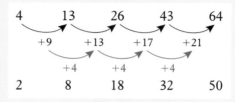

  The formula is $3n - 1$

  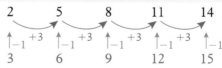

  Put the two parts together to get the
  formula for the sequence you started with.

  The formula is $2n^2 + 3n - 1$

- **Highest common factor (HCF)**

  The factors of 12 are 1, 2, 3, 4, 6, 12   The common factors of 12 and 20 are 1, 2 and 4
  The factors of 20 are 1, 2, 4, 5, 10, 20   The HCF of 12 and 20 is 4

- **Lowest common multiple (LCM)**

  The multiples of 3 are 3, 6, 9, 12, 15, 18, 21, 24, 27, 30, 33 …
  The multiples of 5 are 5, 10, 15, 20, 25, 30, 35 …
  The common multiples of 3 and 5 are 15, 30 …
  The LCM of 3 and 5 is 15

Level 7

1 Find the formula for the nth term of this sequence

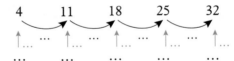

The formula contains ...... n

The formula is ....

2 The formula for the nth term of a sequence is $4n - 3$.
Write down

   a the first term $4 \times 1 - 3 =$ ....

   b the sixth term $4 \times ... - 3 =$ ....

   c the 20th term   .... = ...

3 Find the formula for the nth term of this sequence.

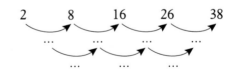

The formula will start ....

To get to the terms of
the sequence you need   ....

The formula is ....

4 The formula for the nth term of a sequence is $3n^2 - n - 2$
Write down

   a the first term ....

   b the fifth term ....

1 This is a series of patterns made out of grey and blue tiles.

Pattern number 1   Pattern number 2   Pattern number 3

a How many grey and blue tiles will there be in pattern number 7?

.... grey tiles   .... blue tiles   1 mark

b How many grey and blue tiles will there be in pattern number 14?

.... grey tiles   .... blue tiles   1 mark

c Write expressions to show the total number of grey and blue tiles in pattern number *n*.

.... grey tiles   .... blue tiles   1 mark

d Write an expression to show the total number of tiles in pattern number *n*.

.... 1 mark

A different series of patterns is made with the grey and blue tiles.

Pattern number 1   Pattern number 2   Pattern number 3

e For this series of patterns write an expression to show the total number of tiles in pattern number *n*.
Show your working and simplify your expression.

Total number of tiles   .... 2 marks

5 Formulas, expressions and equations

Letters can be used to represent numbers.

- **A formula is a set of instructions. It tells you how to work something out.**

- **A formula can be written using words or letters.**

  This formula tells you how to work out the cost, in pounds, of hiring a videotape.

  Cost = 3 × number of nights

  To hire a video for 2 nights

  Cost = 3 × 2 = £6

  This formula tells you how to work out the time, in minutes, needed to roast a turkey.

  Time = 25 + 15 × weight in pounds

  To roast a 12 lb turkey

  Time = 25 + 15 × 12 = 25 + 180 = 205 mins

- **This formula uses letters.**
  The perimeter, p, of a square
  is given by $p = 4\,l$
  l is the length of a side of the square.
  Use the formula to find the perimeter
  of a square with sides of length 8 cm.

  $p = 4 \times 8 = 32$ cm

- **You need to be able to write formulas yourself.**
  Pick out the important words and numbers.
  Choose letters to stand for the important words.
  The **cost** of a class trip to a theme park is **£8** for each **pupil** and **£100** for the coach.
  Use C for the cost and p for the number of pupils.
  The formula is $C = 100 + 8p$

- **Algebraic expressions can be simplified.**
  $2a + 3a$ simplifies to $5a$
  $6b - 3b + b$ simplifies to $4b$

- **Always use correct notation.**
  Write a not $1a$ Write $3 + x$ not $3 + 1x$
  Write $2y$ not $y + y$ Write $4x$ not $x4$, $4 \times x$ or $x \times 4$
  Write $\dfrac{x}{4}$ not $x \div 4$

Level 6

- **Collecting like terms**
  $5p + 6q - 2p + 5q = 3p + 11q$
  $7x - 2 - 9x + 6 = -2x + 4$

- **Multiplying out a bracket**
  Multiply each term in the bracket by the term outside the bracket.
  $4(x + 2) = 4x + 8$ $5g(g + 5) = 5g^2 + 25g$

- **Factorising**
  This is the reverse of multiplying out a bracket.
  $12p - 18 = 6(2p - 3)$ 6 is the highest common factor of 12 and 18.
  $3x^2 + 2x = x(3x + 2)$ This time you take an x out.
  $d^3 + 5d^2 - 12d = d(d^2 + 5d - 12)$ Make sure you have the same number of terms inside the bracket as there were in the question.

- **Using factorising for proof**
  Three consecutive whole numbers are $n, n + 1$ and $n + 2$
  The sum of these numbers $= n + n + 1 + n + 2$
  $$= 3n + 3$$
  $$= 3(n + 1)$$
  The common factor 3 proves that this answer is always a multiple of 3.

- **You can use algebra to solve equations.**
  You need to get the letter by itself on one side of the equation. Look at what is being done to the letter. Do the opposite of this to both sides of the equation.

$x + 4 = 7$ take 4 from both sides $x + 4 - 4 = 7 - 4$ $x = 3$	$p + 8 = 2$ take 8 from both sides $p + 8 - 8 = 2 - 8$ $p = -6$
$5r = 35$ divide both sides by 5 $\dfrac{5r}{5} = \dfrac{35}{5}$ $r = 7$	$\dfrac{y}{6} = 4$ multiply both sides by 6 $\dfrac{y}{6} \times 6 = 4 \times 6$ $y = 24$

- **Some equations are more difficult.** More than one step is needed.

$2x + 7 = 16$ First, take 7 from both sides $2x + 7 - 7 = 16 - 7$ $2x = 9$ Now, divide both sides by 2 $\dfrac{2x}{2} = \dfrac{9}{2}$ $x = 4\frac{1}{2}$	$7x + 4 = 5x + 10$ This equation has xs on both sides First, take $5x$ from both sides $7x - 5x + 4 = 5x - 5x + 10$ $2x + 4 = 10$ Now take 4 from both sides $2x + 4 - 4 = 10 - 4$ $2x = 6$ divide both sides by 2 $x = 3$

- **When you have a bracket in an equation, multiply the bracket out first.**

Multiply out the bracket.

$$2(x + 7) = 15$$
$$2x + 14 = 15$$
$$2x = 1 \quad \text{so } x = \tfrac{1}{2}$$

Levels 3–5

1 **a** A plumber charges a call out charge of £25.
He then charges £15 an **hour**.
Write down the formula for the total **cost**. ....

b Find the cost if the plumber is working for 4 hours.

....

2 Write down a formula for the perimeter, P,
of this rectangle.

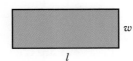

w

l

....

Level 6

Simplify
3 **a** $6c + 5d - c + d$
= ...... + ...

Factorise
c $9p - 12$
= ...... (...... − ......)

Multiply out the bracket
b $5(2q + 7)$
= ...... + ...

Factorise
d $z^3 + 4z^2 - 8z$
= ...... (...... + ... − ......)

4 Solve these equations

a $x + 7 = 13$

$x + 7 \ldots = 13 \ldots$

$x = \ldots$

c $5x - 28 = x - 6$

$5x \ldots - 28 = x \ldots - 6$

$\ldots - 28 = -6$

$\ldots = \ldots$

$x = \ldots$

b $\dfrac{x}{6} - 3 = 4$

$\dfrac{x}{6} - 3 \ldots = 4 \ldots$

$\dfrac{x}{6} = \ldots$

$\dfrac{x}{6} \times \ldots = \ldots \times \ldots$

$x = \ldots$

d $4(x - 3) = 28$

$\ldots = \ldots$

$4x = \ldots$

$x = \ldots$

1 Here are some expressions:

$$x \div 2 \quad x + 2 \quad x^3 \quad x + x \quad x^2 \quad 3x \quad x \times 2 \quad x \div 3 \quad x \div x \quad 2 + x$$

a Write down the expression that is the same as $x \times x$

.... 1 mark

b Write down the expression that is the same as $\dfrac{x}{3}$

.... 1 mark

c **Two** expressions are the same as $2x$.
Write down these two expressions.

.... 1 mark

d Write down a **new** expression which will always be the same as $3x + x$.

.... 1 mark

2 There are n counters in a bag.

a Two of these bags, each with n counters, are put together to make a new bag.
Write an expression for the number of counters that are in the new bag.

.... 1 mark

b **Five** counters are then removed from the new bag.
Write an expression for the number of counters that are now in the new bag.

.... 1 mark

3 This **square** tile has edges of length n centimetres.
Six of the square tiles are put together to make a shape.

a Write an expression for the **perimeter** of the shape.
Simplify your expression.

.... cm   2 marks

52

b The perimeter of the shape is **60** cm.
Use your answer to part **a** to write an equation using n.
Solve your equation to find the **value of n**.

$n =$ .... 2 marks

4 Sapna had **3m** meal vouchers, but has used **4** of them.
Dale had **2m** meal vouchers, has used none, but has gained **one extra** voucher.

a Write down **expressions**, in m, for the number of meal vouchers that
Sapna and Dale each have.

Sapna .... Dale .... 2 marks

b Sapna and Dale now have the **same** number of meal vouchers.
Write down an equation to show this.

.... 1 mark

c Solve the equation to find **m**.

$m =$ .... 1 mark

5 $y = x^2 + x - 3$

Find a value of x, to 1 dp, that gives the value of y closest to 0.
Two values for x have already been worked out.

x	1	2					
y	-1	3					

$x =$ ....

WHAT YOU NEED TO KNOW

- **The signs $<$ $\leqslant$ $>$ $\geqslant$ are all called inequality signs.**
  $<$ means less than $>$ means greater than
  $\leqslant$ means less than or equal to $\geqslant$ means greater than or equal to

- **You can show inequalities on a number line.**

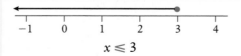

$$x \leqslant 3$$

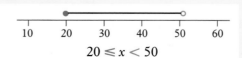

$$20 \leqslant x < 50$$

- **You solve inequalities like equations.**

$$4x - 6 \geqslant 11$$

$$4x - 6 + 6 \geqslant 11 + 6$$

$$4x \geqslant 17$$

$$x \geqslant \tfrac{17}{4}$$

$$\frac{x}{3} + 4 < 2$$

$$\frac{x}{3} + 4 - 4 < 2 - 4$$

$$\frac{x}{3} < -2$$

$$x < -6$$

- **Sometimes you have to give possible values.**
  If $-4 \leqslant x < 3$ and x is an integer
  then x can take the values $-4, -3, -2, -1, 0, 1, 2$.
  An integer is a whole number.

- **Changing the subject of a formula**
  This works like solving equations.
  Get the new subject letter by itself.
  Write the new formula with the subject letter on the left hand side.

Make s the subject.

$$p = 3s - r$$

$$p + r = 3s$$

$$\frac{p + r}{3} = s$$

$$s = \frac{p + r}{3}$$

Make b the subject.

$$a = \sqrt{b + 3c}$$

$$a^2 = b + 3c$$

$$a^2 - 3c = b$$

$$b = a^2 - 3c$$

Level 8

- **Inequalities can have two variables, usually x and y.**

  These can be shown using a graph
  The red line is $y = 2x + 1$
  The red shading shows $y \geqslant 2x + 1$

  The blue line is $y = x - 2$
  The blue shading shows $y < x - 2$
  The line is dashed to show that
  it is not included.

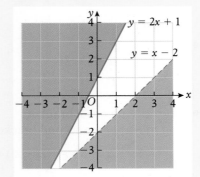

- **A region can be described using more than one inequality.**

  Show the region given by

  $$-2 < x \leqslant 3 \qquad y < 1 \qquad y \geqslant x - 2$$

  You can shade the parts that you don't want.
  The answer is the region, R, which is not shaded.

  Always make it clear on your diagram
  which is the required region.

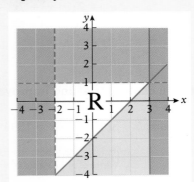

- **Substituting into formulas**

  You need to be able to deal with fractions, decimals and negative numbers.
  If $y = 4x^2 - 3$ find y when $\quad$ **a** $x = \frac{3}{4}$ $\quad$ **b** $x = 2.7$ $\quad$ **c** $x = -5$

  a $\quad y = 4 \times (\frac{3}{4})^2 - 3$ $\qquad$ **b** $\quad y = 4 \times (2.7)^2 - 3$ $\qquad$ **c** $\quad y = 4 \times (-5)^2 - 3$

  $\qquad = 4 \times \frac{9}{16} - 3$ $\qquad\qquad\qquad = 4 \times 7.29 - 3$ $\qquad\qquad\quad = 4 \times 25 - 3$

  $\qquad = -\frac{3}{4}$ $\qquad\qquad\qquad\qquad = 26.16$ $\qquad\qquad\qquad\quad = 97$

- **Solving complicated equations**

  $\dfrac{17 - x}{4} = 2 - x \qquad$ Multiply by the 4 to get rid of the fraction.

  $17 - x = 4(2 - x) \quad$ Now solve in the usual way.

  $17 - x = 8 - 4x \qquad$ So $3x = -9$ and $x = -3$

55

- **Brackets and powers**

$x^3(4x^2 - 7) = 4x^5 - 7x^3$

$2a^2b(a^2 + 3b) = 2a^4b + 6a^2b^2$

- **Factorising**

$6t^4 + 9t^3 = 3t^3(2t + 3)$

$12a^3 - 4a^2 = 4a^2(3a - 1)$

- **Multiplying out 2 brackets**

You multiply the second bracket by each term in the first bracket.

$$\begin{aligned}(s + 3)(2s - 5) &= s(2s - 5) + 3(2s - 5)\\ &= 2s^2 - 5s + 6s - 15\\ &= 2s^2 + s - 15\end{aligned}$$

$$\begin{aligned}(x + 4)^2 &= (x + 4)(x + 4)\\ &= x^2 + 4x + 4x + 16\\ &= x^2 + 8x + 16\end{aligned}$$

$$\begin{aligned}(x - 7)(x + 7) &= x^2 + 7x - 7x - 49\\ &= x^2 - 49\end{aligned}$$

$$\begin{aligned}(2a + b)^2 &= (2a + b)(2a + b)\\ &= 4a^2 + 2ab + 2ab + b^2\\ &= 4a^2 + 4ab + b^2\end{aligned}$$

- **You can use trial and improvement to solve more complicated equations.**

Example Solve $x^3 + x = 1590$ giving your answer to 1 dp.

Value of x	Value of $x^3 + x$	
11	1342	too small
12	1740	too big
11.5	1532.375	too small
11.6	1572.496	too small
11.7	1613.313	too big
11.65	1592.817 125	too big

x is between 11 and 12

x is between 11.5 and 12

x is between 11.6 and 12

x is between 11.6 and 11.7

x is between 11.6 and 11.65

x must be somewhere in the green part of the number line. Any number in the green part rounds down to 11.6 to 1 dp.

Answer: $x = 11.6$ to 1 dp.

Level 7

1 Solve these inequalities and show your answers on number lines.

a $2x + 3 \leqslant 11$

$2x \leqslant \dots$

$\dots$

$$\begin{array}{c|c|c|c|c|c|c|c} \hline -1 & 0 & 1 & 2 & 3 & 4 & 5 \end{array}$$

b $\dfrac{x}{5} - 2 > 1$

$\dots > \dots$

$\dots$

$$\begin{array}{c|c|c|c|c|c|c|c} \hline 0 & 5 & 10 & 15 & 20 & 25 & 30 \end{array}$$

2 If $-1 < x \leqslant 4$ and x is an integer then x can take the values $\dots$

3 Make r the subject of

a $x = 2r - c^2$

$\dots = 2r$

$\dots$

$r = \dots$

b $p = (r - s)^2$

$\dots = (r - s)$

$\dots$

$\dots$

4 Factorise

a $14q - 8$

$\dots$

b $16a^3 - 8a$

$\dots$

Level 8

5 Write down the inequalities shown by the shading.

a

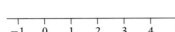

b

c

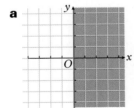
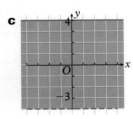

6 Multiply out

a $(x + 4)(x - 3)$

$\dots$

$\dots$

b $(2x - 3)(x - 6)$

$\dots$

$\dots$

1 The table shows the result of adding pairs of expressions.
Complete the table.

A	B	A + B
x	y	
$3a$	$5a$	
$2p$		$2p - 5q$
$5x + 2y$	$3y - 4w$	
	$6k$	$2k$
x^2	$3x^2$	

3 marks

2 A weatherman reported, 'The temperature this
summer never quite reached 24 degrees.'
  a Shade the temperature scale to show
  the **maximum** temperature.

1 mark

  b T = temperature
  Write down an inequality, using T,
  to show the statement of the weatherman.

....

1 mark

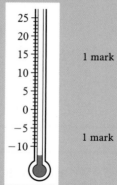

  c The temperature for the winter months
  could be represented by the diagram

Temperature, T [number line from −10 to 15, filled dot at −10, open dot at about 12]

  Write down an inequality, using T,
  to show this range of temperature.

....

1 mark

3 Find the values of P and Q when $x = 5$ and $y = 3$

  a $P = \dfrac{x^2(x - 1)}{4}$

  $P = \text{.........}$

  b $Q = \dfrac{5y^3}{6}$

  $Q = \text{.........}$

2 marks

4 The diagram shows a **square**.
The expressions show the length of a
side of the square, in centimetres.

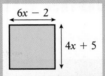

Calculate the value of x, and use it to
find the area of the square.

.... cm^2 2 marks

Level 8

5 The diagram shows
some straight line graphs.

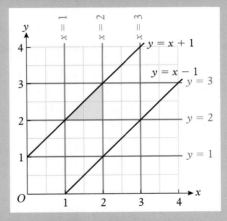

  a Write down **three** inequalities
      which can be used to describe
      the shaded region.   3 marks

  b On the diagram shade the region
      which is described by the inequalities

      $y \geqslant 1$ $y \leqslant x - 1$ $x \leqslant 3$ 2 marks

6 Multiply out and simplify these expressions:

  a $2(x - 3) - (x - 7)$ **b** $(x - 2)(x + 3)$ **c** $(x + 5)^2$ 3 marks

7 Solve these equations.

  a $5 - 3x = 6x + 11$ **b** $2(x - 1) = 6$ **c** $\dfrac{3x}{x - 1} = 5$

      $x = \ldots\ldots\ldots$ $x = \ldots\ldots\ldots$ $x = \ldots\ldots\ldots$ 6 marks

6 Functions and graphs

You use co-ordinates to find
the position of a point.

- **You need two co-ordinates to describe the
position of a point.**

The co-ordinates are
Sun   (0, 0)
Mercury (−1, 1)
Venus   (2, −1)
Earth   (−2, −2)

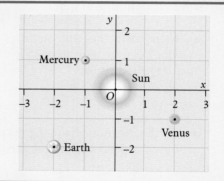

- **To draw a graph**
  (1) Make a table of values.
  (2) Plot the points and join them up.
  Draw the graph of $y = 2x + 1$

x	−1	0	1	2
y	−1	1	3	5

$2 \times (-1) + 1$ ↗   ↖ $2 \times (1) + 1$

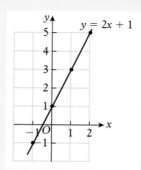

The line $y = 2x + 1$ carries on forever in both
directions. What you have drawn is part of
the line. It is called a line segment.

- **The equation of any straight line can be written as $y = mx + c$.**

  m is the gradient of the line. It tells you how steep the line is. c is where the line crosses the y axis.

  The red line has gradient 1 and crosses the y axis at 3.

  The blue line has gradient -2 and crosses the y axis at 1.

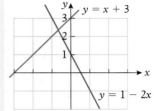

- **Gradient $= \dfrac{\text{vertical change}}{\text{horizontal change}}$**

- **Vertical lines have equations starting $x =$**

- **Horizontal lines have equations starting $y =$**

- **Parallel lines have the same gradient.**

- **If the gradient of a line is m, the gradient of any perpendicular line is $-\dfrac{1}{m}$**

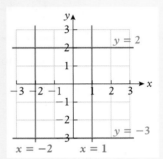

- **Checking to see if a point lies on a line.**
  Does the point $(2, 5)$ lie on the line $y = 3x - 2$?
  When $x = 2$, $\quad y = 3 \times 2 - 2 = 4$
  so $(2, 4)$ lies on the line. $(2, 5)$ does not lie on the line.

- **Finding missing co-ordinates**
  The point $(5, a)$ lies on the   When $x = 5$, $\quad y = 4 \times 5 - 1 = 19$
  line $y = 4x - 1$. Find a.   so $a = 19$

  The line $y = x + 2$ crosses the line   When $y = 1$, $\quad 1 = x + 2 \quad$ so $x = -1$,
  $y = 1$ at P. Find the co-ordinates of P.   The co-ordinates of P are $(-1, 1)$.

- **Some equations do not have y on its own.**
  To draw the graph of $3x + 4y = 12$
  find where the graph crosses each axis

  When $x = 0$ When $y = 0$
  $\quad 4y = 12$ $\quad 3x = 12$
  $\quad\ y = 3$ $\quad\ x = 4$
  This gives $(0, 3)$ This gives $(4, 0)$

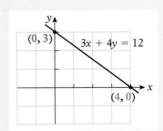

1 Fill in the co-ordinates.

    A (......, ...) B (......, ...) C (......, ...)

2 Plot these points
    D (1, 3) E (4, 5) F (3, 0)

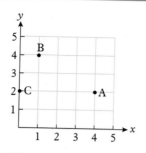

3 Write down the equation of the red line.

    ....

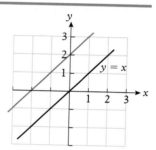

4 Write down the equation of each of these lines.
    Choose from
    $y = -x$, $y = 2x + 2$, $x = 2$, $y = -x - 3$

    A ....   C ....

    B ....   D ....

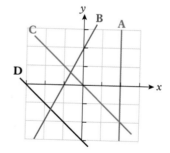

5 Draw the graph of $3x - 2y = 6$

    When $x = 0$ When $y = 0$

    .... = ... = ...

    .... = ... = ...

    This gives (......, ...)   This gives (......, ...)

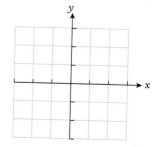

Levels 3–5

1 These triangles make a pattern on a grid.
Each triangle is numbered.
The **bottom right hand corner** of each
triangle is marked with a letter.

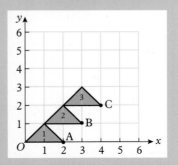

a Write down the co-ordinates of the
corner marked

A (,   ) B (,   ) C (,   )

2 marks

b What are the co-ordinates of the bottom right hand corner of triangle **number 10**?

(,   )

Explain how you worked out your answer.

2 marks

c Explain why **(10, 9) cannot** be a **corner** of a triangle.

1 mark

2 a Plot each of the points P, Q, R and S
on the grid. Join the points together
with straight lines.

P (0, 0)   R (2, 2)
Q (0, 2)   S (2, 0)

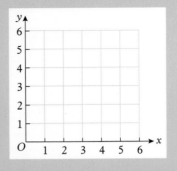

2 marks

b Give the name of the **shape** that you have drawn.

.... 1 mark

63

c Multiply each of the co-ordinates P, Q, R and S **by 3**, and plot these points on the same axes

$$P\ (0, 0) \times 3 \rightarrow (\quad , \quad)$$

$$Q\ (0, 2) \times 3 \rightarrow (\quad , \quad)$$

$$R\ (2, 2) \times 3 \rightarrow (\quad , \quad)$$

$$S\ (2, 0) \times 3 \rightarrow (\quad , \quad)$$

2 marks

d How many **times larger** is the **area** of this shape, compared with the area of the original shape?

.... 1 mark

Level 6

3 The diagram shows the graph of the straight line $y = x + 1$.

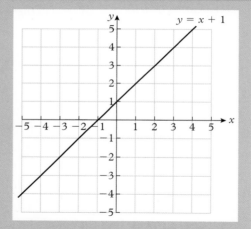

a Draw the graph of the straight line $y = x + 2$. Label your graph.

1 mark

b Draw the graph of the straight line $y = 2x + 2$. Label your graph.

1 mark

c Write down the equation of any straight line which goes through $(0, 0)$.

$y =$ .... 1 mark

d Write down the equation of a straight line which is parallel to $y = x + 1$, and goes through $(-2, 5)$.

$y =$ .... 1 mark

e Write down the gradient of a line that is perpendicular to the line $y = 5x - 1$.

.... 1 mark

- **The point where two lines cross is called the point of intersection.**
  These lines cross at the point (2, 3).

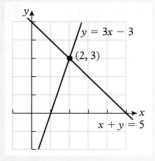

- $x = 2$, $y = 3$ is the solution to the simultaneous equations
  $$y = 3x - 3$$
  $$x + y = 5$$

- **Mid-point of a line**

  To find the mid-point of a line, add the co-ordinates of the end points and divide by 2.

  $$\text{Mid-point of AB is } \left(\frac{1 + 5}{2}, \frac{3 + 13}{2}\right)$$
  $$= (3, 8)$$

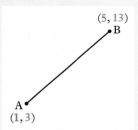

- **To solve a pair of simultaneous equations**

  either   draw the graphs of the 2 equations and find where they cross
  or   use algebra.

- **Solving simultaneous equations using algebra**

Solve (1) $5x + y = 20$
       (2) $2x + y = 11$
	Solve (1) $3x - y = 19$
	       (2) $\;\;x + y = 1$

Subtract the equations to get rid of y $$3x = 9$$ $$x = 3$$	Add the equations to get rid of y $$4x = 20$$ $$x = 5$$
Put $x = 3$ into (1) to find y $$5 \times 3 + y = 20$$ $$y = 5$$	Put $x = 5$ into (1) to find y $$3 \times 5 - y = 19$$ $$y = -4$$
The solution is $x = 3, y = 5$	The solution is $x = 5, y = -4$
Use (2) to check your answer $$2x + y = 2 \times 3 + 5$$ $$= 11 \checkmark$$	Use (2) to check your answer $$x + y = 5 - 4$$ $$= 1 \checkmark$$

- **You sometimes need to multiply one or both of the equations before you add or subtract.**

Solve this pair of simultaneous equations

$$2x + 6y = 13$$
$$4x - 2y = 5$$

Number the equations

(1) $\quad 2x + 6y = 13$
(2) $\quad 4x - 2y = 5$

You need to multiply equation (2) by **3**
so that you have $6y$ in
each equation

$$2x + 6y = 13$$
$(2) \times 3 \quad \underline{12x - 6y = 15}$

Add to get rid of y
This finds x

$$14x \qquad = 28$$
$$x = 2$$

Use equation (1) to find y 　　Put $x = 2$ in equation (1)

$$2 \times 2 + 6y = 13$$
$$4 + 6y = 13$$
$$6y = 9$$
$$y = 1.5$$

The answer is $x = 2, \ y = 1.5$

Use equation (2) to
check your answer

Check　$4x - 2y = 4 \times 2 - 3$
$$= 5 \checkmark$$

Solve this pair of simultaneous equations

$$3x + 5y = 30$$
$$2x + 3y = 19$$

Number the equations

(1) $\quad 3x + 5y = 30$
(2) $\quad 2x + 3y = 19$

Multiply equation (1) by 2
Multiply equation (2) by 3

$$6x + 10y = 60$$
$$\underline{6x + \ 9y = 57}$$

You can now subtract to get rid of x
Put $y = 3$ in equation (1)

$$y = 3$$
$$3x + 15 = 30$$
$$3x = 15$$
$$x = 5$$

The answer is $x = 5, \ y = 3$

Check using equation (2)　Check　$2x + 3y = 2 \times 5 + 3 \times 3$
$$= 19 \checkmark$$

- **You need to be able to recognise these graphs.**

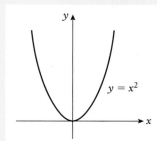 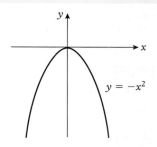

Any quadratic graph will look like $\cup$ or $\cap$
An equation for a quadratic graph will have an x^2 term but no higher powers of x.

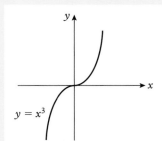 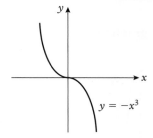

Other cubic graphs will look like one of these or $\mathcal{N}$ or $\mathcal{W}$
An equation for a cubic graph will have an x^3 term but no higher powers of x.

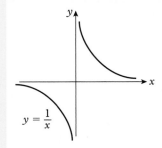 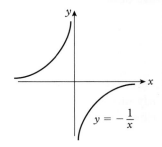

All reciprocal graphs will look like one of these.
Reciprocal graphs always have two parts.

- **Look for these features when describing or sketching graphs that model real situations**, e.g. filling containers with liquid, speed around a track.

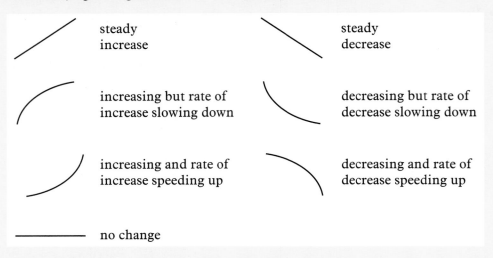

steady increase

steady decrease

increasing but rate of increase slowing down

decreasing but rate of decrease slowing down

increasing and rate of increase speeding up

decreasing and rate of decrease speeding up

no change

- **You can describe a graph using these features.**

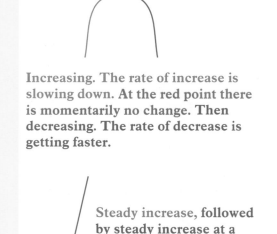

Increasing. The rate of increase is slowing down. At the red point there is momentarily no change. Then decreasing. The rate of decrease is getting faster.

Decreasing. The rate of decrease is slowing down. Momentarily no change at the red point. Then increasing. The rate of increase is getting faster.

Steady increase, followed by steady increase at a faster rate.

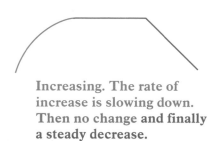

Increasing. The rate of increase is slowing down. Then no change and finally a steady decrease.

1 Solve these pairs of simultaneous equations:

a (1) $2x + y = 14$
(2) $3x - y = 6$

Adding   ...... = ...

$x = ...$

Put $x = ...$ into (1)

$2 \times ...... + y = ...$

$y = ...$

the solution is $x = ...$, $y = ...$

Check in (2)

$3 \times ...... - ...... = ...$

b (1) $4x + 2y = 10$
(2) $5x + 3y = 12$

Multiply (1) by ...... and (2) by ......

...... = ...

...... = ...

Subtracting   ...... = ...

...... = ...

Put ...... = ... into (1)

...... = ...

...... = ...

the solution is ....

Check in (2) ....

2 Write down the letter of the graph by its equation.

A

$y = x^3 - 6x^2 + 11x - 6$

Graph ......

B

$y = 4 - x^2$

Graph ......

C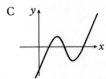

$y = x^2 - 4x + 7$

Graph ......

D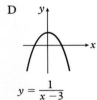

$y = \dfrac{1}{x - 3}$

Graph ......

3 This flask is filled with water at a constant rate.
Sketch the graph to show how the height of the water changes and explain the features of your graph.

Height of water

Time

....

....

....

....

69

1 a Write down the **equation** of the line

through A and B ....

Write down the **equation** of the line

through B and C ....

2 marks

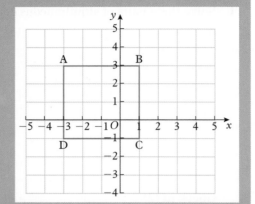

b Fill in the gaps below:

$y - x = 2$ is the equation of the line

through .... and .... 1 mark

c One of the lines of symmetry of the square is $x = -1$.
On the diagram, **draw and label** the line $x = -1$. 1 mark

Write down the equation of **one other** line of symmetry.

.... 1 mark

d The line $y - x = 2$ crosses the line $2y + x = 22$

Solve the simultaneous equations (1) $2y + x = 22$
Show your working. (2) $y - x = 2$

$x = $ .... $y = $ .... 2 marks

e Write down the co-ordinates of the point where the line $y - x = 2$ crosses the
line $2y + x = 22$.

(......, ...) 1 mark

2 Solve these simultaneous equations to find the value of x and y.

(1) $8x + 6y \quad = 10$
(2) $30x - 6y + 1 = 10$

Show your working.

$x = $ .... $y = $ .... 3 marks

3 The diagram shows the graphs of the equations

$$4y = x + 2$$
$$4y = -x + 6$$

Use the diagram to write down the solutions to these simultaneous equations.

$x = \ldots\ldots \quad y = \ldots\ldots$ 2 marks

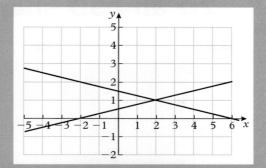

Level 8

4 The diagram shows the graph with the equation $y = 2x^2$.

  a On the same axes draw the graph with the equation $y = x^2$.

  b On the same axes draw the graph with the equation $y = 2x^2 + 2$

  c On the same axes draw the graph with the equation $y = -2x^2$.

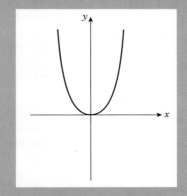

3 marks

5 The graph shows the journey of a car between two sets of traffic lights.

Describe in detail what happened during the journey of the car, as shown by the graph.

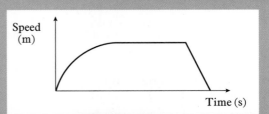

....

....

....

3 marks

7   2D and 3D shapes

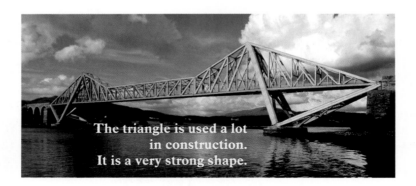

The triangle is used a lot
in construction.
It is a very strong shape.

Levels 3–5

- **Types of angle**

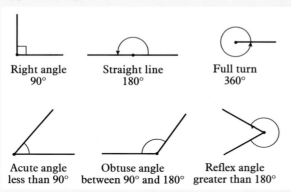

Right angle
90°

Straight line
180°

Full turn
360°

Acute angle
less than 90°

Obtuse angle
between 90° and 180°

Reflex angle
greater than 180°

- **Points of the compass**

- **Directions of turn**

clockwise   anti-clockwise

- **Angles on a straight line
add up to 180°.**

100°

the red angle
must be 80°
because
$100 + 80 = 180$

- **The angles in a triangle
add up to 180°.**

40°

the blue angle
must be 50°
because
$90 + 40 + 50 = 180$

- **Types of triangle**

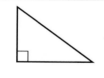

Right-angled triangle

Equilateral triangle
All three sides are equal
All three angles are equal

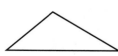

Scalene triangle
No equal sides
No equal angles

Isosceles triangle
Two sides are equal
Two angles are equal

- **Constructing triangles**

  Always leave your construction lines on your diagram.

  Given three sides:
  Draw the longest side
  Use compasses to draw the two red arcs
  Join up the triangle

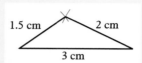

  Given one side and two angles:
  Draw the side
  Use a protractor to draw the two angles
  This will complete the triangle.

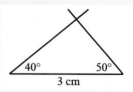

  Given two sides and one angle:
  Draw the longest side
  Use a protractor to draw the angle
  Mark the length of the other side
  Join up the triangle.

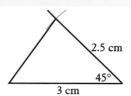

- **Two shapes are congruent if they are exactly the same.**

- **Parts of the circle**

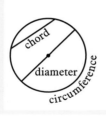

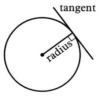

- **Bearings are always measured clockwise starting from North.**
  A bearing must always have three figures.

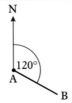

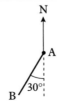

Bearing of
B from A = 120°

Bearing of
B from A = 050°

Bearing of
B from A = 210°

Bearing of
B from A = 300°

- **Constructions**

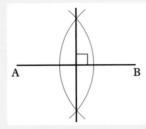

Perpendicular bisector of AB

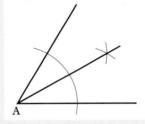

Bisector of angle A

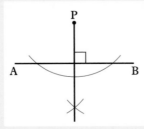

Perpendicular from P onto AB

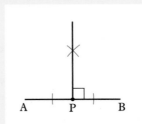

Perpendicular at P

- **Constructing a right-angled triangle**
  Start by drawing a line.
  Construct an angle of 90° from a point on the
  line where you want the right angle to be.
  Use your compass to mark the base length
  with an arc.
  From this first arc use your compasses to
  draw a second arc to show where the
  hypotenuse meets the vertical.

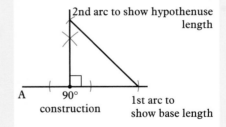

2nd arc to show hypothenuse
length

90°
construction

1st arc to
show base length

- **Types of quadrilateral**
  A shape with four straight sides is a quadrilateral.

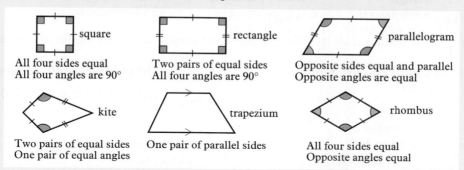

square	rectangle	parallelogram
All four sides equal All four angles are 90°	Two pairs of equal sides All four angles are 90°	Opposite sides equal and parallel Opposite angles are equal
kite	trapezium	rhombus
Two pairs of equal sides One pair of equal angles	One pair of parallel sides	All four sides equal Opposite angles equal

- **Drawings of 3D shapes**

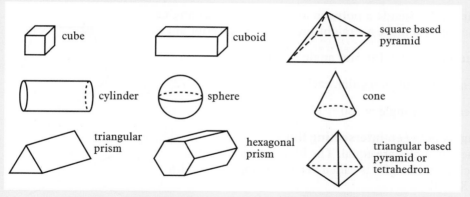

cube · cuboid · square based pyramid

cylinder · sphere · cone

triangular prism · hexagonal prism · triangular based pyramid or tetrahedron

- **When a solid is opened out and laid flat, the shape that you get is called a net of the solid.**

This net   would make   this cube.

Plans and elevations

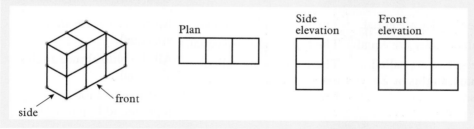

side   front

Plan   Side elevation   Front elevation

BROOKFIELD COMMUNITY SCHOOL

- **Names of polygons**
  - 3 sides – triangle
  - 4 sides – quadrilateral
  - 5 sides – pentagon
  - 6 sides – hexagon
  - 8 sides – octagon
  - 10 sides – decagon

- **A polygon is regular if all its sides are the same length and all its angles are equal.**

- **The angles of a quadrilateral add up to 360°.**

  The red angle is 80° because

  $$110 + 50 + 120 + 80 = 360$$

- **The exterior angles of a polygon add up to 360°.**
  If the hexagon is regular,
  each red angle $= \dfrac{360}{6} = 60°$

  The red angles add up to 360°

- **The angles inside a polygon are called interior angles.**
  They always make a straight line with the exterior angle.

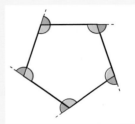

  Exterior angle + Interior angle = 180°

  If the pentagon is regular, each red angle $= \dfrac{360}{5} = 72°$

  so each blue angle $= 180 - 72 = 108°$

- **Angles between intersecting lines**
  The red angles are equal. The blue angles are equal.
  Each pair of angles is called vertically opposite angles or X angles.

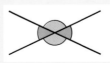

- **Angles between parallel lines**

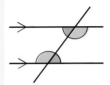 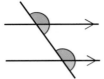 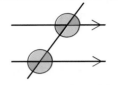

  The red angles are equal. The blue angles are equal.

  These angles are called **alternate angles** or Z angles.

  The red angles are equal. The blue angles are equal.

  These angles are called **corresponding angles** or F angles.

  All the red acute angles are equal.

  All the blue obtuse angles are equal.

  A red and a blue angle together add up to 180°.

Levels 3–5

1 Write down the name of each of these angles.

a    **b**    **c**

....

2 An aeroplane is flying due south. What direction will it be flying if it turns

a 90° clockwise   ....   **c** 270° clockwise   ....

b 45° anticlockwise ....   **d** 135° anticlockwise ....

3 Find the red angle.

a    **b**   **c**

....

Level 6

4 Sketch each of these.
   a Cuboid   **b** Cylinder   **c** Square-based pyramid

5 Find
   a the red angle   **b** the blue angle

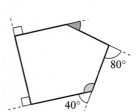

....

6 Find each of the coloured angles.

   a red angle = ...

   b blue angle = ...

   c green angle = ...

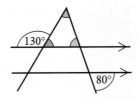

Levels 3–5

1 A cardboard box is being made for a small toy. A plan of the **net** of the box is drawn first.

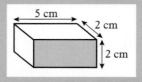

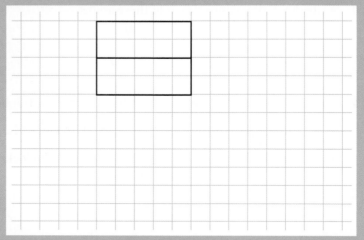

a **Complete** the plan of the **net**. 3 marks

b A **flap** is to be added so the box can have a **top** which closes. Add the **flap** to your plan of the **net**. 1 mark

2

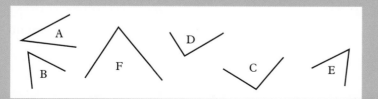

a Which is the **smallest** angle? .... 1 mark

b Which is the **largest** angle? .... 1 mark

c Which **two** angles are the **same size**? .... and .... 1 mark

d Which angle is a **right angle**? .... 1 mark

e Draw an angle which is an **obtuse** angle.

1 mark

3 a John is facing **South**.
He turns **clockwise** through **2 right angles**.
In which direction will he now be facing?

.... 1 mark

b Louise is facing **East**.
She turns **anticlockwise** through **3 right angles**.
In which direction will she now be facing?

.... 1 mark

Level 6

4 a

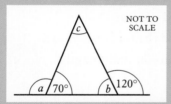

NOT TO SCALE

Calculate angles *a*, *b* and *c*.

a = ...   *b* = ...   *c* = ...   3 marks

b

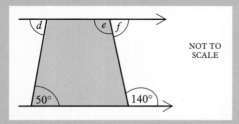

NOT TO SCALE

Calculate angles *d*, *e* and *f*.

d = ...   *e* = ...   *f* = ...   3 marks

What is the name of the blue shape?

.... 1 mark

5 This is an accurate scaled plan of a classroom.

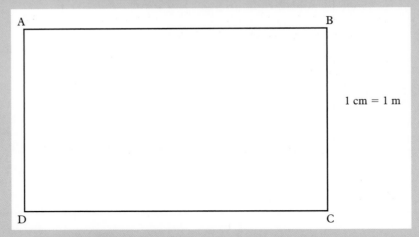

Using ruler and compasses only

a construct a line to bisect angle D, and extend the line to meet AB

b construct a line to bisect side DC, and extend the line to meet AB

Measure both lines, and write down the difference in their lengths.

.... 3 marks

6 In the space below, using ruler and compasses only, draw an accurate equilateral triangle with side of length 3.5 cm.

2 marks

Level 7

- **Pythagoras' theorem is used to find the length of a side in a right-angled triangle.**
  You use it when you know the length of two of the sides.

- **The hypotenuse, h, is the longest side of a right-angled triangle.**
  Pythagoras' theorem tells you
  $$h^2 = a^2 + b^2$$

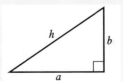

  The square of the hypotenuse = the sum of the squares of the other two sides

- **Finding the hypotenuse**
  $$h^2 = 8^2 + 11^2$$
  $$= 64 + 121$$
  $$= 185$$
  $$h = \sqrt{185}$$
  $$= 13.6 \text{ cm} \quad (3 \text{ sf})$$

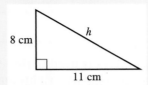

  Check that your answer for the hypotenuse is longer than each of the other two sides.

- **Finding one of the shorter sides**
  Always start by writing Pythagoras' theorem in the usual order starting with hypotenuse^2 = ...
  $$25^2 = x^2 + 9^2$$
  $$25^2 - 9^2 = x^2$$
  so $\quad x^2 = 625 - 81 = 544$
  $$x = \sqrt{544} = 23.3 \text{ cm} \quad (3 \text{ sf})$$

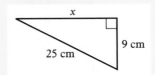

  Check that your answer is shorter than the hypotenuse.

- **Finding the distance between two points**
  Draw a diagram showing the two points.
  Use the co-ordinates to find the lengths of the short sides of the triangle.
  Use Pythagoras to find the hypotenuse.

  $$h^2 = 4^2 + 5^2$$
  $$= 41$$
  $$h = 6.4 \text{ units} \quad (1 \text{ dp})$$

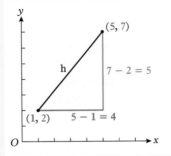

81

- **Angles in circles**

 The **tangent** is perpendicular to the radius.

 The red triangle is isosceles. The blue line forms two congruent right angled triangles.

Angles in the same segment are equal.

Angle at centre is twice angle at circumference.

Angle in a semicircle is 90°

Level 8

- **Trigonometry is used to find the length of a side or an angle in a right-angled triangle.**

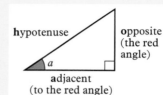
hypotenuse   opposite (the red angle)
a
adjacent (to the red angle)

- **The three trig ratios are**

$$\sin a = \frac{\text{opp}}{\text{hyp}} \quad \cos a = \frac{\text{adj}}{\text{hyp}} \quad \tan a = \frac{\text{opp}}{\text{adj}}$$

- **Finding a length**

$$\sin 40° = \frac{x}{5}$$
$$5 \times \sin 40° = x$$
$$x = 3.21 \text{ m} \quad (3 \text{ sf})$$

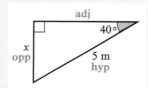
adj   40°
x opp   5 m hyp

- **Finding an angle**

$$\tan a = \frac{12}{18}$$
$$a = 33.7° \quad (1 \text{ dp})$$

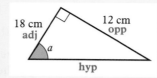
18 cm adj   12 cm opp
a
hyp

- **Bearings are often used in trigonometry questions.**
  Use the bearing to find the angle to work with.

  A ship travels 100 miles on a bearing of **204°**. How far South does it travel?

$$\cos 24° = \frac{x}{100} \qquad x = 91.4 \text{ miles } (3 \text{ sf})$$

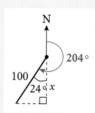
N
204°
100
24° x

Level 7

1 Find x in each of these.

a

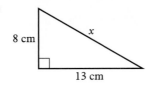

8 cm
x
13 cm

$x^2 = \ldots\ldots + \ldots\ldots$

$\quad = \ldots\ldots$

$x = \sqrt{\ldots\ldots}$

$x = \ldots\ldots$ (3 sf)

b

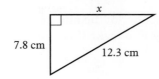

x
7.8 cm
12.3 cm

$\ldots\ldots = \ldots\ldots + \ldots\ldots$

$\ldots\ldots - \ldots\ldots = \ldots\ldots$

$x^2 = \ldots\ldots$

$x = \sqrt{\ldots\ldots}$

$x = \ldots\ldots$ (3 sf)

Level 8

2 Find p in each of these.

a

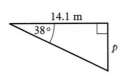

14.1 m
38°
p

$\ldots\ldots\, 38° = \dfrac{p}{\ldots\ldots}$

$\ldots\ldots\ldots = p$

$p = \ldots\ldots$ m (3 sf)

b

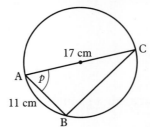

17 cm
C
A
p
11 cm
B

The angle at B is 90° because $\ldots\ldots\ldots\ldots\ldots\ldots$

$\ldots\ldots\, p = \dfrac{\ldots\ldots}{\ldots\ldots}$

$p = \ldots\ldots$ ° (3 sf)

3 A plane flies 500 miles on a bearing of 306° from A. How far West does it travel?

$\ldots\ldots\ldots\ldots\ldots\ldots\ldots\ldots\ldots\ldots\ldots\ldots\ldots\ldots\ldots\ldots\ldots\ldots\ldots\ldots$

$\ldots\ldots\ldots\ldots\ldots\ldots\ldots\ldots\ldots\ldots\ldots\ldots\ldots\ldots\ldots\ldots\ldots\ldots\ldots\ldots$

$\ldots\ldots\ldots\ldots\ldots\ldots\ldots\ldots\ldots\ldots\ldots\ldots\ldots\ldots\ldots\ldots\ldots\ldots\ldots\ldots$

N

A

1 This shape is a **square-based** pyramid.

Write down the letter of the **one** net
which can be used to make this pyramid.

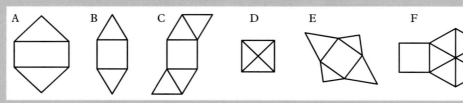

1 mark

2 A boat is to sail around a hexagonal
course ABCDEF, past six buoys.
The boat starts from point A.

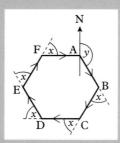

a Through what angle *x* should the boat turn at each of the buoys?

$x =$ .... 1 mark

b What bearing *y* should the boat sail on at the start of the race?

$y =$ .... 1 mark

3 **Calculate** the area of the triangle.

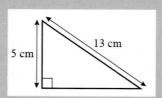

5 cm

13 cm

Area = ... cm² 3 marks

5 A boat is sailed around a lake.

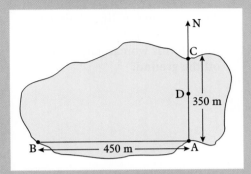

Point C is 350 metres due North of A.
Point B is 450 metres due West of A.

a Calculate the direct distance from point B to point C.

.... m   2 marks

b Calculate the bearing the boat must sail on to travel from point B to point C.

.... °   2 marks

c Calculate the bearing the boat must sail on to travel from point C to point B.

.... °   1 mark

d The boat sails on a bearing of 60° from point B, across the lake until it reaches point D, due North of A.
Calculate the distance from B to D.

.... m   2 marks

8   Position and movement

The window acts like a mirror. The reflection makes it look as though this woman has both feet off the ground.

Levels 3–5

- **A line of symmetry divides a shape into two identical halves. Each half is a reflection of the other.**
  If you fold a shape along a line of symmetry each half fits exactly on top of the other.

- **A shape can have more than one line of symmetry or none at all.**

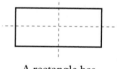

A rectangle has
two lines of symmetry

A square has
four lines of symmetry

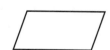

A parallelogram does not
have any lines of symmetry

The dashed red lines are the lines of symmetry.
They are sometimes called mirror lines.

- **To reflect a shape in a mirror line**
  (1) Reflect each corner in turn.
     The new position must be the same distance on the other side of the mirror line.
     Use the squares to help you.
  (2) Join these points to get the reflected shape.

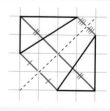

- **You can reflect 3D shapes in a mirror.**
  This shape is symmetrical about the mirror.

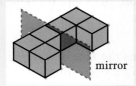

- **A shape has rotational symmetry if it fits on top of itself more than once as it makes a complete turn.**

- **The order of rotational symmetry is the number of times the shape fits on top of itself.**

- **The centre of rotation is the point at the centre of the shape that stays still as the shape turns.**

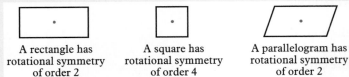

| A rectangle has rotational symmetry of order 2 | A square has rotational symmetry of order 4 | A parallelogram has rotational symmetry of order 2 |

- **To rotate a shape about any point.**
  (1) You need to know the angle and the direction of turn.
  (2) Trace the shape.
  (3) Put your pencil on the centre of rotation and rotate the tracing paper.
  (4) Draw the shape in its new position.

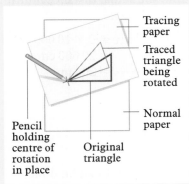

You can use a cross on the tracing paper to help you see when you have rotated through 90°, 180°, 270°.

- **A translation is a movement in a straight line.**
  The shape A has been moved three squares to the right and one square down to get to B.
  You can write this as $\begin{pmatrix} 3 \\ -1 \end{pmatrix}$

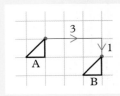

87

- **When you are doing more than one transformation on a shape make sure you do them in the right order.**

- **An enlargement changes the size of a shape.**
  The change is the same in all directions.

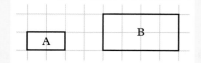

- **The scale factor tells you how many times bigger the enlargement is.**
  Rectangle B is an enlargement of rectangle A, scale factor 2.

- This map shows some streets.
  The real streets are an enlargement of the map.
  The scale of the map tells you the scale factor of the enlargement.
  The distance between the church and the school on the map is 2 cm.
  To find the actual distance multiply by the scale factor

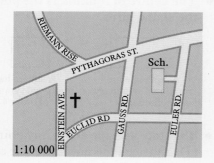

  Actual distance $= 2 \times 10\,000$ cm
  $ = 20\,000$ cm
  $ = 200$ m

Level 6

- **An enlargement can be done from a point.**
  This point is called the centre of enlargement, C.
  Look at the corner of the small triangle marked ●
  ● is 1 square from C.
  The new position will be $1 \times 3 = 3$ squares from C.
  Do the same for the other corners of the shape.

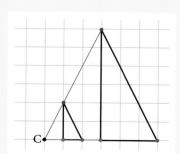

- **Symmetry of the regular polygons.**

Equilateral triangle

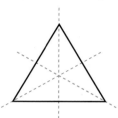

three lines of symmetry
rotational symmetry
of order 3

Square

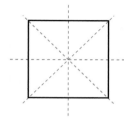

four lines of symmetry
rotational symmetry
of order 4

Regular pentagon

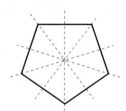

five lines of symmetry
rotational symmetry
of order 5

Regular hexagon

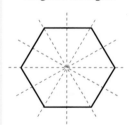

six lines of symmetry
rotational symmetry
of order 6

Regular octagon

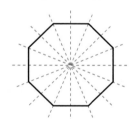

eight lines of symmetry
rotational symmetry
of order 8

Regular decagon

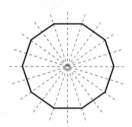

ten lines of symmetry
rotational symmetry
of order 10

- **Symmetry of solids**
  This is a cuboid.
  You can see the three possible
  places to put a mirror so that
  the two halves are
  symmetrical.
  When you put a mirror into a
  shape like this the mirror is
  called a plane of symmetry.

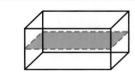

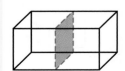

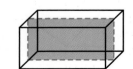

1 For each of these shapes draw the lines of symmetry and write down the order of rotational symmetry.

a   **b**   **c**   **d**

order ......   order ......   order ......   order ......

2 a Translate triangle A 6 squares to the right and 2 squares up.
b Rotate triangle A 90° clockwise about ●
c Reflect triangle A in the blue line.

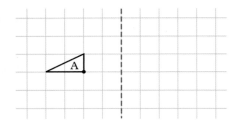

3 Enlarge this shape using centre C and scale factor 2.

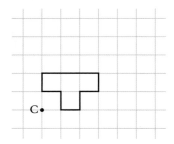

4 Write down the number of planes of symmetry.

a   **b**   **c**

square-based pyramid

....

Levels 3–5

1 a Shade in **one more square** to make a shape which has line AB as a **line of symmetry**.

1 mark

b Shade in **one more square** to make a shape with line CD as a **line of symmetry**.

1 mark

c Shade in **three more squares** to make a shape which has **two lines of symmetry**.

1 mark

d Shade in **one more square** to make a shape which has **rotational symmetry**.

1 mark

e Shade in three more squares to make a shape which has **two lines of symmetry** and **rotational symmetry** about the marked point.

1 mark

f Shade A has been **rotated clockwise** onto shape B. Mark with a clear cross the **centre of rotation**.

Write down the angle of rotation.

....

2 marks

2 For each of these patterns draw in **all** the **lines of symmetry**.

a   **b** **c**

3 marks

91

3 Reflect this triangle in the mirror line.

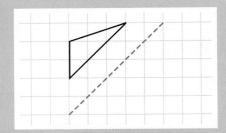

2 marks

Level 6

4 Write down the number of **planes of symmetry** in the following solids.

a Cube ....

b Prism ....

2 marks

5 Draw an **enlargement** of this shape by a **scale factor** of **2**.

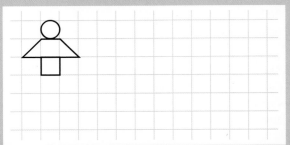

3 marks

6 Draw an **enlargement** of this shape by a **scale factor** of **3** from the centre of enlargement A.

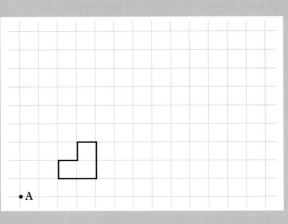

2 marks

Level 7

- **An enlargement can also make a shape smaller.**
  This happens when the scale factor is between 0 and 1. Shape A has been enlarged by scale factor $\frac{1}{2}$.

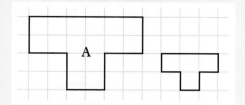

- **The locus of an object is all the possible positions that the object can take as it moves according to a rule.**
  You can describe a locus in words or with a diagram.
  The red line shows the locus in each of these.

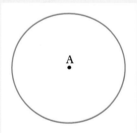

Points that are
1.5 cm from A.

A circle, centre A
radius 1.5 cm.

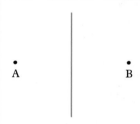

Points that are equidistant
from the two points A and B.

The perpendicular bisector
of the line AB.

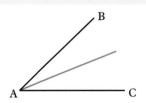

Points that are equidistant
from the lines AB and AC.

The bisector of angle BAC.

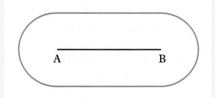

Points that are 1 cm from
the line AB.

Pair of parallel lines with a
semicircle at each end.

- **Use ruler and compasses and the constructions on page 74 to draw loci accurately. Show your construction lines.**

- **You can also shade regions to show where something can be.**
The red region shows the points that are nearer to A than to B.

- **Two triangles are similar if they have the same angles.**
Triangles P and Q are similar.

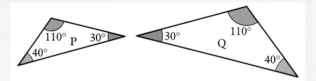

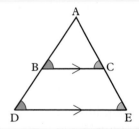

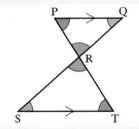

The red angles are corresponding angles so they are equal.
The blue angles are corresponding angles so they are equal.
Triangles ABC and ADE are similar.

The red and blue angles are alternate angles so they are equal.
The green angles are opposite angles and so they are equal.
Triangles PQR and TSR are similar.

- **Similar triangles are enlargements of each other.**
Use the scale factor to find missing lengths.
Make sure you're working with corresponding sides.

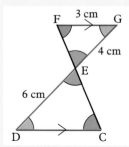

Triangles CDE and FGE are similar.
GE and ED are corresponding sides as they are both opposite the red angles.
The scale factor for the enlargement from FGE to CDE is 6 ÷ 4 = 1.5.
GF and CD are corresponding sides
Length CD = 3 × 1.5
= 4.5 cm.

- **Congruent**

  Two shapes are congruent if they are identical.

  Use one of these rules to show that two triangles are congruent.

  Rule 1   All three pairs of sides are equal

  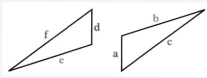

  Here   a = d
               b = e
  and   c = f

  Remember this rule as **SSS**.

  Rule 2   Right angle, hypotenuse and side are equal

  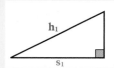 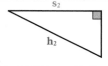

  Here $h_1 = h_2$
               $s_1 = s_2$

  and both triangles
  have a right angle

  Remember this rule as **RHS**.

  Rule 3   Two pairs of corresponding sides are equal and
          the angles *between* the pairs of sides are also equal

  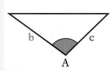 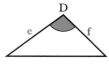

  Here $\hat{A} = \hat{D}$
               b = e
  and   c = f

  Remember this rule as **SAS**.
  You write the A in the middle to remind you that
  the equal angles must be *between* the two sides.

  Rule 4   Two pairs of angles are equal and a pair of
          corresponding sides is also equal

  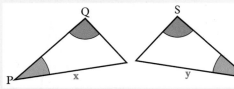

  Here $\hat{Q} = \hat{S}$
               $\hat{P} = \hat{R}$
  and   x = y

  Remember this rule as **AAS**.
  You must remember that the equal sides must be in
  the same place.

Once you have proved that two triangles are congruent
remember that all corresponding sides and angles are equal.

Level 7

---

1 Enlarge the shape using centre C and scale factor $\frac{1}{2}$.

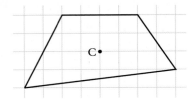

2 The diagram shows a wheel.
  a Draw the locus of the red point on the rim of the wheel as the wheel rolls along the line.
  b Draw the locus of the blue point at the centre of the wheel.

3 An ambulance station must be less than 4 km from the hospital and less than 3 km from the motorway. Show the region where it could be.

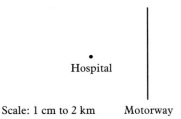

Scale: 1 cm to 2 km

Hospital

Motorway

Level 8

---

4 a Mark the pairs of equal angles.
  b Write down the corresponding side to

    (1) PQ ......   (2) SR ....

  c Find the scale factor for the enlargement from RST to PQR.

    ...... ÷ ...... = ...

  d Find the length SR.

    ...... ÷ ...... = ... cm

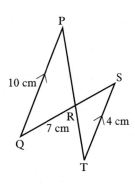

Levels 5–7

1 This is a logo measuring 7 cm by 10 cm.
June wants to use a photocopier to reproduce
the logo on three different sizes of paper.
The logo needs to be as large as possible
on each sheet of paper. Find the scale factor
she should use for each size of paper.
Give your answers correct to 2 dp.

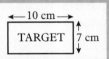

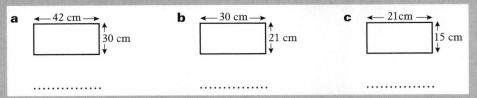

a ⟵ 42 cm ⟶ 30 cm

b ⟵ 30 cm ⟶ 21 cm

c ⟵ 21cm ⟶ 15 cm

....

3 marks

2

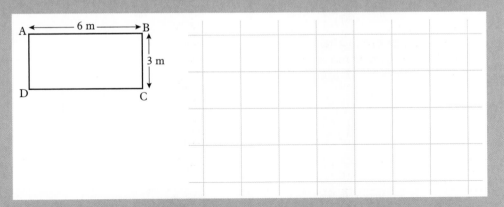

This is a plan of a garden plot.
Draw an **accurate scale plan** of the plot.
Use a scale of 1 square to represent 1 m.   *1 mark*

  a A row of flowers is planted in a **straight line** exactly **1.5 m** from the side BC.
     Show the location of the line of flowers on your scale plan.   *1 mark*

  b The plot is divided by a small fence. The fence starts in corner D, and runs
     across the plot so as to be the same distance from side AD and side DC.
     On your scale plan show the position of the fence.   *1 mark*

  c Seeds are sown in such a way as to be no more than 1 metre from corner A.
     On your scale plan shade the location in which the seeds can be sown.   *1 mark*

3 This is an accurate plan of a garden pond.
It has been drawn using a scale of 1 cm to represent 1 m.

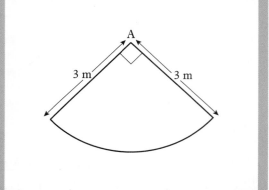

a A fence is to be put up which is **exactly 1 metre** from the edge of the pond. Draw **accurately** the position of the fence on the scale plan. 3 marks

b A small fountain is at the corner A of the pond. It sprays water up to one metre away. On the scale plan shade the part of the pond which is sprayed by the fountain.

1 mark

Level 8

4 These two tins are mathematically similar. The external dimensions are shown. Calculate the height h of the larger tin.

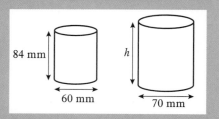

h = ... mm

2 marks

5 A 10 metre high pole is held in place by two metal struts, AE and BC.
The position of the struts is described in the diagram.
AD = 10 m, BC = 6 m, DE = 12 m, AC = 8.5 m
BC is parallel to the level ground DE.
Calculate the length of CE.

CE = ... m

2 marks

6

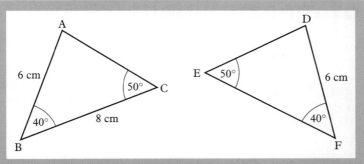

ABC and DEF are two congruent triangles.

a Explain why ABC and DEF are congruent.

1 mark

b Use both triangles to find the length DE.

3 marks

7

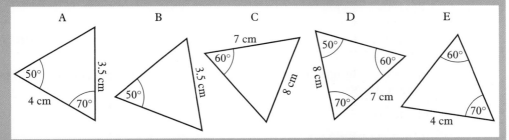

a Write down the letters of two triangles that are mathematically **similar** to each other, but **not** congruent.

……… ………

Explain why they are only similar.

2 marks

b Write down the letters of two triangles that are **congruent** to each other.

……… ………

Explain why they are congruent.

2 marks

c Write down the letters of two **different** triangles that are **congruent** to each other.

……… ………

Explain why they are congruent.

2 marks

9   Units of measurement

French scientists worked out the distance from the North Pole to the Equator and divided by 10 million. They called this distance 1 metre.

Levels 3–5

- **The metric units of length are millimetres (mm), centimetres (cm), metres (m) and kilometres (km).**

  10 mm = 1 cm   100 cm = 1 m   1000 m = 1 km

- **The metric units of capacity are millilitres (m*l*), centilitres (c*l*) and litres (*l*).**

  10 ml = 1 c*l*   100 cl = 1 *l*   1000 m*l* = 1 *l*

- **The metric units of mass are milligrams (mg), grams (g), kilograms (kg) and tonnes (t).**

  1000 mg = 1 g   1000 g = 1 kg   1000 kg = 1 t

- **To convert between units you need to know the above conversion facts.**

  Convert 4800 g to kilograms.
  Look for the conversion fact that you need.
  To go from the larger unit to the smaller unit you multiply.
  To go from the smaller unit to the bigger unit you divide.

  > 1000 g = 1 kg
  >
  > g → kg
  > smaller → bigger
  > so divide by 1000

  4800 g ÷ 1000 = 4.8 kg

- **The Imperial units of length are inches (in), feet (ft), yards (yd) and miles.**

  12 in = 1 ft   3 ft = 1 yd   1760 yd = 1 mile

- **The Imperial units of mass are ounces (oz), pounds (lb) and stones (st).**

  16 oz = 1 lb   14 lb = 1 st

- **The Imperial units of capacity are fluid ounces (fl oz), pints (pt) and gallons (gal).**

  20 fl oz = 1 pt   8 pt = 1 gal

- **Converting between metric and Imperial units of length**

  You need to remember these conversion numbers and when to multiply and divide.

	Conversion number
1 in is about 2.5 cm	2.5
1 ft is about 30 cm	30
1 yd is about 90 cm	90
1 mile is about 1.6 km	1.6

  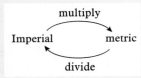

  Convert 3 yd to cm
  Look for the conversion number
  that you need.

  3 yds = 3 × 90 = 270 cm

  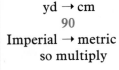

- **Converting mass and capacity**

	Conversion number
1 oz is about 30 g	30
1 lb is about 450 g	450
1 st is about 6.5 kg	6.5
1 pt is about 600 m*l*	600
1 gal is about 4.5 *l*	4.5

- **Converting from metric to Imperial units**

  You may find it easier to remember these:
  1 metre is about 3 feet.   8 kilometres is about 5 miles.
  1 kilogram is about 2.2 pounds.   1 litre is just less than 2 pints.

- **To read a scale**

  (1) Work out what each division represents.
  (2) Work out the reading.

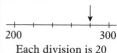

Each division is 20
The reading is 280

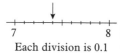

Each division is 0.1
The reading is 7.4

- **Time can be written using am and pm or the 24-hour clock**

morning
7.20 am
07:20

afternoon
5.50 pm
17:50

night
12.15 am
00:15

- You need to be able to estimate in both Imperial and metric units. Remember these familiar objects to help you.

Length

1 in
1 cm

2 m   6 ft

1 ft
30 cm

Mass

CRISPS
30 g or 1 ounce

sugar
1 kg or 2.2 lb

100 kg or 15 st

Capacity

250 ml or ½ pt

Coke
2 l or 3½ pt

90 l or 20 gal

1 **a** 1 m = ... cm   **e** ...... pt = 1 gal   **i** 400 c*l* = ... *l*

  b ...... in = 1 ft   **f** 1 *l* = ... m*l*   **j** ...... oz = 3 lb

  c ...... oz = 1 lb   **g** 2 cm = ... mm   **k** 6 yd = ... ft

  d 1 kg = ... g   **h** ...... kg = 3t   **l** 24 in = ... ft

2 **a** 1 mile is about ...... km   **c** 1 yd is about ...... cm   **e** 1 oz is about ...... g

  b 1 pt is about ...... m*l*   **d** 1 gal is about ...... *l*   **f** 1 lb is about ...... g

3 **a**

10 20
Each division is ...
The reading is ...

  b

5 6
Each division is ...
The reading is ...

  c

10 20
Each division is ...
The reading is ...

4 **a** 6:50 am = ...   **c** 01:45 = ...

  b 23:10 = ...   **d** 4:36 pm = ...

5 **a**

length is about ...... m

  b

mass is about ...... oz

  c

width is about ...... in

  d

capacity is about ...... m*l*

1

BUS TIMETABLE

Underhill	depart	07:30	08:15	09:00	09:45	10:30
Bramley	arrive	08:05	08:50	09:35	10:20	11:05

a A bus leaves **Underhill** at **09:45**.
At what time does it arrive at **Bramley**? .... 1 mark

b A bus arrives at **Bramley** at **10:20**.
At what time did it leave **Underhill**? .... 1 mark

c How long does the bus journey take from **Underhill** to **Bramley**?

.... minutes 1 mark

d Which buses could you catch to get to **Bramley** by **10:00**?

.... or .... or .... 1 mark

e Vincent needs to be in **Bramley** by **09:00**.
What is the time of the **latest** bus he can catch from **Underhill**?

.... 1 mark

f The last evening bus from
Underhill is at **23:15**.
Draw hands on this clock
face to represent this time.

1 mark

2

a Write down the **length** of the pencil

in centimetres ....   in millimetres .... 2 marks

b Another pencil of length 5.3 cm has 16 mm cut from its length.
What is the new length of the pencil?
Give your answer in centimetres. .... cm 1 mark

3 a A piece of cheese is weighed.
Write down the mass shown
by the scale.

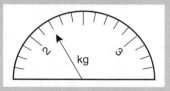

.... **kg**   1 mark

b 600 g of cheese is cut off.
How much cheese remains?
Give your answer in kilograms.   .... **kg**   2 marks

4 Write down your estimate of each of the following:

a The mass of a bag of sugar   .... kg

b The capacity of a milk bottle   .... *l*

c The length of an ant   .... mm

5 The conversion graph shown on the grid is for centimetres and inches.

a Change **2 inches** into
centimetres.

.... cm

b Change **20 centimetres**
into **inches**.

.... inches

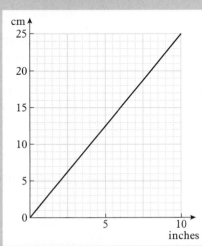

2 marks

Level 7

- **Lower and upper limits**
  Any number in the red part of the
  number line rounds to 7 to the nearest
  whole number.

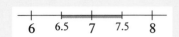

  6.5 is called the lower limit.
  7.5 is called the upper limit.

- $\text{Speed} = \dfrac{\text{Distance}}{\text{Time}}$ $\text{Time} = \dfrac{\text{Distance}}{\text{Speed}}$ $\text{Distance} = \text{Speed} \times \text{Time}$

  This triangle can help you to remember these.
  Cover up the letter you're trying to find.
  What is left is the rest of the equation.

  An object moves 300 m in 2 mins
  Find the average speed in metres per second.
  To get the speed in metres per second you must work in metres and seconds.
  So the object moves 300 m in 120 s.

  $\text{Speed} = \dfrac{300}{120} = 2.5$ m/s.

- **Travel graphs**
  The **red** part shows movement away
  from home. 50 km in 2 hours is a speed
  of 25 km/h.
  The **blue** part shows a stop lasting 1 hour.
  The **green** part shows the journey home.
  There is a further 1 hour stop 30 km from
  home.

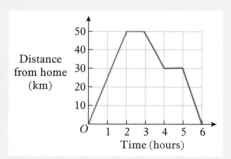

  The average speed = total distance ÷ total time = $100 \div 6 = 16\frac{2}{3}$ km/h

- **Density** $= \dfrac{\text{Mass}}{\text{Volume}}$ $\text{Volume} = \dfrac{\text{Mass}}{\text{Density}}$

  Mass = Density × Volume.

Level 7

1 The sides of this box are
correct to the nearest
whole number.

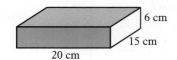

6 cm
15 cm
20 cm

  a The lower limits of each length are

    ...... cm, ... cm, ... cm.

  b The upper limits of each length are ...... cm, ... cm, ... cm.

2 The travel graph shows Tim's cycle
journey from Cranley to Marsh.

  a How far is it from Cranley to Marsh?

    ....

  b How long did Tim stop for a rest?

    ....

  c Did Tim travel faster before or after
his rest? Explain your answer.

    ....

    ....

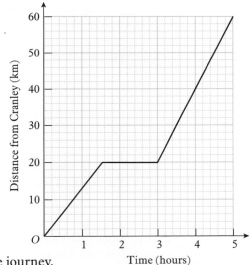

  d Find Tim's average speed for the whole journey.

    ....

    ....

3 Complete the table.

	Speed	Distance	Time
a		13 m	2 s
b	5 m/s		2.5 mins
c	12 km/h	4 km	
d	mph	40 miles	$1\frac{1}{4}$ hours

4 Complete the table.

	Density	Mass	Volume
a		50 g	10 cm³
b	50 kg/m³	100 kg	
c	15 g/cm³		20 cm³
d	g/cm³	2.5 kg	100 cm³

Levels 5–7

1 Estimate the readings on the following scales.
Give the units of measurement with your answer.

a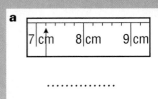

b

c

....

....

....   3 marks

2 The scales show the mass of a man in stones.

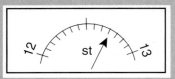

a Write down, in **stones and pounds**, the reading on the scales.

.... st .... lb   1 mark

b The man has lost $1\frac{1}{2}$ stones while on a diet.
How much did the man weigh **before** he went on the diet?

.... st .... lb   1 mark

3 A 600 *l* tank is being filled with water.
The table shows some readings taken while the tank is being filled.

Time (min)	1	6	10	15	25	30	
Capacity (litres)		72		180			600

a Complete the table.   2 marks

b *C* is the capacity of the tank in litres,
and *T* is the time in minutes.
Write an equation using symbols to connect *C* and *T*.   .... 1 mark

c A tank of capacity **5000 *l*** is to be filled at the same rate as before.
How long, in hours and minutes, does it take to fill the tank?

.... hours .... minutes   2 marks

4 Janet exchanges £550 for 880 euro.

   a Work out the exchange rate.

                                     £1 = ... euro   1 mark

   b While on holiday Janet buys a leather
      bag for 26.40 euro.
      Work out how much this is in pounds.

                                     £ ....   2 marks

5 The travel graph represents
the journeys of two cyclists,
Adam and Belinda.
Adam is travelling from
Crook to Debens.
Belinda is travelling from
Debens to Crook.

   a How many minutes after Belinda did Adam start his journey?

                                .... minutes   1 mark

   b Describe briefly what happened at point X.

                                                             1 mark

   c Work out the average speed for Adam's entire journey, in kilometres per hour.

                                  .... km/h   1 mark

   d Work out Belinda's average speed using only the amount of time during which
      she was actually moving.

                                  .... km/h   1 mark

   e Between which two times was Adam's speed the fastest?

                                .... and ....   1 mark

10 Perimeter, area and volume

The world record for the number of people in a phone box is 23.
This is a lot of people in a very small space!

Levels 3–5

- **The total distance around the outside of a shape is called its perimeter.**
  The perimeter of this shape is
  $5 + 8 + 6 + 10 = 29$ cm

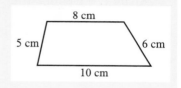

- **Area is measured in squares.**
  The area of this shape is 5 squares.
  If each square is 1 cm by 1 cm then the area is 5 cm^2.

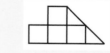

- **You can count squares to estimate an area.**
  Count all the squares which are more than half inside the outline.
      Area = 10 cm^2

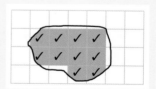

- **The area of a rectangle = length × width**
  The area of this rectangle is
      $5 \times 3 = 15$ cm^2

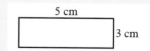

- **Units of area are always square units.**

- **Volume is measured in cubes.**
  The volume of this solid is 7 cubes.
  If each cube is 1 cm by 1 cm by 1 cm then the volume is 7 cm^3.

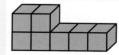

- **The capacity of a hollow object is the volume of space inside it.**
  Capacity is measured in millilitres and litres. 1 ml is the same as 1 cm^3.

- **The area of a triangle** $= \dfrac{\text{base} \times \text{height}}{2}$

  The area of this triangle is

  $$\frac{6 \times 5}{2} = \frac{30}{2} = 15 \text{ cm}^2$$

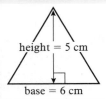

The base and the height must always be at right angles like these.

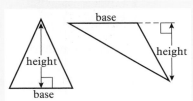

- **Circumference of a circle** $= \pi \times \text{diameter}$
  The circumference of this circle is $\pi \times 6 = 18.9$ cm (1 dp)
  The value of π is 3.14159265 ...

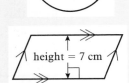

- **Area of a circle** $= \pi \times \text{radius}^2 = \pi \times \text{radius} \times \text{radius}$
  The area of this circle is $\pi \times 3 \times 3 = 28.3 \text{ cm}^2$ (1 dp)
  The radius is half the diameter.

- **Area of a parallelogram** $= \text{base} \times \text{height}$
  The area of this parallelogram is
  $10 \times 7 = 70 \text{ cm}^2$

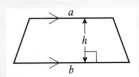

- **The area of a trapezium** $= \frac{1}{2}(a + b)h$

  You add the two parallel sides, divide by 2 and then multiply by the height.

  The area of this trapezium is

  $\frac{1}{2}(7 + 5) \times 3 = 6 \times 3 = 18 \text{ cm}^2$

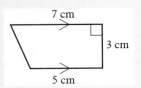

- **Volume of a cuboid** $= \text{length} \times \text{width} \times \text{height}$
  The volume of this cuboid is
  $8 \times 4 \times 3 = 96 \text{ cm}^3$
  Units of volume are always cube units.

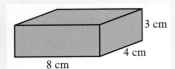

Levels 3–5

1 The perimeter of this shape is

...... + ... + ... = ... cm

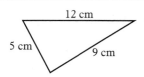

2 The area of this shape is

...... squares

3 The area of this rectangle is

...... cm × ...... cm = ... cm²

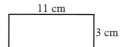

4 The area of this triangle is

$$\frac{\dots \times \dots}{\dots} = \frac{\dots}{\dots} = \dots \text{ cm}^2$$

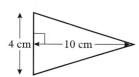

5 The volume of this solid is

...... cubes

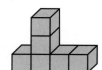

Level 6

6 The circumference of this circle is

π × ...... = ...   cm (1 dp)

The area of this circle is

π × ...... × ...... = ...   cm² (1 dp)

7 The area of this trapezium is

......(...... + ...) × ...... = ... × ...... = ... cm²

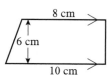

8 The volume of this cuboid is

...... × ...... × ...... = ... cm³

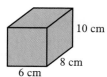

1 These shapes have been drawn on a 1 cm grid.

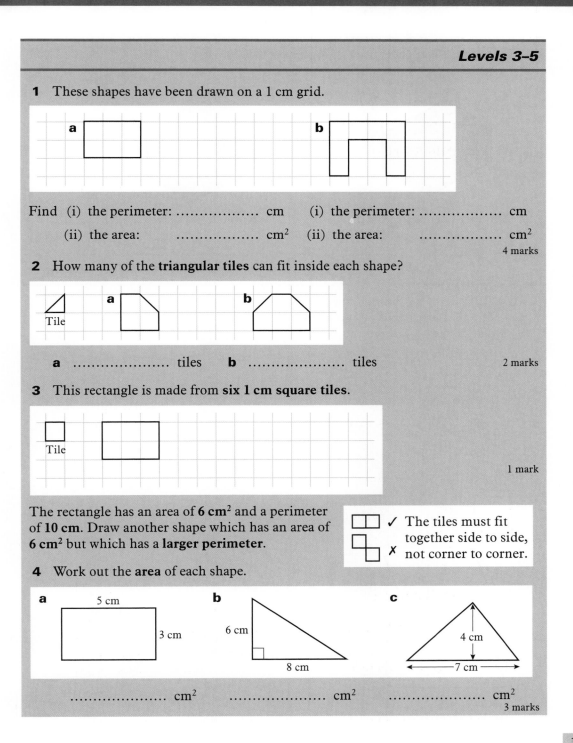

Find (i) the perimeter: .... cm   (i) the perimeter: .... cm

 (ii) the area: .... cm² (ii) the area: .... cm²

4 marks

2 How many of the **triangular tiles** can fit inside each shape?

a .... tiles   **b** .... tiles   2 marks

3 This rectangle is made from **six 1 cm square tiles**.

1 mark

The rectangle has an area of **6 cm²** and a perimeter of **10 cm**. Draw another shape which has an area of **6 cm²** but which has a **larger perimeter**.

✓ The tiles must fit together side to side, ✗ not corner to corner.

4 Work out the **area** of each shape.

a 5 cm 3 cm

b 6 cm 8 cm

c 4 cm 7 cm

.... cm²   .... cm²   .... cm²

3 marks

113

5 These shapes are made from small cubes of side 1 cm.
Write down how many small cubes there are in each shape.

a

b

Number of cubes: ....

Number of cubes: ....

2 marks

Level 6

6 a This coin has a **diameter** of **12 mm**.
The coin is pushed round exactly **twice**.
Work out how far the coin has moved.

12 mm

.... mm   1 mark

b This coin has a **diameter** of **16 mm**.
The coin has been moved **201 mm**.
How many times has it been pushed round?

16 mm

201 mm

.... times   1 mark

7 The area of this square is **9 cm²**.
What is the **perimeter** of the square?

.... cm   1 mark

8 Find the **area** of this parallelogram.

5 cm   4 cm

7 cm

.... cm²   1 mark

9 The **area** of the trapezium is **24 cm²**.
What is its vertical **height**, *h* cm?

5 cm

h cm

7 cm

.... cm   1 mark

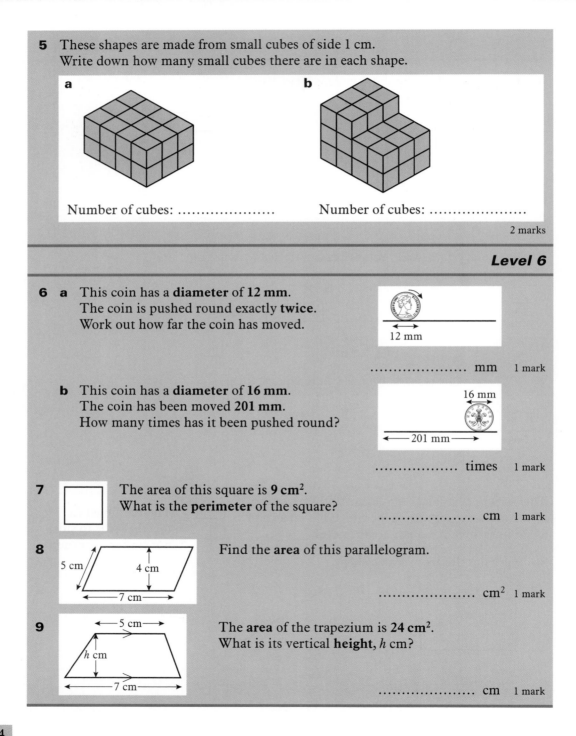

114

- **To find the area of this shape, find the area of the two parts and add them together.**

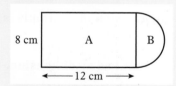

  Area A = $12 \times 8 = 96$ cm^2

  Area B = $\dfrac{\pi \times 4^2}{2} = 25.1$ cm^2 (1 dp)

  Total area = $96 + 25.1 = 121.1$ cm^2 (1 dp)

- **To find the area of the red shape you have to subtract the areas.**

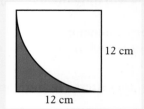

  = $12 \times 12 - \dfrac{\pi \times 12^2}{4}$

  = $144 - 113.1$

  = 30.9 cm^2 (1 dp)

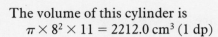

  12 cm

  12 cm

- **Volume of a prism = area of cross section × length**
  A prism is a solid which is exactly
  the same shape all the way through.

  The volume of this prism is
  $15 \times 20 = 300$ cm^3

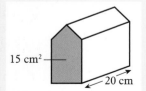

  15 cm^2

  20 cm

- **Volume of a cylinder = area of cross section × length**
  $= \pi r^2 \times h$

  The volume of this cylinder is
  $\pi \times 8^2 \times 11 = 2212.0$ cm^3 (1 dp)

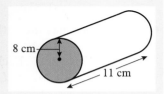

  8 cm

  11 cm

- **Converting area and volume units**

  1 m$^2 = 10\,000$ cm^2 1 m$^3 = 1\,000\,000$ cm^3

  ×10 000

  m^2 cm^2

  ÷10 000

  ×1 000 000

  m^3 cm^3

  ÷1 000 000

- The dimension of a formula is the number of lengths that are multiplied together.

- A constant has no dimension.

- Length has one dimension.
  Formulas for length will only involve constants and lengths.

- Area has two dimensions.
  Formulas for area will only involve constants and length × length.

- Volume has three dimensions.
  Formulas for volume will only involve constants and length × length × length.

In these formulas the letters x, y and x are lengths, k is a constant.

$P = 4xy$ This is constant × length × length
so P is an area.

$Q = \pi y^2 z$ This is constant × length² × length
= constant × length × length × length
so Q is a volume.

$R = kx$ This is constant × length
so R is a length.

- If a formula has more than one term, each term must have the same dimension.

$U = cx + \pi y$ Each term has dimension one
so U is a length.

$V = x^2 y - \pi xyz$ Each term has dimension three
so V is a volume.

$W = 2y^2 - 4\pi x$ $2y^2$ has dimension two
$4\pi x$ has dimension one
so W is an incorrect formula for length or area.

Level 7

1 The area of this shape is

...... $+$ $\dfrac{...... \times ......}{......}$

$= ...... + ... = ...$ cm² (1 dp)

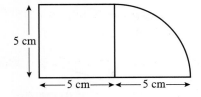

2 The red area is

...... $-$ ...... $\times$ ......

$= ...... - ...... = ...$ cm² (1 dp)

3 The volume of this prism is

$\dfrac{...... \times ......}{......} \times 15 = ...$ cm³

4 The volume of this cylinder is

...... $\times$ ...... $\times$ ......

$= ......$ cm³ (1 dp)

5 The length of this prism is

...... $\div$ ...... $=$ ...... cm

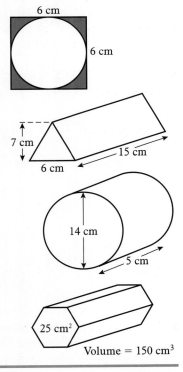

Volume = 150 cm³

Level 8

6 p, q and r are lengths. c and k are constants.
Write 'length', 'area', 'volume' or 'incorrect' for each of these formulas.

$B = cpq$ ....

$D = p^2q + 4pqr$ ....

$C = 2kq + \pi r$ ....

$E = 4\pi p^2 + ckr$ ....

Levels 5–7

1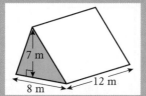

    a Calculate the area of the shaded face.

                                .... m^2 2 marks

    b Calculate the volume of the prism.

                                  .... m^3 1 mark

2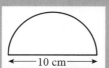

    For this semicircle find:

    a the area   .... cm^2 1 mark

    b the perimeter .... cm 1 mark

3 These two triangular prisms have the
same cross-sectional area.

    What is the height of prism B?

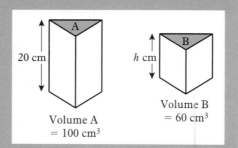

    Height: .... cm   2 marks

4

    This rectangle has a perimeter of **48 cm**.
The length is three times the width.
Calculate the **area** of the rectangle. .... cm^2 1 mark

5 A box has internal dimensions as shown.
What is the maximum number of cubes,
of side 2 cm, that can be stacked inside
the cuboid?

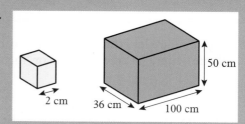

    Number: .... 2 marks

6 Calculate the area of the shaded region.

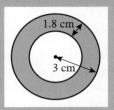

Area: .... cm²   2 marks

7 Calculate the surface area of this triangular prism.

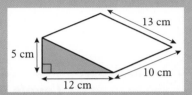

13 cm

5 cm

10 cm

12 cm

Area: .... cm²   2 marks

Level 8

8

8 cm

The surface area of a sphere is calculated using the formula $4\pi r^2$, where r is the radius of the sphere.
This hemisphere has a diameter of 8 cm.
Calculate the total surface area of the entire hemisphere.

Area: .... cm²   3 marks

9 Some of the expressions in the table can be used to calculate lengths, areas or volumes of some shapes.
The letters b, h, l and r represent lengths.
π, 2, 3, and 4 are numbers which have no dimension.
Put a tick in a box underneath each expression to show whether the expression represents a length, area or volume.

$4\pi r^2$	lbh	$\frac{1}{2}bh$	$\frac{4}{3}\pi r^3$	$4(r + b)$	$\dfrac{\pi h^2}{b}$	
						Length
						Area
						Volume

2 marks

11 Organising data

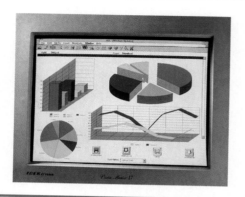

You can get information from lists of data but graphs and charts show it in a more eye-catching way.

Levels 3–5

- Tally marks are done in groups of five ⧄. The total number of tally marks is called the frequency.

- Organise data by making a frequency table.
  This is a frequency table.
  It shows what 30 people have for breakfast.

Breakfast	Tally	Frequency
cereal	⧄ ⧄ ‖	12
toast	⧄ ‖‖	8
cooked	‖‖‖	4
drink only	⧄ ‖	6

- A pictogram is a diagram which uses pictures to show the data. It must always have a key to show what each picture represents.
  The pictures must all be the same size and in line.

represents 4 people

so represents 2 people.

- A bar-chart uses bars instead of pictures to show the frequency.
  The bars must all be the same width and the same distance apart. The heights of the bars are the frequencies. You can add up all the heights to find the total number of people.

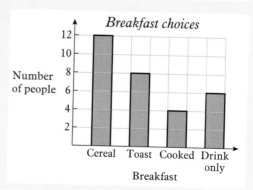

- **A stem and leaf diagram uses the data to form the bars.**
  This data is shown on the stem and leaf diagram.

  33, 18, 25, 23, 31, 20, 19, 28, 35, 22

  You must always include a key to show you've split the data into stems and leaves.

Stem	Leaf
1	8 9
2	0 2 3 5 8
3	1 3 5

Key: 2 | 3 means 23

- **You can use a vertical line instead of a bar. This is called a vertical line graph.**

- **Instead of a bar-chart or vertical line graph you can draw a frequency polygon.**
  The table shows the KS3 Maths results for 30 pupils.

Level	3	4	5	6
Number of pupils	7	8	10	5

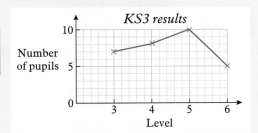

Plot the points like co-ordinates.
Join them up with straight lines.

- **When data is put into groups you can still draw bar-charts and frequency polygons.**
  The table shows the percentage test results for 30 pupils.

Score	Number of pupils
50–59	3
60–69	8
70–79	10
80–89	7
90–99	2

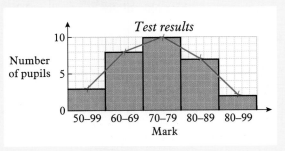

The bars in the bar-chart now touch.
The red graph is the frequency polygon.
Each point is plotted in the middle of the group.

- **A conversion graph is a graph that you can use to change from one unit to another.**

  Conversion graphs are always straight lines.
  This graph lets you convert between miles and kilometres.
  To change miles into kilometres you go up to the line and then across.
  To convert 15 miles into km follow the red lines.
  15 miles is 24 km.

  To convert 32 km into miles follow the blue lines.
  Go across and then down.
  32 km is 20 miles.

  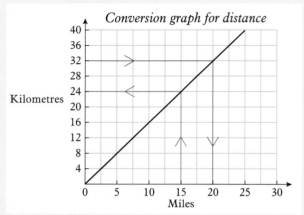
  Conversion graph for distance

- **Another type of diagram is a pie-chart.**
  The angle of the slice represents the frequency.

  The pie-chart shows that:
  $\frac{1}{2}$ of the chocolates are milk
  This is the same as 50%
  $\frac{1}{4}$ of the chocolates are plain
  This is the same as 25%

  If the total number of chocolates is **40**

  Number of milk chocolates $= \frac{1}{2} \times 40 = 20$
  Number of white chocolates $= \frac{1}{4} \times 40 = 10$

  Contents of box of chocolates

- **You can only estimate the sizes of the slices for some pie-charts.**

  The slice for Fat is a bit more than 25%.
  An estimate is 30%.
  The slice for Carbohydrate is a bit more than 50%.
  An estimate is 60%.

  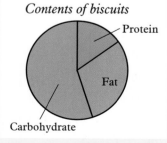
  Contents of biscuits

- **All diagrams must be properly labelled and given a title.**

- **Drawing pie-charts**

120 students were asked what they want to do when they leave school.
Here are the results:

Go to university	Go to college	Get a job	Don't know
50	35	25	10

Draw a pie-chart to show this data.

First you need to work out the angles for the pie-chart.
There are 360° to share between the 120 students.
Each student gets 360° ÷ 120 = 3°
Now work out the angle for each slice.

	Number of students	Angle
University	50	50 × 3° = 150°
College	35	35 × 3° = 105°
Job	25	25 × 3° = 75°
Don't know	10	10 × 3° = 30°

Check the angles add up to 360°.
  150° + 105° + 75° + 30° = 360° ✔

You can now draw the pie-chart.

(1) Draw a circle. Mark the centre.
Draw a line to the top of the circle.
Draw the first angle (150°).

(2) Measure the next angle
from the line that you
have just drawn (105°).

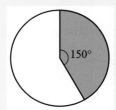

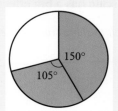

(3) Carry on until you have drawn all
the angles.
Label the pie-chart.
You need to label each slice like this.
You also need a title.

*What students
hope to do when
they leave school*

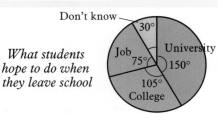

- **There are two types of data.**
  When data can only take certain individual values it is called discrete data.
  Number of people is discrete data. You can't have 2.8 people.
  When data can have any value it is called continuous data.
  Length, area, mass, time and temperature are all examples of continuous data.

- **To draw diagrams for continuous data you must label the horizontal axis as a scale.**

Journey times	Number of pupils
5 mins but < 10 mins	5
10 mins but < 15 mins	8
15 mins but < 20 mins	10
20 mins but < 25 mins	7

Time	10:00	12:00	14:00	16:00	18:00	20:00
Temp. (°C)	12	19	20	18	15	10

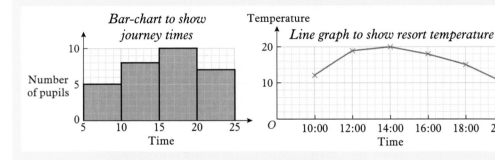

- **Sometimes graphs are used to mislead people.**
  Changing the scale has a big effect.

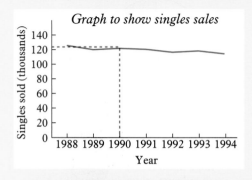

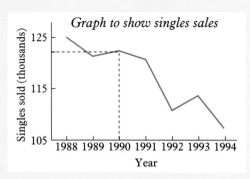

The two graphs show exactly the same information.
They look very different because of the scales.

Levels 3–5

1 This data gives you the number of TVs in 30 families.

   2 2 3 1 2 3 1 3 2 1 4 2 1 2 2
   1 2 2 1 3 2 3 1 3 2 2 4 2 3 1

a Tally these results.

Number of TVs	Tally	Frequency
1		
2		

b Draw a pictogram.
Use 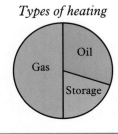 to represent two TVs.

Number of TVs

1	
2	
3	
4	

c Draw a bar-chart of the data.

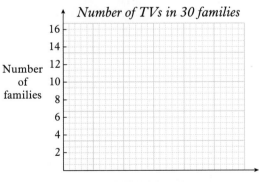

Number of TVs in 30 families

Number of families

16
14
12
10
8
6
4
2

Number of TVs

2 **a** The fraction for gas is ………

b ……% use gas.

c About ……% use storage.

50 households are represented.

d …… households use gas.

Types of heating

Oil

Gas

Storage

3 Complete this pie-chart for these sales of hot drinks

Coffee   40
Tea   80
Chocolate   60

Total number of drinks = ...

Each drink gets 360° ÷ ...... = ...°

Angle for coffee = ...

Angle for tea = ...

Angle for chocolate = ...

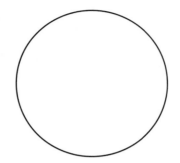

4 Draw a bar-chart for this data.

Masses of tomatoes (g)	Frequency
0 to less than 10	6
10 to less than 20	12
20 to less than 30	13
30 to less than 40	4

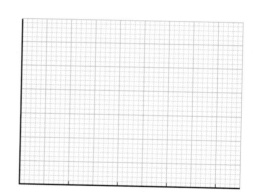

5 This bar-chart shows a company's profits in 1995 and 1996. Why is the chart misleading?

....

....

....

....

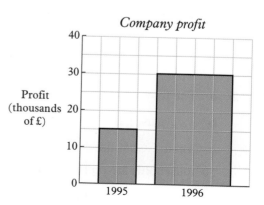

Company profit

1 The **pictogram** shows the number of CDs sold on a market stall.
Each symbol represents **4 CDs**.

Number of CDs sold

Monday	⊙ ⊙ ⊙ ⊙ ⊙ ⊙ ⊙
Tuesday	⊙ ⊙ ⊙ ⊙ ⊙ ◖
Wednesday	⊙ ⊙ ⊙ ◖
Thursday	
Friday	

a How many CDs were sold on

   Monday .... Tuesday .... Wednesday ....   3 marks

b CDs were also sold on **Thursday** and **Friday**.
   Show these sales figures on the pictogram as symbols.
      9 CDs were sold on Thursday
      24 CDs were sold on Friday.   2 marks

c The market was closed for half a day during the week.
   On which day was the market closed for half a day?   ....   1 mark

The **following** week a **tally-chart** was used to record the sales.

Monday	ЖЖЖ II	Tuesday	ЖЖ II	Wednesday	Ж III
Thursday	ЖЖ IIII	Friday	ЖЖЖ III		

d Give one reason why the **pictogram** is a good way of recording the sales figures.

   ....

   ....   1 mark

e Give one reason why the **tally-chart** is a good way of recording the sales figures.

   ....

   ....   1 mark

2 Kim did a survey of **two** types of television programme, on **two** different channels, during a week.

	Channel 1	Channel 3
Films	16	12
Quiz shows	11	13

a How many programmes did Kim record in the week?

.... 1 mark

b What was the **total** number of films shown on **both** channels?

.... 1 mark

c Kim also recorded details of two other types of programme in her survey.

	Mon	Tues	Wed	Thur	Fri
Channel 1	soap, comedy	soap, soap	soap, comedy	soap, comedy	soap, soap, comedy
Channel 3	soap, soap, comedy	soap, soap soap	soap, soap comedy	soap, comedy soap, comedy	soap, comedy comedy

Record this data in the table below.

	Channel 1	Channel 3
Soap		
Comedy		

2 marks

3 Malika did a survey of pets in her class. She drew a pie-chart to show her results.

a Which pet was the most popular?

....

b Which two pets were equally popular?

.... and ....

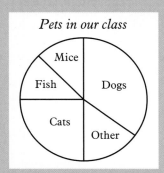

Pets in our class

Malika recorded **40** pets in her survey.

c How many of the pets were cats? ....

d Estimate how many of the pets were dogs? .... 4 marks

Level 6

4 A surveyor in a street asked people to say which one of five different types of holiday they liked best.
The results are shown below.

Ski	𝍸 𝍸 |||
Winter abroad	𝍸 𝍸 𝍸 𝍸 𝍸 𝍸 𝍸
Summer sun	𝍸 𝍸 𝍸 𝍸 𝍸 𝍸 𝍸 𝍸 𝍸 𝍸 𝍸 𝍸 𝍸 𝍸 𝍸 𝍸 𝍸 ||
Touring	𝍸 𝍸 𝍸 𝍸 ||
UK holiday	𝍸 𝍸 𝍸 𝍸 |||

a Give a reason why this display of the information is **not** clear.

.... 1 mark

b How many people were questioned? .... 1 mark

c Give a reason why a **pie-chart** rather than a **bar-chart** is a clearer way to show this information?

.... 1 mark

d Draw a pie-chart to show the holiday information.
Label each section of your pie-chart and give it a title.

3 marks

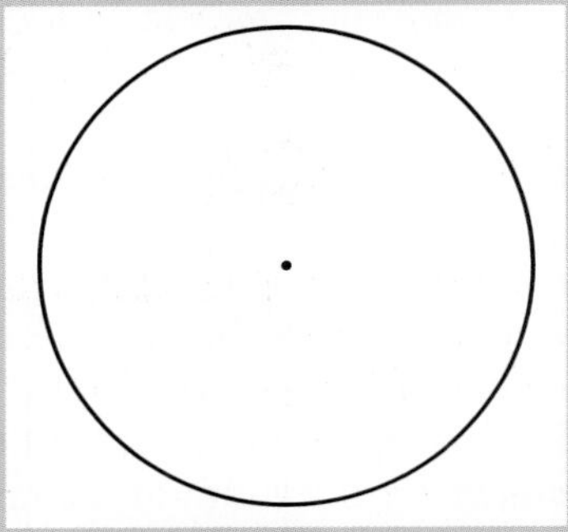

- **Questionnaire design.**

  (1) Questions should not be biased or upset people.

  (2) Questions should be clear and useful to your survey.

  (3) Don't ask questions that give a lot of answers. Structure them so that you can give a choice of possible answers such as

  (a) Yes ☐ No ☐ Don't know ☐

  (b) Agree ☐ Disagree ☐ Don't know ☐

  (c) 0–2 ☐ 3–5 ☐ More than 5 ☐

  (d) Strongly agree 1 2 3 4 5 Strongly disagree

- **Frequency polygons can be used to compare two sets of data.**

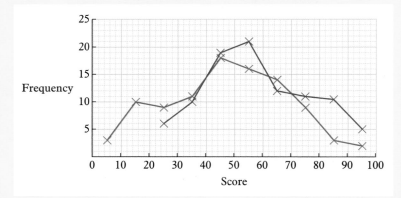

The red and blue frequency polygons show the exam results of 100 pupils at two schools.

The blue results are higher in general than the red results. This is shown by the blue frequency polygon being generally to the right of the red frequency polygon and being above the red polygon for higher marks.

The red results are more spread out than the blue.

This is shown by the width of each polygon.

1 Say what is wrong with each of these questions.

    a Intelligent people watch the TV news. Do you?

    ....

    b How much do you weigh?

    ....

    c What do you think about smoking in restaurants?

    ....

2 50 words are sampled from each of two books and the number of letters in each word counted.

Number of letters	1	2	3	4	5	6	7	8
Number of words, Book A	3	9	14	17	6	1	0	0
Number of words, Book B	4	5	6	10	8	9	5	3

    a Draw a frequency polygon for each book on these axes.

Frequency

Number of letters

    b Describe the differences between the two books.

    ....

    ....

    ....

    ....

1 Two snack bars keep a record of their sales for a day. The pie-charts show the sales of certain items.

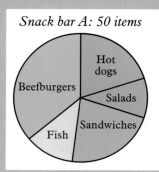
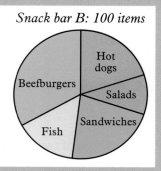

Snack bar A: 50 items *Snack bar B: 100 items*

a Estimate the **percentage** of people in **Snack bar A** who bought a beefburger.

...............% 1 mark

b **100** items were recorded for **Snack bar B**.
Estimate the number of hot dogs that were sold.

.... 1 mark

c Explain why the pie-charts do **not** show that more beefburgers were sold in Snack bar A than Snack bar B.

....

.... 1 mark

d This table shows the data collected from a third snack bar.

Snack bar C	
Beefburgers	70
Hot dogs	50
Salads	30
Sandwiches	30
Fish	20

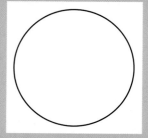

Draw a pie-chart to show the information in the table.
Label each section of your pie-chart and give it a title.

3 marks

2 Some pupils wanted to find out how much pupils at their school spend on crisps and chocolate. They wrote a questionnaire.

   a One of their questions is shown below.
'On average, how much do you spend on crisps and chocolate per day?'

☐   ☐   ☐   ☐   ☐   ☐

50p or less   5–10p   10–15p   15–20p   20–30p   30p or over

Write down **three** ways in which these boxes could be improved.

....

....

.... 3 marks

   b One pupil said, 'We can't give a questionnaire to everyone, so let's just give them to our class to complete.'
Explain what is wrong with this method of collecting the data.

....

....

.... 2 marks

3 The frequency polygon shows the number of TV sets sold by shop assistants Ali and Gary in a shop, over a 10 week period.

   a 'It is easy to predict Gary's sales in week 11.' Explain why this statement is true.

.... 1 mark

   b 'Ali has the greatest number of sales overall.' Explain why this statement is false.

.... 1 mark

12 Averages and spread

A famous politician once said, 'We want everyone to be better than average.'
You need to understand averages better than he did!

Levels 3–5

- **There are three types of average – the mode, the median and the mean.**

- **The mode is the most common or most popular data value.**
  It is sometimes called the modal value.
  The mode is the easiest average to find if there is one.
  The mode of   90 90 95 91 89 91 84 90   is 90

- **The median is the middle value when the data is given in order of size.**
  To find the median of   29 25 0 32 14 22 14

  (1) Put the numbers in order.   0 14 14 22 25 29 32

  (2) Write down the middle number.   Median = 22

  If the number of data values is even you will have two middle numbers. Add these two numbers together and divide by 2 to find the median.
  To find the median of   95 91 89 84 90 88

  (1) Put the numbers in order.   84 88 89 90 91 95

  (2) Add the 2 middle numbers and divide by 2.   Median = $\dfrac{89 + 90}{2} = 89.5$

134

- **To find the mean of a set of data**

  (1) Find the total of all the data values.

  (2) Divide the total by the number of data values.

  To find the mean of   88 90 79 94 86 91

  (1) Add them all up. $88 + 90 + 79 + 94 + 86 + 91 = 528$

  (2) Divide by 6 $528 \div 6 = 88$

  The mean is 88

- **The range of a set of data is the biggest value take away the smallest value.**

  The range of   72 **43** 62 57 **75** 63   is $75 - 43 = 32$

  The range is a single number not 43 to 75 or 43−75 which you might see in a newspaper.

  The range tells you how spread out the data is.

- **To compare two sets of data you need**

  (1) A measure of average. This will usually be the mean.

  (2) The range.

  Here are the runs scored by two cricketers in their last six innings.

Ian	44	73	39	60	68	40
Gavin	120	7	84	26	9	90

Ian's mean is 54 runs. His range is 34 runs.

Gavin's mean is 56 runs. His range is 113 runs.

The means are very similar but Gavin's range is much bigger. The bigger range shows that Gavin may score a lot of runs but he may score very few. Ian's smaller range means that he is more consistent.

Level 6

- **You can find averages from frequency tables.**

The frequency table shows the number of pit stops in a race.

Number of stops	Frequency	Stops × Frequency
1	2	1 × 2 = 2
2	11	2 × 11 = 22
3	10	3 × 10 = 30
4	1	4 × 1 = 4
	Total = 24	Total = 58

This row shows that 10 drivers stopped 3 times

To find the mean add the red column to the table.

$$\text{Mean} = \frac{58}{24} = 2.4\,(1\,\text{dp})$$

The mode is the number of stops with the highest frequency.

$$\text{Mode} = 2$$

The median is the middle value. The 24 values are

1 1 2 2 2 2 2 2 2 2 2 2 2 3 3 3 3 3 3 3 3 3 3 4 $\text{Median} = \dfrac{2+2}{2} = 2$

- **A scatter graph is a diagram that is used to see if there is a connection between two sets of data.**

Plot pairs of values like co-ordinates and look for a pattern.

Weight | Height

As the height increases so does the weight.
This is positive correlation.

Value | Age

As the age increases the value decreases.
This is negative correlation.

Height | Test score

There is no connection between height and test score.
This is zero correlation or no correlation.

- **Correlation can be strong or weak.**

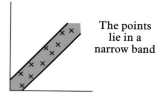

The points lie in a narrow band

Strong positive correlation

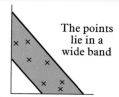

The points lie in a wide band

Weak negative correlation

1   24   18   15   21   19   18

    a   The mode is ....

    b   ....

    The median is $\dfrac{...... + ...}{2}$ = ...

    c   Total = ...

    Mean = ... ÷ ....

           = ... (1 dp)

    d   Range = ... – .... = ...

2   These are the means and ranges for the times that it takes two taxi companies to get a taxi to a customer.

You have to leave to catch a train in 16 mins. Which company would you call? Explain your answer.

	Mean (min)	Range (min)
Terry's Taxis	12.3	13
Chris' Cabs	12.4	4

....

....

....

3   This table shows the age and sale value of 10 cars.

Age (years)	3	6	5	4	2	6	5	3	6	5
Value (thousands of £)	6.0	2.5	2.9	3.5	6.5	2.3	3.1	5.8	2.1	3.3

    a   Draw a scatter graph.

    b   The scatter graph shows

    .... correlation

    As .... increases

    ....

    ....

Value (1000s)

Age (years)

1 Use the stem and leaf diagram to work out

   a the mode of the data

   .... 1 mark

   b the range of the data

   .... 1 mark

   c the median of the data

   .... 1 mark

   d the mean of the data

   .... 1 mark

Ages of members					
stem	leaf				
1	2	3	5		
2	0	4	4	7	8
3	0	2	6		
4	1	9			
Key 3│6 means 36 years					

2 Over three games Jerry needs to score an average of **12** points to win.
At his first two attempts he has scored **8** points and **15** points.
What is the **minimum** number of points he must score in his final game to win?

.... 2 marks

3 Helen conducts a survey to find the number of pets kept in the homes of pupils. She draws a graph of the results of her survey.

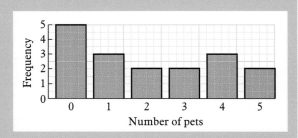

   a Use the graph to calculate the mean number of pets per pupil.

.... 1 mark

   b What is the modal number of pets?

.... 1 mark

   c Find the median number of pets.

.... 1 mark

4 A teacher records the number of errors on each test paper marked.
The results are recorded in the table.

Errors	1	2	3	4	5
Frequency	5	6	7	5	3

  a Calculate the **mean** number of errors per pupil.
    Show your working.

.... 2 marks

  b Find the **median** number of errors per pupil.

.... 2 marks

  c Explain why the **mean** and the **median** give different values.

....

.... 1 mark

5 The owner of a cafe keeps a record of the number of cups of hot soup, and the
number of cups of coffee that he sells per day, and the temperature on that day.

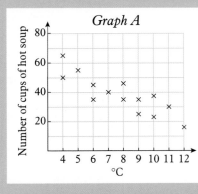
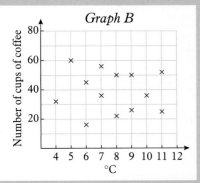

  a What does **graph A** show about the relationship between the number of cups
    of hot soup sold, and the temperature on each day.

.... 1 mark

  b What does **graph B** show about the relationship between the number of cups
    of coffee sold, and the temperature on each day.

.... 1 mark

- **When a scatter graph shows correlation the points will look as though they lie around a straight line. This line is called the line of best fit. You can use this line to estimate values.**

This scatter graph shows weights and heights of 6-month-old babies.

The red line is the line of best fit. You draw this with a ruler. Try to have about the same number of points on each side of the line.

To estimate the weight for a height of 65 cm draw the blue lines and read off the answer **6.8** kg.

To estimate the height for a weight of 6 kg draw the green lines and read off the answer **62** cm.

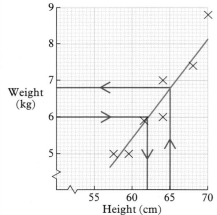

- **Finding mean, mode, median, and range for grouped data.**

Here are the results of a test.

Mark	31–40	41–50	51–60	61–70	71–80	81–90	91–100
Number of pupils	5	14	28	35	24	16	8

Look at the first column of data. You can see that 5 pupils scored between 31 and 40 but you do not know exactly what each of them scored.

To work out an **estimate** for the mean you have to assume that all 5 of them scored the middle mark of the group. This middle mark is $\dfrac{31 + 40}{2} = 35.5$

You can work out all the mid-points and show these in a new table.

Mark	35.5	45.5	55.5	65.5	75.5	85.5	95.5
Number of pupils	5	14	28	35	24	16	8

You can now **estimate** the mean as

$$\frac{35.5 \times 5 + 45.5 \times 14 + 55.5 \times 28 + 65.5 \times 35 + 75.5 \times 24 + 85.5 \times 16 + 95.5 \times 8}{5 + 14 + 28 + 35 + 24 + 16 + 8}$$

$$= \frac{8605}{130} = 66.2 \text{ marks (1 dp)}.$$

- **When data is grouped you cannot tell which data value is the most common. You can only say which group has the highest frequency. This group is called the modal group.**
  For the test results the modal group is 61–70 marks.

- **When data is grouped you can only say which group the median is in.**

  For the 130 test results the median would be the $\dfrac{65^{\text{th}} + 66^{\text{th}}}{2}$ data value.

  The 65th and 66th values lie in the group 61–70 because the first 3 groups contain 47 data values and the first 4 groups contain 82 data values.

  The median is in the 61–70 group.

- **An estimate for the range is the biggest possible value take away the smallest possible value.**
  For the test marks an **estimate** for the range is $100 - 31 = 69$ marks.

- **Equation of line of best fit.**

  y intercept $= 1$

  gradient $= \dfrac{10}{5} = 2$

  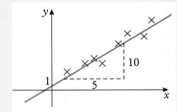

  The equation of the line of best fit is $y = 2x + 1$

- **Assumed mean**
  You can find a mean quickly by guessing the answer first. This guess is called the assumed mean.

Look at this data.	307, 325, 315, 309, 322, 318
You might guess the mean is 315.	
Now work out the differences between each value and this assumed mean.	$-8, \quad 10, \quad 0, -6, \quad 7, \quad 3$
Add these differences.	$-8 + 10 + 0 - 6 + 7 + 3 = 6$
Divide by the number of data values.	$6 \div 6 = 1$
Add this amount to the assumed mean to get the true mean.	mean $= 315 + 1$ $= 316$

- **Cumulative frequency is a running total.**
  This table shows the lifetimes, in hours, of 375 light bulbs.

The red part of the table is a cumulative frequency table. The red lifetime column shows the upper end of each class.

Lifetime	Frequency	Lifetime	Cumulative frequency
201–400	56	400 or less	56
401–600	124	600 or less	180
601–800	101	800 or less	281
801–1000	63	1000 or less	344
1001–1200	31	1200 or less	375

It is often useful to draw a curve from a cumulative frequency table.

The graph is called a **cumulative frequency curve**.
It allows you to estimate cumulative frequencies for points that are not at the ends of the groups.

A cumulative frequency curve is drawn with the values on the horizontal axis and the cumulative frequency on the vertical axis.
The points are always plotted at the **end** of each range.
The points are joined with a smooth curve.

If you are asked to draw a cumulative frequency diagram you can join the points with straight lines instead of a curve.

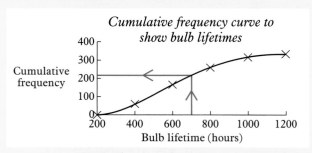

Cumulative frequency curve to show bulb lifetimes

Notice how the curve is joined back to the beginning of the first range in the original table. This is the point (200, 0).

To estimate the number of bulbs that lasted less than 700 hours:
(1) Draw the red line up from 700 on the horizontal axis to the curve and then across to the vertical axis.
(2) Read the value from this axis.
In this example this is approximately 220 bulbs.

- **The median is the middle data value.**

  To get an estimate of the median:
  (1) Find half the total frequency on the cumulative frequency axis.
  (2) Draw a line across to the curve.
  (3) Draw down to the horizontal axis.
  (4) Read off the estimate of the median.

- **The lower quartile is the value one quarter of the way through the data values.**

  To find the lower quartile:
  (1) Find one quarter of the total frequency on the cumulative frequency axis.
  (2) Draw lines as you did for the median.

- **The upper quartile is the value three quarters of the way through the data.**

- **The interquartile range is the difference between the upper quartile and the lower quartile. This tells you how spread out the central half of the data is.**

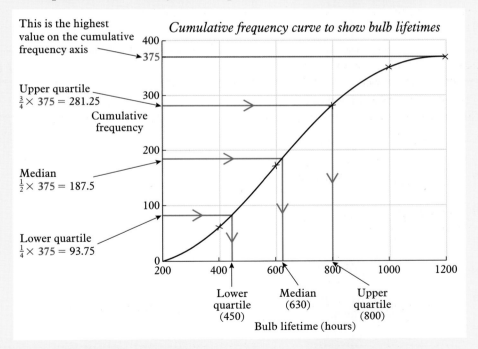

Cumulative frequency curve to show bulb lifetimes

Median = 630   Lower quartile = 450   Upper quartile = 800
Interquartile range = 800 − 450 = 350

- **You can use the median and the interquartile range to compare two sets of data.**

TEST YOURSELF

1 The table shows the wages of people who work in a car factory.

Wages, £000s	1–10	11–20	21–30	31–100
Wages, mid-points	......	......	......	......
Number of people	25	39	10	6

a Fill in the mid-points in the table.

b Estimate of mean wage $= \dfrac{...... \times ...... + ... \times ...... + ... \times ...... + ... \times ......}{...... + ... + ... + ...}$

$= \dfrac{......}{......} = ...$ to nearest £1000

c The modal group is ....

2 The cumulative frequency diagrams show the waiting times at a clinic and a surgery.

	Surgery	Clinic
a Median	......	......
b Lower quartile	......	......
c Upper quartile	......	......
d Interquartile range	......	......

e Compare the waiting times for the clinic and surgery.

....

....

....

1 Barry is doing a geography project.
He records on a graph the number of hours of clear sky on certain days, and the
temperature at a certain time on these days.

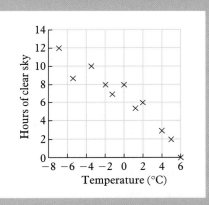

a What does the graph show about the relationship between the hours of clear
sky and the temperature in °C?

....

....

....

.... 1 mark

b Draw a **line of best fit** on the scatter diagram.   2 marks

Use your line to find an estimate of the hours
of clear sky when the temperature is **2°C**.

.... hours   1 mark

Use your line to find an estimate of the
temperature on a day when there are
4 hours of clear sky.

...........°C   1 mark

2 Kim counts the number of paces between each of the houses on her paper round. She groups and records the information in a table.

Number of paces	Midpoint (x)	Frequency (f)	fx
30–39	34.5	3	103.5
40–49	44.5	8	
50–59	54.5	11	
60–69	64.5	9	
70–79	74.5	13	
80–89	84.5	6	
Totals		50	

a Calculate an estimate of the **mean** number of paces per house.

.... 2 marks

b Write down the group within which the **median** will lie.

.... 1 mark

3 The cumulative frequency graph shows the distribution of ages for 200 people in a village.

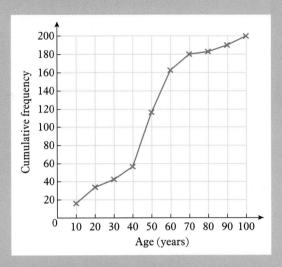

a Use the graph to estimate the **median** age of the people in the village.

.... years   1 mark

b Use the graph to estimate the **interquartile range** of the ages.

.... years   2 marks

c Estimate the **percentage** of the village population who are under 50 years of age.

.... %   1 mark

13 Probability

People would like to be certain about whether a hurricane is coming their way. Forecasts can only tell them how likely it is. They use probabilities.

Levels 3–5

- **Probability tells you how likely something is to happen.**
- **You can show probabilities on a scale.**

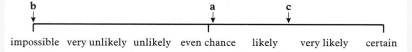

The scale shows the probabilities that
(a) a newly born baby will be a girl
(b) you will live to be 300
(c) the next person to come into the room will be right handed.

- **You can use probability to decide whether something is fair or not.**
  This spinner is being used by two friends to see who eats the last Rolo.
  One person eats it if the spinner lands on blue, the other person eats it if the spinner lands on yellow.

  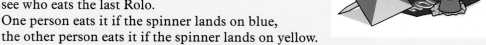

  This is not fair. There is a greater chance that the spinner will land on blue. If you spin it four times you would expect to get three blues and one yellow.

- **Probability is written as a number between 0 and 1.**
  You can only use fractions, decimals, or percentages to show probabilities.

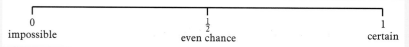

- **Events are equally likely if they have the same chance of happening.**

  You can use equally likely events to work out probabilities.

  100 tickets are sold for a raffle.
  The probability that you will win if you have **1** ticket is $\frac{1}{100}$.

  The probability that you will win if you have **5** tickets is $\frac{5}{100}$ because each of the tickets is equally likely to win.

- **There are three methods for working out probabilities.**

  (1) Use equally likely outcomes.
      The probability of getting a 4 with a fair dice is $\frac{1}{6}$

  (2) Use a survey or do an experiment.
      If the events are not equally likely you need to do a survey or experiment to see which is more likely.

  (3) Look back at data.
      If the events are not equally likely and you can't do an experiment, then you look back at data. To find the probability that it will snow in London on Christmas Day look back at the records to see how likely it is.

Level 6

- **Probabilities must add up to 1.**
  If the probability of rain is 0.4 then the probability of no rain is $1 - 0.4 = 0.6$

- **A sample space is a list of all the possible outcomes.**
  A table showing these is called a **sample space diagram**.

  The sample space diagram for the possible
  outcomes of using this spinner and coin is

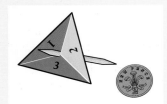

		Spinner		
		1	2	3
Coin	H	H, 1	H, 2	H, 3
	T	T, 1	T, 2	T, 3

The probability of getting a tail and an odd number $= \frac{2}{6} = \frac{1}{3}$

149

Levels 3–5

1 Mark these probabilities.
   a The sun will rise tomorrow.
   b Ice will be found on the sun.
   c The sun will shine on the first day of spring.

```
├────────────────┼────────────────┤
0               0.5               1
```

2 Sue puts these counters into a bag.
   She picks a counter at random.

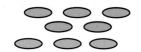

   a What colour is she more likely to get? ....

   b What is the probability that she will get a blue counter? ....

   c Sue picks out a counter and replaces it. She does this 16 times.

   How many red counters does she expect to get? ....

   d She wants to make it equally likely that she will get a red or a blue counter.

   What extra counters does she need to put in the bag? ....

3 Choose the method to find each probability.
   Method 1   Use equally likely outcomes.
   Method 2   Use a survey or do an experiment.
   Method 3   Look back at data.

   a The next car passing will be red.   Method ......

   b You will get an even number when you roll a fair dice.   Method ......

   c There will be an earthquake somewhere in the world today.   Method ......

Level 6

4 a Fill in the sample space diagram.

					Dice			
		1	2	3	4	5	6	
Coin	H				H, 4			
	T							

   b Find the probability of getting a head and an even number. ....

   c Write down the probability of not getting a head and an even number. ....

Levels 3–5

1 A box contains cubes which are **five** different colours –
red, green, blue, orange and brown.

There are the same number of cubes of each colour in the box.
Bill takes a cube out of the box without looking.

a What is the **probability** that Bill will get a **red** or a **blue** cube?

.... 1 mark

b What is the **probability** that Bill will get a **yellow** cube?

.... 1 mark

c Draw a cross on the probability scale to show the probability that Bill will get
a **blue** or a **brown** cube.

0 ├──┼──┼──┼──┼──┼──┼──┼──┼──┤ 1

.... 1 mark

d Draw a cross on the probability scale to show the probability that Bill will **not**
get a **green** cube.

0 ├──┼──┼──┼──┼──┼──┼──┼──┼──┤ 1

.... 1 mark

2 This wheel is spun around.
It will stop with the arrow
pointing at a colour.

a Liam says that **red** is more likely than any other colour.
Explain why Liam is **wrong**.

....

.... 1 mark

b The wheel is spun, and stops with the arrow pointing at **yellow**.
What is the **probability** that the wheel will stop on the **yellow** when it is
spun again?

.... 1 mark

151

c Colour or shade this spinner so that it will be **certain** that the arrow will land on the **same colour** each time.

1 mark

d Colour or shade this spinner so that there is a **0.5 chance** the spinner will land on **one colour**.

1 mark

3 A coin is thrown and lands on heads **four** times in a row.

a Draw a cross on the probability scale to show the probability of it landing on heads on the **fifth** throw.

0 ————————————————— 1

1 mark

b **Two** coins are thrown together.
What is the probability that you will throw two heads together?

.... 1 mark

c What is the probability that you will **not** throw two tails with two coins?

.... 1 mark

Level 6

4 Julie has a bag containing 20 coloured counters.
She takes four red counters out of the bag without looking.

a Julie says, 'The bag must only contain red counters.'
Explain why Julie may be **wrong**.

....
.... 1 mark

b Julie then takes out two blue and one green counter.
She says, 'As I have four red, two blue and one green counter then the probability in the future of me picking a red is $\frac{4}{7}$, picking a blue is $\frac{2}{7}$, and a green $\frac{1}{7}$.'
Explain why Julie is **wrong**.

....
....
.... 1 mark

Level 7

- **The frequency of an event is the number of times that it happens.**

- **The relative frequency of an event** $= \dfrac{\text{frequency of the event}}{\text{total frequency}}$

The relative frequency gives an estimate of the probability.
This estimate can be improved by increasing the number of times the experiment is repeated.

A drawing pin is dropped 100 times.
It lands point up or point down.
The table shows the results.

The relative frequency of up $= \frac{67}{100}$

$= 0.67$

Position	Frequency
up	67
down	33

An estimate of the probability that the drawing pin will land point up is 0.67
This estimate will get closer to the true probability as the pin is dropped more times.

Level 8

- **Events are mutually exclusive if they cannot happen at the same time.**

When a coin is thrown it can land showing either a head or a tail. It cannot show a head and a tail at the same time. They are mutually exclusive events.
When a playing card is chosen from a pack getting an ace and getting a heart are not mutually exclusive. The ace of hearts satisfies both events.

- When combining mutually exclusive events you add the probabilities

  $P \, (\text{diamond}) = \frac{1}{4} \qquad P \, (\text{club}) = \frac{1}{4}$
  $P \, (\text{diamond or club}) = \frac{1}{4} + \frac{1}{4} = \frac{1}{2}$

- The word 'or' means **add** the probabilities.

- **Two events are independent if the outcome of one has no effect on the outcome of the other.**

  When you roll a dice and throw a coin the outcome from the dice has no effect on the outcome of the coin. These are independent events.

- **When combining independent events you multiply the probabilities.**

  P (getting a 4 on a dice) $= \frac{1}{6}$ P (getting head on a coin) $= \frac{1}{2}$
  P (getting a 4 **and** a head) $= \frac{1}{6} \times \frac{1}{2} = \frac{1}{12}$

- The word '**and**' means **multiply** the probabilities.
  Watch for other words like 'both' being used instead of 'and'.

- **You can use tree diagrams to show the outcomes of more than one event.**

  This is a tree diagram for throwing two dice when you want to know how many 6s you get.

  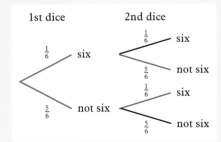

  P (getting two 6s) $= \frac{1}{6} \times \frac{1}{6} = \frac{1}{36}$

'Getting two 6s' is the same as 'getting a 6 **and** getting a 6'.
This is also the same as 'getting a 6 on **both** dice'
The probability of only getting one 6 is shown by the green routes through the tree.

P (getting one 6) $=$ P(6 **and** not 6) **or** P (not 6 **and** 6)
$$= \frac{1}{6} \times \frac{5}{6} \quad + \quad \frac{5}{6} \times \frac{1}{6}$$
$$= \frac{10}{36}$$
$$= \frac{5}{18}$$

- **You multiply the probabilities along the branches. You add the probabilities if you use more than one route.**

1 The table shows the colours of cars passing a school.

Colour	Frequency
black	8
red	35
white	28
other	29

a The total number of cars = ………

b Relative frequency of black = ………

c An estimate of the probability that the next car to pass the school will be red = ………

d How can the estimate in **c** be made more accurate?

....

2 These two dice are thrown.
Find the probability that

a the red dice will show a 3 or a 5 ………

b the red dice will show a 3 and the green dice will show an even number ………

c both dice will show a 6 ………

3 The probability that a pupil has chips for lunch is 0.6

    a Fill in the tree diagram to show the choices of the next two pupils.

Use the tree diagram to find the probability that

b the next two pupils both have chips

....

c only one of the next two pupils has chips

....

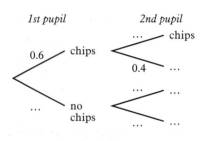

1st pupil   2nd pupil

… chips

0.6 chips

0.4 …

… no chips

… …

… …

155

1 Amanda and Gurjeet each have a spinner.
They **add** the scores on their spinners.

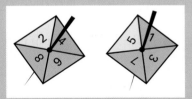

a Complete the table below to show all their possible answers.

+	2	4	6	8
1				
3				
5				
7				

1 mark

b What is the **probability** that their answer is a number **greater than 9**?

.... 1 mark

c What is the **probability** that their answer is a number which is a **square number**?

.... 1 mark

d What is the **probability** that their answer is an **even** number?

.... 1 mark

2 This **biased** cube has coloured faces.
Tony throws the cube **60** times, and
records the following results.

Red	Blue	Green	Yellow	Orange	Purple
30	5	6	8	7	4

a Write down an estimate of the probability of throwing a **red** with this cube.

.... 1 mark

b How many times would you expect to get a red if you threw the cube **20 times**?

.... 1 mark

c Tony threw the cube **20 times**, but only got a red on **4** occasions.
Can you explain this?

....

.... 1 mark

d How could Tony improve the accuracy of his results?

....

.... 1 mark

Level 8

3 A road traffic survey showed that the probability of a car having to stop at a traffic light is **0.7**
On a particular road there are two sets of traffic lights.

a Calculate the probability that a car will pass through **both** sets of traffic lights without having to stop.

.... 1 mark

b Calculate the probability that a car will be stopped at **only one** of the sets of traffic lights as it passes along the road.

.... 2 marks

c Karen passes through the traffic lights **80 times** in a month.
How many times during the month should she expect to be stopped at the **first set** of traffic lights?

.... 1 mark

1 Whole numbers

Levels 3–5 (p. 8)

1 a 30   **b** 100

2 a 28   **b** 54   **c** 3

3 a 260   **b** 4100   **c** 10

4 a 36   **b** 80   **c** 10

5 a
```
   2 6 0
 + 1 2 3
 -------
   3 8 3
```
c
```
   1 7 4
 -   5 1
 -------
   1 2 3
```

b
```
   1 8 7
 +   3 5
 -------
   2 2 2
    1 1
```
d
```
   4 5¹⁰0̸ 9
 -     4 6
 ---------
     4 6 3
```

6 a
```
     2 3 7
 ×     2 5
 ---------
   1 1 8 5
   4 7 4 0
 ---------
   5 9 2 5
        1
```
b
```
      2 3
 14)32⁴2
```
$1 \times 14 = 14$
$2 \times 14 = 28$
$3 \times 14 = 42$

7 $-6, -4, 0, 5, 12$

8 $3\,°C$

Level 6 (p. 8)

9 a 10   **d** -5 **g** -3
b -11 **e** 20   **h** 6
c 28   **f** -18 **i** 50

Level 7 (p. 13)

1 a $\div$ **b** $\times$ **c** $\times$ **d** $\div$

2 a

`( 4 . 8 6 × 1 . 6 3 ) ÷`
`( 4 . 3 7 + 1 . 9 4 ) =`

b

`( 4 . 2 + 3 . 6 x² ) ÷`
`( 4 . 9 1 − 2 . 8 7 ) =`

3 a 625   **b** 9   **c** 3   **d** 64

Level 8 (p. 13)

4 a p^9 **b** m^5 **c** r^{21} **d** $\dfrac{1}{4^3} = \dfrac{1}{64}$

5 a 5×10^{-3} **b** 1.2×10^7

6 a 281 000   **b** 0.000 000 83

7

`4 . 2 EXP 6 ÷ 2 . 1 EXP`
`+/− 4 =`

2 Fractions, decimals and percentages

Levels 3–5 (p. 22)

1 a
```
   2 . 1 4
 + 1 . 7 9
 ---------
   3 . 9 3
        1
```
c
```
     2 . 5 3
 ×       2 4
 -----------
   1 0 . 1 2
   5 0 . 6 0
 -----------
   6 0 . 7 2
```

b
```
   ¹1̸2 .⁶7̸¹6
 -    8 . 5 8
 -----------
      4 . 1 8
```
d
```
      1 . 7 9
  5)8 .³9⁴5
```

2 a $224 \div 8 = 28$
$28 \times 5 = £140$
b $900 \div 100 = 9$ or $72 \div 100 = 0.72$
$9 \times 72 = 648\,g$ $0.72 \times 900 = 648$

3 a   **b** or any 6 sectors

Level 6 (p. 22)

4

Fraction	$\frac{1}{2}$	$\frac{1}{4}$	$\frac{1}{5}$	$\frac{3}{4}$	$\frac{3}{5}$	$\frac{81}{100}$
Decimal	0.5	0.25	0.2	0.75	0.6	0.81
Percentage	50%	25%	20%	75%	60%	81%

5 a $\dfrac{16}{40} = \dfrac{2}{5}$

b 35 p as a percentage of 250 p

$= \dfrac{35}{250} \times 100\% = 14\%$

6 Total number of parts = 9
Value of 1 part = 180 ÷ 9 = £20
Value of each share
2 × £20 = £40   3 × £20 = £60
4 × £20 = £80

7 a $\frac{3}{5}$ **c** $\frac{3}{7}$

b $\frac{8}{12} + \frac{9}{12} = \frac{17}{12} = 1\frac{5}{12}$ **d** $\frac{8}{9} - \frac{6}{9} = \frac{2}{9}$

8 a $\frac{6}{35}$ **b** $\frac{24}{36} = \frac{2}{3}$

c $\frac{7}{3} \times \frac{3}{2} = \frac{21}{6} = 3\frac{1}{2}$

d $\frac{3}{4} \times \frac{8}{1} = \frac{24}{4} = 6$

e $\frac{5}{2} \div \frac{4}{3} = \frac{5}{2} \times \frac{3}{4} = \frac{15}{8} = 1\frac{7}{8}$

9 $\frac{1}{2} = \frac{15}{30}$ $\frac{7}{15} = \frac{14}{30}$ $\frac{3}{5} = \frac{18}{30}$

$\frac{7}{15}, \frac{1}{2}, \frac{3}{5}$

Level 7 (p. 27)

1 a 20% of 650 g = 130 g
New amount = 780 g
b $\frac{2}{5}$ of £460 = £184
New amount = £644

2 a 15% of 370 cm = 55.5 cm
New amount = 314.5 cm

b $\frac{3}{8}$ of 2400 kg = 900 kg
New amount = 1500 kg

3 17.5% of 60 = £10.50
Total bill = £70.50

Level 8 (p. 27)

4 Year 1
15% of £8600 = £1290
New value = 8600 − 1290 = £7310
Year 2
15% of £7310 = £1096.50
New value = 7310 − 1096.50 = £6213.50
Year 3
15% of £6213.50 = £932.03
New value = 6213.50 − 932.03
= £5281.47

5 100% + 7% = 107%
1% = 2568 ÷ 107 = 24
100% = 24 × 100 = 2400

6 $\frac{3}{17}$ is 420 so $\frac{1}{17}$ is 140
Number of people now is
140 × 17 = 2380

3 Estimating

Levels 3–5 (p. 32)

1 a 15 + 3
= 18   **d** 7 × 4
= 28

b 26 − 15
= 11   **e** 14 ÷ 2 + 7
= 7 + 7 = 14

c 24 − 4
= 20   **f** 9 + 24
= 33

2 a 2   **c** 140   **e** 100
b 50   **d** 400

3 a $34 \times 176 = 5984$
$34 = 30$ to the nearest 10
$176 = 200$ to the nearest 100
$30 \times 200 = 6000$

b $858 \div 33 = 26$
$858 = 900$ to the nearest 100
$33 = 30$ to the nearest 10
$900 \div 30 = 30$

4 a 7.9   **c** 13.4   **e** 4.857
b 6.32   **d** 29.09   **f** 4.70

5 1 tape costs £11.50 ÷ 8 = £1.44

Level 7 (p. 37)

1 a 4   **c** 30   **e** 7000
b 0.07   **d** 0.007   **f** 10 000

2 a 500 000   **f** 150
b 24 000   **g** 300
c 0.0003   **h** 20
d 0.000 42   **i** 7000
e 80   **j** 30 000

3 a $\dfrac{48 \times 35}{6 \times 7}$ **b** $\dfrac{30 \times 42}{5 \times 7}$

$\quad = \dfrac{48}{6} \times \dfrac{35}{7} \qquad\qquad = \dfrac{30}{5} \times \dfrac{42}{7}$

$\quad = 8 \times 5 \qquad\qquad\quad = 6 \times 6$

$\quad = 40 \qquad\qquad\qquad = 36$

Level 8 (p. 37)

4 a $\sqrt{17} \simeq \sqrt{16} = 4$ **b** $\sqrt{87} \simeq \sqrt{81} = 9$

5 $\sqrt{\dfrac{5^2 \times 62}{2^4}} = \sqrt{\dfrac{25 \times 62}{16}} \simeq \sqrt{\dfrac{25 \times 64}{16}}$

$\quad = \sqrt{25 \times 4} = \sqrt{100} = 10$

---

4   Patterns and sequences

Levels 3–5 (p. 42)

1 a 7, 21, 42   **c** 1, 3, 10, 21
b 2, 3, 7, 13, 23   **d** 1, 8, 64

2 a 4, 8, 12, 16, 20, 24, 28, 32, 36, 40
b 9, 18, 27, 36, 45, 54, 63, 72, 81, 90
c 36

3 a 49   **b** 216   **c** 10   **d** 14

Level 6 (p. 42)

4 a add 5   **c** $3 + 49 \times 5 = 248$
b 5   **d** $5n - 2$

Level 7 (p. 46)

1
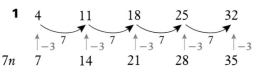

The formula is $7n - 3$

2 a $4 \times 1 - 3 = 1$
b $4 \times 6 - 3 = 21$
c $4 \times 20 - 3 = 77$

3

$$
\begin{array}{ccccc}
2 & 8 & 16 & 26 & 38 \\
\end{array}
$$

n^2 1   4   9   16   25

     1   4   7   10   13

The formula is $n^2 + 3n - 2$

4 a $3 - 1 - 2 = 0$
b $3 \times 25 - 5 - 2 = 68$

5 Formulas, expressions and equations

Levels 3–5 (p. 51)

1 a $c = 25 + 15h$
b $25 + 15 \times 4 = £85$

2 $P = 2l + 2w$

Level 6 (p. 51)

3 a $5c + 6d$
b $10q + 35$
c $3(3p - 4)$
d $z(z^2 + 4z - 8)$

4 a $x + 7 - 7 = 13 - 7$
$x = 6$

b $\dfrac{x}{6} - 3 + 3 = 4 + 3$
$\dfrac{x}{6} = 7$
$\dfrac{x}{6} \times 6 = 7 \times 6$
$x = 42$

c $5x - x - 28 = x - x - 6$
$4x - 28 = -6$
$4x = 22$
$x = 5.5$

d $4x - 12 = 28$
$4x = 40$
$x = 10$

Level 7 (p. 57)

1 a $2x \leqslant 8$
$x \leqslant 4$

[number line: 1 2 3 4 5, filled point at 4, line going left]

b $\dfrac{x}{5} > 3$
$x > 15$

[number line: 5 10 15 20 25, open point at 15, line going right]

2 $0, 1, 2, 3, 4$

3 a $x + c^2 = 2r$
$r = \dfrac{x + c^2}{2}$

b $\sqrt{p} \leqslant r - s$
$r = \sqrt{p} + s$

4 a $2(7q - 4)$
b $8a(2a^2 - 1)$

Level 8 (p. 57)

5 a $x \geqslant 0$
b $y \leqslant x + 3$
c $-4 < y \leqslant 4$

6 a $x^2 - 3x + 4x - 12 = x^2 + x - 12$
b $2x^2 - 12x - 3x + 18 = 2x^2 - 15x + 18$

6 Functions and graphs

Levels 3–5 (p. 62)

1 A $(4, 2)$ B $(1, 4)$ C $(0, 2)$

2

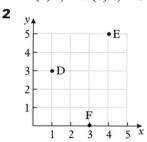

Level 6 (p. 62)

3 $y = x + 2$

4 A $x = 2$ C $y = -x$
B $y = 2x + 2$ D $y = -x - 3$

5 When $x = 0$ When $y = 0$
    $-2y = 6$ $3x = 6$
     $y = -3$ $x = 2$
This gives $(0, -3)$ This gives $(2, 0)$

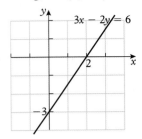

Level 7 (p. 69)

1 **a** Adding gives $5x = 20$
                 $x = 4$
Put $x = 4$ into (1)
      $2 \times 4 + y = 14$
            $y = 6$
Solution is $x = 4, y = 6$
Check in (2)
    $3 \times 4 - 6 = 12 - 6 = 6$ ✓

   b Multiply (1) by 3 and (2) by 2
        $12x + 6y = 30$
        $10x + 6y = 24$
Subtracting $2x = 6$
             $x = 3$
Put $x = 3$ into (1)
    $4 \times 3 + 2y = 10$
           $y = -1$
The solution is $x = 3, y = -1$
Check in (2) $5 \times 3 + 3 \times -1 = 12$ ✓

Level 8 (p. 69)

2 A $y = x^2 - 4x + 7$

   B $y = \dfrac{1}{x - 3}$

   C $y = x^3 - 6x^2 + 11x - 6$
   D $y = 4 - x^2$

3

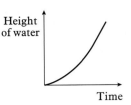

Height increases slowly at first but then rate of increase gets bigger. Then constant rate of increase for the last part.

---

7 2D and 3D shapes

. . . .

Levels 3–5 (p. 77)

1 **a** obtuse   **b** acute   **c** reflex

2 **a** W   **c** E
   b SE   **d** NE

3 **a** $70 + 110 = 180$ $110°$
   b $35 + 55 + 90 = 180$ $55°$
   c $80 + 20 + 80 = 180$ $80°$

Level 6 (p. 77)

4 **a**   **b**   **c**

5 **a** $90 + 90 + 40 + 80 = 300$
      $360 - 300 = 60°$
   b $40 + 140 = 180$ $140°$

6 **a** Angles on straight line
      $130 + 50 = 180$ $50°$
   b Opposite angles $80°$
   c Angles in triangle
      $50 + 80 + 50 = 180$ $50°$

Level 7 (p. 83)

1 a $x^2 = 8^2 + 13^2$
$= 233$
$x = \sqrt{233}$
$x = 15.3$ (3 sf)

b $12.3^2 = x^2 + 7.8^2$
$12.3^2 - 7.8^2 = x^2$
$x^2 = 90.45$
$x = \sqrt{90.45} = 9.51$ (3 sf)

Level 8 (p. 83)

2 a $\tan 38 = \dfrac{p}{14.1}$

$14.1 \times \tan 38 = p$
$p = 11.0$ cm (3 sf)

b because it is an angle in a semicircle

$\cos p = \dfrac{11}{17}$
$p = 49.7°$ (3 sf)

3 $\sin 54 = \dfrac{x}{500}$
$x = 500 \times \sin 54$
$= 405$ miles (3 sf)

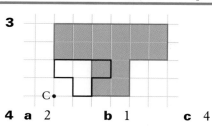

8 Position and movement

Levels 3–5 (p. 90)

1 a

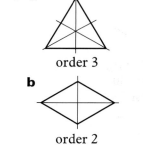

order 3

b

order 2

c

order 4

d

order 3

2

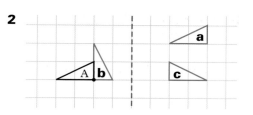

Level 6 (p. 90)

3

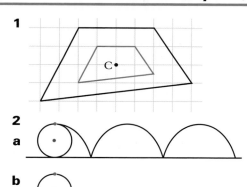

4 a 2 **b** 1 **c** 4

Level 7 (p. 96)

1

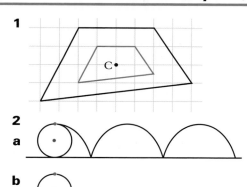

2
a

b

3 The region is shaded.
The boundaries are not included.

Scale: 1 cm to 2 km

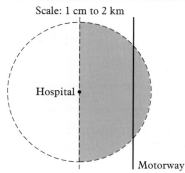

163

Level 8 (p. 96)

4 a

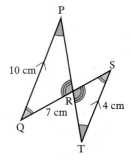

b (1) ST   (2) QR
c $10 \div 4 = 2.5$ (or $2\frac{1}{2}$)
d $7 \div 2.5 = 2.8$ cm

9   Units of measurement

Levels 3–5 (p. 103)

1 **a** 100   **e** 8   **i** 4
   b 12   **f** 1000   **j** 48
   c 16   **g** 20   **k** 18
   d 1000   **h** 3000   **l** 2

2 **a** 1.6   **c** 90   **e** 30
   b 600   **d** 4.5   **f** 450

3 **a** 2, 18   **b** 0.1, 5.6   **c** 2, 13

4 **a** 06:50   **c** 1:45 am
   b 11:10 pm   **d** 16:36

5 **a** Any in range 3 to 6 m.
   b Any in range 3 to 8 oz.
   c Any in range 2 to 4 in.
   d Any in range 30 to 100 ml.

Level 7 (p. 107)

1 **a** 19.5 cm, 14.5 cm, 5.5 cm
   b 20.5 cm, 15.5 cm, 6.5 cm

2 **a** 60 km   **b** $1\frac{1}{2}$ hours
   c After. The gradient is steeper after his rest.
   Speed before $= 20 \div 1\frac{1}{2} = 13\frac{1}{3}$ km/h
   Speed after $= 40 \div 2 = 20$ km/h
   d $60 \div 5 = 12$ km/h

3 **a** $13 \div 2 = 6.5$ m/s
   b $5 \times (2.5 \times 60) = 750$ m
   c $4 \div 12 = \frac{1}{3}$ h $= 20$ mins
   d $40 \div 1\frac{1}{4} = 32$ mph

4 **a** $50 \div 10 = 5$ g/cm^3
   b $100 \div 50 = 2$ m^3
   c $15 \times 20 = 300$ g
   d $(2.5 \times 1000) \div 100 = 25$ g/cm^3

10   Perimeter, area and volume

Levels 3–5 (p. 112)

1 $12 + 9 + 5 = 26$ cm

2 6 squares

3 $11 \times 3 = 33$ cm^2

4 $\dfrac{4 \times 10}{2} = \dfrac{40}{2} = 20$ cm^2

5 6 cubes

Level 6 (p. 112)

6 $\pi \times 16 = 50.3$ cm (1 dp)
   $\pi \times 8 \times 8 = 201.1$ cm^2 (1 dp)

7 $\frac{1}{2}(8 + 10) \times 6 = 9 \times 6 = 54$ cm^2

8 $6 \times 8 \times 10 = 480$ cm^3

Level 7 (p. 117)

1 $25 + \dfrac{(\pi \times 5^2)}{4}$

$= 25 + 19.6349 \ldots$

$= 44.6 \text{ cm}^2 \text{ (1 dp)}$

2 $36 - \pi \times 3^2$

$= 36 - 28.2743 \ldots$

$= 7.7 \text{ cm}^2 \text{ (1 dp)}$

3 $\dfrac{6 \times 7}{2} \times 15 = 315 \text{ cm}^3$

4 $\pi \times 7^2 \times 5 = 769.7 \text{ cm}^3 \text{ (1 dp)}$

5 $150 \div 25 = 6 \text{ cm}$

Level 8 (p. 117)

6 B   Area   D   Volume
C   Length   E   Incorrect

11 Organising data

Levels 3–5 (p. 125)

1 a

Number of TVs	Tally	Frequency
1	IIII III	8
2	IIII IIII III	13
3	IIII II	7
4	II	2

b *Number of TVs*

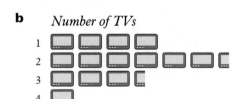

c   *Number of TVs in 30 families*

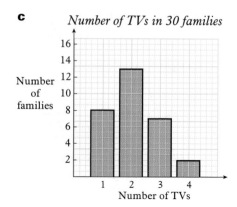

2 a $\frac{1}{2}$ **b** 50%   **c** 20%   **d** 25

Level 6 (p. 126)

3 Total number of drinks $= 180$
Each drink gets $360 \div 180 = 2°$
Angle for coffee $= 80°$
Angle for tea $= 160°$
Angle for chocolate $= 120°$

Sales of hot drinks

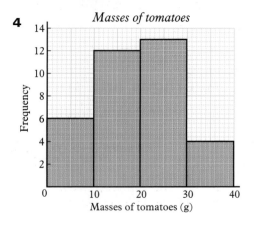

4

Masses of tomatoes

5 Chart is misleading because the bar for 1996 is twice as wide as the 1995 bar. The area is affected by more than the change in profits and the eye will register the area rather than just the height.

Level 7 (p. 131)

1 a Biased because people will answer Yes as they want to appear intelligent.

b There will be a wide variety of answers – they could well be all different.

c People will give opinions and these will be impossible to analyse properly.

2 a

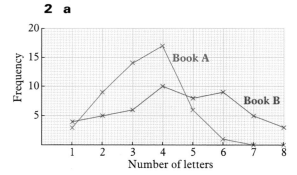

b There are more shorter words in A than in B. B has a greater range of the number of letters in words.

12 Averages and spread

Levels 3–5 (p. 137)

1 a The mode is 18

b 15, 18, 18, 19, 21, 24

The median is

$$\frac{18 + 19}{2} = 18.5$$

c Total = 115
Mean = $115 \div 6 = 19.2$ (1 dp)

d Range = $24 - 15 = 9$

2 Chris' Cabs because the times are more consistent and more likely to be less than 16 mins.

Level 6 (p. 137)

3 a

b Negative correlation. As the age increases the value decreases.

Level 7 (p. 144)

1 a 5.5, 15.5, 25.5, 65.5 (these are in £1000s)

b

$$\frac{25 \times 5500 + 39 \times 15\,500 + 10 \times 25\,500 + 6 \times 35\,500}{25 + 39 + 10 + 6}$$

$$= \frac{1\,390\,000}{80} = £17\,375$$

c The modal group is 11–20

Level 8 (p. 144)

		Surgery	Clinic
a	Median	20	22
b	Lower quartile	14	13
c	Upper quartile	27	32
d	Interquartile range	13	19

e The waiting times at the surgery are generally shorter than those at the clinic. They are also more consistent in length of waiting times.

13 Probability

Levels 3–5 (p. 150)

1

2 a red
  b $\frac{3}{8}$
  c 10
  d 2 blue counters

3 a Method 2
  b Method 1
  c Method 3

Level 6 (p. 150)

4 a

Coin	Dice					
	1	2	3	4	5	6
H	H, 1	H, 2	H, 3	H, 4	H, 5	H, 6
T	T, 1	T, 2	T, 3	T, 4	T, 5	T, 6

  b $\frac{3}{12} = \frac{1}{4}$ c $1 - \frac{1}{4} = \frac{3}{4}$

Level 7 (p. 155)

1 a 100   b $\frac{8}{100} = \frac{2}{25}$
  c $\frac{35}{100} = \frac{7}{20}$ (or 0.35)
  d By surveying more cars

Level 8 (p. 155)

2 a $\frac{2}{6} = \frac{1}{3}$
  b $\frac{1}{6} \times \frac{1}{2} = \frac{1}{12}$
  c $\frac{1}{6} \times \frac{1}{6} = \frac{1}{36}$

3 a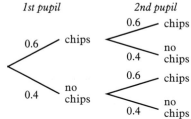

  b $0.6 \times 0.6 = 0.36$
  c $(0.6 \times 0.4) + (0.4 \times 0.6)$
     $= 0.24 + 0.24 = 0.48$

At appropriate stages the marks to be awarded are shown as (✓).

1 Whole numbers

Levels 3–5 (p. 9)

1 **a** 2345 (✓)   **b** 5432 (✓)   **c** 0 (✓)

2 **a**
$$\begin{array}{r} £13 \\ \times\ 25 \\ \hline 260\ (✓) \\ 65 \\ \hline £325\ (✓) \end{array}$$
25 CDs cost £325

b
$$18\overline{)3\ 0^{12}0}\quad 1\ 6\ \text{r}12$$
(✓ *if remainder 12 shown*)

16 packs of video tapes can be bought with £300 (✓)

3 **a** −3°C (✓)   **b**   **c** −2°C (✓)

8 °C →

Level 6 (p. 10)

4 **a** −4 − 5 = −9 (✓)   **b** −4 − −5 = 1 (✓)

5 $T = \dfrac{4 \times 15}{-2} = \dfrac{60}{-2} = -30$ (✓)

Levels 5–7 (p. 14)

1 **a** 821 − 647 = **174** (✓)
b $a \times b \times 5 = 40$, where $a \times b = 8$ (e.g. 2 × 4) (✓)
c 1400 ÷ **100** = 14 (✓)
d 182 ÷ 7 = **26** (✓)
e $a − b = 31$ (e.g. 32 − 1) (✓)
f 37 × 9 = **333** (✓)

2 **a**
$$\begin{array}{r} £27 \\ \times\ 34 \\ \hline 810\ (✓) \\ 108 \\ \hline £918\ (✓) \end{array}$$
34 candles sell for £918

b
$$12\overline{)2\ 0^{8}0}\quad 1\ 6\ \text{r}8$$
(✓ *with remainder 8*)

16 full boxes can be packed (✓)

3 $K = \dfrac{14.2 \times 37.4}{80.4 − 13.53} = \dfrac{531.08}{66.87} = 7.941\,977$ (✓)

4 A   86 850 000 ÷ 347 400 = £250
B   119 945 000 ÷ 521 500 = £230
C   98 784 000 ÷ 403 200 = £245
D   170 977 500 ÷ 670 500 = £255

a Town B has the lowest tax per person (✓)
b Town D has the highest tax per person (✓)

Level 8 (p. 15)

5 **a** 1.5×10^{10} (✓)
b $1.5 \times 10^{10} \times 9.46 \times 10^{12}$ (✓) $= 1.419 \times 10^{23}$ (✓)
6 $10^{600} \div 10^{303}$ (✓) $= 10^{600−303} = 10^{297}$ (✓)

2 Fractions, decimals and percentages

Levels 3–5 (p. 24)

1 **a** 16 ÷ 2 = 8 (✓)   **c** 16 − **a** or 16 − 8 = 8 (✓)
b $\frac{4}{16} = \frac{1}{4}$ (✓)   **d** 16 − 4 = 12 (✓)

2 To find the quantities needed for 9 people, first divide by 6 and then multiply by 9 (i.e. multiply by 1.5).
Garlic: 2 ÷ 6 × 9 = 3 cloves
Chick peas: 4 ÷ 6 × 9 = 6 ounces
Olive oil: 4 ÷ 6 × 9 = 6 tablespoons
Paste: 5 ÷ 6 × 9 = $7\frac{1}{2}$ (fluid ounces) (2✓)

3 **a** $\frac{9}{12} = \frac{3}{4}$ (✓)
b $\frac{3}{4} \times 100 = 75\%$ (✓)
c $\frac{2}{3} \times 12 = 8$ shaded triangles (✓)
4 **a** $\frac{5}{100} \times 30 = £1.50$ (✓)
b $\frac{2}{5} \times 4 = £1.60$ (✓)
c £1.50 (✓)

Level 6 (p. 25)

5 **a** Quantity of one 'part' of paint = 12 ÷ 3
= 4 litres (✓)
So 2 × 4 = 8 litres of red paint are needed. (✓)
b Total quantity of orange paint made
= 12 + 8 = 20 litres (✓)

Levels 5–7 (p. 28)

1 **a** 0.36 (✓)   **b** 0.1 (✓)   **c** 0.08 (✓)
2 **a** $\frac{1}{2} + \frac{1}{4} + \frac{1}{8} = \frac{4}{8} + \frac{2}{8} + \frac{1}{8} = \frac{7}{8}$
So fourth piece is $1 − \frac{7}{8} = \frac{1}{8}$ of cake (✓)
b $\frac{1}{4} = \frac{4}{16}$ (✓)
So weight of $\frac{1}{4}$ of cake = weight of $\frac{1}{16} \times 4$
= 20 × 4 = 80 g (✓)
3 **a** Percentage of pupils in Year 9
$= \dfrac{(90 + 70)}{295} \times 100 = 54.2\%$ (✓)
b Boys : girls = 150 : 145 (✓)
= 150 ÷ 150 : 145 ÷ 150 = 1 : 0.967 (✓)
4 **a** $1 − \frac{3}{8} = \frac{8}{8} − \frac{3}{8} = \frac{5}{8}$ (✓)
b $\frac{5}{8} \times 100 = 62\frac{1}{2}\%$ (✓)
c $\frac{3}{8} \times 24 = £9$ (✓)

Level 8 (p. 29)

5 **a** Value of computer after 2 years
$= £800 \times \dfrac{80}{100} \times \dfrac{80}{100}$ (✓) $= £512$ (✓)
b Value of computer when new
$= £704 \times \dfrac{100}{80} \times \dfrac{100}{80}$ (✓) $= £1100$ (✓)
c **i** 0.8^2 or 0.64 (✓)   **ii** 0.8^n (✓)
d Value after 4 years = £1500 × 0.8^4 (✓) = £614.40 (✓)
e $0.8^3 = 0.512\ (>\frac{1}{2})$, $0.8^4 = 0.4\ (<\frac{1}{2})$ (✓ *for method*)
So it will take 4 years for the value of any computer to fall by half its original value.

At appropriate stages the marks to be awarded are shown as (✓).

3 Estimating

Levels 3–5 (p. 33)

1 350 000 or 346 000 (✓)
2 a $x \div y = 5$ where $5 \times y = x$ (✓), e.g. where $x = 10, y = 2$
   b $24 \div 3 + 1 = 9$ (✓)
3 Any two of 2, 36; 3, 24; 4, 18; 6, 12; 8, 9 (2✓)
4 a e.g. 8, 9 (✓)   b e.g. 15, 3 (✓)
5 a $3 + 6 + (2 \times 4)$ (✓)   b $(6 + 4 + 2) \times 3$ (✓)
6 7 (2✓)
7 9 (2✓)
8 a

School	Number of pupils	To the nearest 100	To the nearest 10
Olney	884	900	880
Mesnes	662	700	660
Heaton	788	800	790
Pendle	906	900	910

(4✓)
   b Any two numbers between 650 and 654 inclusive. (2✓)
9 a $4667 \div 359 (=13)$ or $4667 \div 13 (=359)$ (✓)
   b $1138 - 377 (=761)$ or $1138 - 761 (=377)$ (✓)
   c $1830 - 1103 (=727)$ or $727 + 1103 (=1830)$ (✓)
   d $17 \times 311 (=5287)$ or $5287 \div 311 (=17)$ (✓)
10 37 (✓)

Levels 5–7 (p. 38)

1 a Cost of 4 garden pots £2.45 × 4 = £9.80 (✓)
   b $12 \div 2.45 = 4.89$
      So you can buy 4 pots with £12.00 (✓)
   c $12 \div 4.49 = 2.67$
      So you can buy 2 pairs of pots with £12.00 (✓)
   d £4.49 × 3 pairs + £2.45 × 1 single = £15.92
      So 7 pots is the greatest number you can buy with £16.00 (✓)

2

Number	Rounded to 1 sf	Rounded to 2 sf	Rounded to 3 sf
0.5182	0.5	0.52	0.518
10.099	10	10	10.1
58.42	60	58	58.4
3486	3000	3500	3490

3 $\dfrac{81 \times 155}{42.4 \times 2.4} \approx \dfrac{80 \times 200}{40 \times 2}$ (1 sf) (✓) = 200 (✓)

Level 8 (p. 39)

4 a 5.115 (✓)   b 5.1249 or 5.125 (✓)
5 $\sqrt{\dfrac{12.2^3 \times 14.3}{440 \times 9.6^2}} \approx \sqrt{\dfrac{10^3 \times 10}{400 \times 10^2}}$ (1 sf) (✓) $= \dfrac{1}{2}$ (✓)

4 Patterns and sequences

Levels 3–5 (p. 43)

1 a Either 16×2 or 32×1 (✓)
   b $32 \div 6$ does not go exactly; 6 is not a factor of 32 (✓)
2 a   (✓)

   b $22 \div 2 \times 5 = 55$ (✓)
   c Number of white tiles in odd pattern
      $= ((\text{Length} + 1) \div 2 \times 5) - 2$ or
      $((\text{Length} - 1) \div 2 \times 5) + 3$ (✓)
3 a 10, 15, 21 (✓)
   b Two prime numbers (e.g. 2, 3, 11, 13, 17, 19, …) (✓)
   c 15 is not prime, it has 2 factors; 3 and 5 as well as 1 and 15 (✓)

Level 6 (p. 44)

4 a 12 grey, 9 red (✓)   c $T = 4N - 3$ (✓)
   b 28 grey, 29 red (✓)

Levels 5–7 (p. 47)

1 a 49 grey, 4 blue (✓)
   b $14^2 = 196$ grey, 4 blue (✓)
   c n^2 grey, 4 blue (✓)
   d $n^2 + 4$ (✓)
   e $n^2 + n^2 + 3$ (✓) $= 2n^2 + 3$ (✓)

5 Formulas, expressions and equations

Levels 3–5 (p. 52)

1 a x^2 (✓)   c $x \times 2, x + x$ (✓)
   b $x \div 3$ (✓)   d e.g. $4x, 2x + 2x$ (✓)
2 a $2 \times n$ (✓)   b $2n - 5$ (✓)
3 a $n + n \ldots + n + n = 12n$ (✓)
   b $12n = 60$ (✓) so $n = 5$ (✓)

Level 6 (p. 53)

4 **a** Sapna : $3m - 4$ (✓) Dale : $2m + 1$ (✓)
  b $3m - 4 = 2m + 1$ (✓)
  c $3m - 4 = 2m + 1$
    $3m - 2m = 1 + 4$
    $m = 5$ (✓)

5

x	y	
1	-1	too low
2	3	too high
1.5	0.75	too high (✓ *for attempt between 1 and 2*)
1.4	0.36	too high
1.3	-0.01	too low
1.35	0.1725	too high (✓ *for attempt at 1.3 and 1.4*)

The value which gives the solution nearest to 0 $x = 1.3$ (1 dp) (✓)

Levels 5–7 (p. 58)

1 $x + y$; $8a$; $-5q$; $5x + 5y - 4w$; $-4k$; $4x^2$ (3✓)

2 **a**
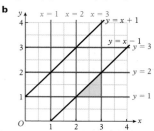
24 °C
  b $T < 24$ (✓)
  c $-9 \leqslant T < 12$ (✓)

3 **a** $P = \dfrac{x^2(x - 1)}{4}$
    $P = \dfrac{5^2(5 - 1)}{4} = \dfrac{25 \times 4}{4} = 25$ (✓)
  b $Q = \dfrac{5y^3}{6}$
    $Q = \dfrac{5 \times 3^3}{6} = \dfrac{5 \times 27}{6} = 22.5$ (✓)

4 $6x - 2 = 4x + 5$
  $6x - 4x = 5 + 2$
  $2x = 7$
  $x = 3.5$ (✓)
  Area of square $= (4x + 5)^2 = (4 \times 3.5 + 5)^2$
          $= 19^2 = 361$ cm^2 (✓)
  or
  Area of square $= (6x - 2)^2 = (6 \times 3.5 - 2)^2$
          $= 19^2 = 361$ cm^2

Level 8 (p. 59)

5 **a** $y \geqslant 2$ (✓) $x \leqslant 2$ (✓) $y \leqslant x + 1$ (✓)
  b
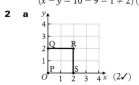

---

6 **a** $2(x - 3) - (x - 7) = 2x - 6 - x + 7$
          $= x + 1$ (✓)
  b $(x - 2)(x + 3) = x^2 + 3x - 2x - 6$
          $= x^2 + x - 6$ (✓)
  c $(x + 5)^2 = x^2 + 5x + 5x + 25$
          $= x^2 + 10x + 25$ (✓)

7 **a** $5 - 3x = 6x + 11$
      $-3x - 6x = 11 - 5$
      $-9x = 6$
      $x = -\frac{6}{9} = -\frac{2}{3}$
  b $2(x - 1) = 6$
      $2x - 2 = 6$ (✓)
      $2x = 8$
      $x = 4$ (✓)
  c $3x = 5(x - 1)$
      $3x = 5x - 5$
      $5 = 2x$
      $x = 2\frac{1}{2}$ (✓)

At appropriate stages the marks to be awarded are shown as (✓).

6 Functions and graphs

Levels 3–5 (p. 63)

1 **a** A(2, 0), B(3, 1), C(4, 2)
          (2✓ *for all 3 correct*, ✓ *for 1 or 2 correct*)
  b (11, 9) (✓)
    The x co-ordinate is one more than the triangle number.
    The y co-ordinate is one less than the triangle number. (✓)
  c There needs to be a difference of two between the x and the y co-ordinates.
    $(x - y = 10 - 9 = 1 \neq 2)$ (✓)

2 **a**
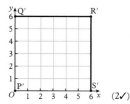
    (2✓)
  b Square (✓)
  c P'(0, 0), Q'(0, 6), R'(6, 6), S'(6, 0)

    (2✓)
  d $36 \div 4 = 9$ times larger
    or (linear scale factor)$^2 = 3^2 = 9$ times larger (✓)

Level 6 (p. 64)

3 a, b

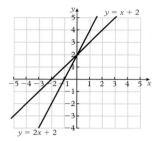

c $y = nx$ (e.g. $y = -2x, y = x, y = \frac{1}{3}x$, etc.) (✓)

d $y = x + 7$ (✓)

e $-\frac{1}{5}$ (✓)

Levels 5–7 (p. 70)

1 a $y = 3$ (✓), $x = 1$ (✓)

b $y - x = 2$ is the equation of the line through D and B. (✓)

c

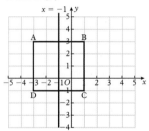

One of $y = 1$ or $y - x = 2$ or $y = -x$ (✓)

d $2y + x = 22$ [1]
$y - x = 2$ [2]
$3y = 24$ [1] + [2]
$y = 8$ (✓)

Putting $y = 8$ in equation [2] gives
$8 - x = 2$
$x = 8 - 2 = 6$ (✓)

e (6, 8) i.e. answers from part **d**

2 $8x + 6y = 10$ [1]
$30x - 6y = 9$ [2] (✓ for rearrangement)
$38x = 19$ ADD [1] + [2]
$x = 0.5$ (✓)

Putting $x = 0.5$ in equation [1] gives
$4 + 6y = 10$
$6y = 6$
$y = 1$ (✓)

3 $x = 2$ (✓), $y = 1$ (✓)

Level 8 (p. 71)

4 $y = 2x^2 + 2$ (✓); $y = x^2$ (✓); $y = -2x^2$ (✓)

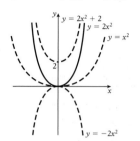

5 i acceleration/increasing speed (✓)

ii level/same or constant speed (✓)

iii constant deceleration/braking (✓)

7 2D and 3D shapes

Levels 3–5 (p. 78)

1 a, b e.g.:

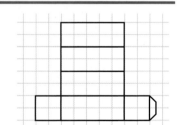

(3✓ for net of cuboid, ✓ for flap)

2 a A (✓) **b** C (✓) **c** B, E (✓) **d** D (✓)

e Pupil's drawing of angle between 90° and 180° (✓)

3 a N (✓) **b** S (✓)

Level 6 (p. 79)

4 a $a = 180° - 70° = 110°$ (✓)
$b = 180° - 120° = 60°$ (✓)
$c = 180° - 70° - b° = 180° - 70° - 60° = 50°$ (✓)

b $d = 50°$ (alternate angles) (✓)
$e = 140°$ (alternate angles) (✓)
$f = 180° - 140° = 40°$ (angles on a straight line) (✓)
Trapezium (✓)

5 2.1 cm (3✓)

6 angles of 60° (✓), lengths correct to within 1 mm (✓)

Levels 5–7 (p. 84)

1 C (✓)

2 a $x = 360° \div 6 = 60°$ **b** $y = 60° + 90° = 150°$

3 Using Pythagoras

Base $= \sqrt{(13^2 - 5^2)}$ (✓)

$= \sqrt{(169 - 25)} = \sqrt{144} = 12$ cm (✓)

Area $= \frac{1}{2}$(base × height)

$= \frac{1}{2}(12 \times 5) = 30$ cm² (✓)

Level 8 (p. 85)

4 a Using Pythagoras

BC $= \sqrt{(450^2 + 350^2)}$ (✓) $= \sqrt{325\,000} = 570$ m (✓)

b To find the bearing, b, from B to C first find angle x.

Using trigonometry

$\tan x = \dfrac{350}{450} = 0.777\ldots$

$x = \tan^{-1} 0.777\ldots = 37.9°$ (3 sf)

Therefore $b = 90° - 37.9° = 52.1°$

Bearing from B to C is 052.1° (✓)

c To find the bearing, c, from C to B first find angle y.

$y = 180 - 90 - 37.9 = 52.1°$ (angles in a triangle)

or $y = 52.1°$ (alternate angles)

Therefore $c = 180° + 52.1° = 232.1°$

Bearing from C to B is 232.1° (✓)

d $\cos 30 = \dfrac{450}{d}$ (✓)

$d = \dfrac{450}{\cos 30} = 520$

Distance from B to D $= 520$ m (✓)

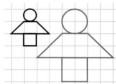

8 Position and movement

Levels 3–5 (p. 91)

1

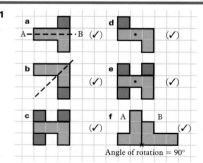

a A—────··B (✓)

b (✓)

c (✓)

d (✓)

e (✓)

f A   B (✓)

Angle of rotation = 90°

2

 a **b**   **c**

(✓)   (✓)   (✓)

3

(2✓)

Level 6 (p. 92)

4 a 12 (✓)   **b** 2 (✓)

5 Circle drawn (✓)

Trapezium drawn (✓)

Square drawn (✓)

6 Correct size (×3) (✓)   Correct position (✓)

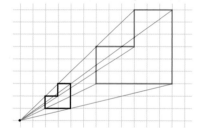

Levels 5–7 (p. 97)

1 a $42 \div 10 = 4.20$

$30 \div 7 = 4.29$

Scale factor $= 4.20$ (2 dp) (✓)

b $30 \div 10 = 3.00$

$21 \div 7 = 3.00$

Scale factor $= 3.00$ (2 dp) (✓)

c $21 \div 10 = 2.10$

$15 \div 7 = 2.14$

Scale factor $= 2.10$ (2 dp) (✓)

2

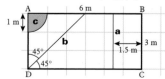

Scale 1 square : 1 m

(✓ for drawing rectangle 6 cm × 3 cm)

a Line 1.5 cm from side BC (✓)

b Line at 45° to side DC (✓)

c Shaded $\frac{1}{4}$ circle radius 1 cm, centre A (✓)

3

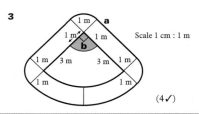

Scale 1 cm : 1 m

(4 ✓)

Level 8 (p. 98)

4 $\dfrac{h}{70} = \dfrac{84}{60}$ (✓)

So $h = \dfrac{84 \times 70}{60} = 98$ mm (✓)

or scale factor = $70 \div 60$ (✓)
so $h = 84 \times 70 \div 60$ (✓)

5 Triangles ADE and ABC are similar.

So $\dfrac{AE}{AC} = \dfrac{DE}{BC}$ (✓)

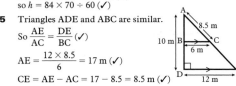

$AE = \dfrac{12 \times 8.5}{6} = 17$ m (✓)

$CE = AE - AC = 17 - 8.5 = 8.5$ m (✓)

6 **a** ASA (✓)
    b BAC = 90° (✓); AC = DE = $\sqrt{(8^2 - 6^2)}$ = 5.29 cm (2✓)

7 **a** A, D (✓); enlargement only (no sides the same) (✓)
    b A, E (✓); AAS (✓)
    c C, D (✓); AAS (✓)

At appropriate stages the marks to be awarded are shown as (✓).

9   Units of measurement

Levels 3–5 (p. 104)

1 **a** 10 : 20 (✓)   **b** 09 : 45 (✓)   **c** 35 minutes (✓)
    d 07 : 30 or 08 : 15 or 09 : 00 (✓)
    e 08 : 15 (✓)
    f

(✓)

2 **a** 6.4 cm (✓) 64 mm (✓)
    b 16 mm = 1.6 cm
        Length of pencil = 5.3 − 1.6 = 3.7 cm (✓)

3 **a** 2.2 kg (✓)
    b 600 g = 0.6 kg (✓)
        Mass of cheese = 2.2 − 0.6 = 1.6 kg (✓)

4 **a** 1 kg (✓)
    b Value between 0.5 and 0.7 litres (✓)
    c Value between 4 and 9 mm (✓)

5 **a** Value between 4.9 and 5.1 cm (✓)
    b Value between 7.7 and 7.9 in (✓)

Levels 5–7 (p. 108)

1 **a** 7.2 cm (✓)
    b Value between 2.6 and 2.8 kg (✓)
    c Value between 5.32 m and 5.34 m (✓)

2 **a** 12 st 10 lb (✓)
    b 14 st 3 lb (✓)

3 **a**

Time (min)	1	6	10	15	25	30	50
Capacity (litres)	12	72	120	180	300	360	600

(2✓)

    b $C = 12T$ (✓)

    c $T = \dfrac{C}{12} = \dfrac{5000}{12} = 416.666\ldots$ minutes
        416.666 ... minutes = 6 hours 57 minutes
                      (rounding to nearest minute)

4 **a** £550 = 880 euro

        So £1.00 = $\dfrac{880}{550}$ = 1.60 euro (✓)

    b 26.40 ÷ 1.60 = £16.50 (2 ✓)

5 **a** 10 minutes (✓)
    b Adam and Belinda passed each other going in
        opposite directions (✓)

    c 50 minutes = $\dfrac{50}{60} = \dfrac{5}{6}$ hours

        Average speed = $\dfrac{\text{Distance}}{\text{Time}}$

        Average speed = $\dfrac{10}{\frac{5}{6}} = \dfrac{10 \times 6}{5} = 12$ km/h (✓)

    d Time Belinda was moving = 20 + 15 + 10
                       = 45 minutes = $\dfrac{3}{4}$ hours

        Average speed = $\dfrac{10}{\frac{3}{4}} = \dfrac{10 \times 4}{3} = 13.3$ km/h (✓)

    e 10 and 20 minutes (✓)

---

10   Perimeter, area and volume

Levels 3–5 (p. 113)

1 **a** **i** Perimeter = 10 cm (✓)   **ii** Area = 6 cm² (✓)
    b **i** Perimeter = 18 cm (✓)   **ii** Area = 8 cm² (✓)

2 **a** 7 (✓)   **b** 10 (✓)

3 **a** Any shape (other than the one shown) with 6 tiles
        connected correctly. (✓)

4 **a** $5 \times 3 = 15$ cm² (✓)
    b $\frac{1}{2} \times 6 \times 8 = 24$ cm² (✓)
    c $\frac{1}{2} \times 4 \times 7 = 14$ cm² (✓)

5 **a** $12 \times 2 = 24$ (✓)   **b** $6 + (12 \times 2) = 30$ (✓)

Level 6 (p. 114)

6 **a** Circumference = $\pi \times$ diameter
                      = $\pi \times 12 = 37.69$ mm (✓)
        Distance moved = $2 \times$ circumference
                        = $2 \times 37.69 = 75.4$ mm (3 sf) (✓)

b Number of turns = $\dfrac{\text{Distance}}{\text{Circumference}}$

$= \dfrac{201}{\pi \times 16} = \dfrac{201}{50.27}$

$= 3.998 = 3.40 \ (3 \text{ sf}) \ (\checkmark)$

7 Length of side = $\sqrt{9} = 3$
Perimeter = $3 \times 4 = 12$ cm $(\checkmark)$

8 $7 \times 4 = 28 \text{ cm}^2 \ (\checkmark)$

9 $\frac{h}{2}(7 + 5) = 24$
$12h = 48$, so $h = 4 \ (\checkmark)$

Levels 5–7 (p. 118)

1 a Area of shaded face $= \frac{1}{2} \times 7 \times 8 \ (\checkmark) = 28 \text{ m}^2 \ (\checkmark)$
b Volume of prism = Area of base × Height
$= 28 \times 12 = 336 \text{ m}^3 \ (\checkmark)$

2 a Area of semicircle $= \frac{1}{2}\pi r^2 = \frac{1}{2}(\pi \times 5^2)$
$= 39.27 \text{ cm}^2 \ (2 \text{ dp}) \ (\checkmark)$
b Perimeter of semicircle $= \frac{1}{2}\pi d + d = 15.708 + 10$
$= 25.71 \text{ cm} \ (2 \text{ dp}) \ (\checkmark)$

3 $\dfrac{h}{60} = \dfrac{20}{100} \ (\checkmark)$ so $h = \dfrac{20 \times 60}{100} = 12 \text{ cm} \ (\checkmark)$
or cross-section area = $100 \div 20 = 5 \text{ cm}^2 \ (\checkmark)$
$5h = 60$ so $h = 12 \text{ cm} \ (\checkmark)$

4 If width is x cm, then length is $3x$ cm and perimeter is
$3x + x + 3x + x = 8x$ cm
$8x = 48$ cm so $x = 6$ cm
Area of rectangle = $x \times 3x = 3x^2$
$= 3 \times (6^2) = 108 \text{ cm}^2 \ (\checkmark)$

5 $36 \div 2 = 18$, $100 \div 2 = 50$, $50 \div 2 = 25 \ (\checkmark)$
Number of cubes that will fit in box = $18 \times 50 \times 25$
$= 22\,500 \ (\checkmark)$

6 Area of shaded region = $\pi(3^2) - \pi(1.2^2) \ (\checkmark)$
$= 28.27 - 4.52 = 23.75 \ (2 \text{ dp}) \ (\checkmark)$

7 Surface area of prism = $(\frac{1}{2} \times 5 \times 12) + (\frac{1}{2} \times 5 \times 12)$
$+ (13 \times 10) + (12 \times 10) + (5 \times 10) = 360 \text{ cm}^2 \ (\checkmark)$

Level 8 (p. 119)

8 Surface area of curved face = $\frac{1}{2}(4\pi r^2) = 2\pi r^2 \ (\checkmark)$
Surface area of face = $\pi r^2 \ (\checkmark)$
Surface area of hemisphere = $2\pi r^2 + \pi r^2 = 3\pi r^2$
$= 3\pi 4^2 = 48\pi$
$= 150.8 \text{ cm}^2 \ (4 \text{ sf}) \ (\checkmark)$

9

$4\pi r^2$	lbh	$\frac{1}{2}bh$	$\frac{4}{3}\pi r^3$	$4(r + b)$	$\dfrac{\pi h^2}{b}$	
				$\checkmark$	$\checkmark$	Length
$\checkmark$		$\checkmark$				Area
	$\checkmark$		$\checkmark$			Volume

$(2\checkmark)$

At appropriate stages the marks to be awarded are shown as $(\checkmark)$.

11 Units of measurement

Levels 3–5 (p. 127)

1 a Monday 28 $(\checkmark)$ Tuesday 22 $(\checkmark)$ Wednesday 15 $(\checkmark)$
b Thursday: $2\frac{1}{4}$ discs $(\checkmark)$ Friday: 6 discs $(\checkmark)$

c Thursday $(\checkmark)$
d The pictogram summarises the data and shows it in
such a way that it is easily understood. Makes it easy
to compare the figures. $(\checkmark)$
e A tally-chart is easy to add to, and to use to collect
the data. $(\checkmark)$

2 a Number of programmes recorded
$= 16 + 11 + 12 + 13 = 52 \ (\checkmark)$
b Number of films recorded = $16 + 12 = 28 \ (\checkmark)$
c

	Channel 1	Channel 3
Soaps	7	10
Comedy	4	6

$(2\checkmark)$

3 a Dog $(\checkmark)$ **b** Fish and mice $(\checkmark)$
c Number of cats = $40 \times \frac{1}{4} = 10 \ (\checkmark)$
d Number of dogs = number between 12 and 15 $(\checkmark)$

Level 6 (p. 129)

4 a There are too many tallies. The tallies needed to be
counted up to make the chart clearer. $(\checkmark)$
b 180 $(\checkmark)$
c A pie-chart will show better a comparison between
the holiday choices, as a fraction of those questioned.
It is not how many who have made a choice that is
important, but the proportion of each that have
shown a preference. $(\checkmark)$
d Ski 26°, Winter abroad 70°,
Summer sun 174°, Touring
44°, UK holiday 46°
(*2 angles correct* $\checkmark$; *all angles
correct* $2\checkmark$; *labels and title* $\checkmark$)

Holiday preferences

Levels 5–7 (p. 132)

1 a Between 30% and 40% $(\checkmark)$
b Between 15 and 25 $(\checkmark)$
c There are many more items included in B than A $(\checkmark)$
d (*2 angles correct* $\checkmark$; *all angles
correct* $2\checkmark$; *labels and title* $\checkmark$)

Snack bar C: 200 items

2 a Any three from:
Amounts overlap
No 'don't know' box
Amounts are too small
Groupings need to be bigger to cover more
amounts $(3\checkmark)$
b Need to include both girls and boys, and pupils of
different ages/year, groups and backgrounds. $(2\checkmark)$

3 a There is little change in Gary's figures. Therefore
his week 11 sales are likely to be similar to his sales
in weeks 1–10.
b Though Ali's sales figures in some weeks are higher
than Gary's, in many more weeks they are lower
than Gary's. Therefore, Ali's overall sales are lower.

12 Averages and spread

Levels 3–5 (p. 138)

1
  a Mode = 24 (✓)
  b Range = 49 − 12 = 37 (✓)
  c Median = 27 (✓)
  d Mean = 351 ÷ 13 = 27 (✓)

2 To score an average of 12, Jerry must score $3 \times 12 = 36$ over three games. In 2 games he has scored $8 + 15 = 23$ points. So he must score $36 − 23 = 13$ points in his final game.

3
  a Mean = $\dfrac{\text{Total number of pets}}{\text{Total number of pupils}}$

  $= \dfrac{(5 \times 0) + (3 \times 1) + (2 \times 2) + (2 \times 3) + (3 \times 4) + (2 \times 5)}{5 + 3 + 2 + 2 + 3 + 2}$ (✓)

  $= \dfrac{35}{17} = 2.06 \,(3\,\text{sf})$ (✓)

  b Modal number = 0 pets (✓)
  c Median number is 9th value = 2 pets (✓)

Level 6 (p. 139)

4
  a Mean number of errors = $\dfrac{\text{Total number of errors}}{\text{Total number of pupils}}$

  $= \dfrac{(1 \times 5) + (2 \times 6) + (3 \times 7) + (4 \times 5) + (5 \times 3)}{5 + 6 + 7 + 5 + 3}$ (✓)

  $= \dfrac{73}{26} = 2.81 \,(3\,\text{sf})$ (✓)

  b Median = 13th value = 3 errors (✓)

  c The mean, as it is the result of a calculation, need not be one of the given number of errors. The median is a given number of errors. (✓)

5
  a As the temperature rises, the number of cups of hot soup decreases (inverse proportion, negative correlation). (✓)

  b No relation (no correlation). (✓)

Levels 5–7 (p. 145)

1
  a As the number of hours of clear sky increases, the temperature decreases (inverse proportion, negative correlation). (✓)

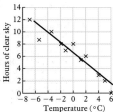

  b Line of best fit drawn ±2 mm (✓)
  $2\,°C \rightarrow 4.8\,\text{h} \pm 1\,\text{h}$ (✓)
  $4\,\text{h} \rightarrow 3\,°C \pm 1\,°C$ (✓)

2
  a Mean = $\dfrac{\sum fx}{\sum f}$

  $\sum fx = (34.5 \times 3) + (44.5 \times 8) + (54.5 \times 11) + (64.5 \times 9) + (74.5 \times 13) + (84.5 \times 6) = 3115$ (✓)

  Mean = $\dfrac{3115}{50} = 62.3$ paces (✓)

  b Median is 25th → group 60–69 (✓)

Level 8 (p. 147)

3
  a Median age = 47 ± 2 (✓)
  b Interquartile range: 150 on vertical axis → 57 ± 2
  50 on vertical axis → 36 ± 2
  Interquartile range = $57 − 36 = 21$ (2 ✓)
  c Percentage of population under $50 \approx \dfrac{116}{200} \times 100$

  $= 58\% \pm 2\%$ (✓)

13 Probability

Levels 3–5 (p. 151)

1
  a $\frac{2}{5}$ (✓)   **b** 0 (✓)
  c Probability of getting a blue or brown cube is $\frac{2}{5} = 0.4$

  (✓)

  d Probability of **not** getting a green cube is $1 − \frac{1}{5} = \frac{4}{5} = 0.8$

  (✓)

2
  a Probability of red = $\frac{3}{8}$
  Probability of green = $\frac{3}{8}$
  So red is no more likely than green. (✓)
  b The wheel is just as likely to stop on yellow the second time as it was the first.
  So probability of yellow = $\frac{1}{8}$ (✓)

  c   **d**

  All segments one colour. (✓)   Any four segments one colour. Remaining four segments a second colour. (✓)

3
  a Coin is just as likely to land on heads the fifth time as it was the other four times. So probability of heads = $\frac{1}{2} = 0.5$

  b Probability of 2 heads = $\frac{1}{2} \times \frac{1}{2} = \frac{1}{4}$ (✓)
  c Probability of not throwing 2 tails
  = 1 − probability of 2 tails = $1 − \frac{1}{4} = \frac{3}{4}$ (✓)

Level 6 (p. 152)

4 a It is possible that the bag contains many different coloured counters and that it is only by chance that she has picked only red counters. (✓)

b The probabilities of picking counters from the bag depend on the colours of the counters in the bag, not on the colours of the counters already taken out of the bag. (✓)

Levels 5–7 (p. 56)

1 a

+	2	4	6	8
1	3	5	7	9
3	5	7	9	11
5	7	9	11	13
7	9	11	13	15

(✓)

b Probability that answer is greater than $9 = \frac{6}{16} = \frac{3}{8}$ (✓)

c Probability that answer is a square number = Probability that answer is $9 = \frac{4}{16} = \frac{1}{4}$ (✓)

d Probability that answer is an even number = 0 (✓)

2 a Estimated probability of red $= \frac{30}{60} = \frac{1}{2}$ (✓)

b 10 times (✓)

c Probability only tells you what is likely to happen, not what actually happens. (✓)

d To improve the accuracy of his results, Tony needs to do more trials, i.e. throw the cube more times. (✓)

Level 8 (p. 57)

3 a Events are independent. So probability of passing through both sets of lights without having to stop = $0.3 \times 0.3 = 0.09$ (✓)

b Probability of being stopped at only one set of lights = $(0.7 \times 0.3) + (0.3 \times 0.7)$ (✓) = $0.21 + 0.21 = 0.42$ (✓)

c Probability of being stopped at first set of lights = 0.7 Number of times Karen can expect to be stopped in 80 journeys = $0.7 \times 80 = 56$ times

Test Tips

In the days before the tests

- Read through the 'What you need to know?' sections for your tier again.

- Read the Test Yourself tests and the Practice Questions for your tier of entry. Check the answers too and make sure that you know how to do all of the questions you have seen.

- Ask your teacher for copies of the Maths Tests from last year and the year before. If you try questions from these papers, ask your teacher for the answers and check your work.

On the day of the tests

Take the right equipment with you: pen, pencil, rubber, ruler, protractor or angle measurer, compasses and a calculator for the calculator paper and anything else that your teacher has told you to bring.

In the examination room

- Read each question carefully. Make sure you understand what the question is about and what you are expected to do.

- In all questions show any working out you do, even if you are using a calculator. You may lose marks if you do not show working.

- When using rulers, protractors or compasses make sure you use them accurately.

- The number of marks for each question is always shown on the paper.

- Give your answers to an appropriate degree of accuracy. **Do not** make them inaccurate by rounding off.

- Always round money answers to the nearest penny and to a given number of significant figures **where this is asked for**.

- If you find a question too hard, go on to the next question. But try to write something for each part of every question.

- If you have spare time at the end, use it wisely to check over your answers and working.